National Academy Press

The National Academy Press was created by the National Academy of
Sciences to publish the reports issued by the Academy and by the
National Academy of Engineering, the Institute of Medicine, and the
National Research Council, all operating under the charter granted to
the National Academy of Sciences by the Congress of the United States.

Biographical Memoirs

NATIONAL ACADEMY OF SCIENCES

NATIONAL ACADEMY OF SCIENCES
OF THE UNITED STATES OF AMERICA

Biographical Memoirs

VOLUME 57

NATIONAL ACADEMY PRESS
WASHINGTON, D.C. 1987

The National Academy of Sciences was established in 1863 by Act of Congress as a private, nonprofit, self-governing membership corporation for the furtherance of science and technology, required to advise the federal government upon request within its fields of competence. Under its corporate charter the Academy established the National Research Council in 1916, the National Academy of Engineering in 1964, and the Institute of Medicine in 1970.

INTERNATIONAL STANDARD BOOK NUMBER 0-309-03729-8
LIBRARY OF CONGRESS CATALOG CARD NUMBER 5-26629

Available from

NATIONAL ACADEMY PRESS
2101 CONSTITUTION AVENUE, N.W.,
WASHINGTON, D.C. 20418

PRINTED IN THE UNITED STATES OF AMERICA

CONTENTS

PREFACE — vii

ARTHUR FRANCIS BUDDINGTON — 3
BY HAROLD L. JAMES

J. GEORGE HARRAR — 27
BY JOHN J. McKELVEY, JR.

PAUL HERGET — 59
BY DONALD E. OSTERBROCK AND P. KENNETH SEIDELMANN

JOHN DOVE ISAACS III — 89
BY WILLARD BASCOM

BESSEL KOK — 125
BY J. MYERS

OTTO KRAYER — 151
BY AVRAM GOLDSTEIN

REBECCA CRAIGHILL LANCEFIELD — 227
BY MACLYN McCARTY

HAROLD DWIGHT LASSWELL — 249
BY GABRIEL A. ALMOND

CONTENTS

JAY LAURENCE LUSH 277
    BY ARTHUR B. CHAPMAN

JOHN HOWARD MUELLER 307
    BY A. M. PAPPENHEIMER, JR.

ROBERT FRANKLIN PITTS 323
    BY ROBERT W. BERLINER AND GERHARD H. GIEBISCH

JOHN ROBERT RAPER 347
    BY KENNETH B. RAPER

KARL SAX 373
    BY CARL P. SWANSON AND NORMAN H. GILES

GERHARD SCHMIDT 399
    BY HERMAN M. KALCKAR

LESLIE SPIER 431
    BY ROBERT F. SPENCER

HANS-LUKAS TEUBER 461
    BY LEO M. HURVICH, DOROTHEA JAMESON, AND
    WALTER A. ROSENBLITH

WARREN WEAVER 493
    BY MINA REES

CUMULATIVE INDEX 531

PREFACE

The *Biographical Memoirs* is a series of volumes, beginning in 1877, containing the biographies of deceased members of the National Academy of Sciences and bibliographies of their published scientific contributions. The goal of the Academy is to have these memoirs serve as a contribution toward the history of American science. Each biographical essay is written by an individual familiar with the discipline and the scientific career of the deceased. These volumes, therefore, provide a record of the lives and works of some of the most distinguished leaders of American science as witnessed and interpreted by their colleagues and peers. Though the primary concern is the members' professional lives and contributions, these memoirs also include those aspects of their lives in their home, school, college, or later life that led them to their scientific career.

The National Academy of Sciences is a private, honorary organization of scientists and engineers elected on the basis of outstanding contributions to knowledge. Established by a Congressional Act of Incorporation on March 3, 1863, the Academy works to further science and its use for the general welfare by bringing together the most qualified individuals to deal with scientific and technological problems of broad significance.

PETER II. RAVEN
Home Secretary

CAROLINE K. McEUEN
Associate Editor

Biographical Memoirs

VOLUME 57

Photograph by Harold L. James

ARTHUR FRANCIS BUDDINGTON
November 29, 1890–December 25, 1980

BY HAROLD L. JAMES

ARTHUR FRANCIS BUDDINGTON was one of the most respected and most effective teachers of geology of his generation and a productive research scientist whose contributions spanned a wide segment of the geologic spectrum. For nearly sixty years he was identified with Princeton University, where he is remembered with pride and honor; he had a parallel career as a field geologist with the New York State Museum and the U.S. Geological Survey, organizations that would also gladly claim him as one of their own. He was a man of parts, and he left his mark on geologic science in America.

Buddington, known affectionately if somewhat irreverently as "Bud" to his friends, colleagues, and ex-students, was born in Wilmington, Delaware, the son of Osmer G. Buddington, a Baptist minister, and Mary Salina Buddington, née Wheeler. Although the family was temporarily domiciled in Delaware, its roots were set firmly in New England: Buddingtons (also spelled Budington or Boddington) and Wheelers had lived in Connecticut since the 1600s, and men from both sides of the family served in Connecticut contingents of the Revolutionary Army. In 1904 Osmer Buddington returned with his family to Connecticut, where he became minister of the country church at Poquonnock Bridge. He augmented his salary with commercial gardening and poultry culture, activities that involved but did not enchant his teenage son.

Young Arthur's early education was in the public schools of Wilmington (Delaware), Mystic (Connecticut), and Westerly (Rhode Island). In 1908 he graduated from Westerly High School and entered Brown University. After a year in the liberal arts curriculum (during which he acquired an often expressed lifelong distaste for Latin and Greek), he began to specialize in the sciences, first in botany and chemistry, then in geology. He graduated in 1912, second in his class, and continued his studies, receiving the M.S. degree in 1913.

Buddington's master's thesis was a geobotanical study of fossiliferous Carboniferous shales exposed in a newly driven tunnel on College Hill—his first and only venture into the arcane realms of paleontological research. The same year—1913—also marked the beginning of his long association with Princeton University, where he had been awarded a fellowship. He became a member of the 1913 Princeton field party in Newfoundland and began a field study that developed into his doctoral thesis. He was awarded the degree in 1916.

At Princeton, Buddington was probably influenced most strongly by two individuals: A. H. Phillips, an able chemist-mineralogist active in both departmental and civic affairs, and C. H. Smyth, a distinguished petrologist of broad interests and—in Buddington's words—"the epitome of a scholar and a gentleman." But it is likely that much of his intellectual growth during this period should be attributed to close association with other budding scientists and scholars in the newly constructed residential Graduate College. This group included men such as Harlow Shapley in astronomy, Alan Waterman and Arthur Compton in physics, and William Cumberland in economics.

For the next several years, however, Buddington's course was irregular, doubtless a direct or indirect reflection of the turmoil of World War I. After receiving the Ph.D. degree from Princeton, he held a postdoctoral fellowship there for a short period and, under the auspices of the New York State Museum, began his first studies in Adirondack geology. In 1917, after briefly considering a career in the burgeoning petroleum industry, he accepted a position at Brown—only to return the following spring to Princeton to teach aerial observation under his friend Edward Sampson. This Princeton tenure was again brief for Buddington: in April 1918, with the United States now in the war, he enlisted as a private in the Signal Corps. Because of his chemistry background, he was transferred within months to the Chemical Warfare Service and assigned research duties under R. C. Tolman. Mustered out at war's end with the rank of sergeant, Buddington returned to Brown to finish the academic year as an instructor.

In 1919 Buddington accepted an appointment to the Geophysical Laboratory of the Carnegie Institution, then (and now) one of the leading experimental geology laboratories in the world. It was a decisive move. Not only did it lead to personal acquaintance and lasting friendship with some of the nation's outstanding geochemists (including N. L. Bowen, C. N. Fenner, H. E. Merwin, and H. S. Washington), but it also expanded his already strong background in chemistry with "hands-on" experience in mineralogical experimentation and the preparation of phase equilibria diagrams. With chemist J. B. Ferguson, he completed what was then a definitive study of the melilite group of minerals before returning to Princeton in 1920 as an assistant professor. Buddington remained at Princeton for the next half century to provide leadership in the study of rocks as chemical and physical systems.

Buddington's parallel career as a field geologist also took shape about this time. His career in this area had sputtered along during the years previous to and during World War I, but in 1921 he received an appointment to the U.S. Geological Survey and began an association that would last for more than forty years. His first assignment for the Survey was the geologic mapping of southeastern Alaska; he attributed this assignment (perhaps rightly) more to his Newfoundland experience in handling small boats than to his technical qualifications. The work occupied five seasons during which some 4,000 miles of rugged coastline were mapped, with traverses up the glacially oversteepened slopes of the Alaskan fjords and occasional ventures across glacial ice. Conditions often were atrocious—Buddington recorded that in 1921 it rained eighty-seven of the ninety days spent in the field. Yet later he would say that these five seasons were the most satisfying of his entire career.

This sort of devotion to field studies is perhaps difficult for a laboratory scientist to understand, and, considering that it often calls for exhausting physical effort under conditions that may be far from benign, perhaps not too easy to explain either. Part of the lure undoubtedly is aesthetic—the deep emotions evoked by close contact with nature in all its variety. Beyond that, however, are the excitement, the challenge, and the intellectual satisfaction that comes from seeing a geologic story emerge, outcrop by outcrop. In any case, field studies were an activity to which Buddington remained devoted throughout his life.

Buddington's teaching load at Princeton, even during his fourteen-year tenure as departmental chairman, was never light. Normally it consisted of one senior-level undergraduate course in petrology and, at the graduate level, courses given in alternate years in chemical geology and petrology. His impact on students, particularly in graduate classes, was profound; yet there was no Buddington "school" of petrologic thought. What was implanted in students was not a set of organized conclusions but a method of approach that would outlast the concepts of any given date. Buddington placed heavy emphasis on the application of theoretical and experimental chemistry to the understanding of natural systems. Such emphasis, however, always carried the expressed recognition that the rocks themselves represent completed experiments of far more complex design.

Because Buddington's petrology had no artificial limits, the coverage in his courses was broad, including ore deposits and chemical sedimentary rocks along with the traditional igneous and metamorphic suites. His graduate-level lectures, generally two hours in length, were meticulously prepared and delivered, even though the class might consist of fewer than a dozen students, and they were illustrated with blackboard diagrams drawn with care and precision. Buddington never resorted to dogmatic assertion: the door was always left open for reconsideration based on new evidence. After presenting an experimentally derived phase diagram—perhaps of sulfate assemblages—and discussing with some enthusiasm its application to certain natural deposits, he might conclude: "But I don't say," he would caution, waving at the blackboard illustration, "that this necessarily pertains. But I do say"—and his voice would become emphatic—"that *this is the sort of thing that pertains!*" It left the student with the zeal to discover for himself just what "sort of thing" might in fact apply.

Robert Hargraves (1984) records that 174 Ph.D. degrees in geology were awarded during the Buddington years. Of these, 100 were in petrology, ore deposits, and related fields. It is safe to say that Buddington's influence, whether direct or indirect, was important to all of them.

Buddington strove mightily during his long tenure as a

lead professor and as departmental chairman (1936–1950) to establish Princeton as a center of excellence in petrology and ore deposits—in general, the study of chemical processes in rock formation. Progress was made, but it was an uphill battle for many years in a department with long-established traditions in vertebrate and invertebrate paleontology. In the mid-1920s Buddington induced Norman L. Bowen, the distinguished petrologist of the Geophysical Laboratory, to present a series of lectures at Princeton, which were published in 1928 by the Princeton University Press. This thin volume, *Evolution of the Igneous Rocks,* is a masterly exposition of the application of experimental data to natural systems. It became a veritable Bible to petrologists of that day, and Princeton shone in reflected glory. By the mid-1930s, with the addition of Harry Hess to the staff, Princeton was recognized as one of the nation's leading schools in "hard rock" geology. But it was not until 1949 that Buddington's ambitions were fully realized, and the department's first program in experimental geology using high-temperature–high-pressure apparatus was inaugurated under John C. Maxwell.

Buddington briefly resumed work with the U.S. Geological Survey in 1930 when he spent a most enjoyable season mapping the Bohemia and North Santiam mining districts of the Oregon Cascades. But his major post-Alaska involvement with the Survey began in 1943, when he accepted the leadership of a program of field research on iron ores of the northeastern states. This program, with some redirection in its later stages, was to continue for the next seventeen years. It involved many geologists, among them H. E. Hawkes, A. W. Postel, Cleaves Rogers, B. F. Leonard, P. K. Sims, P. E. Hotz, and D. R. Baker. (The latter four subsequently earned the Ph.D. degree at Princeton using material derived from the Survey studies as bases for doctoral dissertations.)

The field studies of regional geology and iron deposits,

coupled with use of the newly available airborne fluxgate magnetometer under the direction of J. R. Balsley, resulted in the discovery of several ore bodies of small to moderate size (Hawkes and Balsley 1946). The economic success of the program was gratifying to Buddington's canny New England instincts. The work also resulted in a plethora of good scientific reports and papers, among them one by Preston Hotz that provided a definitive answer to the question of the origin of Cornwall-type magnetite deposits (Hotz 1950). The field program also nurtured two other significant developments in geology. One (noted above) was aerial magnetic surveying using equipment that had been developed for wartime submarine detection; it was first used systematically on low-level flights in the Adirondacks in 1944, often with Buddington aboard as an observer. The other significant development was exploration geochemistry, in large part the brainchild of project member H. E. Hawkes (Hawkes 1976).

Buddington's contributions to regional geology are recorded in a number of major documentary-type publications, notably: *Geology and Mineral Deposits of Southeastern Alaska* (U.S. Geological Survey Bulletin 800, with T. Chapin); *Metalliferous Mineral Deposits of the Cascade Range in Oregon* (U.S. Geological Survey Bulletin 893, with E. Callaghan); *Geology and Mineral Resources of the Hammond, Antwerp, and Lowville Quadrangles, N.Y.* (New York State Museum Bulletin 296); *Regional Geology of the St. Lawrence Magnetite District, N.Y.* (U.S. Geological Survey Professional Paper 376, with B. F. Leonard); *Ore Deposits of the St. Lawrence Magnetite District, N.Y.* (U.S. Geological Survey Professional Paper 377, with B. F. Leonard); and *Geology of the Franklin and Part of the Hamburg Quadrangles, N.J.* (U.S. Geological Survey Professional Paper 638, with D. R. Baker). These data-laden reports are not stimulating reading and are rarely referenced; nevertheless they are recognized as the stuff of which the nation's geologic data base has been built. Not so evident, and often overlooked, is the linkage between these field studies and Buddington's better known topical papers in which new concepts and new ideas are introduced. A few illustrative examples follow.

Buddington's 1959 paper delineating and explaining depth-related differences among igneous intrusives—a most useful and illuminating concept—is based on his perceptive field observations of igneous intrusives in the greatly different geologic environments of Newfoundland, the Alaska Coast Ranges, the Oregon Cascades, and the Adirondacks of New York. (Buddington's additional observation of the progressive changes, west to east, in the dominant composition of the Coast Range batholith of Alaska would have to wait forty years for explanation. Not until the concepts of plate tectonics and subduction zone geometry were developed would this progressive change be understood.) Another paper, published in *Economic Geology* in 1935, introduced the concept of a "xenothermal" (shallow depth, high-temperature) class of hydrothermal ore deposits, an idea clearly based on observations of the character of the shallow intrusives and associated ore deposits of the Oregon Cascades. This represents perhaps the first formal break with the then-dominant but now largely superseded Lindgren-Emmons classification, in which depth of emplacement and temperature of formation were assumed to vary sympathetically. Buddington's pioneer contribution was explicitly noted in R. W. Hutchinson's 1983 presidential address to the Society of Economic Geologists (Hutchinson 1983).

The systematic descriptions of and distinctions between anorthosite of Grenville-type massifs and that of layered gabbroic complexes were expressed most completely in Buddington's 1960 paper published by the Geological Survey of India. These findings obviously derive from field studies in the Adirondacks, coupled with observations on the Stillwater Complex of Montana that were made during his supervision of the thesis studies of Princeton graduate students A. L. Howland and J. W. Peoples. Buddington's conclusions were summarized in a 1970 symposium paper: massif-type anorthosite is derived by fractional crystallization of gabbroic anorthosite magma, genetically distinct from associated rocks of the quartz syenite-mangerite series. Although this finding was challenged by other workers in the 1960s, it has since been affirmed by studies of rare-element distribution.

Buddington also produced a series of papers, variously coauthored with J. R. Balsley, D. H. Lindsley, and others, that described mineralogical variations in the Fe-Ti-O system and their significance. These contributions stemmed from the extensive field program of the U.S. Geological Survey in New York–New Jersey, which was led by Buddington. Many concepts of value were produced, among them the relationship between mineralogy and magnetic anomalies. (For example, it was discovered that reverse remanent magnetism was a characteristic property of Ti-bearing hematite, information of great value in the interpretation of measured magnetic anomalies in the region.) Buddington himself valued most highly the 1964 paper with D. H. Lindsley of the Geophysical Laboratory in which it was shown that compositions of minerals of the ilmenite-titaniferous magnetite suite could be used as a measure of partial pressure of oxygen and of temperature at the time of origin. The paper drew worldwide attention and stimulated extensive follow-on research.

Buddington tended to be somewhat orthodox and conservative in his scientific thinking—disciplined rather than venturesome; yet he was not bound by orthodoxy. New concepts were examined critically and without bias; those aspects that were found to be supported by empirical data or cogent theoretical analysis were woven into existing theory, expanding rather than replacing. For example, without changing his basic thesis that massif-type anorthosite originated by fractionation of gabbroic anorthositic magma, he found that the concept of "flow differentiation," which was advanced in the late 1950s by W. R. A. Baragar in Canada (Baragar 1960), provided an acceptable mechanism for separation of a plagioclase-rich fraction. He consequently incorporated the concept into his model for origin.

During the great "granitization" debate of the 1940s and 1950s, a number of well-known geologists in Europe and North America were converted to the radical doctrine that large bodies of granitic rock were formed by metasomatic replacement of pre-existing materials rather than by crystallization from silicate melts. Buddington, however, emerged as he had entered; a staunch magmatist. But even so, his rejection of the hypothesis as a major geologic process was not out-of-hand; it came only after the examination of possible examples of granitization in the Adirondacks and the viewing of cited field evidence elsewhere—and after many a spirited discussion with more "heretical" colleagues. It is likely that most geologists and geochemists today would share Buddington's skepticism of the importance of the granitization process. Somewhat ironically, however, with respect to the Adirondacks, it is also likely that Buddington's strictly magmatic interpretation of certain bodies of alaskite and layered gneiss in the dominantly metasedimentary terrane of the Adirondack Lowlands will have to yield to a more complex model: one that involves partial melting, diapiric movement, and at least some degree of high-temperature metasomatic replacement.

Exclusive of abstracts, medal presentations, and the like, Buddington's bibliography consists of about seventy papers, twenty-three of them published after his formal retirement in 1959. What is impressive about this list is not the number of papers but the tremendous range of subject matter and its extraordinarily high quality. Few if any are trivial, many are important, and some are recognized as true classics. Among the latter is *Adirondack Igneous Rocks and Their Metamorphism* (Geological Society of America Memoir 7), a monumental work that contains a vast amount of first-class data and dozens of significant geological conclusions. With few exceptions the petrologic concepts expressed in the Memoir—many of which were expanded or further developed in later papers— have proved remarkably sound. Buddington's colleague in later Adirondack work, B. F. Leonard, has remarked that the Memoir is "a contribution that still seems to me a full generation ahead of its time," a conclusion that is eminently justified by the record.

Buddington earned many honors and awards during his distinguished career. Most seemed to surprise him, although he was human enough to be deeply gratified. In 1942 Brown University recognized its distinguished alumnus with an honorary Sc.D. degree. He was elected to the National Academy of Sciences in 1943, to the American Academy of Arts and Sciences in 1947; in 1954 he was awarded the Penrose Medal of the Geological Society of America—America's highest honor in geology—and in 1956 the Roebling Medal of the Mineralogical Society of America. Franklin and Marshall College granted him an honorary L.L.D. degree in 1958, and in 1960 he received the André H. Dumont Medal of the Geological Society of Belgium. *Petrologic Studies: A Volume in Honor of A. F. Buddington,* written and edited by former students, was published by the Geological Society of America in 1962. The Department of the Interior, at the instigation of the U.S. Geological Survey, presented him with its highest honor, the Distinguished Service Award, in 1963. In 1964 came a different kind of honor, one that pleased Buddington greatly: a new mineral discovered by his former student Donald E.

White was given the name buddingtonite (Erd et al. 1964). The University of Liège in 1967 presented him with an honorary degree in "applied science." And finally the symposium volume *The Origin of Anorthosite and Related Rocks,* which was published in 1970 by the New York State Museum and Science Service, is dedicated most appropriately to Arthur F. Buddington in honor of his geologic work in the Adirondacks and his more than fifty years of association with the Museum.

Buddington was inclined to be impatient with formal rules and procedures, whether of stratigraphic nomenclature or management practice. His long stint—from 1936 to 1950—as departmental chairman at Princeton was notable for a minimum of formality and officiousness; to the student and the outsider the department appeared simply "to run itself." It didn't, of course; there were many problems to be solved and many serious decisions to be made. But most were handled quietly and effectively on a person-to-person basis. After fourteen years of his administrative leadership the department was one of increased strength and status.

As a responsible member of a number of professional societies, Buddington was often called upon to serve on committees and advisory panels. He did so willingly, enjoying the opportunities to become acquainted with fellow geologists, but he never actively sought high office. Some of his major areas of service included membership on the Council (1939–41) and the vice-presidency (1943 and 1947) of the Geological Society of America (breaking with custom, Buddington declined the semiautomatic move into the presidency of the society after serving as vice-president); membership on the Council (1936–40) and the presidency (1942) of the Mineralogical Society of America; the presidency of the Volcanology Section (1941–44) of the American Geophysical Union;

the chairmanship of the Geology Section (1954–57) of the National Academy of Sciences; and membership on the Advisory Board (1950–61) of the *Geochimica et Cosmochimica Acta*. He also served as associate editor of *American Journal of Science* (1950–69) and *American Scientist* (1961–62).

In 1924 Arthur Buddington married Jene Elizabeth Muntz of David City, Nebraska, whom he had met while with the Geophysical Laboratory in Washington, D.C. She was to be his loved and treasured helpmate until her death in 1975. Buddington depended on her absolutely in social affairs, and she was a gracious hostess to generations of Princeton graduate students—for years the Buddingtons regularly visited and in turn entertained incoming students and their wives, engendering an esprit de corps at Princeton rarely matched in academic circles. Mrs. Buddington also served as a loyal chauffeur during Adirondack field work, "driving over all kinds of roads in all kinds of weather," because Buddington, oddly enough, never learned to drive a car—even though he was entirely at ease at the helm of a motor-driven small boat in rough water. The Buddingtons had one daughter, Elizabeth Jene (Mrs. Lyle Branagan), who now lives in Cohasset, Massachusetts.

Honesty and integrity are two of the best remembered elements of Buddington's character. He was a man of true modesty, a trait that led him to give fair hearing to views with which he disagreed, whether expressed by lowly student or professional peer. He did enjoy—both as a participant and as a listener—a brisk exchange of opinions, particularly in the field, but he was not of an argumentative disposition. He had a loud and gusty laugh that often echoed down the corridors of Guyot Hall, and even if sometimes it seemed at odds with his quiet speech and manner, it was nonetheless entirely genuine. These personal characteristics, coupled with a complete lack of pomp and ceremony, endeared Buddington to students. That his influence was lasting can be illustrated by a passage in Harry Hess's touching tribute in the 1962 Buddington Volume (Hess 1962). The words are from a letter sent to Harry by a former student—unnamed, but at the time of writing a distinguished professor in his own right:

> He always has been the greatest man I know in science, and I don't lead an isolated life. To me he is, to use his expression, "the pure quill." If I ever do anything worth a damn, it will be largely due to his influence on me. There is nothing like Bud on the market—and I go shopping every day.

IN PREPARING THIS MEMOIR I have had the advantage of access to autobiographical notes prepared by Buddington in his later years and to a draft of a memorial being prepared by B. F. Leonard. I have drawn freely from both sources, generally without attribution. I have also incorporated, again without specific credit, thoughts and comments received from others—notably, P. E. Hotz, A. E. J. Engel, P. K. Sims, J. C. Maxwell, and M. P. Foose—all of whom shared my good fortune in having had Bud as a teacher and as a friend.

REFERENCES

Baragar, W. R. A. 1960. Petrology of basaltic rocks in part of the Labrador Trough. Geol. Soc. Am. Bull., 71:1589–1644.

Erd, R. C., D. E. White, J. J. Fahey, and D. E. Lee. 1964. Buddingtonite, an ammonium feldspar with zeolitic water. Am. Mineral., 49:831–50.

Hargraves, R. B. 1984. Memorial to Arthur Francis Buddington. Geol. Soc. Am. Mem.

Hawkes, H. E. and J. R. Balsley. 1946. Magnetic exploration for iron ore in northern New York. U.S. Geological Survey Strategic Minerals Investigations, Preliminary Report, 3–194.

Hawkes, H. E. 1976. The early days of exploration geochemistry. J. Geochem. Explor., 6:1–11.

Hess, H. H. 1962. (A. F. Buddington) An appreciation. In: *Petrologic Studies* (a volume in honor of A. F. Buddington), ed. A. E.

J. Engel, H. L. James, and B. F. Leonard, pp. vii–xi. Boulder, Colorado: Geological Society of America.

Hotz, P. E. 1950. Diamond-drill exploration of the Dillsburg magnetite deposits, York County, Pennsylvania. U.S. Geol. Surv. Bull., 969-A.

Hutchinson, R. W. 1983. Hydrothermal concepts: the old and the new. Econ. Geol., 78:1734–41.

BIBLIOGRAPHY

1916

Pyrophyllitization, pinitization and silicification of rocks around Conception Bay, Newfoundland. J. Geol., 24:130–52.

1917

Report on the pyrite and pyrrhotite veins in Jefferson and St. Lawrence Counties, New York. N.Y. State Defense Council Bull. no. 1. 40 pp.

1919

Foliation of the gneissoid syenite-granite complex of Lewis County, New York. In: 14th Report of the Director, N.Y. State Museum, 1917, pp. 101–10.

Pre-Cambrian rocks of southeast Newfoundland. J. Geol., 27:449–79.

1920

With J. B. Ferguson. The binary system akermanite-gehlenite. Am. J. Sci., 199:131–40.

1922

On some natural and synthetic melilites. Am. J. Sci., 203:35–87.

Mineral deposits of the Wrangell district, southeastern Alaska. U.S. Geol. Surv. Bull., 739-B:51–75.

1924

Alaskan nickel minerals. Econ. Geol., 19:521–41.

1925

Mineral investigations in southeastern Alaska. U.S. Geol. Surv. Bull., 773-B:71–139.

1926

Submarine pillow lavas of southeastern Alaska. J. Geol., 34:824–28.

With C. H. Smyth, Jr. Geology of the Bonaparte quadrangle. N.Y. State Mus. Bull. no. 269. 103 pp.

Mineral investigations in southeastern Alaska. U.S. Geol. Surv. Bull., 783-B:41–62.

1927

Geology and mineral deposits of the Salmon River area. Eng. Min. J. Press, pp. 525–30.
Coast range intrusives of southeastern Alaska. J. Geol., 35:224–46.
Coincident variations of types of mineralization and of Coast Range intrusives. Econ. Geol., 22:158–79.

1929

With T. Chapin. Geology and mineral deposits of southeastern Alaska. U.S. Geol. Surv. Bull. no. 800. 398 pp.
Geology of Hyder and vicinity, southeastern Alaska. U.S. Geol. Surv. Bull. no. 807. 124 pp.
Granite phacoliths and their contact zones in the northwest Adirondacks. N.Y. State Mus. Bull., 281:51–107.

1930

Molybdenite deposit at Shakan, Alaska. Econ. Geol., 25:197–200.

1931

The Adirondack igneous stem. J. Geol., 39:240–63.

1932

With J. G. Fairchild. Some Eocene volcanics in southeastern Alaska. Am. J. Sci., 224:490–96.

1933

Correlation of kinds of igneous rocks with kinds of mineralization. In: *Ore Deposits of the Western States* (Lindgren Volume), pp. 350–85. New York: American Institute of Mining and Metallurgical Engineers.
Gravity stratification as a criterion in the interpretation of the structure of certain intrusives of the northwestern Adirondacks. Int. Geol. Congr. 16th Rep., 1:347–52.

1934

Geology and mineral resources of the Hammond, Antwerp, and Lowville quadrangles. N.Y. State Mus. Bull. no. 296. 215 pp.

1935

High-temperature mineral associations at shallow to moderate depth. Econ. Geol., 30:205–22.

1936

With E. Callaghan. Dioritic intrusive rocks and contact metamorphism in the Cascade Range in Oregon. Am. J. Sci., 31:421–49.

Review of geology and ore deposits of the Montezuma quadrangle, Colorado. Econ. Geol., 31:318–21.

Memorial to Alexander Hamilton Phillips. Geol. Soc. Am. Proc., pp. 241–48. (Also in: Am. Mineral., 22:1094–98.)

1937

With H. H. Hess. Layered peridotitic laccoliths in the Trout River area, Newfoundland. Am. J. Sci., 33:380–88.

Geology of the Santa Clara quadrangle, New York. N.Y. State Mus. Bull. no. 309. 56 pp.

1938

Memorial to Charles Henry Smyth, Jr. Geol. Soc. Am. Proc., pp. 195–202.

With E. Callaghan. Metalliferous deposits of the Cascade Range in Oregon. U.S. Geol. Surv. Bull. no. 893. 141 pp.

1939

Adirondack igneous rocks and their metamorphism. Geol. Soc. Am. Mem. no. 7. 354 pp.

1941

With L. Whitcomb. Geology of the Willsboro quadrangle, New York. N.Y. State Mus. Bull. no. 325. 137 pp.

1943

Some petrological concepts and the interior of the earth. Am. Mineral., 28:119–40.

1948

Origin of granitic rocks of the northwest Adirondacks. Geol. Soc. Am. Mem., 28:21–43.

1950

Composition and genesis of pyroxene and garnet related to Adirondack anorthosite and anorthosite-marble contact zones. Am. Mineral., 35 (Larsen Volume):659–70.

1952

Chemical petrology of some metamorphosed Adirondack gabbroic, syenitic, and quartz syenitic rocks. Am. J. Sci. (Bowen Volume), part I:37–84.

1953

With B. F. Leonard. Chemical petrology and mineralogy of hornblendes in northwest Adirondack granitic rocks. Am. Mineral., 38 (Ross-Schaller Volume):891–902.

Geology of the Saranac quadrangle, New York. N.Y. State Mus. Bull. no. 346. 84 pp.

1954

With J. R. Balsley. Correlation of reverse remanent magnetism and negative anomalies with certain minerals. J. Geomagn. Geoelectr., 6:176–81.

1955

With J. Fahey and A. Vlisidis. Thermometric and petrogenetic significance of titaniferous magnetite. Am. J. Sci., 253:497–532. (Discussion [1956], 254:511–15.)

1956

Correlation of rigid units, types of folds, and lineation in a Grenville Belt. In: *The Grenville Problem*, R. Soc. Canada Spec. Publ., 1:99–118.

1957

With J. R. Balsley. Remanent magnetism of the Russell belt of gneisses, northwest Adirondack Mountains. Philos. Mag. Suppl., 6:317–22.

With J. R. Balsley and J. W. Graham. Stress induced magnetization of some rocks with analyzed magnetic minerals. J. Geophys. Res., 62:465–74.

Interrelated Precambrian granitic rocks, northwest Adirondacks. Geol. Soc. Am. Bull., 68:291–306.

1958

Geologic section at Hibernia Mine, N.J. U.S. Geol. Surv. Prof. Pap., 287:147–59.

With J. R. Balsley. Iron-titanium oxide minerals, rocks, and aeromagnetic anomalies of the Adirondack area, New York. Econ. Geol., 53:777–805.

1959

Granite emplacement with special reference to North America. Geol. Soc. Am. Bull., 70:671–747.

1960

With J. R. Balsley. Magnetic susceptibility, anisotropy, and fabric of some Adirondack granites and orthogneisses. Am. J. Sci., 258-A (Bradley Volume):6–20.

Norman Levi Bowen. Am. Philos. Soc. Yearb., pp. 113–18.

The origin of anorthosite re-evaluated. Geol. Surv. Indian Rec., 86:421–32.

1961

With J. R. Balsley. Microintergrowths and fabrics of iron-titanium oxide minerals in some Adirondack rocks. In: Mahadevan Volume, pp. 1–16. Hyderabad, India: Osmania University Press.

With D. R. Baker. Geology of the Franklin and part of the Hamburg quadrangles, New Jersey. U.S. Geol. Survey Misc. Geol. Inv., Map I-346.

1962

Iron and iron-titanium oxide minerals and concentrations in Precambrian rocks in New York and New Jersey, U.S.A. In: Korzhinsky Volume. Moscow.

With B. F. Leonard. Regional geology of the St. Lawrence County magnetite district, N.Y. U.S. Geol. Surv. Prof. Pap. no. 376. 145 pp.

1963

With J. Fahey and A. Vlisidis. Degree of oxidation of Adirondack iron oxide and iron-titanium oxide minerals in relation to petrogeny. J. Petrol., 4:138–69.

Isograds and the role of H_2O in metamorphic facies of orthogneisses of the northwest Adirondacks area, New York. Geol. Soc. Am. Bull., 74:1155–81.

Metasomatic origin of large parts of the Adirondack phacoliths— A discussion. Geol. Soc. Am. Bull., 74:353.

1964

With D. H. Lindsley. Iron-titanium oxide minerals and synthetic equivalents. J. Petrol., 5:310–57.

With B. F. Leonard. Ore deposits of the St. Lawrence County magnetite district, northwest Adirondacks, New York. U.S. Geol. Surv. Prof. Pap. no. 377. 259 pp.

Esper S. Larsen, Jr. In: *Biographical Memoirs of the National Academy of Sciences,* vol. 37, pp. 161–84. New York: Columbia University Press for the National Academy of Sciences.

Distribution of MnO between coexisting ilmenite and magnetite. In: *Advancing Frontiers in Geology and Geophysics* (Krishnan Volume), ed. A. P. Subramaniam and S. Balakrishna, pp. 233–48. Hyderabad, India: Osmania University Press.

1965

The origin of three garnet isograds in Adirondack gneisses. Mineral. Mag., 34 (Tilley Volume):71–81.

1966

The occurrence of garnet in the granulite-facies terrane of the Adirondack Highlands—A discussion. J. Petrol., 7:331–35.

The Precambrian magnetite deposits of New York and New Jersey. Econ. Geol., 61:484–510.

1969

With M. L. Jensen and R. C. Mauger. Sulfur isotopes and origin of northwest Adirondack sulfide deposits. Geol. Soc. Am. Mem. no. 115 (Poldervaart Volume), pp. 423–51.

Some problems in estimation of physical conditions for development of Adirondack rocks. N.Y. State Ed. Dept. Geogram, 7:7–16.

1970

Adirondack anorthositic series. In: *The Origin of Anorthosite and Related Rocks,* ed. Y. W. Isachsen. N.Y. State Mus. Sci. Serv. Mem. no. 18, pp. 215–31.

With R. B. Hargraves. Analogy between anorthositic series on the earth and moon. Icarus, 13:371–82.

With D. R. Baker. Geology of the Franklin and part of the Hamburg quadrangles, N.J. U.S. Geol. Surv. Prof. Pap. no. 638.

1972

Differentiation trends and parental magmas for anorthositic and quartz mangerite series, Adirondacks, New York. Geol. Soc. Am. Mem. no. 132, pp. 477–88.

1973

Memorial to Harry Hammond Hess. Geol. Soc. Am. Mem., 1:18–26.

1975

Anorthosite bearing complexes: Classification and parental magmas. In: *Studies in Precambrians,* ed. C. Naganna, pp. 115–41. Bangalore, India: Bangalore University Press.

Karsh of Ottawa

J. GEORGE HARRAR
December 2, 1906–April 18, 1982

BY JOHN J. McKELVEY, JR.

J GEORGE HARRAR led from strength—from many strengths. He loved a battle; he expected to win, and few indeed were the battles that he lost. Intuitively and with uncanny accuracy, he assessed his odds for success in whatever endeavor he contemplated. Quick in mind, he reached decisions easily—a quality most evident in the formative years of his career. He never lost this quality, but sometimes it was masked later in his life by the subtleties of many situations he had to face.

Born on December 2, 1906, in Painesville, Ohio, George shared with his brother Ellwood Scott, Jr., two years older, and his sister Marjorie, three years younger than he, the parental guidance typical of an Ohio family at that time. Regular attendance at church school was a must. There, as in his high school, the younger children in the group would cluster around him. E. S. Harrar, Sr., George's father, had earned his degree in electrical engineering from Lehigh University. When the family lived in Painesville, he worked to establish ore docks in nearby Ashtabula. When George was three years old, the family moved to Ashtabula; six years later, Youngstown became their permanent home. In Youngstown Mr. Harrar was instrumental in the electrification of steel mills for the Youngstown Sheet and Tube Company. George's mother, Lucetta Sterner, taught school briefly but gave up teaching after her marriage to devote herself exclusively to her family.

George's father was a Boy Scout leader and stimulated his sons' interest in nature. Both relished the merit badge challenges of the program and went beyond Eagle Scout rank. As a Boy Scout, George became the troop bugler. His interest in the bugle led him to cornet lessons, and soon he was playing in the school band. He loved good music; he could identify almost any composition and its composer after hearing only a few measures. The Scout sports program also appealed to George. Through its activities he became a fine swimmer and diver. A nearby tennis court sparked his interest, and he spent many hours practicing there. He also managed the basketball team in high school. From riflery and target practice he developed a penchant for hunting. During the summer months, George turned his interest in sports to good advantage, earning his spending money as a golfer's caddie—and trying golf himself with his own homemade golf club. George also read from the best of the literature in the family library, but at an early age his reading interests turned to biology and the sciences.

The two brothers chose Oberlin for college, George enrolling at age sixteen in 1923, a year after his brother. Scott, as a sophomore, suffered a serious automobile accident that took him out of Oberlin; but he went on to study forestry at Syracuse University and ultimately to serve as dean of the College of Forestry at Duke University. George stayed at Oberlin; he could have graduated in 1927 after the customary four-year period but remained for a fifth year to take additional courses and to captain the track team.

Throughout his life, George was "George" to almost everyone, but he was "Dutch" to the few who knew of his prowess on the Oberlin track team. At college he earned the sobriquet "The Flying Dutchman" (shortened to Dutch) for the records he set in 1928 in the 440-yard dash and as anchorman on the record-setting mile relay team. One of his classmates wrote recently, "I remember 'Dutch' Harrar very well and always enjoyed attending track meets when he ran. He seemed to give every ounce of energy to it and I always feared whether his endurance could hold out"—an assessment of performance that was characteristic of George's entire career.

Oberlin taught George academic rigor; it blessed him also with the love and friendship of two persons who were to influence his entire life—Georgetta (Georgie) Steese, then a student in the Conservatory of Music, and Frederick Grover, emeritus head of the botany department. Georgie became his wife, whose love and support he thoroughly appreciated. Grover, a classical botanist and an impressive teacher, recognized George's intellectual talents and cultivated his interest in botany. An intense mutual admiration developed between the two. The twinkle in Grover's eye when he later spoke of George told of the human as well as of the intellectual traits he knew George possessed and that he, Grover, understood. (Perhaps from his Oberlin classmates or from his colleagues at the Youngstown steel mills—where he earned money sharpening tools during the summer months—he further acquired a colorful vocabulary and the art of telling stories—risqué ones—that might deceive those who were unaware of his high moral standards.)

Following graduation from Oberlin, George had hoped to enroll in medical school, but the Depression precluded such a long and expensive period of education. Instead he won a teaching fellowship in plant pathology at Iowa State University where he studied under the direction of I. E. Melhus, the head of the department, and John Aikman, a plant ecologist. Within nine months he completed the requirements for the master's degree and was on his way to the University of Puerto Rico as professor of biology in the College of Agriculture; shortly thereafter, Georgie, his bride, joined him. His subsequent four years in Puerto Rico gave him a love of the Latin temperament and facility with the Spanish language.

George left Puerto Rico in 1934 to accept a Firestone fellowship and to become an instructor in plant pathology at the University of Minnesota. He went there because he wanted to work toward his Ph.D. degree with E. C. Stakman (Stak), the eminent wheat pathologist and a man with international interests who would later receive world recognition as the elder statesman in his discipline. As in the case of Frederick Grover, George and Stak became fast friends; once again a relationship of mutual admiration and loyalty developed—each would pick on the other's weaknesses but passionately defend the other from outside attack.

Like George, Stak had a powerful and intensely competitive intellect. One day when Stak and I were sitting in the lobby of a hotel in New Delhi, India, amidst the haze of blue smoke from his pipe, he blurted out, "John, have you ever had an argument with George?" I answered, "No, not a real argument. After all, first as one of his graduate students and now in his employ, I have never been in a position to have an argument with George." After a long silence, Stak offered, "Well, an argument with George is not an argument—it's a battle." And Stak—halfway around the globe from George who was then in New York—must have been nursing some wounds from an "argument" he had lost and mulling over what he should have said and did not.

George went from the University of Minnesota to Virginia Polytechnic Institute (VPI) in Blacksburg in 1935 to teach plant pathology. I first met George in 1939 at the International Microbiology Congress in New York. A melange of impressions struck me then: his youthfulness; his slight build and small features; his thinning hair, fine, slightly reddish, and wavy; his conservative dark-blue suit; and eyes, as blue and sharp as I had ever encountered, that divined instantly what one might be thinking.

Seated in the back of George's classroom at VPI, one had difficulty in following his lectures because he spoke in such a steady, low voice. Yet discipline never got out of hand in his classes—an amazing fact given the nonacademic interests of most of the VPI cadet corps—"Highty Tighties," as they called themselves in the 1930s. George said to me one day, "If trouble is brewing in my class, I just look for the biggest and roughest in the bunch and take him on; then the others behave." No smart aleck lasted long in George's graduate studies program, either. He demanded loyalty and work to the best of one's ability. Whether or not an individual was an A student did not matter as long as one strove to do one's best. And George cared deeply about his graduate students. He insisted that they participate at national scientific meetings, where he made certain to introduce them to his colleagues. He sought job opportunities for them diligently, even if an available job would carry a student into a different but related discipline.

George, Georgie, and their two children—Cynthia Ann and Georgetta Louise, born in Roanoke—loved Blacksburg. Although for George the academic pace set by the easygoing head of the Department of Biology I. D. Wilson was too slow, the surroundings nevertheless offered a spectacular succession of black locust, red bud, dogwood, azalea, and rhododendron in blossom. In the fall, the hunting for quail and grouse was good. As a volunteer, George coached the VPI track team.

The Harrars built a home in Blacksburg, but by 1941 the challenges clearly lay elsewhere. So after six years at VPI,

George accepted the positions of professor and head of the Department of Plant Pathology and head of the Division of Plant Pathology of the Agricultural Experiment Station at Washington State College. (This prestigious set of posts had previously been held by F. D. Heald, whose text on plant pathology had become the Bible of plant pathologists.) During these years, George and his brother Scott at Durham, North Carolina, worked intensively on their book, *Guide to Southern Trees*.

The Harrars stayed less than two years at Washington State College because George accepted an offer to become the local director of the Mexican Agricultural Program, which the Rockefeller Foundation had decided to initiate in 1943. This program had originated in discussions among the U.S. Vice-President Elect Henry Wallace, certain Mexican officials, and the Foundation's president (then Raymond B. Fosdick). The talks explored how the Rockefeller Foundation might be able to help bring Mexico out of its slump in agricultural production to the point where it could produce the basic foods it needed—corn, beans, and wheat. The Foundation called on three eminent agriculturists—E. C. Stakman, who was the project's leader; P. C. Mangelsdorf, professor of botany at Harvard University; and Richard Bradfield, head of the Department of Agronomy at Cornell University—to advise on the feasibility of the Foundation's entering into an agreement with the Mexican government to build a program of research dealing with the basic food crops.

Strange that the Foundation should have chosen George to head a practical program in agriculture. He was city bred; he had no farm experience; he had graduated from a liberal arts college; and in his research in graduate school and his subsequent assignments at the University of Puerto Rico and VPI, he had focused—and published—mainly on mycological problems associated with plant disease agents rather than on pragmatic problems of producing basic food crops. The choice was not so strange, however, when one considers three things: George's total dedication to a task at hand; his growing awareness through his land-grant college assignments of the vital importance of a healthy agriculture to the welfare of a country; and his reputation as a proven scientist.

Free to build a program in Mexico, George sharpened his talents in administration and diplomacy. He exercised his inspirational leadership abilities, his deftness in the choice of colleagues, and his ability to maintain a cool exterior while burning inside. Innate patience never figured among George's strengths, but he did have a miraculous control—in public—of a fiery temperament. He hated to be kept "on hold" outside the offices of Mexican officials, but he would wait and burn. While he burned, he would exercise his charm, wit, and diplomacy on the junior functionaries who ofttimes held the keys to the inner sancta, whether of the secretary, subsecretary, or other agricultural official. George often got past those doors when others could not.

In selecting the scientists and other staff for the Mexican Agricultural Program, George exhibited one of his strongest suits: the ability to choose the right person for the right job. Most of those he selected spent their entire careers in one or another of the Foundation's programs. One of his earliest choices, Norman E. Borlaug, later received the Nobel Peace Prize for his contributions—not only in Mexico but worldwide—to the alleviation of hunger through the production of varieties of high-yielding wheat resistant to disease.

No one, however, can achieve a perfect score in the choice of individuals for specific assignments. Once in a while a staff member had to go. In such cases George would feel a responsibility toward that individual's career, and he would invariably work out an easy transition for the person leaving the Foundation. The Mexican civil service system, from which it was almost impossible to fire an individual, may have reinforced this compassionate feeling. In that system an individual who was unsatisfactory in his post likewise would eventually find himself transferred to another.

George set the life-style, the ethic, of the Mexican Agricultural Program; to wit, "work hard, play hard, but above all, work hard." Even socializing at frequent house parties (discotheques in a sense) and at bowling parties took on value greater than merely releasing tensions engendered during the work of a highly competitive group of colleagues. It was a mechanism for achieving interdisciplinary cooperation and for bringing wives into a full knowledge of and participation in program activities.

Although George had found his métier in Mexico, toward the close of his nearly ten years there he had obviously outgrown the program. By 1952 the Mexican Agricultural Program had proliferated. A similar effort was under way in Colombia, and arrangements had been made to create an additional program in Chile. Brazil, Ecuador, and Peru, among other countries, were clamoring for assistance for their agricultural, educational, and research institutions; and a program in India was under consideration. Warren Weaver, director of the Foundation's Natural Sciences Division, decided he needed George at headquarters in New York.

Reluctantly, George went to New York; but his heart never left Mexico. The move to New York meant that those occasional sorties at dawn, slogging through the marshes of Toluca Valley to hunt ducks, would have to go. So would the lilt of the mariachi music from the itinerant bands of Mexico City. Something else would have to replace the satisfaction of outfoxing the foxes who might try to torpedo parts of his program, the occasional lesser officials who did not always appreciate George's motives and those of his colleagues. The lightheartedness, the *compañerismo,* among staff families would have to give way to a New York sedateness and formality. Nevertheless, in New York his drive to inform staff wives and to involve them in Foundation affairs lingered. It cropped up in the occasional get-togethers at George's house in Scarsdale and in the banquets at the Tower Suite of the Time and Life Building in New York.

In New York as deputy director for agriculture, George sometimes chafed under Warren Weaver's direction. Weaver's program on molecular biology was well established, and the two programs were in a sense competitive for the same funds. Moreover, Weaver, of diminutive physique, was another intellectual giant, a mathematician with sparkling clarity in his thinking and writing. He was charming, but he, too, could indulge in intellectual skirmishes with punitive results to his adversary. It tickled George that E. C. Stakman could exasperate Weaver, who would lay a neat trap in an argument only to find that Stak was "batting on another wicket" by the time Weaver thought he had him in his clutches. "Ouchy" about pain himself, George admired Weaver for his inurement to it. For example, Weaver—in shorts—would tramp through the brambles of his seven acres on Second Hill in New Milford, Connecticut, unmindful of the blood trickling down his legs from his brush with the thorns of those bushes.

Weaver had become the most powerful of the directors of his time within the Foundation. He accepted the groundswell of trustee and public concern about agricultural research and development, even though it promised to engulf his cherished program in molecular biology. Shrewdly he developed companion interests that he labeled "nonconventional agriculture," which was somewhat competitive with George's practical program. Under this rubric, Weaver could support research on solar energy for agricultural uses; on *Chlorella,* an alga, for producing proteinaceous food under laboratory conditions; on discarded pea pods and vines ground and compressed into pellets that when liberally doused with curry were supposed to be palatable; and on *Torula* yeasts for converting sawdust and similar cellulose waste products into highly proteinaceous foods for human consumption.

During his years as Weaver's deputy director for agriculture (1952–55), and subsequently as director of agriculture (1955–59) in his own right, George brought to realization his concept of international institutions devoted to practical research for the improvement of basic food crops. The first of these, the International Rice Research Institute (IRRI) in the Philippines, had its origin partly in the successes of the Mexican Program on wheat improvement. It also came partly from the idea that an international effort might offer freedom from the constraints of operating at national levels through the bureaucracies of foreign countries; but mainly IRRI arose out of the need to improve rice production in Asia. Harrar, whose vision always sought the financial horizon beyond existing monetary barriers, knew that the Rockefeller Foundation could not by itself finance the first of the international agricultural research centers—let alone those to follow. Since Vice-President F. F. Hill of the Ford Foundation shared George's belief that something should be done about rice jointly, with USAID and other donor agencies participating later, they could and did establish IRRI.

Once a professional, always a professional. While involved with the administration and execution of the Foundation's agricultural program, George collaborated with Stak to produce their text, *Principles of Plant Pathology.*

George and Warren Weaver never developed a "Frederick Grover" relationship, although Warren became one of George's most ardent mentors. When in 1955 Weaver became vice-president for medical, natural, and agricultural sciences under President Dean Rusk's administration of the Foundation, George became director for the agricultural sciences. When Warren Weaver retired in 1959, George followed in his shoes as vice-president. In that capacity one of his major accomplishments was to open up for the Foundation (and for the U.S. government through USAID as well) the potential for developing programs in Africa. In consultation with many experts, he developed the initial pattern for the improvement of science, technology, and education throughout Africa in a study that he led and USAID financed through the Foreign Office of the National Academy of Sciences. What George really set in motion within the National Academy, however, was a long-term effort of assistance to developing countries. This proliferated to embrace the South Pacific and Latin American, as well as the African Science Board, and culminated in the creation of the Board of Science and Technology for International Development.

In 1961 George succeeded Dean Rusk as president of the Foundation when Rusk left to become President Kennedy's Secretary of State. Two years later, in 1963, the Foundation celebrated its 50th anniversary. George took advantage of that moment to reflect on the Foundation's past accomplishments and to lead in recasting its program.

George carried into the presidency his "do it yourself" philosophy sharpened by his land-grant college experiences and by the successes of the Mexican Agricultural Program. He also brought his penchant for integrating programs that had become diffuse and disconnected and his insistence that programs express purposeful objectives. Thus, early in his administration he called upon the social, agricultural, natural, and medical sciences to interdigitate in a university development program for the developing world. The agricultural, medical, and social sciences were to forge linkages embodying crop production, nutrition, economics, and agricultural policy in a program entitled "Toward the Conquest of Hunger." The medical and natural sciences division was to embrace population stabilization. These growing in-house programs required a vast expansion of field staff on whose importance Harrar laid special stress; he was mindful of the great achievements of such staff in the days when the Foundation was combating hookworm in the southern United States and malaria and yellow fever abroad, as well as of his own experiences in Mexico. By 1968 George and the trustees had woven into the social sciences division an action program entitled "Toward Equal Opportunity for All," which was directed toward disadvantaged racial groups in the United States. Finally, in the last several years of his presidency, he sneaked through a Foundation program called "Allied Interests," his concern, as expressed in one of the first annual reports of his presidency, for the quality of the environment. By 1971 this concern had become a full-fledged program entitled "Natural and Environmental Sciences," dealing not only with the noxious chemicals applied to agricultural crops but with those spewing from industry as well.

The 1960s—the decade of George's presidency—were halcyon days for the philanthropic foundations. The economy was robust, inflation was insignificant, and the Rockefeller Foundation's assets rose to nearly a billion dollars, a level not to be reached again until the early 1980s. The Foundation trustees were relaxed; they dipped into capital annually—at times to the extent of $10 million to $15 million—to finance especially worthwhile projects.

Congressional uneasiness about tax-exempt institutions soon impaired that aura of well-being. The Committee on Finance of the U.S. Senate and the Committee on Ways and Means of the House of Representatives requested that the Treasury examine the activities of private foundations for tax abuses and report its findings and recommendations. While these investigations revealed that the preponderance of private foundations performed their functions without tax abuse, evidence accrued to indicate that a very few such organizations did abuse the tax exemption privilege: through self-dealing, retaining contributions as capital and thus delaying the benefits to charity, involvement in business enterprises, family use of foundations to control corporate and other property, the performance of financial transactions unrelated to charitable functions, and in other ways. The report led to recommendations for legislation that would have seriously cramped all of the foundations in their efforts to provide wise and responsible philanthropy. Against this background, George, among other foundation presidents, felt it imperative to plead the case for the foundations—albeit some foundation executives seemed complacent about the report and about the proposed legislation. Indeed, in his oral history George reported:

> The Chairman of the Board [of the Rockefeller Foundation] said, "Well, George, if you're worrying as much as you are, we won't worry any more," or something like that. Well, that was nice to let me worry alone. I *did* worry a great deal, and it was at that point that I decided on my own that, yes, I was going to write a good deal more and I was going to have other people writing and I was going to appear on television and radio and in every way that I could, with dignity and within reason, that we'd try to get our case before the public in a more effective fashion.
>
> By the end of the year 1969, we were right into it and we were doing everything we could to try to offset some of the threats which we knew existed. One was that should not all foundations be given what I called a death sentence? Should they have a fixed life? And that ranged from 25 years to 45 years, as I remember it. The various suggestions came in and we really protested to the maximum of our ability and did succeed in getting those provisions knocked out of the bill. I had a few colleagues who said, in the foundation world, "Well, within 45 years, who knows? Or in 25 years a thing can turn around," et cetera, et cetera. I said, "We're under the gun right now. Let's not put up with this. We know it's wrong...."

The responsibilities of the presidency weighed heavily on George. He seemed not to enjoy that post as he had his early ones. He retained his thoroughness in researching matters upon which he had to reach decisions. But his inclination increased, in fact, to let officers proceed far down a trail in expecting one decision only to find ultimately that George had reached an alternative one.

George's collateral responsibilities burgeoned during his tenure as president of the Rockefeller Foundation. He was elected to the National Academy of Sciences in April 1966 and shortly thereafter served on its Committee on Science and Public Policy. His alma mater, Oberlin College, elected him a trustee. President Johnson appointed him to his General Advisory Committee on Foreign Assistance Programs from 1965 to 1969. These and others, together with his academic and social affiliations and with the honors that he received, required that much of his time be spent in writing and in speaking engagements.

When George retired, the trustees of the Foundation took the unprecedented action of recognizing his achievements by designating him a life fellow, the first in the fifty-eight years of Foundation history. George himself had stabilized many of the Foundation programs with staff he had so artfully acquired over the years. In the program "Toward the Conquest of Hunger," for example, soil scientist R. F. Chandler, Jr., was serving as director of the Rice Research Institute; Norman E. Borlaug had won his Nobel Peace Prize and was continuing his research in Mexico on wheat as an associate director in New York; Dorothy Parker, trained as a botanist, was specializing in library development; Sterling Wortman, a plant breeder, had become the Foundation's vice-president for the natural, environmental, and agricultural sciences; plant breeder E. J. Wellhausen was director of the corn and wheat improvement center, CIMMYT, in Mexico; and John A. Pino was director for agricultural sciences, the post that Harrar once held. All had at one time or another been staff members in the Mexican Agricultural Program. These staff and their colleagues gathered at Williamsburg in 1979 to honor George and Georgetta. They presented him with a silver sword embedded in crystal, a facsimile of King Arthur's Excalibur—incidentally to recognize George's abiding interest in collecting knives, symbolically to pay tribute to his mastery over his profession, agriculture.

The many responsibilities that came George's way in retirement may have deprived him of time with his family and the opportunity to take the frequent dips he enjoyed in his swimming pool at his Scarsdale home. He wrote; he participated in an early scholarly exchange mission to China sponsored by the National Academy of Sciences, the Social Science Research Council, and the Council of Learned Societies; he served as director of several corporations; he lectured as an Andrew D. White Professor-at-Large at Cornell University; and above all, he still engaged in institution building. Sterling Wortman, vice-president of the Rockefeller Foundation, called on George to become a trustee and chairman of the board of the newly created International Agricultural Development Service to help that institution meet its mandate to promote the application of modern agricultural research to problems of development among the nations of Latin America, Asia, and Africa. Slowed in his seventies, however, by decades of burning his candle at both ends—in the best sense of that figure of speech—in his seventy-fifth year, George succumbed to a heart attack in his home on April 18, 1982.

J. George Harrar's strength—his many strengths—sprang from his intrinsic capabilities. Certain extrinsic forces, however, helped him to make the most of those capabilities. The perfect marriage, synchrony in philosophy, of a man and an institution figured among the strongest of those forces. The Rockefeller Foundation offered George flexibility and scope for formulating and executing his programs—which then became Foundation programs—from the conquest of hunger through equality of opportunity, quality of the environment, population stabilization, and improvement of health to promotion of the arts and of the humanities and development of social sciences and educational opportunities in the universities of the developing worlds. And George offered the Rockefeller Foundation leadership with loyalty and distinction, enabling it to satisfy its mandate—which was George's mandate as well—"toward the well-being of mankind throughout the world," during the thirty years of that marriage that culminated in the decade of his presidency: inspiring times, troubled ones, too, in a great Foundation.

IN THE PREPARATION OF MY MEMOIR of J. George Harrar, I have drawn on communications from his sister, Mrs. Marjorie Filmer, and I have virtually quoted material that she sent to me in her letter of May 16, 1983, about his life prior to college days. I have also quoted Miss Gertrude Jacobs, a volunteer research assistant at Oberlin College, from a postscript of a letter that she wrote to me verifying George's track records at Oberlin. His wife, Georgetta, contributed much information about his entire life and work. Dorothy Parker, a lifelong associate of Dr. Harrar, verified information with respect to his career. Mr. William J. Hess, archivist of the Rockefeller Foundation, supplied me with information on George's testimony before the House Ways and Means Committee; and from the material he gave me I have excerpted quotations from George's oral history. Anne E. Newbery, editor; Henry Romney, director of information services, the Rockefeller Foundation; and my wife, Josephine Faulkner McKelvey, helped with specific editorial suggestions. Others have read the manuscript and offered suggestions. Anna Starr, my secretary, has been involved in the preparation of the manuscript and in assembling the bibliography. Marie Dooling, librarian, checked the references. I acknowledge with deep gratitude the help of these people.

HONORS AND DISTINCTIONS

EDUCATION

A.B., Oberlin College, 1928
M.S., Iowa State University, 1929
Ph.D., University of Minnesota, 1935

HONORARY DEGREES

1962 Doctor of Laws, Oberlin College
1963 Doctor of Laws, University of California
1971 Doctor of Laws, Columbia University
1971 Doctor of Laws, Utah State University
1964 Doctorate, Agrarian University, Lima, Peru
1966 Doctor Honoris Causa, University of the Andes, Bogotá, Colombia
1966 Doctor Honoris Causa, Central University, Quito, Ecuador
1964 Doctor of Science, University of Florida
1964 Doctor of Science, West Virginia University
1964 Doctor of Science, Ohio State University
1967 Doctor of Science, Clemson University
1968 Doctor of Science, University of Illinois
1968 Doctor of Science, University of Arizona
1968 Doctor of Science, Rockefeller University
1969 Doctor of Science, Washington University
1975 Doctor of Science, Ripon College

PROFESSIONAL APPOINTMENTS

1928–1929 Teaching Fellow, Iowa State University
1929–1933 Professor and Head of the Department of Biology, University of Puerto Rico, College of Agriculture
1934–1935 Instructor in Plant Pathology and Firestone Fellow (1935), University of Minnesota
1935–1937 Assistant Professor, Biology, Virginia Polytechnic Institute
1937–1941 Associate Professor, Biology, Virginia Polytechnic Institute
1941 Professor, Virginia Polytechnic Institute
1941–1942 Professor and Head, Department of Plant Pathology, and Head, Division of Plant Pathology, Agricultural

	Experiment Station, Washington State College, Pullman, Washington
1943–1951	Local Director, Mexican Agricultural Program, The Rockefeller Foundation
1951–1955	Deputy Director for Agriculture, Division of Natural Sciences and Agriculture, The Rockefeller Foundation
1955–1959	Director for Agriculture, The Rockefeller Foundation
1959–1961	Vice-President, The Rockefeller Foundation
1961–1972	Trustee and President, The Rockefeller Foundation
1973–1979	Member, Governing Council, The Rockefeller Archive Center
1960–1972	Trustee, General Education Board
1961–1971	President, General Education Board
1971–1972	Chairman of the Board, General Education Board

DIRECTORSHIPS

1971–1982	Dreyfus Third Century Fund
1968–1982	International Flavors and Fragrances, Inc.
1962–1978	Campbell Soup Company
1971–1979	Merck and Company
1971–1978	Viacom International, Inc.
1970–1976	Kimberly-Clark Corporation
1964–1978	Nutrition Foundation (Chairman of the Board, 1972–78)

TRUSTEESHIPS

1973–1962	Chairman, Draper World Population Fund
1960–1962	The International Rice Research Institute
1962–1973	Oberlin College, Oberlin, Ohio
1972–1978	The Near East Foundation, New York
1975–1982	Chairman of the Board, International Agricultural Development Service

MEMBERSHIPS

1966–1982	National Academy of Sciences, Washington, D.C.
1972–1975	Citizen's Commission for Science, Law, and the Food Supply, New York

1972	Overseas Development Council, Washington, D.C.
1973–1979	Rockefeller University Council, New York
1973	Scientific Delegation to visit the People's Republic of China
1973–1975	Panel II on Food, Health, World Population, and Quality of Life, Commission on Critical Choices for Americans
1974–1976	Commission on U.S.–Latin American Relations
1974–1977	Corporation Visiting Committee, Department of Nutrition and Food Science, Massachusetts Institute of Technology
1967–1973	Visiting Committee to Harvard Medical School and School of Dental Medicine
1960	President Eisenhower's Science Advisory Committee
1975–1979	President's General Advisory Committee on Foreign Assistance Program
1966–1972	Mayor's Science and Technology Advisory Council, New York City
1973–1978	Advisory Board, New Perspective Fund, Inc.
1952–1982	American Academy of Arts and Sciences
1962–1982	American Philosophical Society
1968–1982	Chairman, National Advisory Council of the Monell Chemical Senses Center, University of Pennsylvania

HONORARY MEMBERSHIPS

1957 Brazilian Society of Geneticists
1966 Asociacion Ecuatoriana de Ingenieros Agronomos, Ecuador

FELLOWSHIPS

1939–1982	American Association for the Advancement of Science
1965	American Phytopathological Society
1972	Royal Society of Arts, London
	Andrew W. Cordier Fellow, Columbia University

LEARNED SOCIETIES

Academy of Arts and Sciences of Puerto Rico
American Academy of Arts and Sciences

American Philosophical Society
Italian National Academy of Agriculture, Bologna
World Academy of Art and Science
Japan Academy of Sciences

OTHER HONORS AND AWARDS

1950 Certificate for Meritorious Service to Agriculture, University of Florida
1952 Medal of Agricultural Merit, Government of Mexico
1952 Medal of Agricultural Merit, Government of the State of Coahuila, Saltillo (Mexico)
1953 Outstanding Achievement Award, University of Minnesota
1953 Distinguished Alumnus Citation from Oberlin College
1954 Cruze de Boyaca, "Caballero," Republic of Colombia
1958 Chilean Order of Merit, "Bernardo O'Higgins"—"Oficial"; "Gran Oficial," 1962
1960 Citation and Medallion of Merit, University of Arizona
1961 Citation and diploma for contributions to agricultural improvement in the Americas, from the Diplomatic Corps in Honduras representing Chile, Colombia, Costa Rica, Ecuador, El Salvador, Guatemala, Mexico, Nicaragua, Panama, Peru, and Venezuela
1962 Presidential Award, American Public Health Association
1963 Public Welfare Medal, National Academy of Sciences
1963 Decoration from the Government of Ecuador, "Caballero," for Agricultural Merit
1964 Order of the Golden Heart, Government of the Philippines
1965 Governor's Award, State of Ohio, for the Advancement of the Prestige of Ohio
1968 Inter-American Agricultural Medal, Inter-American Institute of Agricultural Sciences of the Organization of American States, Costa Rica
1969 Elvin Charles Stakman Award, University of Minnesota
1970 Distinguished Achievement Citation, Iowa State University
1971 The first Edward W. Browning Award, presented annually by the American Society of Agronomy
1971 Knight Commander of the Most Nobel Order of the Crown of Thailand authorized by King Bhumidol Adulyadej and conferred by the Prime Minister, Bangkok, Thailand

1973	"Rafael Uribe Uribe" Order of Merit in Agriculture, Republic of Colombia
1974	Wilbur O. Atwater Medal
1974	Americas Award
1975	Underwood-Prescott Memorial Award, Massachusetts Institute of Technology
1980	Harrar Hall (training and dormitory complex of the International Rice Research Institute) named in honor of Dr. J. George Harrar
1980	Order of the Aztec Eagle, Government of Mexico, Mexican Embassy, Washington, D.C.

BIBLIOGRAPHY

1930

With M. M. Evans. Germination of the oospores of *Sclerospora graminicola* (Sacc.) Schroet. Phytopathology, 20.

1935

Boxwood diseases in Virginia. In: *The Virginia Fruit*, col. 23.

1936

Powdery mildews in Virginia. Plant Dis. Rep., 20.
Cercospora leaf spot of *Calendula* in Virginia. Plant Dis. Rep., 20.
Hyphal structures of *Fomes lignosus* Klotzsch. (Abstract.) Proc. Va. Acad. Sci.:40.
With J. M. Grayson. Boxwood blight in Virginia. (Abstract.) Proc. Va. Acad. Sci.:36–37.
With R. S. Mullin. *Cercospora* leaf spot of *Calendula* spp. (Abstract.) Proc. Va. Acad. Sci.:40–41.
With S. A. Wingard. Boxwood diseases in Virginia. Plant Dis. Rep., 20.

1937

Some unusual diseases of ornamentals in Virginia. Plant Dis. Rep., 21.
Cladosporium leaf and stem disease of snapdragons. (Abstract.) Proc. Va. Acad. Sci.:52.
Infection of *Buxus sempervirens* by *Verticillium* sp. (Abstract.) Proc. Va. Acad. Sci.:42–43.
Cercospora leaf spot of *Calendula*. (Abstract.) Phytopathology, 27.
Factors affecting the pathogenicity of *Fomes lignosus* Klotzsch. Minn. Tech. Bull., 123.
With S. A. Wingard. Diseases of Virginia ornamental trees. Plant Dis. Rep., 21.

1938

Blue rot of boxwood. (Abstract.) Phytopathology, 28.
With J. B. Clark. Inhibition of the growth of *Mycobacterium tuberculosis hominis* on protein media by sulfur and its compounds. (Abstract.) Proc. Va. Acad. Sci.:83.

With L. I. Miller. Studies in the morphology and physiology of a species of *Entomophthora* on *Typhlocyba pomaria*. (Abstract.) Proc. Va. Acad. Sci.:41.

With L. I. Miller. *Phoma* (*phyllosticta*) *artirrhini* in Virginia. (Abstract.) Phytopathology, 28.

With L. I. Miller. A *Phoma* leaf spot and stem canker of *Artirrhinum* spp. (Abstract.) Phytopathology, 28.

1939

With S. A. Wingard and L. I. Miller. Cultural studies on a species of *Entomophthora* from the apple leaf hopper (*Typhlocyba pomaria*). (Abstract.) Phytopathology, 29.

1945

With E. C. Stakman. Plant pathology in Mexico. In: *Plants and Plant Science in Latin America*. Waltham, Mass.: Chronica Botanica.

1946

With E. S. Harrar. *Guide to Southern Trees*. New York: McGraw-Hill. 709 pp. (Reissued, New York: Dover Publications, 1962.)

1947

With N. E. Borlaug. Stem rust of wheat in Mexico. Paper presented at the 39th annual meeting of the American Phytopathology Society, Chicago, Illinois, December 30. Phytopathology, 27(1):12.

1949

With N. E. Borlaug and J. A. Rupert. *Nuevos Trigos para Mexico*. Folleto de Divulgacion no. 5. Mexico: Oficina de Estudios Especiales, Secretaria de Agricultura y Ganaderia.

1950

With E. C. Stakman, W. Z. Loegering, and N. E. Borlaug. *Razas Fisiologicas de Puccinia Graminis Tritici en Mexico*. Folleto Tecnico no. 3. Mexico: Oficina de Estudios Especiales, Secretaria de Agricultura y Ganaderia.

Mexican Agricultural Program. New York: The Rockefeller Foundation. 35 pp.

1953

Science and Human Needs. Nellie Heldt lecture presented at Oberlin, Ohio, April 30. Oberlin College. 19 pp.
Meeting human needs through agriculture. In: *Transactions of the Eighteenth North American Wildlife Conference,* March 9–11, pp. 46–50. Washington, D.C.: Wildlife Management Institute.

1954

A pattern for international collaboration in agriculture. Adv. Agron., 6:95–119.
Book review of *Indian Corn in Old America* by Paul Weatherwax. New York Times Book Review, August 1, p. 12.
International collaboration in food production. In: *Proceedings of the Third Annual Meeting of the Agricultural Research Institute,* pp. 21–27. Washington, D.C.: National Research Council.
Book review of *New Life in Old Lands* by Kathleen McLaughlin. New York Times Book Review, November 21, p. 4.
Food for the future. A speech at the symposium, "Natural Resources: Power, Metals, Food," which comprised the first part of the AAAS symposium, "Science and Society," Berkeley, California, December 27.

1955

Food for the future. Science, 122(3164):313–16.
Fertilizer, pesticide use in Mexico. Agric. Chem., 10(2):26–28; 137–38.
Technical aid and agricultural chemistry. J. Agric. Food Chem., 3:395–98.

1956

Practical suggestions to carry out a well-considered program. In: *University Projects Abroad,* pp. 23–31. Washington, D.C.: American Council on Education.
Alimentos para el futuro. Turrialba, 6(1–2)(June):6–12.
Food and agriculture and man's health. (Speech at Massachusetts Institute of Technology Alumni Day, June 11.) Technol. Rev., 58:479–80; 508–14.

1957

With E. C. Stakman. *Principles of Plant Pathology.* New York: The Ronald Press. 581 pp. (Also in Russian, Spanish, and Polish translations.)

1958

Food, science, and people. (A speech at a meeting of the New York Academy of Sciences, December 9, 1957.) Trans. N.Y. Acad. Sci., 20:263–77.

New scientific developments in the area of food. (A speech at Sarah Lawrence College, August.) In: *The American Economy: An Appraisal of its Social Goals and the Impact of Science and Technology,* pp. 132–38. New York: Joint Council on Economic Education. (Also in: Paper no. 107 of the Agricultural Journal Series Papers of The Rockefeller Foundation.)

1959

Agricultural horizons. (A speech at the 51st annual meeting of the American Society of Agronomy, Purdue University, August 5, 1958.) Agronomy, 51:187–90.

An international approach to the study and control of plant disease. (An address at the American Phytopathological Society, Golden Jubilee Meeting, Bloomington, Indiana, August 24–28, 1958.) In: *Plant Pathology, Problems and Progress, 1908–1958.* Madison: University of Wisconsin Press.

1960

Cooperation in the training of scientists and engineers. In: *Science in the Americas: Cooperation of the Scientists and Engineers of the Americas in Furthering Scientific Training and Research,* pp. 13–16. Washington, D.C.: National Research Council.

Will there be enough? The Club Dial (magazine of the Woman's Club of White Plains, New York).

Portions of articles on plant disease control and bananas. In: *McGraw-Hill Encyclopedia of Science and Technology.* New York: McGraw-Hill.

Food in national and international welfare. (Reprinted from N.Y. State Agric. Exp. Stn. Geneva Bull., no. 790:44–49, as part of the dedication program for the station's new food research building, May 5.

1961

Unhappy paradox. (Editorial.) Science, 133(March 10):671.
The influence of current social and economic trends on international health. In: *Industry and Tropical Health*, vol. 4, pp. 79–83. Cambridge, Mass.: Harvard School of Public Health.
Socio-economic factors that limit needed food production and consumption. (An address to the 5th International Congress on Nutrition, Symposium on World Needs and Food Resources, Washington, D.C., September 6, 1960.) Fed. Proc., 20 (Suppl. 7, no. 1, part III):381–83.
Technologic revolution in agriculture; Contributions of science. (An address to a symposium of the Food Protection Committee, Washington, D.C., December 8, 1960.) In: *Science and Food; Today and Tomorrow*, pp. 5–8. Washington, D.C.: NAS-NRC Publ. 877.
Principles and problems of increasing food crops and animals in low production areas. (An address to the Conference on Nutrition, arranged by New York Academy of Medicine, Arden House, Harriman, New York, December 15, 1958.) In: *Human Nutrition, Historic and Scientific*, pp. 171–77. New York: International Universities Press.

1962

Making the most of human resources. (An address to the 90th annual meeting of the American Public Health Association, Miami Beach, October 15.) Am. J. Public Health, 53(March):375–81.
Bread and Peace. (An address to the spring meeting of the Nutrition Foundation, March 6.) New York: The Rockefeller Foundation. 16 pp. (Also in: C & E News, April 29, pp. 126–31.)
New Ventures for Private Philanthropy. New York: The Rockefeller Foundation. 9 pp. (Reprinted from New York Times Magazine, June 9, p. 29.)
Nutrition and numbers. In: *Sixth International Congress of Nutrition*, Edinburgh, August 9, pp. 1–6. New York: The Rockefeller Foundation.

1963

Aid abroad: Some principles and their Latin American practice. Foundation News, September, pp. 1–3.

Selected papers of J. G. Harrar. In: *Strategy for the Conquest of Hunger.* New York: The Rockefeller Foundation. (Revised edition, 1967.)

1964

Moving frontiers of applied microbiology. (An address to the conference, Global Aspects of Applied Microbiology, Stockholm, Sweden, August 1963.) In: *Global Impacts of Applied Microbiology,* ed. Mortimer P. Starr, pp. 19–27. New York: John Wiley & Sons.
A Commencement Perspective. (Commencement address at the University of Florida, Gainesville, April 19.) New York: The Rockefeller Foundation. 11 pp.
Foundations and the Public Interest. (Adapted from an address given at the Cosmos Club, Washington, D.C., November 16.) New York: The Rockefeller Foundation. 11 pp.
New nations and new universities. (Paper presented at the general session of the 78th annual convention of the Association of State Universities and Land-Grant Colleges, November 8–11.) In: *Proceedings of the Association of State Universities and Land-Grant Colleges,* pp. 9–13.

1965

The Race Between Procreation and Food Production. (Paper presented at the spring meeting of the American Philosophical Society, Philadelphia.) New York: The Rockefeller Foundation. 29 pp.

1966

Statement of J. George Harrar. Hearings: War on Hunger, House Committee on Agriculture, February 16, 1966. New York: The Rockefeller Foundation. 13 pp.
Foundations for the Future. (An address to the 17th annual conference of the Council on Foundations, Inc., Denver, Colorado, May 11.) New York: The Rockefeller Foundation. 18 pp.
The Quality of the Future. (Commencement address at Emory University, Atlanta, Georgia, June 13.) New York: The Rockefeller Foundation. 8 pp.
Agricultural Development in Latin America. (Statement of J. George Harrar before the Subcommittee on International Finance of the House Committee on Banking and Currency, August 29.) New York: The Rockefeller Foundation. 15 pp.

Principles for Progress in World Agriculture. (An address to the 33rd annual meeting of the National Agricultural Chemicals Association, White Sulphur Springs, West Virginia, September 8.) New York: The Rockefeller Foundation. 16 pp.

1967

Survival or Fulfillment. (An address to the California Institute of Technology Conference on The Next Ninety Years, March 7.) New York: The Rockefeller Foundation. 15 pp.
Education and responsibility. (Commencement address at Clemson University, Clemson, South Carolina, May 6). Clemson, S.C.: Clemson University.

1968

Crises in human ecology. (Banquet address to the annual meeting of the National Academy of Sciences, Washington, D.C., April 23.) Proc. Natl. Acad. Sci. USA, 61:357–62. (Also: New York: The Rockefeller Foundation; World Agric., 18[October]:3–5.)
Increasing Food Supplies Through Adaptive Research. (Principal address, 25th Anniversary Celebration of Texas Research Foundation at Renner, Texas, May 22.) Texas Research Foundation, Special Series, no. 5.
United States public policy with regard to world food problems. In: *The Potential Impact of Science and Technology on Future U.S. Foreign Policy* (papers presented at a Joint Meeting of the Policy Planning Council, Department of State, and a Special Panel of the Committee on Science and Public Policy, National Academy of Sciences, Washington, D.C., June 16–17).

1969

With Sterling Wortman. Expanding food production in hungry nations: The promise, the problems. (Paper presented at a meeting of the American Assembly, Columbia University, October 31, 1968.) In: *Overcoming World Hunger,* ed. Clifford M. Hardin. Englewood Cliffs, New Jersey: Prentice-Hall. (Also in French as *Vaincre la Faim,* Paris: Editions France-Empire, 1970, pp. 89–135.)
Plant Pathology and World Food Problems. (Discourse given before the First International Congress of Plant Pathology, London, July 16, 1968.) New York: The Rockefeller Foundation. 21 pp.

Statement on foundations and tax exemption before the House Committee on Ways and Means, Washington, D.C., February 19. New York: The Rockefeller Foundation.

Supplementary statement on foundations and tax exemption before the House Committee on Ways and Means, Washington, D.C., July 9. New York: The Rockefeller Foundation.

Statement of J. George Harrar on effects of population growth on natural resources and the environment at hearings before a Subcommittee of the Committee on Government Operations, House of Representatives, 91st Congress, 1st session, September 16. (Published in complete hearings by the U.S. Government Printing Office, Washington, D.C., 1969, #35–506, pp. 52–56.)

The challenge of hunger. (Banquet address to the annual meeting of the American Chamber of Commerce of Mexico, Mexico City, August 21.) Mex. Am. Rev., October:31–35.

1970

The Green Revolution as an historical phenomenon. In: *Symposium on Science and Foreign Policy: the Green Revolution*, pp. 16–23. Washington, D.C.: U.S. Government Printing Office.

The global food supply. (A talk given at the Symposium on Aids and Threats to Society from Technology, National Academy of Sciences, Washington, D.C., April 29.) Proc. Natl. Acad. Sci. USA, 67(October):900–907.

Ecological crisis demands new ethic of responsibility. Catal. Environ. Qual., 1:22–24.

Education and human ecology. Western Bulletin (Western College for Women, Oxford, Ohio), Summer:1–4.

1971

Human behavior and the environment. (Commencement address at Utah State University, June 5.) 17 pp.

1972

Raymond Blaine Fosdick. Yearb. Am. Philos. Soc.: 157–65.

1973

Toward the conquest of hunger and malnutrition: The Rockefeller Foundation's worldwide efforts to increase food supplies and improve nutrition. U.S. Information Service–Voice of America series on nutrition, May 8.

Impressions of China (based on a visit to the People's Republic of China on a scientific and scholarly exchange mission under the auspices of the National Academy of Sciences, the Social Science Research Council, and the Council of Learned Societies, May 11–June 17).

1975

Nutrition and Numbers in the Third World: The 1974 W. O. Atwater Memorial Lecture. Washington, D.C.: Agricultural Research Service. 18 pp.

Agricultural Initiative in the Third World: A Report on the Conference "Science and Agribusiness in the Seventies." Lexington, Mass.: Lexington Books for The Agribusiness Council.

1979

E. C. Stakman Memoir. Yearb. Am. Philos. Soc.: 107–12.
Warren Weaver Memoir. Yearb. Am. Philos. Soc.: 113–17.

PAUL HERGET

January 30, 1908–August 27, 1981

BY DONALD E. OSTERBROCK
AND P. KENNETH SEIDELMANN

YOUTH AND EDUCATION

PAUL HERGET was born on January 30, 1908, in Cincinnati, Ohio. He was to live, study, and do research there nearly all his life; he was one of the most outstanding scientists ever produced in that pleasant Midwestern city. His father, Conrad Frederick Herget, had emigrated from Germany to Cincinnati in 1893, at the age of eighteen—just ahead of a summons to military duty, according to Paul's memory. His mother, Clara Brueckner Herget, was born of immigrant parents in the old "Over the Rhine" area of Cincinnati, just north of downtown. By the time Paul was born, his parents were living in Fairview, a district on the brow of one of the hills overlooking the central city and the Ohio River. When he was four, they moved to Oakley, an eastern suburb of the city; they stayed there until his father died in 1938. Paul was christened, in the tradition of German Protestantism, as Paul Frederick Ernst Herget—Frederick for his father, who was called Fred, and Ernst for an uncle. But he dropped the middle names as soon as he learned to read and write and always signed himself Paul Herget. He liked to assert that "he was his own person and did not want the name of someone else tagging along with him."

Paul's father Fred never went to school in America; he had to go right to work to support himself, first in a laundry, where he soon became a foreman, then in a machine-tool factory. Clara Herget finished two years of high school; she was a firm believer in education, and she always encouraged her only son (Paul had two younger sisters) to go as far as he could. Paul believed that the most influential factor in his childhood was his Erector set, which stimulated his geometrical thinking, mechanical abilities, and sense of order. He also benefited from his Boy Scout experiences and from the mobility and skill with tools that came from owning a bicycle. Paul's mother supported him in everything he wanted to do, especially schoolwork; he remembered his father as a harsh taskmaster, a "typical German father," who often disciplined him. Paul resented it then, but in later life felt that it had shaped his character.

Paul went to Oakley Public School and then to Withrow High School. He was a good student in all subjects, especially in mathematics. In his last two years at Withrow he was greatly inspired by his mathematics teacher, Helen Swineford, whom he later considered the greatest single influence on his career. Paul worked in summer jobs at the machine tool factory with his father; after he graduated from high school in 1926 he got a temporary position as a surveyor with the Cincinnati Gas and Electric Company. That fall he entered the University of Cincinnati as a civil engineering student. He had never considered going anywhere else; his family had little money, and he could not afford to go away from home to college. All the students in the Engineering College of the University of Cincinnati were automatically enrolled in a "co-operative program." The program alternated terms of going to school and working in industry; students earned their tuition and living expenses at the same time they started putting their engineering education to practical use. Civil engineering was at least close to mathematics, Paul thought.

But after only a few weeks he realized that it was not close enough for him. He withdrew from the university and got a full-time job as a surveyor. By rigid economy, he was able to save a thousand dollars in one year. That sum enabled him to enter the College of Liberal Arts in 1927 as a full-time mathematics student, as he had wanted to do from the first.

Teaching was the only future he could envision in mathematics; he took a minor in education so that he could get a high school teacher's certificate and follow in Helen Swineford's path. He disliked and resented the education courses he had to take, but he graduated in 1931—the worst part of the Great Depression—with an A.B. degree. Paul was offered a job as an assistant at the Cincinnati Observatory, which paid $1,020 a year. To him the job was just like a "real good fellowship" that would pay his living expenses and allow him to continue his education as a part-time graduate student. He snapped it up.

GRADUATE STUDIES

The Cincinnati Observatory is the oldest astronomical research observatory west of the Alleghenies. It was founded in 1843 by Ormsby McKnight Mitchel under the auspices of the Cincinnati Astronomical Society and was originally funded by small contributions from the general public. Its 12-inch refractor was a big telescope by the standards of the time. Former President John Quincy Adams came west to speak at its dedication; later the observatory became part of the University of Cincinnati. By 1931 the 12-inch and the newer 16-inch refractors were not significant research instruments, and the main program of the Cincinnati Observatory was the accurate meridian-circle measurement of the positions of stars in order to determine their proper motions. On the recommendation of his mathematics professors, Paul Herget was hired as a computer to reduce these observations.

Paul was always fascinated by computing. As an undergraduate he was intrigued by the idea of numerically evaluating π to high precision. Using what he considered the best rapidly convergent series, he took a large sheet of wrapping paper, and with a lead pencil as his only computational device calculated π to thirty-two decimal places. Years later he checked it—he had kept a copy, as he did of most of his computations—and found that he had gotten the first twenty-eight places correct. As a graduate student, after studying higher-order interpolation, he produced a two-page table that gave sines and cosines of any angle correct to eight decimal places. This was his first scientific publication.

Working at the Cincinnati Observatory under director Everett I. Yowell and Elliott S. Smith, Paul still considered himself a mathematics graduate student. He took courses from Charles N. Moore and Harris Hancock, who had recommended him for the assistantship at the observatory. He was strongly influenced by Louis Brand, a younger mathematics professor, who emphasized the power of vectors to express complicated formulae in simple terms. Herget was to use them extensively in all his work, and his book, *The Computation of Orbits*, is written completely in terms of vectors. He always claimed that spherical trigonometry is not a subject but only two vector equations, the dot and cross product, repeated over and over again.

As Paul became more proficient in the reduction of the meridian-circle observations, he found himself with spare time on his hands at the observatory. He began reading research publications, especially the *Astronomical Journal*. He became interested in orbit theory and studied it on his own. As a result, by 1933, when he received his M.A. degree, he considered himself a student of astronomy rather than mathematics. Paul was almost completely self-taught in his new subject, with practically no graduate courses and very little in the way of guidance, except on old-fashioned observational methods. He was especially attracted by the papers of Leslie J. Comrie, the leading exponent of punched-card machines in astronomy, who was revamping the work of the Nautical Almanac Office in Great Britain.

There were no punched-card machines at the Cincinnati Observatory in the 1930s, but Paul became an expert computer, using the old hand-operated, mechanical desk calculators. He did his thesis on the computation of orbits almost entirely without advice or direction, and earned his Ph.D. in 1935. Soon afterward he married Harriet Louise Smith, his high school classmate, longtime sweetheart, and the daughter of Elliot S. Smith, his superior at the Cincinnati Observatory.

Paul then received an Alexander Morrison Fellowship and spent one year at the University of California as a postdoctoral research associate. Armin O. Leuschner was the head of the Berkeley Astronomy Department and a very senior expert in orbit computation. As a young man he had developed "Leuschner's method" for calculating the orbit of a new comet, and Herget delighted in pointing out the situations in which it failed in practice and in which his own method, based on Gauss's original scheme, was better. Leuschner in the end told Herget that he was too opinionated and that he acted as if his name were "Herr Gott" [the Lord God]. Nevertheless, Herget—supremely self-confident—learned what he could from Leuschner and continued to go his own way.

At the end of his year in California, Paul nearly got a job as a lecturer at the Griffith Planetarium in Los Angeles, which would have taken him out of research. Fortunately for astronomy, another candidate was judged a better speaker.

Paul, however, let the University of Cincinnati administration know that he was thinking of going elsewhere, and they promptly raised his salary to $1,650 a year to bring him home.

MINOR PLANET CENTER

After his return to Cincinnati in 1936, Paul undertook the project of determining the orbit of one of the minor planets discovered by James C. Watson. A pioneer American student of asteroids, Watson had left in his will an endowment fund to support research on the ones he had found. Leuschner had been directing work on them over the years. Aethra (132)—the most difficult because it had the largest eccentricity—was the one Herget tackled first. After he had completed its orbit he continued to work on one minor planet at a time, in cooperation with Gustav Stracke at the Rechen Institut in Berlin. Herget was what the Germans called a *Mitarbeiter*, or collaborator.

After World War II, the personnel of the Rechen Institut were split between the Russian and Western occupation zones. Dirk Brouwer, president of Commission 20 of the International Astronomical Union, was responsible for getting the minor planet work organized again. After discussions with H. Spencer Jones, president of the International Astronomical Union, Brouwer asked Herget to operate a minor planet center. Paul was familiar with what was required from his previous activities, and he readily agreed. President Raymond Walters of the University of Cincinnati supported his decision. Herget then arranged for Eugene Rabe, one of the younger Rechen Institut members in the Western zone, to join him in Cincinnati. He also obtained an appointment at the Observatory for Peter Musen, who was a native of Yugoslavia.

They began their work by recording each minor planet

observation made after 1939 on a punched card so that all their computations could be carried out on punched-card equipment. To obtain observations of the minor planets, Herget loaned the 10-inch astrographic camera that the University of Cincinnati owned to Frank Edmondson at Indiana University. Edmondson built a blink machine and acquired a measuring engine so that he could provide accurate measurements of asteroids upon request. This program provided the Indiana students with a continuing project and a means of learning the processes of taking and measuring minor planet positional observations.

From 1947 to 1978 Herget was director of the Minor Planet Center of the International Astronomical Union. During that period, 4,390 *Minor Planet Circulars* were published. The best computer—or punched-card—equipment to which he had access was used for the computations of the elements and ephemerides of the minor planets included in these circulars.

U.S. NAVAL OBSERVATORY

Recognizing that the astronomer Forest R. Moulton had contributed greatly to ballistic computations during World War I, Herget sought to do the same during World War II. He began by contacting government officials at the Ballistic Research Laboratory at Aberdeen Proving Grounds and at the Naval Weapons Center at Dahlgren, Virginia. At Dahlgren he inquired about the Weapons Center's plans to use punched-card equipment; he was told that punch cards were used for preparing the payroll, "but they ain't no good" for calculations. So he figured "Boy, if you think they ain't no good, I'm not going to work for you." He went instead to Washington. There he joined Wallace J. Eckert at the Nautical Almanac Office of the U.S. Naval Observatory from 1942 until after the war ended. Prior to Eckert's arrival in 1939, all calculations had been performed by hand on paper. He arranged for the acquisition of an IBM tabulator, summary punch, and sorter, which were used to prepare the *Air Almanac*. Herget's job was to convert the preparation of parts of the *American Ephemeris and Nautical Almanac* by means of the punched-card equipment.

During this period he also performed the computations for the "submarine book," a task that gave him the greatest satisfaction of his lifetime. In 1943 the losses of Allied convoys had reached 30 percent. The German submarines would radio their headquarters when they sighted convoys. The Allies had 108 listening posts around the world that could pick up the directions of these radio signals. With tabulated solutions of about a quarter of a million spherical triangles, these observations were used to pinpoint the locations of the submarines to within five miles. Destroyers could then use sonar equipment to locate them and drop depth charges. Herget and Eckert did all the necessary calculations within three months, working only at night because the punched-card machines were in use all day on the *Air Almanac* and *Nautical Almanac*. Once the submarine book had been printed and put into use, Allied losses went down to about 6 percent. After returning to the University of Cincinnati in 1946, Herget continued to maintain a close working relationship with the Naval Observatory. His research results—"Rectangular Coordinates of Ceres, Pallas, Juno, and Vesta," "The Solar Coordinates, 1800–2000," and the "Coordinates of Venus, 1800–2000"—were all published in the *Astronomical Papers of the American Ephemeris*.

COMPUTER APPLICATIONS

In 1928 Ernest W. Brown, the eminent celestial mechanician and author of *Lunar Theory* and *Tables of the Moon*, visited Europe. He saw that Leslie J. Comrie was using punch cards to compute the lunar ephemeris and proceeded to support Eckert's acquisition of punched-card equipment. Herget recognized the advantages of such equipment and followed Eckert's leadership. From 1947 to 1951 the Cincinnati Observatory had an IBM tabulator, multiplier, sorter, and reproducer; after 1951 Herget used computing equipment—when it was available—at the Procter & Gamble Company, the General Electric Company, and the Cincinnati Gas & Electric Company. He worked with the computers only when company employees were not using them—usually at night or on weekends. He would also exchange computer time for lectures to the employees or technical advice on their problems. As a result of such cooperation, the Cincinnati Gas & Electric Company still uses the Julian Day Number system in preparing its bills.

Over the years Herget used many different models of tabulating equipment and computers, progressing from the multiplier through the IBM 603, 650, 1620, Naval Ordnance Research Calculator (NORC), and 360. The NORC was his favorite machine, "the greatest love of my life, after my wife and daughter." Herget found that by spending two weeks at the NORC he could get a full year's work done. Throughout his career the common thread was the application of computer technology to real problems. It was in this area that he advised the Air Force Mapping and Charting Laboratory and also maintained the Cancer Registry at the University of Cincinnati. But it also led to a number of larger projects. In 1944 and 1945 Herget was a consultant for the Manhattan Project at Oak Ridge, Tennessee. And from 1951 to 1957 he was a consultant for the Project Atlas Intercontinental Ballistic Missile effort at Convair. In this effort he formulated the system for computing the ballistic trajectory for the missiles, including all the known effects that would perturb the trajectories.

In 1955 President Dwight D. Eisenhower announced that

America would have a space program. Following that announcement, each of the organizations that wanted to set up and operate the satellite computing program contacted Herget. He reasoned that only one of them was going to win, and agreed that he would participate in the proposals from Univac, the Army Map Service, and the Naval Research Laboratory. That way no matter who managed the program, he would be on the team. In 1959 he spent a week with IBM writing their proposal for the Mercury Project. After IBM got the contract, he set up the computer program for calculating the orbits for Mercury launches.

THE CINCINNATI OBSERVATORY

The research of Paul Herget centered around orbit computations and the use of computer programs. Early in his work he realized that the site of the Cincinnati Observatory was not ideal for observations because it was surrounded by a large industrial city. Therefore he entered into cooperative activities with Indiana University so that the required observing could be done there. He strongly supported public use of the Cincinnati Observatory; amateur astronomers came to the observatory to make mirrors, and public tours were held on a regular basis. The observatory library and punched-card files were well kept up, but the telescopes were maintained only to satisfy the public tour requirements. Most of the effort of the personnel at the Cincinnati Observatory was directed toward the Minor Planet Center and related research. Herget responded to educational requirements in a manner consistent with his own background and philosophy.

An outstanding research professor, Herget enjoyed the confidence and support of University of Cincinnati presidents Raymond Walters and Walter C. Langsam. Paul always financed his research chiefly from outside sources. His well-timed news releases and newspaper stories, his outgoing personality, and his background and sympathies—so much in tune with those of the engineering executives of many large Cincinnati industrial plants—brought him support on the local scene. Astronomers recognized him as a top expert in celestial mechanics, and he had no trouble getting modest NSF and NASA grants for travel and publication costs. If he needed a little seed money for a project he could usually count on getting it from the president's office.

THE TEACHER

At an informal astronomy neighborhood meeting in Cincinnati after World War II, a number of scientists discussed the problems of textbooks. For almost ten years only a few new advanced textbooks had been published. The astronomers urged Herget to publish his lecture notes; the result was *The Computation of Orbits*, one of the first astronomy texts written using vector notation. In addition to writing the book, he typed it himself in camera-ready copy so that it could be printed inexpensively. Thus it was made available at a very low price—but only by purchase directly from its author.

Paul followed the earlier masters of celestial mechanics by heading each chapter with a formal Greek motto. But in his book these mottoes were actually translations, provided by a friend, of English-language quotations or phrases. The chapter on spherical astronomy is headed by the Greek words for "Abandon hope, all ye who enter here," the chapter on the calculus of finite differences by those for "His numbers will conquer the world," and the one on improvement of the orbit by "If at first you don't succeed, try, try again."

In response to the launching of *Sputnik*, the University of Cincinnati established its Institute of Space Sciences, with Herget as director. At the same time, a related graduate teaching program was initiated. There were a limited number of students, and their courses were restricted to dynamical astronomy and applied mathematics, directly reflecting Paul's own education. He was a firm believer in teaching and learning by doing: he taught students to operate the computer by taking them into the computer room, showing them how the computer performed a given program, handing them decks of cards, telling them to "do it yourself," and leaving the room. In this graduate program Herget supervised the M.S. theses of James D. Wray and Conrad M. Bardwell and the Ph.D. dissertations of J. Derral Mulholland and P. Kenneth Seidelmann. Rabe supervised the Ph.D. dissertations of S. C. Pilet and Allen F. Schanzle. The program was discontinued, however, after only four years.

Paul was seen by many of his colleagues on the University of Cincinnati faculty as a great scholar who did not make much of a contribution to the teaching program. He did not believe astronomy should be taught at the undergraduate level. Without a doubt, however, he was the most influential person at the university in the development of its computing facilities and its Computer Laboratory from the 1950s through the early 1970s. His knowledge of computers and their use, and his close relationship with the manufacturers of computing equipment, were invaluable in determining the route the university took in this field. Of equal or greater importance was the instruction, both formal and informal, that Paul gave to faculty members and graduate students regarding the importance and use of computers. He was thus extremely influential in the development of computers for education and research at the University of Cincinnati.

THE SCIENTIST

Herget always maintained that he was fortunate: throughout his life he was able to do what he wanted to do and be paid for doing it. In 1971 he stated: "A lot of people spend their time playing bridge. I'd rather program a computer." He never really saw any need for vacations, for he felt that he traveled enough on business to see everything he wanted to see. If he were to be gone for a long period of time, he would take his wife with him so that she could enjoy the trip as a vacation. He often emphasized that he did what was within his own competence, and he sought to develop that competence. He was not particularly interested in the origin of the solar system or in how the universe began. He took them as they were, and tried to perfect his ability to calculate their motions. In response to questions concerning the interests of other astronomers and what other scientists were doing, he would say: "To each his own."

Although Paul expressed little if any interest in the physical properties of asteroids—or in their origin or evolution—his work played a part in the renaissance of physical studies of these objects that began in the 1960s. For twenty years when there was very little interest in minor planets elsewhere, he had archived the positional observations and used them to calculate orbits and ephemerides. His powerful self-confidence did much to keep the subject alive in the face of the massive indifference of most other astronomers. Moreover, he had so improved the standards of orbit determination that there is now no significant chance that a numbered asteroid will ever be lost. This was not always the case in earlier years.

Herget acted as an adviser to Gerard P. Kuiper, who organized the survey (with a 10-inch Ross camera at McDonald Observatory) that provided good statistical data on minor planets as faint as sixteenth magnitude. Later Paul participated in the Palomar-Leiden survey, based on observational material obtained with the 48-inch Schmidt telescope, that extended these statistics down to twentieth magnitude. He did all the reductions of the positional measurements (with an IBM 1620) and also calculated (with the NORC) the orbital elements for the 1,800 asteroids found in this survey. Subsequent discussions of asteroid size distributions, collision rates, and orbital-parameter distribution functions depend almost completely on these data.

Herget was a great asset at astronomical meetings. During the scientific sessions he never hesitated to ask questions or to express criticisms. He did not do this in a vicious or belittling fashion but in a way designed (or at least intended) to develop the best method or to indicate the weaknesses and fallacies of other ideas. During the evenings at these meetings, Herget was a great raconteur. In the 1930s the American Astronomical Society featured speakers at its banquets; Joel Stebbins and Philip Fox were two of the regulars. In 1939 the Society officers decided that one of the younger members should also go on the program, and Herget was selected. As he told it, he started out by saying: "I am at a tremendous disadvantage because I am unable to take a poor, weak story and stretch it as thin or long as Joel Stebbins can." Over the years, he demonstrated his very real talent for telling stories. Fortunately, his lifetime provided him with a rich history of experiences upon which to draw.

In small groups Herget was a vivid conversationalist. He had strong opinions and enjoyed defending them. A memory many of his friends have of Paul is of him sitting at his worktable calculating with his left hand on an old Friden machine, doing long products by ear without ever looking at the multiplier register, recording the results in pencil on a huge computing form with his right hand, and all the while delightedly telling, in his marked Cincinnati accent, stories of which he was invariably the hero.

HONORS

Over the course of his long professional life, Paul Herget received many honors. In 1962 he became the sixth Ohioan to be elected to the National Academy of Sciences in its century-long history. In 1970 the president of Commission 20 of the International Astronomical Union, Frank Edmondson, used his authority to name minor planet 1751 "Herget." Paul received the Academy's James Craig Watson Gold Medal in 1965 and the Dirk Brouwer Award of the Division on Dynamical Astronomy of the American Astronomical Society in 1980.

In his hometown Herget was widely recognized as "Cincinnati's best known astronomer," the acknowledged local expert who was always interviewed by the newspapers on any astronomical story from artificial satellites to the distant reaches of the universe. The Cincinnati Technical and Scientific Council, of which he was a longtime member, named him Engineer of the Year in 1957, and the University of Cincinnati Alumni Association awarded him its William Howard Taft Medal in 1965. Paul considered this award especially significant because as a high school student he had received financial aid from the Cincinnati Scholarship Foundation, an organization headed (and financed) by Louise Taft Semple, niece of the former president and chief justice.

The university recognized his outstanding research work by appointing Herget a fellow of the Graduate School in 1957. At the 1965 commencement exercises, he received the title of Distinguished Professor of the University of Cincinnati. Only one other faculty member had a similar appointment—Albert B. Sabin of the Medical School, the developer of the polio vaccine. In 1973 Herget received the Governors' Award from his home state, and in 1974 his fellow faculty members at the University of Cincinnati gave him its George Rieveschl Award for Distinguished Scientific Research. In 1969 he had received the first honorary Sc.D. degree granted by Edgecliff College (formerly Our Lady of Cincinnati College); in 1978, when he retired, the University of Cincinnati awarded him its Sc.D.

FINAL YEARS

Paul was not happy with his alma mater in his last few years. He could not succeed in convincing the University of Cincinnati to ensure the continuity of the Cincinnati Observatory according to his own wishes. Although he had many scientific friends, business contacts with industry, and friendships within the university, there had been a change in the times and a change in attitude among faculty members. There had also been a significant change in the University of Cincinnati. It was a municipal university supported largely by city taxes. As the cost of quality education went up, the taxpayers—as they tend to everywhere—rebelled. The university's graduates had become accustomed to looking further afield for jobs, and the city's machine-tool, chemical, and electrical companies had begun recruiting engineers nationwide. Cincinnati was no longer dependent on its university and its College of Engineering. The University of Cincinnati gave up its close financial ties with the city and became part of the Ohio state university system. A small tax rate that had been written into the city charter years before as a permanent source of income for the Cincinnati Observatory was also given up by the university negotiators—over Paul's bitter objections—in the act that transferred ownership to the state.

With Herget's retirement imminent and the future of the Cincinnati Observatory uncertain, in 1977 the International Astronomical Union decided that it had to arrange for the continuity of the Minor Planet Center. The IAU subsequently moved it from Cincinnati to the Smithsonian Astrophysical Observatory of the Center for Astrophysics in Cambridge, Massachusetts. Moreover, after Paul's retirement, the university administration decided to merge the observatory into a new department of physics and astronomy and to make future appointments in astrophysics. Thus the proud reputation of the Cincinnati Observatory as a center for excellence in celestial mechanics and a leading source of research results in that field ended with the retirement of Paul Herget.

In 1965 Harriet Herget had developed cancer, and in the course of her treatment Paul met many of the outstanding physicians on the University of Cincinnati Medical School faculty. Deeply moved by his wife's illness, Paul worked directly with doctors at Holmes Hospital in developing a computer program for the Cancer Control Council Neoplastic Disease Registry, which contained data on tens of thousands of patients. He also contributed a very large sum of money (particularly for a university professor) to help establish a Cobalt Therapy Unit at Holmes Hospital, and personally solicited two other large donors for it. After several remissions and several renewed bouts of illness, Harriet died on March 12, 1972.

Later that year Paul married Anne Lorbach, the secretary of the Cincinnati Observatory, who had lived just down the street from it since childhood. After his retirement Paul and Anne did more traveling around the country—now that his job was no longer his hobby. One event that was particularly memorable to him was a Symposium on Star Catalogues, Positional Astronomy, and Celestial Mechanics and a testimonial dinner in his honor in Washington in 1978, which was organized by Paul's friends at the U.S. Naval Observatory.

Paul died in his sleep at his home at 3522 Herschel View, near the Cincinnati Observatory, on August 27, 1981. He was survived by his widow and by his daughter, Marilyn Jean Herget, of Cleveland.

CONCLUSION

Paul Herget was an outstanding practitioner of a very specialized but highly important branch of astronomy. His orbit calculations were widely known, trusted, and used. He was not only an expert at numerical computation, but a skilled theoretician with the insight necessary to cast practical astronomical problems into forms well suited for solution with available computers. During his lifetime he converted a little observatory, at a poor site, and without a large telescope, into a briefly important research center known throughout the world for its scientific results.

THIS BIOGRAPHY is based on Paul Herget's published papers; his scientific correspondence, now mostly on deposit at the U.S. Naval Observatory in Washington; his correspondence with various Lick Observatory astronomers, preserved in the Mary Lea Shane Archives of Lick Observatory; his autobiographical sketch, on file at the National Academy of Sciences; the file of newspaper clippings and news releases about him at the Office of Information Services of the University of Cincinnati; and the transcript of a far-ranging interview he gave David DeVorkin in 1977, which is on file at the American Institute of Physics. We also benefited from the recollections of his friends and colleagues—and not least from the memories of two once-young Cincinnati boys whom he inspired to become astronomers.

BIBLIOGRAPHY

1933

A table of sines and cosines of eight decimal places. Astron. J., 42:123–25.
Note on table of sines and cosines. Astron. J., 42:196.
Elements of the orbit of comet 1932c Carrasco. Astron. J., 43:39.

1934

Elements—comet 1932c Carrasco. Astron. J., 43:128.
A note on the computation of orbits. Astron. Nachr., 251:53–54.

1935

Comets 1931 V Carrasco—elements. Iberica (Barcelona), 21 no. 1037, suppl. 18.
The determination of orbits. Astron. J., 44:153–61.
Elements of Hubble Object = 1935 QN. Harv. Coll. Obs. Circ. 348 and 351. (Also in: U.A.I. Circulaire 557; Nature, 6:110.)
Ephemerides of Hubble Object = 1935 QN. Harv. Coll. Obs. Circ. 348, 349, 351, and 354. (Also in: Planetenzirkulare nos. 1246 and 1274.)

1936

Elements and ephemeris of Peltier's comet. Harv. Coll. Obs. Circ. 378.
With D. Davis. New Delporte object. Publ. Astron. Soc. Pac., 48:104–6.
A method for determining preliminary orbits adopted to machine computation. Publ. Cincinnati Obs., 21:1–9.
Improved orbit of Biarmia (1146). Publ. Cincinnati Obs., 21 (unnumbered).
Tables for true anomaly and perihelion passage in nearly parabolic orbits. Publ. Cincinnati Obs., 21:9–11.

1937

With S. Arend. Elements and ephemeris of minor planet 1935 OA ([1361] Leuschneria). Astron. J., 45:126–28.

1938

Elements of Jupiter X. Harv. Coll. Obs. Circ. 457.
Elements and ephemeris of Jupiter XI. Harv. Coll. Obs. Circ. 461 and 463.
Elements of Jupiter X and XI. Harv. Coll. Obs. Circ. 464.
Elements of Jupiter X–XI. Pop. Astron., 46:509–11.
Elements (1285) Julietta, (1286) Banachiewicza, and (1287) Lorcia. Astron. J., 46:39.
Elements and ephemeris of (657) Gunlod = 1936 YI. Astron. J., 46:156.
Elements and approximate perturbations of (1175) Margo. Astron. Nachr., 265:369–72.

1939

Elements and ephemeris of Cosik-Peltier comet. Harv. Coll. Obs. Circ. 470 and 471.
Elements and ephemeris of comet Vaisala. Harv. Coll. Obs. Circ. 477.
Ephemeris of Jupiter XI. Harv. Coll. Obs. Circ. 491.
Ephemeris of Jupiter X. Harv. Coll. Obs. Circ. 493.
The orbit and perturbations of (132) Aethra. Astron. J., 47:17–23.
Elements and general perturbations of (1274) Delportia. Astron. J., 47:122–24.
Planetary motions and Lambert's theorem. Pop. Astron., 47:310–14.
The differential correction of orbits. Astron. J., 48:105–8.
Indeterminate cases in the Laplacian orbit method. Astron. J., 48:122–24.
Orbits of the new satellites of Jupiter. Publ. Am. Astron. Soc., 9:156–57.
Ephemeris of comet 1939b Vaisala. Pop. Astron., 47:282.
Elements and approximate perturbations of (300) Geraldina. Astron. Nachr., 267:1–4.
On the group theory of general perturbations. Publ. Am. Astron. Soc., 9:261.

1940

Ephemeris of Jupiter X and XI. Harv. Coll. Obs. Circ. 523.

1941

Ephemeris of Jupiter X. Harv. Coll. Obs. Circ. 591.
Ephemeris of Jupiter XI. Harv. Coll. Obs. Circ. 592.
With J. E. Kline. On the accuracy of first order general perturbations. Astron. J., 49:121–24.
Ephemeris of Jupiter XI. Harv. Coll. Obs. Circ. 592. (Also in: U.A.I. Circ. 885; Beobachtungzirkular der Astron. Nachr., 23:119.)
Elemente von kleinen Planeten. Astron. Nachr., 272:82.

1942

Ephemeris of Jupiter X and XI. Harv. Coll. Obs. Circ. 620.
The orbit of Jupiter XI. Publ. Am. Astron. Soc., 10:164.
The accuracy of approximate general perturbations. Publ. Am. Astron. Soc., 10:225.

1943

Ephemeris of comet Oterma II. Harv. Coll. Obs. Circ. 642, 643, 649, and 654.
Ephemeris of comet Schwassmann-Wachmann 1925 II. Harv. Coll. Obs. Circ. 658, 683, and 716.

1944

Ephemeris of comet 1944b Vaisala. Harv. Coll. Obs. Circ. 684.
Ephemeris of comet Oterma (1943A). Harv. Coll. Obs. Circ. 687 and 741.
Elements of comet Oterma (1943A). Harv. Coll. Obs. Circ. 698.
Elements and ephemeris of comet Vaisala (1944A). Harv. Coll. Obs. Circ. 695.
Ephemeris of comet Vaisala (1944B). Harv. Coll. Obs. Circ. 702 and 722.
Search ephemeris for Adonis. Astron. J., 50:68.
Elements and approximate perturbations of (657) Gunlod. Astron. J., 50:69–70.
Positions of asteroids. Astron. J., 50:71.
With G. M. Clemence. Optimum-interval punched-card tables. Mathematical tables and other aids to computation. Math. Tables Aids Comput., 1:173–76.

With G. M. Clemence. Editorial changes in scientific papers. Science, 99:241.
Multiplication of Fourier series. Astron. J., 51:20.
Comet 1943b Oterma = 1942 VII. Harv. Coll. Obs. Circ. 741. (Also in: U.A.I. Circ. 1036.)

1946

Catalogue of 2300 stars for the equinox 1925.0. Publ. Cincinnati Obs., 22.
Numerical integration with punched cards. Astron. J., 52:115–17.
The orbits of comet 1925 II (Schwassmann-Wachmann) and comet 1943a (Oterma). Astron. J., 52:124.

1947

Comet Schwassmann-Wachmann 1925 II ephemeris. Harv. Coll. Obs. Circ. 777.
Comet Schwassmann-Wachmann(1), 1925 II. Br. Astron. Assoc. Handb. 1948:48–49.
Comet Oterma (1943A) ephemeris. Harv. Coll. Obs. Circ. 812.
Comet Oterma 1942 VII (= 1943a). Br. Astron. Assoc. Handb. 1948:49–50.
A device in satellite perturbation computations. Astron. J., 52:177–78.
Approximate general perturbations of (1361) Leuschneria. Astron. J., 52:198–200.
On the higher order effects of a differential rotation. Astron. J., 53:15–16.
Elements and ephemeris of comet Schwassmann-Wachmann 1925 II. Astron. J., 53:16–17.
The orbit of comet 1943a (Oterma). Astron. J., 53:18–21.

1948

Ephemeris of Otermascher comet (1942 VII). Br. Astron. Assoc. Handb. 1948. (Also in: Int. Astron. Union Circ. 1162.)
The Computations of Orbits. Ann Arbor, Mich.: Edwards Brothers, Inc., Press. ix + 177 pp.
Ephemeris of erster Schwassmann-Wachmann comet (1941 VI). Br. Astron. Assoc. Handb. 1949. (Also in: Nachrichtenblatt As-

tron. Zentralstells 2, 26, and 32; Int. Astron. Union Circ. 1183 and 1193.)
Comet Oterma, 1942 VII (= 1943a). Br. Astron. Assoc. Handb. 1949:56–57.

1949

Ephemeris of erster Schwassmann-Wachmann (1941 VI). Nachrichtenblatt Astron. Zentralstells 3 and 25. (Also in: U.A.I. Circ. 1228; Astr. Circ. UDSSR, 82:7; Astr. Circ. UDSSR, 90/91:13.)
With G. M. Clemence and Hans G. Hertz. Rectangular coordinates of Ceres, Pallas, Juno, Vesta 1920–1960. Astron. Pap. Am. Eph. 11, part 4. Washington, D.C.: U.S. Government Printing Office. 67 pp.

1950

Reports on the progress of astronomy. Minor planets. Mon. Not. R. Astron. Soc., 110:167–69.
Solutions of the wave equation. In: *Proceedings—Seminar on Scientific Computation, Nov. 1949*, pp. 79–86. New York: International Business Machines Corporation.
Current minor planet problems. Astron. J., 55:165.

1951

Notes on magnitude. Minor Planet Circ. 603.
Reports on the progress of astronomy. Minor planets. Mon. Not. R. Astron. Soc., 111:232–33.
The constructions of tables. In: *Proceedings—Computation Seminar, Dec. 1949*, pp. 62–66. New York: International Business Machines Corporation.
Coordinates of the Sun. Astron. J., 56:128.

1952

Reports on the progress of astronomy. Minor planets. Mon. Not. R. Astron. Soc., 112:332.
Methods for minor planet perturbations. Astron. J., 57:13.

1954

Reports on the progress of astronomy. Minor planets. Mon. Not. R. Astron. Soc., 114:358.

1955

Solar coordinates, 1800–2000. Astron. Pap. Am. Eph. 14. xi + 735 pp.

Coordinates of Venus, 1800–2000. Astron. Pap. Am. Eph. 15, part 3. x + 523 pp.

1956

Reports on the progress of astronomy. Minor planets. Mon. Not. R. Astron. Soc., 116:218.

Resume of minor planet perturbation computations at the Cincinnati Observatory. Minor Planet Circ. 1423–31.

The computation of minor planet perturbations. Minor Planet Circ. 1504–6.

1957

With G. M. Clemence and R. L. Duncombe. Ephemeris of satellite 1957 A 2. Int. Astron. Union Circ. 1626.

With G. M. Clemence and R. L. Duncombe. Satellite 1957 A 2 ephemeris. Harv. Coll. Obs. Circ. 1380.

The return of comet Pons-Brooks 1884 I. Astron. J., 57:160.

1958

The computation of minor planet perturbations. Minor Planet Circ. 1695.

With P. Musen. A modified Hansen lunar theory for artificial satellites. Astron. J., 63:430–33.

Opposition dates for new minor planets. Sonderdruck Real Acad. Ciencias Artes Barcelona, 1957.

With R. L. Duncombe. Elements of satellite 1958A. Int. Astron. Union Circ. 1640.

With R. L. Duncombe. Satellite 1958 A elements. Harv. Coll. Obs. Circ. 1393.

1959

With P. Musen. The calculation of literal expansions. Astron. J., 64:11–20.

Partial astronomical refraction. Astron. J., 64:334–35.

General theory of oblateness perturbations. In: *Proc. Symposium Applied Math.*, 9:29–35.

With P. Musen. Erratum: A modified Hansen lunar theory for artificial satellites. Astron. J., 64:73.

1960

The elements and ephemeris of comet Wirtanen 1948b. Astron. J., 65:385–86.
Parabolic orbit calculations on the IBM 650. Astron. J., 65:491–92.

1961

The orbit of comet Schwassmann-Wachmann 1. Astron. J., 66:266–71.
Keeping track of the minor planets. I.C.S.U. Rev., 3:125–29.

1962

On the variation of arbitrary vectorial constants. Astron. J., 67:16–18.

1963

With C. Bardwell. Potter object = 1963A. Harv. Coll. Obs. Circ. 1629.
Rectangular coordinates of Ceres, Pallas, Juno, Vesta, 1960–1980. Astron. Pap. Am. Eph., 16:341–95.

1965

Computation of orbits. Astron. J., 70:1–3.

1966

The Minor Planet Center at the Cincinnati Observatory. Bull. Cincinnati Hist. Soc., 24:175–87.
With C. J. Van Houten and J. Van Houten-Groeneveld. Periodic comet Van Houten. Int. Astron. Union Circ. 1973.
With F. Barlein, S. Lauret, C. Bertaud, J. Verdier, A. D. Andrews, S. J. Arend, and L. E. Cunningham. Andrews object. Int. Astron. Union Circ. 1900.

1967

Revised plate constants for the Bordeaux astrographic zone. Astron. J., 72:575–81.

1968

Ephemerides of comet Schwassmann-Wachmann 1 and the outer satellite of Jupiter with text. Publ. Cincinnati Obs., 23:1–62.
The outer satellites of Jupiter. Astron. J., 73:737–42.
Revised orbit of comet Schwassmann-Wachmann 1. Astron. J., 73:729–30.

1969

Index to minor planet elements. Minor Planet Circ. 3001–3007.

1970

With C. J. Van Houten, I. P. Van Houten-Groeneveld, and T. Gehrels. The Palomar-Leiden survey of faint minor planets. Astron. Astrophys., Suppl. Ser., 2:339–448.
The physical distortion of Schmidt Plates. In: *I.A.U. Colloquium No. 7: Proper Motions,* ed. W. J. Luyten, p. 93. Minneapolis: University of Minnesota.
The solution of overlapping plates by iteration. In: *I.A.U. Colloquium No. 7: Proper Motions,* ed. W. J. Luyten, pp. 94–95. Minneapolis: University of Minnesota.
With H. J. Carr. The probable error of mass determination. Bull. Am. Astron. Soc., 2:245–46.
Minor planet circulars. Cincinnati Obs. 3023–3126.
Comet 1957 I. Schwassmann-Wachmann 1. Int. Astron. Union Circ. 2295.

1971

The work at the Minor Planet Center. In: *Physical Studies of Minor Planets,* NASA SP-267, ed. T. Gehrels, pp. 9–12. Washington, D.C.: NASA SP-267.
Seth Barnes Nicholson. In: *Biographical Memoirs of the National Academy of Sciences,* vol. 42, pp. 201–27. Washington, D.C.: The National Academy of Sciences.
An analysis of the AGK3 companion star positions. In: *Conference on Photographic Astrometric Technique,* ed. H. Eichhorn, pp. 169–71. Washington, D.C.: NASA CR-1825.

1972

On the differential correction of nearly parabolic orbits. In: *The Motion, Evolution of Orbits, and Origin of Comets,* ed. G. Chebotarev, E. I. Kazimirchak-Polonskaya, and B. G. Marsden, p. 123. Dordrecht: D. Reidel.

With H. J. Carr. The motion of periodic comet Pons-Brooks, 1812–1954. In: *The Motion, Evolution of Orbits, and Origin of Comets,* ed. G. Chebotarev, E. I. Kazimirchak-Polonskaya, and B. G. Marsden, pp. 195–99. Dordrecht: D. Reidel.

On the determination of planetary masses. In: *The Motion, Evolution of Orbits, and Origin of Comets,* ed. G. Chebotarev, E. I. Kazimirchak-Polonskaya, and B. G. Marsden, pp. 244–45. Dordrecht: D. Reidel.

New determination of the plate constants of the Bordeaux zone of the Astrographic Catalogue. In: *Asteroids, Comets, Meteoric Matter,* ed. C. Cristescu, W. J. Klepcynski, and B. Milet, pp. 69–70. Bucharest: Editura Academici Republicii Socialiste Romania.

Cometary research. Vistas Astron., 13:144–51.

1973

Plate constants for the Bordeaux zone of the Astrographic Catalogue. Publ. Cincinnati Obs., 24:1–42.

Comet 1925 II Schwassmann-Wachmann 1. Periodic comet Schwassmann-Wachmann 1. Int. Astron. Union Circ. 2501.

Elementary dynamical astronomy. In: *Recent Advances in Dynamical Astronomy.* Proceedings of the Advanced Study Institute, Cortina d'Ampezzo, Italy, August 9–21, 1972.

1974

Minor planets. In: *Encyclopaedia Britannica,* 15th ed., vol. 14, pp. 491–94.

Minor planet motions. Celestial Mech., 9:315–19.

With R. S. Harrington and M. Miranian. 433 Eros. Int. Astron. Union Circ. 2735.

Comet 1925 II Schwassmann-Wachmann 1. Periodic comet Schwassmann-Wachmann 1. Int. Astron. Union Circ. 2652.

1975

Occultation of K Gem by Eros. Harv. Coll. Obs. Circ. 2735 and 2737.

Gerald M. Clemence—the keeper of Mars. Sky and Telescope, 49:215–16.

With R. S. Harrington and H. L. Giclas. Occultation of K Geminorum A by 433 Eros on 1975 January 24. Int. Astron. Union Circ. 2737.

1976

Comet 1974 II Schwassmann-Wachmann 1. Periodic comet Schwassmann-Wachmann 1. Int. Astron. Union Circ. 2962.

Minor planets. In: *Reports on Astronomy, 16A, Part 1,* ed. G. Contopoulous, pp. 118–20. Dordrecht: D. Reidel.

1977

Errata in the Paris and Toulouse zones of the astrographic catalog. Centre Données Stellaires, Inf. Bull. no. 12, pp. 32–40.

1978

Armin Otto Leuschner. In: *Biographical Memoirs of the National Academy of Sciences,* vol. 49, pp. 129–47. Washington, D.C.: The National Academy of Sciences.

1980

Of computing and astronauts. Sky and Telescope, 60:374–75.

With E. Bowell and B. G. Marsden. Comet Bowell (1980B). Int. Astron. Union Circ. 3465.

1984

With C. J. Van Houten and B. G. Marsden. The Palomar-Leiden survey of faint minor planets: Conclusion. Icarus, 59:1–19.

Scripps Institution of Oceanography Photo Lab
University of California, San Diego

JOHN DOVE ISAACS III
March 28, 1913–June 6, 1980

BY WILLARD BASCOM

JOHN DOVE ISAACS III was born in Spokane, Washington, and he was raised in Oregon where his maternal grandparents had located after crossing the plains by wagon train. His paternal grandfather, John D. Isaacs, Sr., was chief consulting engineer for the Southern Pacific and Union Pacific systems, which was of particular import to John who vastly enjoyed travels with his grandfather in his private railroad car. A bronze plaque at Stanford University credits the senior Isaacs with conceiving and developing the principle of making motion pictures; the first photographic experiments were carried out with Edward Muybridge at Leland Stanford's farm in Palo Alto, California. John's father, also a railroad engineer, died in a hunting accident when John was six.

During his childhood, John lived on the 120,000-acre Hay Creek Ranch in central Oregon with his mother, his sister Emily, and his favorite aunt and uncle. Later he moved to his pioneer grandparents' first ranch home near Pendleton, Oregon. Ranch life gave him a solid background in practical ecology as well as an opportunity for his strong naturalist instincts to develop.

Early in life John showed intense scientific curiosity and a capacity for invention. As a Pendleton High School student in the early 1930s, he proposed to his physics teacher a way of detecting distant objects by means of reflected radio waves. (Unfortunately, the fellow did not grasp the possibilities and thereby lost an opportunity to become a coinventor of radar.) To his chemistry teacher, he had to confess that his chemistry lab was the scene of the production of the hydrogen-plus-acetylene balloons that had recently been exploding over Pendleton and that had even ripped the shingles off the minister's roof.

Young John enjoyed reading encyclopedias, and he had an excellent memory. As an adult he would sometimes launch into detailed dissertations on esoteric subjects—such as the complex life cycles of oriental parasites—that he had read twenty to thirty years earlier.

In 1933 he joined the new Civilian Conservation Corps. He became a camp office manager and—because there was a good supply of logging and construction accidents as well as stabbings and shootings—an accident investigator. Two years later John became camp manager at Cape Perpetua, Oregon, a Resettlement Administration facility. (The Resettlement Administration was a New Deal agency that resettled low-income local families on more productive lands.) By the following year he had saved enough money to return to college at Oregon State, where one of the attractions was Mary Carol Zander.

When school was out, John got a job as a forestry service lookout on Mt. Hebo in the Siuslaw National Forest. When it wasn't raining, this meant twenty-four hours a day atop a high tower accompanied only by Sampson, his trusty cat. During the period Isaacs spent in Oregon's coastal forest, he learned not only the names of all the trees and the undergrowth plants but also the intricate relationship among them and how it changed with logging and fires. In later life when he would drive along the highway, he would amuse himself, and sometimes his companions, by intoning the Latin names of each species of passing tree. One of the monuments he leaves behind is the stand of one thousand trees he planted on his estate in Rancho Santa Fe, California.

In 1938 he moved to Astoria, Oregon, just as a great run of albacore tuna appeared offshore. It was said that everyone in Oregon who had a lettuce crate went after the albacore; John was no exception. He joined with a friend who owned a small boat just a little bigger than a lettuce crate. After long hours of work to make it ready for fishing, John took the boat well out to sea for a test run. Coming back into the Columbia River entrance—always a scary experience in a small boat—events occurred that almost proved fatal. The boat's engine coughed and stopped dead in the turbulent waters of the bar. After frantic work, John realized there was no chance of getting it running again and that the boat would soon crash on the jetty. He stripped off his shoes and pants, put on a life jacket, and committed himself to the river. He vaguely remembered seeing one large wave fling the boat on the unforgiving rocks and watching splinters drift away. After half an hour in the icy waters he was picked up by a passing tug. The crew put him in a cold shower to warm him up; he remembered it as scalding in relation to the river. It was thought at the time that one could not survive in those rough frigid waters more than 10 minutes, but he knew by his watch otherwise. His body was black and blue, totally bruised from head to foot, and he was hardly able to walk for some time after the ordeal.

The next day John and Mary Carol walked out on the jetty. She found the only surviving relics of the wreck: his trousers with his wallet in the pocket, and in it his social security card. He carried the card for the rest of his life as a reminder of his good luck that near-tragic day. Later in that year the two were married. The young pair occupied the captain's cabin and officer's quarters aboard the sailing ship *William Taylor,* which was moored in Young's Bay near Astoria.

As a young commercial fisherman working out of the Columbia River, Isaacs was outraged one day by a passing tourist who said something to the effect that "these fishermen don't know much about what they're doing." John—with a 6-foot 3-inch frame and one of the highest recorded I.Q.'s in the state of Oregon—rather firmly suggested that this unwary soul sit down and observe while he dissected a salmon and explained in detail the function of each organ and tissue.

John Isaacs was a fisherman throughout his life, and he appeared to enjoy cold, wet, miserable weather as long as he could fish. He felt he could think better with a fishing pole in hand. Some of his best thoughts about who eats whom in the sea, under what conditions, and how the sea's biological energy is distributed were developed over fifty years of random observations. These were set down finally in a landmark piece in *Scientific American* entitled "The Nature of Oceanic Life"—illustrated, of course, with photos of deep sea creatures taken by his monster camera. But that was much later.

As a commercial fisherman with a boat that was considered large for the pre-World War II period, John—and occasionally Mary Carol—would fish out of the Columbia River, sometimes going north to Grays Harbor or the Quillayute River, or south to Tillamook Bay. It was the perfect school for a future oceanographer and it left him with an ever-ready bag of stories, as well as a good sense of the lore of the sea.

After two years of commercial fishing John and Mary Carol returned to school and spent the academic year of 1940–41 at Oregon State University. Afterward John took a job with a survey crew on the construction of Tongue Point Naval Air Station near Astoria, Oregon. As various construction problems arose, John devised solutions that moved him rapidly up the job ladder. For example, the ceiling beams in one of the buildings under construction flexed excessively because of poor design. To solve the problem, Isaacs derived the formula for computing bending stresses in beams and redesigned the offending structure "so the plaster below would stay on." When the chief engineer unexpectedly quit, he was offered the job. In 1943–44 Isaacs studied at the University of California at Berkeley, receiving a B.S. in civil engineering, his only degree. While at Berkeley he came to know and appreciate Dean Morrough (Mike) O'Brien who greatly influenced his life.

Thereafter he spent his life with the University of California, beginning as a research engineer on the WAVES Project at Berkeley, which is where I met him. John's enthusiasm for the sea and his sense of humor attracted me to him at once. After listening to him for two hours on our first encounter in 1945, I switched immediately from mining to oceanography. The following week we began surveying the beaches of northern California, Oregon, and Washington using amphibious trucks (DUKWS), seaplanes, radio-controlled cameras, and a small party of men who didn't mind daily dousings in cold seawater. In the late 1940s at Berkeley he invented such things as a wave direction indicator using a Rayleigh disc, several varieties of wave meters, a wave-propelled "sea-sled" to carry surveying rods through the surf zone, and a means of measuring and modeling stress in torpedo nets. Later he and I worked together measuring the effects of nuclear explosions in Eniwetok and Bikini.

John Isaacs was present at four nuclear test series; he especially distinguished himself during two of them. The first was Crossroads in 1946 for which John's job was to measure waves from the blasts. For this purpose he arranged to have large aerial cameras (with a film size of 9 by 18 inches) set up on two camera towers on Bikini Island. These cameras were to be started a little before the explosion, simultaneously taking a picture every three seconds for several minutes. This wave-measuring technique had previously been tested on the northern California coast, but at Bikini the problem was a little different.

Because the objective of that first test was to learn the effects of an airburst and an underwater burst on a fleet of warships, it was necessary to know the exact distances between the explosions and specific parts of each ship. The ships were to be anchored, and the original plan had been to run aerial photo sorties over the fleet a day or two before the shot. These were to have been assembled in a mosaic in order to determine the distances from ship to shot. As any seaman knows, however, ships at anchor move about in a "watch circle" whose radius is the anchor line, which is at least three times the depth of the water (some 200 feet in Bikini lagoon). As a result, matching successive lines of pictures was impossible; between photo runs some ships had moved several hundred feet. Weapons effects decrease as the cube root of the distance; thus such errors in position were unacceptable.

At the uncomfortable moment when this fundamental flaw in the great test was discovered, Isaacs' proposal to use the wave-measuring cameras to triangulate ship positions was gratefully accepted. For months afterward he had a group of people using a traveling microscope mounted on a large steel micrometer stage measuring photos and precisely computing the position of ships in the test fleet. The wave measurements became almost incidental. Using automatic cameras that fire every three seconds he had the fantastic luck to get a picture of the Baker shot's lighted bubble breaking the surface.

During the Castle series at Bikini in 1954, John became very concerned about the possibility of the shots causing a tidal wave that would wash over some of the islets on which people were intending to stay during the shot. Some of us thought there was little likelihood of that happening because John was jokingly known as a "calamatologist" (who often foresaw unlikely calamities). Nevertheless, he had the ear of the admiral, and at the last minute, just to be on the safe side, that worthy ordered everyone except the firing team off the atoll.

The first shot of the series (Bravo) went with about twice the expected yield. When it did, it destroyed many camp buildings on the islands and dumped heavy radioactivity on the atoll. The firing party was trapped in the bunker for a time, and no one went back ashore for several days. There was no substantial tidal wave, but I am convinced that if Isaacs' hunch had not been followed, lives would have been lost both to the blast and the subsequent radioactivity.

John Isaacs liked to think, and the more complex the subject, the better he liked it. Some of his favorite topics were far from oceanography. They included such diverse matters as black holes in space, the groundwaters of the upper Indus valley, growing food plants in saline water, and esoteric aspects of mine warfare. He did not think in mathematical terms, but in later life he wrote equations for ideas that to him were self-evident.

John philosophized about a great many diverse subjects including economics ("The more money is expended for nothing, the more it approaches nothing as a value," and Whitehead's universe where "the possibilities are not only infinite but actual"). He revitalized Epimetheus, the hind-thinker, rampant on a field of greenbacks, who proposed panaceas for vaguely defined scientific problems. And he worried about the communications disjuncture between those who possess scientific understanding and those who are responsible for the direction of governmental action.

John was a big man with quick reactions, but he was not

especially athletically inclined. Instead he played games like "slaphands" in which two persons face each other and extend their hands, each parallel to the other's, but with the hands below, palms up. The object is for the hands below to slap the back of the hands above. No one came close to beating Isaacs at this. He was also expert at ping pong and delighted in "teaching" it to graduate students who had an overly high opinion of their prowess. He loved chess, including blind chess, Kriegspiel, and triple cylindrical chess, but he often had a hard time finding worthy opponents.

Isaacs had a marvelous sense of humor that began with outrageous puns and extended upward to jokes that were so sophisticated that almost no one would get the point. Having delivered some such witicism he would cautiously look around the audience to see if anyone had caught on. On such occasions I would just perceptibly move my head from side to side to show that his remarks had not gone completely unnoticed—but as a matter of principle I never cracked a smile. Isaacs was in his glory when it became fashionable to devise a horrid form of joke known as a Tom Swifty. As with puns he was always trying to invent ones with double and triple meanings. These were marvelously idiotic, and when we all laughed he would be encouraged to attempt an even more outrageous version.

John Isaacs moved from Berkeley to the Scripps Institution of Oceanography in 1948. From this vantage point he could involve himself wholly in all aspects of sea studies.

About that time he heard of the existence of huge freshwater icebergs in the Antarctic, some ten miles long and a mile wide. He promptly set about thinking of ways in which they could be used to increase California's water supply. Isaacs posited that they could be towed into the Peru current, which would move them north to the equatorial currents, which would carry them westward and into the Kuro Siwa, which would move them eastward toward Vancouver and eventually south along the California coast. The ice would take on a streamlined form as it moved, powered by a temperature-difference "engine"; and it would produce more water from rain than from ice melt. Eventually—somehow—the berg would be parked behind Catalina Island. The worst objection to this plan was that it would change the weather in southern California. In a year or so we found that this idea had been invented several times before, but by then Isaacs had gone on to bigger schemes.

Isaacs' curiosity about the animals that live in the depths led to the development (with Lewis Kidd) of the Isaacs-Kidd midwater trawl. This net had a hydrodynamic depressor across the bottom to hold it down while being towed at a depth of several hundred meters. He was also keen on making photos of the animals that live on the deep-sea bottom. In the late 1960s, in association with Richard Schwartzlose, Richard Shutts, and others, he developed baited automatic cameras that were freely released in water as much as 7 km deep and recovered a day later. In several places he photographed a surprisingly large number of active invertebrates, fishes, and some gigantic sharks that changed man's thinking about the sparsity of life at such depths. The nets and the cameras were extensions of his senses as he sought to find out: What's going on down there?

In 1958 he became head of the Marine Life Research Program, which was concerned with discovering whether man's overfishing or pollution had caused sardines to disappear from California waters in the early 1950s. His unconventional approach was to examine (with Andrew Soutar) the yearly layers of undisturbed sediment layers in the Santa Barbara Basin. These layers contained the scales of fish species going back for some 1,200 years. Counting the scales, year by year, showed that sardines had—for natural reasons—

come and gone many times before man arrived. This led to a new question: Why were sardines so plentiful when they were present? The answer is not yet known.

In 1950 I invented the deep taut-moored buoy and used it for wave measurements at the nuclear shots. The buoy was held about 100 feet beneath the sea surface by a slender steel wire some 6,000 feet long; the wire connected the buoy to a heavy anchor clump installed on a sea-mount, which furnished a steady platform for instruments in deep water. John always wanted to "go me one better," and in 1966 he devised the "sky hook." The sky hook was a taut-moored earth satellite that was to be held just beyond synchronous orbit by a wire. If it could be built it would permit large amounts of material to be moved into space without the use of rockets. Aside from the problem of actually constructing this device, however, the wire into space required a tensile strength far beyond any known material. Someday it may be possible; in the meantime the idea has been duly credited in Arthur Clarke's book, *The Fountains of Paradise*.

While thinking about how to deal with sea mines activated by a ship's pressure signal, Isaacs also devised a ship hull that trapped its own waves. This was basically an ordinary hull, "sliced" down the middle, with the pieces transposed and separated by a closed bottom so that only straight sides were exposed. The propeller was between the hulls, and the ship carried a substantial breaking wave just inside the stern, the forward part being a raceway. I piloted a model of it through a number of test runs without disturbing the surface of a glassy reservoir.

Later, Isaacs and Hugh Bradner proposed that the earth might be appreciably heated by neutrinos. John Isaacs also gave a good deal of thought to the matter of extracting power from the sea. In 1954 he studied the Claude thermal difference process and started to build a resonant wave pump for the end of the Scripps pier. Later he reinvestigated tidal power schemes, pointing out that much of what seemed to be available head (usable water height) in an estuary would be lost as soon as any structure was built because the kinetic run-up would be much reduced.

In the 1970s he and various associates at the Institute of Marine Resources, including Walter Schmitt, Gerald Wick, and David Castel, reexamined the utilization of energy from ocean waves. John liked to remind his listeners that more power is expended by waves in heaving—that is, vertically moving—a ship up and down as it crosses the ocean than by the thrust of its screws. He noted that waves are a form of solar energy; as such their very nature requires that a great number of small devices be used if much energy is to be extracted. Their special feature is that if waves are cropped by some extraction device, the wind builds them up again; thus there could be a hundred times more power available than is observed in a steady-state condition.

Isaacs and his associates established design criteria for wave-powered machines and then proceeded to construct a wave-powered pump. A photo of a small version of this pump appeared on the cover of *Science* (January 18, 1980) spouting water some 6 meters into the air in waves of only 0.6 meter. The advantages of zero fuel costs and only one moving part led him to suggest that a 50-kilowatt plant of this type in trade-wind seas using a pipe 0.9 meter in diameter and 153 meters long would be very efficient—if only there were a suitable application.

Next Isaacs (and Wick) looked into salinity gradient energy. This is a potentially large source of usable energy that can be tapped if the osmotic pressure between two fluids of different salinity can be harnessed. Where a stream flows into the ocean, this pressure is equivalent to 240 meters of head; it is more than ten times that much if it flows into the Great

Salt Lake. Several schemes for tapping salinity gradient energy were reviewed, most of which required better and cheaper semipermeable membranes than currently exist. John pointed out that there may be greater amounts of energy available from the salt in salt domes than in the oil and gas that has been extracted from them.

At the end of his paper on the forms of and prospects for using the ocean for human power needs, Isaacs concluded: "The most important . . . will be in the employment of seawater for heat rejection and of the deep region below the sea floor for the disposal of nuclear wastes."

Isaacs the whimsical philosopher also liked to consider the positions of events and energy in perspective. He and Walter Schmitt constructed an energy "ladder" and made order-of-magnitude estimates that included some of the following:

Big bang	10^{75}
Sun's radiation (one year)	10^{41}
Ice age latent heat	-10^{33}
Marine biomass (one year)	10^{28}
Large salt dome	10^{26}
Largest H-bomb	10^{24}
Tornado	10^{22}
Lightning flash	10^{17}
Human daily diet	10^{14}
Melting ice cube	-10^{9}
Striking typewriter key	10^{5}
Flea hop	10^{0}

After carefully considering the implications of the above, he concluded (in *Science*) that the sun's radiation for one year could fuel the leap of 10^{41} fleas.

One of his inventions was an elegantly simple means of controlling heat and moisture loss in divers, mountain climbers, or other individuals subjected to cold–dry stress. In normal breathing, inhaled air is warmed and humidified as it moves toward the lungs; with exhalation, most of that heat and moisture is lost. Under extreme conditions, the heat–moisture losses are 250 times those that occur at rest at room temperature. As Isaacs pointed out, by far the largest part of the heat lost is that required to vaporize water, and divers and climbers can have a serious problem of dehydration.

Previously existing techniques were complex and heavy, and required some stored water. His solution was to equip the explorer with a small cylinder of hydrogen under high pressure. The hydrogen is then premixed with incoming air in a breathing mask and passed over a catalytic metal where it is combusted. This provides a supply of warm, moist air. As long as the amount of hydrogen is less than 3 percent, there is no danger of explosion.

The patent for this device is held by the Foundation for Ocean Research. Isaacs' name does not appear on it but, as he liked to say, "There's no limit to what a man can accomplish if he doesn't care who gets the credit."

John Isaacs was committed to the conservation and protection of natural resources, but he was incensed by regulations that attempted to control the discharge of human wastes into the sea. It was his opinion that:

> The return of organic waste and plant nutrients resulting from the most natural of acts to the sea is most probably beneficial. The benefits of putting the same material on land is clear to any farmer but the advantages to the sea are not so easily appreciated. The sea is *starved* for basic plant nutrients and it is a mystery to me why anyone should be concerned with their introduction into coastal seas in any quantity we can generate in the forseeable future. (Testimony of October 19, 1973.)

On other occasions Isaacs liked to note that if the human population of the southern California coast (about 10 million persons) were compared on a weight basis with the anchovy populations (then about 3.5 million tons), the anchovies would produce about ten times as much fecal material. "Why should the human product be worse?" he would ask dramatically. "Don't you know that most sea animals live in a soup of fecal material and feed on it directly?"

During the first decade of work by the Southern California Coastal Water Research Project (of which this writer is director), Isaacs was the chairman of the scientific consulting board that guided its efforts. His wise counsel in the beginning established the attitude that has continued to this day. He believed that we should try to understand the overall picture—including all sources of contaminants—against the background of changing sea conditions. The project's contribution to man's knowledge of marine food webs, toxicity, and the understanding of marine biological processes derives in part from John's intuitive suggestions.

One of his more dramatic ideas was based on the sixfold increase in the recorded incidence of tornadoes in the United States over the forty years prior to 1975. He claimed that part of the increase was caused by streams of motor vehicles moving in opposite directions on highways: these vehicles imparted angular momentum as a counterclockwise torque to the atmosphere. He suggested that the center of tornado activity had steadily moved eastward in recent decades and that there were fewer tornadoes on Saturdays when two-way truck and commuter traffic is at a minimum. Subsequent study by James Stork substantiated this forecast and showed specifically that there were, on the average, 300 less tornadoes per year on Saturdays than on other days.

Publication of this novel thesis in *Nature* created a storm of controversy at first, but after extensive exchanges Isaacs' views seem to have prevailed. His position was that shear, caused by the flow of autos and trucks, is the largest identifiable source of nonrandom cyclonic vorticity. His analysis showed that rotating storms of the dimensions of hurricanes are energy limited, whereas those of tornadoes are limited by angular momentum.

Isaacs loved Beethoven, Brahms, Tchaikovsky, Mozart, and Rimski-Korsakov—when he wrote or studied at home it was often to the accompaniment of great music. In literature his tastes remained consistent throughout his life; the Bible, Shakespeare, Omar Khayyām, Mark Twain, and Kipling were his favorites. He constantly quoted the first three, often used analogues to Mark Twain scenes (seeing himself as a latter-day Huck Finn), and traded many a quote from Kipling with me. He was very fond of writing quotes from Omar Khayyām on blackboards or reciting them to students—carefully noting which of the five editions was used.

In 1961 Isaacs became a full professor at the University of California. In 1971 he was named director of the University's statewide Institute of Marine Resources, and in 1976 he was elected president of the Foundation for Ocean Research of San Diego. He was elected to the National Academy of Sciences in 1974 and to the National Academy of Engineering in 1977. He was also a member of the World Academy of Arts and Sciences and was president of the Pacific Division of the American Association for the Advancement of Science. In addition to these affiliations, he was involved in dozens of other clubs, societies, committees, and chairmanships.

Among the posthumous tributes he received were the naming of a research vessel after him (the RV *John Isaacs*); the establishment, by the National College Sea Grant Program, of the annual John D. Isaacs Memorial Scholarship for excellence in marine science by a high school student; and the endowment of the John D. Isaacs Chair of Natural Philosophy at the University of California at San Diego.

John and Mary Carol produced four children: Ann Katherine, who is professor of modern history at the University of Pisa, Italy; Caroline Marie, a research sedimentary geologist at the U.S. Geological Survey, Menlo Park, California; Jon Berkeley, a student at the University of California at San Diego; and Kenneth Zander, a neurologist in private practice and research in Walla Walla, Washington. There are also two grandchildren: Alessandro Marcello and Jessica Ann Marie.

Only rarely do scientists leave a clear, succinct statement of their opinions about the state of science and its relation to government and education. Fortunately, John Isaacs recorded his for a plenary address to the Pacific Science Congress at Vancouver, British Columbia, in 1975. Those who remember his unique manner of expression will recognize the following excerpts from that speech as pure vintage Isaacs:

> I believe that the vast reaches of the Pacific Ocean, covering more than one-third of the planet, hold and conceal minerals, energy, food, aesthetic resources, and intellectual challenges of immense potential to the peoples of the Pacific Basin—can we but learn to discern these possibilities and intelligently approach them.
> I believe that there are many remarkably simple but undiscovered ways of achieving understanding of and dealing with the resources and forces of this great realm.
> The scientific hierarchy demands deeper penetration of nature, not broader and broader comprehension! Yet it is the development of increasing breadth and comprehension as well as penetration, that we must espouse with open-eyed, broad, undogmatic intellectual fervor, confidence and devotion if we are to understand the complexity of nature. It is increasingly clear that our crucial task is now to learn how the pieces fit together, for it is interaction on this planet, rather than its components, that form the limiting problem of mankind.
> Our educational system in science and technology tends to train only those faculties of the human intellect that are readily testable: memory and formal reasoning. Untaught, unevaluated and, indeed, often suppressed, since they are so challenging to teachers, are those other vast components of intellectuality: conceptualization, that allows one to conceive of complex interactions as a system; intuition, the mysterious quality

that leaps to truths through a jungle of confusing detail; the trilogy: mental adventurousness and fervor, attention to the unexpected, and curiosity, those intellectual attributes that can challenge established dogma by discerning its underlying flaws, and judgment, the equally mysterious faculty of recognizing the "likelihood" of something, a mental quality that went out of fashion a hundred years ago.

My point is, of course, that the intellectual qualities that we neither teach nor know how to teach, and hence tend to suppress, are precisely the ones essential to dealing with the complex systems of this planet, and since these qualities are suppressed in our educational system, untutored people often possess them in more highly developed form than do the educated.

I have much greater faith in simple observations and untrammeled thinking than I have in sophisticated observations and simplistic thinking! And I have much greater confidence that man's relationship to the sea and its resources will be enhanced by thoughtful and observant people closely involved and broadly acquainted with the sea—scientist and non-scientist alike—than by frantic bureaucratic responses to public hysteria or by the pontification of the scientific hierarchy.

John Isaacs spent his last few months fighting cancer. He tried to live a reasonably normal life, doing the teaching that he loved in his regular seminars at the Foundation for Ocean Research. He committed his major energies, however, to work on a book that he envisioned as presenting a total conceptualization of current multidisciplinary knowledge of the sea. It was his belief that a broad and penetrating study of the sea and man's interventions and relationships there could provide some guidance in solving the complex problems threatening man's future.

In his own words lies his theme: "It was largely the challenge of the seas that brought medieval man out of the dark ages and into the modern world. His discoveries of the oceans and continents, and his development of navigation instruments and ships, gave him new confidence in his ability to surpass the achievements of the ancients, the darkness of his times, and the inadequacies of his institutions.

"The sea again challenges our sciences and our institutions and presents again those same opportunities to guide ourselves out of the present age and into a new and future world."

On June 6, 1980, John Isaacs passed—as Mark Twain put it—"to that mysterious country from whose bourne no traveler returns."

BIBLIOGRAPHY

1945

Memorandum on drawing refraction diagrams directly by orthogonals. Fluid Mechanics Laboratory, University of California, Berkeley, report nos. HE-116-47 and HE-116-47b.

Memorandum on sighting bar discrepancies. Fluid Mechanics Laboratory, University of California, Berkeley, report no. HE-116-57.

A device for traversing the surf zone of ocean beaches. Fluid Mechanics Laboratory, University of California, Berkeley, report no. HE-116-90.

A revised rudder for the LCVP. Fluid Mechanics Laboratory, University of California, Berkeley, report no. HE-116-91.

Plans for the study of beaches—I. Fluid Mechanics Laboratory, University of California, Berkeley, report no. HE-116-92.

Plans for the study of beaches—II. Fluid Mechanics Laboratory, University of California, Berkeley, report no. HE-116-125.

Memorandum on proposed change in sighting bar procedure. Fluid Mechanics Laboratory, University of California, Berkeley, report no. HE-116-129.

Report on survey at Surf. Fluid Mechanics Laboratory, University of California, Berkeley, report no. HE-116-130.

Survey and reconnaissance of miscellaneous Pacific Coast beaches. Fluid Mechanics Laboratory, University of California, Berkeley, report no. HE-116-131.

Littoral current at Estero Bay. Fluid Mechanics Laboratory, University of California, Berkeley, report no. HE-116-132.

Report on survey with sea sled and mast at Pismo, California. Fluid Mechanics Laboratory, University of California, Berkeley, report no. HE-116-135.

Plans for the study of beaches—III. Fluid Mechanics Laboratory, University of California, Berkeley, report no. HE-116-138.

Report on survey at Pismo. Fluid Mechanics Laboratory, University of California, Berkeley, report no. HE-116-139.

Hydrography at Coronado. Fluid Mechanics Laboratory, University of California, Berkeley, report no. HE-116-141.

Report on survey at Oceano. Fluid Mechanics Laboratory, University of California, Berkeley, report no. HE-116-149.

Hydrography at Estero Bay. Fluid Mechanics Laboratory, University of California, Berkeley, report no. HE-116-154.

Beach and surf conditions at Carmel Beach on July 24, 1945. Fluid Mechanics Laboratory, University of California, Berkeley, report no. HE-116-178.

Analysis of elements of a breaker by two sighting bars. Fluid Mechanics Laboratory, University of California, Berkeley, report no. HE-116-179.

Beach and surf conditions at Half Moon Bay. Fluid Mechanics Laboratory, University of California, Berkeley, report no. HE-116-181.

Beach and surf conditions at Point Joe Bight. Fluid Mechanics Laboratory, University of California, Berkeley, report no. HE-116-183.

Beach and surf conditions at Carmel River Bight, July 26, 1945. Fluid Mechanics Laboratory, University of California, Berkeley, report no. HE-116-185.

1946

Hydrography at Monterey Bay. Fluid Mechanics Laboratory, University of California, Berkeley, report no. HE-116-200.

Notes on reconnaissance of miscellaneous Pacific beaches, May 21–September 29, 1946. Fluid Mechanics Laboratory, University of California, Berkeley, report no. HE-116-223.

Preliminary report on harbors, havens and anchorages of the Pacific coast from San Francisco to the Straits of Juan de Fuca. Fluid Mechanics Laboratory, University of California, Berkeley, report no. HE-116-225.

Field report on the reconnaissance of beaches of the island of Oahu. Fluid Mechanics Laboratory, University of California, Berkeley, report no. HE-116-231.

1947

Beach and surf conditions on beaches of the Oregon and Washington coast between August 27 and September 27, 1945. Fluid Mechanics Laboratory, University of California, Berkeley, report no. HE-116-229.

With D. L. Foight and W. N. Bascom. Report on amphibious operation at Oceanside. Fluid Mechanics Laboratory, University of California, Berkeley, report no. HE-116-235.

With W. N. Bascom. Water-table elevations in some Pacific coast beaches. Fluid Mechanics Laboratory, University of California, Berkeley, report no. HE-116-238.

Memorandum on the use of magnesium rod as a release device. Fluid Mechanics Laboratory, University of California, Berkeley, report no. HE-116-251.

With R. Wiegel. Investigation of torpedo net. Part II. Fluid Mechanics Laboratory, University of California, Berkeley, report no. HE-116-254.

With A. J. Chinn. Investigation of torpedo net. Part III (revised model "zippering" effect). Fluid Mechanics Laboratory, University of California, Berkeley, report no. HE-116-255.

With S. Schorr. Memorandum of analysis of pressure records from Mark III Model II, shore wave recorder. Fluid Mechanics Laboratory, University of California, Berkeley, report no. HE-116-257.

With S. Schorr. Records of waves on the Pacific coast of California and Oregon. Fluid Mechanics Laboratory, University of California, Berkeley, report no. HE-116-263.

With S. Schorr. General information on wind waves and swells (marine operations). Fluid Mechanics Laboratory, University of California, Berkeley, report no. HE-116-263, addendum I.

With W. N. Bascom. Report on operation and characteristics of U.S. Army DUKWS in oceanographic investigations. Fluid Mechanics Laboratory, University of California, Berkeley, report no. HE-116-266.

Graphical construction of refraction diagrams directly by orthogonals. Fluid Mechanics Laboratory, University of California, Berkeley, report no. HE-116-273.

1948

With J. W. Johnson. Action and effect of waves. West. Constr News, 23(4):97–102, 116.

Discussion of "Refraction of surface waves by currents" by J. W. Johnson (in Trans. Am. Geophys. Union, 28[1947]:867–74). Trans. Am. Geophys. Union, 29(5):739–41.

With J. W. Johnson and M. P. O'Brien. *Graphical Construction of Wave Refraction Diagrams*. U.S. Navy Hydrological Office Publication no. 605. 45 pp.

With R. L. Wiegel. The measurement of wave heights by means of a float in an open-end pipe. Fluid Mechanics Laboratory, University of California, Berkeley, report no. HE-116-271.

With E. Winkler. Preliminary report on the modification of the Esterline Angus one milliampere movement for recording long period swell. Fluid Mechanics Laboratory, University of California, Berkeley, report no. HE-116-277.

With J. P. Frankel. The design and operation of an underwater deflection meter. Fluid Mechanics Laboratory, University of California, Berkeley, report no. HE-116-284.

With J. W. Johnson. Action and effect of waves. West. Constr. News, 23(4):97–102.

With T. Saville, Jr. The comparison between recorded and forecast waves on the Pacific coast. Fluid Mechanics Laboratory, University of California, Berkeley, report no. HE-116-285.

With A. J. Chinn. Preliminary report on the Mark II wave direction indicator and recorder. Fluid Mechanics Laboratory, University of California, Berkeley, report no. HE-116-290.

1949

The forecasting of sea and swell and open water protection from waves in coastal waters. Explor. J., 27(1):1–9, 59.

With W. N. Bascom. Water-table elevations in some Pacific Coast beaches. Trans. Am. Geophys. Union, 30(2):293–94.

With R. L. Wiegel. The measurement of wave heights by means of a float in an open-end pipe. Trans. Am. Geophys. Union, 30(4):501–6.

With T. Saville, Jr. A comparison between recorded and forecast waves on the Pacific Coast. Ann. N.Y. Acad. Sci., 51, art. 3:502–10.

1950

With J. M. Snodgrass. Underwater electrical signals. In: *Proceedings of the Fifth Undersea Symposium,* Washington, D.C., May 1950. National Research Council, Committee on Undersea Warfare Publ. 0095.

With R. L. Wiegel. Thermopile wave meter. Trans. Am. Geophys. Union, 31(5):711–16.

1951

With E. A. Williams and C. Eckart. Total reflection of surface waves by deep water. Trans. Am. Geophys. Union, 32(1):37–40.
With L. W. Kidd. A midwinter trawl. Scripps Institution of Oceanography, SIO Reference no. 51-51.

1952

With C. O'D. Iselin, ed. Oceanographic instrumentation. (By Office of Naval Research, Rancho Santa Fe, California, June 1952.) NAS–NRC Publ. 309.
With D. L. Fox and E. F. Corcoran. Marine leptopel, its recovery, measurement and distribution. J. Mar. Res., 11(1):29–46.
With A. E. Maxwell. The ball-breaker, a deep water bottom signalling device. J. Mar. Res., 11(1):63–68.
With E. A. Williams. The refraction of groups and of the waves which they generate in shallow water. Trans. Am. Geophys. Union, 33(4):525–30.
With R. S. Arthur and W. H. Munk. The direct construction of wave rays. Trans. Am. Geophys. Union, 33(6):855–65.

1953

With L. W. Kidd. Isaacs-Kidd midwater trawl. Oceanographic Equipment Report no. 1, ed. R. F. Devereux. Scripps Institution of Oceanography, SIO Reference no. 53-3.
With L. W. Kidd. High-speed diving dredge. Oceanographic Equipment Report no. 4, ed. R. F. Devereux. Scripps Institution of Oceanography, SIO Reference no. 53-37.

1955

With T. R. Folsom. Mechanism and extent of the early dispersion of radioactive products in water. Preliminary report, Operation Wigwam, Project 2.6, Armed Forces Special Weapons Project ITR-1064.
Oceanography and engineering. J. Mar. Res., 14(4):323–32.

1956

With R. Revelle, T. R. Folsom, and E. D. Goldberg. Nuclear science and oceanography. In: *Proceedings of the International Conference on Peaceful Uses of Atomic Energy,* Geneva, August 1955, vol. 13, *Legal, Health, and Safety Aspects of Large-Scale Use of Nuclear Energy,* pp. 371–80. New York: United Nations.

With R. L. Wiegel. Thermopile wave meter. In: *Proceedings of the First Conference on Coastal Engineering Instruments,* Berkeley, California, 1955, pp. 101–10. (Revision of 1950 article.)

1957

With R. P. Huffer and L. W. Kidd. Instrument stations in the deep sea. Science, 125(3243):341.

1958

With J. L. Faughn, T. R. Folsom, F. D. Jennings, DeC. Martin, Jr., L. E. Miller, and R. L. Wisner. A preliminary radioactivity survey along the California coast through disposal areas. In: *Proceedings of the Ninth Pacific Science Congress,* Thailand, 1957, vol. 16, pp. 152–58.

With E. H. Ahlstrom, J. R. Thrailkill, and L. W. Kidd. High-speed plankton sampler. Fish. Bull., 58:187–214.

1959

With O. E. Sette. Unusual conditions in the Pacific. Science, 129(3351):787–88.

1960

With O. E. Sette, eds. The changing Pacific Ocean in 1957 and 1958. (Presented at California Cooperative Oceanic Fisheries Investigations Symposium, Rancho Santa Fe, California, June 1958.) Calif. Coop. Oceanic Fish. Invest. Rep., 7:13–217.

With G. B. Schick. Deep-sea free instrument vehicle. Deep-Sea Res., 7:61–67.

With J. E. Tyler. On the observation of unresolved surface features of a planet. Publ. Astron. Soc. Pac., 72(426):159–66.

1961

Underwater inspection methods. In: *Syllabus of On-Site Inspection of Unidentified Seismic Events*, pp. 141–50. Stanford, Calif.: Stanford Research Institute.

Capacity of the oceans. Int. Sci. Technol. (prototype):38–43.

With G. B. Schick. Underwater remote programming. Undersea Technol., 2(6):29–32.

1962

With L. M. K. Boelter, D. M. Bonner, L. A. Bromley, D. E. Carritt (chairman), B. F. Dodge, E. Epstein, H. P. Gregor, G. A. Jeffrey, J. J. Katz, K. A. Kraus, G. W. Murphy, and T. K. Sherwood. *Desalination Research and the Water Problem*. (Presented at Desalination Research Conference, Woods Hole, Massachusetts, June–July 1961.) NAS–NRC Publ. no. 941. 85 pp.

Note on an association of cumulus clouds and turbid water. J. Geophys. Res., 67(5):2076–77.

Editor. *Disposal of Low-Level Radioactive Waste into Pacific Coastal Waters*. (A report of a working group of the Committee on Oceanography.) NAS–NRC Publ. no. 985. 87 pp.

Mechanism and extent of the early dispersion of radioactive products in water. (Revision of 1955 report.) Operation Wigwam, May 1955, Proj. 2.6-1. Defense Atomic Support Agency Report WT-1014.

1963

With J. L. Faughn, G. B. Schick, and M. C. Sargent. Deep-sea moorings: Design and use with unmanned instrument stations. Bull. Scripps Inst. Oceanogr., 8(3):271–312.

Deep-sea anchoring and mooring. In: *The Sea*, vol. 2, ed. M. N. Hill, pp. 516–27. New York: Interscience; John Wiley & Sons.

The water dilemma. In: *The Impact of Science*, pp. 41–49. (Proceedings of conference no. 4 of the conference series, California and the Challenge of Growth, San Diego, University of California, Berkeley, June 1963.)

With W. R. Schmitt. Resources from the sea. Int. Sci. Technol., June:39–45.

Atmospheric jet streams. Science, 141(3585):1045–46.

World Book Encyclopedia contributions (since 1958): Aegean Sea, Sea of Azov, Bay of Biscay, Bosporus, Caspian Sea, River Derwent, English Channel, Fiord (Fjord), Inchcape Rock, Ionian Sea, Sea of Marmara, Strait of Messina, North Sea, Ruhr River, Scapa Flow, and White Sea. New York: McGraw-Hill.

1964

Discussion of "Considerations on the siting of outfalls for the sea disposal of radioactive effluent in tidal waters" by R. T. P. Whipple. In: *Advances in Water Pollution Research,* vol. 3, ed. E. A. Pearson, pp. 26–35. (Proceedings of the International Conference, London, September 1962.) Oxford: Pergamon Press.
California and the world ocean. In: *Proceedings of the Governor's Conference, Colloquy, and Forum,* Los Angeles, January 31–February 1, pp. 97–106.
Explosively created harbors. In: *Engineering with Nuclear Explosives,* pp. 335–54. (Proceedings of the Third Plowshare Symposium, University of California, Davis, April 1964.) U.S. Atomic Energy Commission, Division of Technical Information no. TID-7695. Washington, D.C.
Night-caught and day-caught larvae of the California sardine. Science, 144(3622):1132–33.
The planetary water problem. In: *Proceedings of the First International Conference of Women Engineers and Scientists,* New York, June, pp. II-1 to II-13.
With H. Bradner. Neutrino and geothermal fluxes. J. Geophys. Res., 69(18):3883–87.

1965

Possible oceanographic and related observations from satellites. In: *Oceanography from Space,* ed. G. C. Ewing, p. 51. (Proceedings of Conference on the Feasibility of Conducting Oceanographic Explorations from Aircraft, Manned Orbital, and Lunar Laboratories, Woods Hole, Massachusetts, August 1964.) Woods Hole Oceanographic Institution Reference no. 65-10.
With B. Polk. New techniques, new esthetic. Landscape, 14(3):3–5.
Larval sardine and anchovy interrelationships. Calif. Coop. Oceanic Fish. Invest. Rep., 10:102–40.

With R. A. Schwartzlose. Migrant sound scatterers: Interaction with the sea floor. Science, 150(3705):1810–13.
With G. B. Schick, M. H. Sessions, and R. A. Schwartzlose. Development and testing of taut-nylon moored instrument stations (with details of design and construction). Scripps Institution of Oceanography, SIO Reference no. 65-5.
An historical study of the eastern North Pacific. In: Final report, Junior College Workshop in Biology, pp. 23–29. California Department of Education.

1966

With A. C. Vine, H. Bradner, and G. E. Backus. Satellite elongation into a true "sky-hook." Science, 151(3711):682–83. (Further discussion in: Science, 152[3723]:800 and 158[3803]:946–47.)
The sea and man. Portal (first edition), pp. 18–28.
With J. L. Reid, Jr., G. B. Schick, and R. A. Schwartzlose. Near-bottom currents measured in 4 kilometers depth off the Baja California coast. J. Geophys. Res., 71(18):4297–303.
With D. M. Brown. Isaacs-Brown opening, closing trawl. Scripps Institution of Oceanography, SIO Reference no. 66-18.

1967

Food from the sea. Int. Sci. Technol., April: 61–68.
Large-scale anomalous sea surface conditions in the North Pacific. In: *Proceedings of the Fourth U.S. Navy Symposium on Military Oceanography*, Washington, D.C., May.
With R. Radok and W. Munk. A note on mid-ocean internal tides. Deep-Sea Res., 14:121–24.
Remarks on some present and future buoy developments. In: *Transactions of the Second International Buoy Technology Symposium*, Washington, D.C., September, pp. 503–29. Marine Technology Society.
The oceans and man. Ariz Eng. Sci., December:4, 6.

1968

With G. B. Schick and M. H. Sessions. Autonomous instruments in oceanographic research. In: *Marine Sciences Instrumentation*, vol. 4, ed. F. Alt, pp. 203–30. (Proceedings of the Fourth National ISA Marine Sciences Instrumentation Symposium, Cocoa Beach, Florida, January.) New York: Plenum Press.

With M. H. Sessions and R. A. Schwartzlose. A camera system for the observation of deep-sea marine life. In: *Proceedings of the Underwater Photooptical Instrumentation Applications Seminar,* San Diego, California, February. Society of Photooptical Instrumentation Engineers.

With D. M. Brown. "Bootstrap" corer. J. Sediment. Petrol., 38(1):159–62.

The North Pacific study. In: *Proceedings of the Third Marine Systems and ASW Meeting,* San Diego, California, April 29–May 1. Am. Inst. Aeronaut. Astronaut., AIAA Paper no. 68-475.

Oceans without megohms (a twenty-year baptism of electronics by seawater—a report). In: *Electronics Serving Mankind,* pp. 1–5. (Proceedings of the Institute of Electrical and Electronics Engineers, Region Six Conference, Portland, Oregon, May.) New York: IEEE.

General features of the ocean. In: *Ocean Engineering,* ed. J. F. Brahtz, pp. 157–201. New York: John Wiley & Sons.

Science and technology: The driving force. In: *Revolution,* ed. M. D. Generales and J. D. Kitchen, pp. 218–35. (Proceedings of the Twenty-Sixth Annual Institute on World Affairs, San Diego, California, August.) San Diego, Calif.: San Diego State College Press.

Probing the birthplace of American weather. Naval Res. Rev., 21(11-12):1–13.

The sea and man. Explor. J., 46(4):260–65.

With M. W. Evans and R. A. Schwartzlose. Data from deep-moored instrument stations. Scripps Institution of Oceanography, SIO Reference no. 68-17.

1969

With A. Soutar. History of fish populations inferred from fish scales in anaerobic sediments off California. Calif. Coop. Oceanic Fish. Invest. Rep., 13:63–70.

With R. F. Devereux and F. D. Jennings. Long-distance telemetry of environmental data for the North Pacific study. In: *Proceedings Oceanology International 69, First International Oceanology*

Conference, Brighton, England, February. London: BPS Exhibitions Ltd.
The North Pacific study. (Revision of 1968 AIAA paper.) J. Hydronaut., 3(2):65–72.
With M. W. Evans and R. A. Schwartzlose. Atmospheric effects on the ocean as measured from deep-moored instrument stations. In: *Proceedings of the Marine Temperature Measurements Symposium,* Miami Beach, June, pp. 71–93. Marine Technology Society.
With A. Fleminger and J. K. Miller. Distributional atlas of zooplankton biomass in the California current region: Spring and fall 1955–1959. Calif. Coop. Oceanic Fish. Invest. Atlas, 10: i–xxv; 1–252.
Role of the NDBS in future variability studies of the North Pacific. In: *Proceedings of the First National Data Buoy Systems Scientific Advisory Meeting,* U.S. Coast Guard Academy, New London, Connecticut. May, pp. 62–78.
With R. A. Schwartzlose. Transient circulation event near the deep ocean floor. Science, 165(3896):889–91.
The nature of oceanic life. Sci. Am., 221(3):146–62. (Also in: *Readings from Scientific American:* "Oceanography," 1971, pp. 214–27; see also para. 4, p. 208, for review; "Ecology, Evolution, and Population Biology," 1973, pp. 239–52; see also para. 2, p. 191, for review; "Life in the Sea," 1981, pp. 4–17; see also para. 6 *et seq.,* p. 2, for review. Available as Sci. Am. Offprint no. 844.)
With W. R. Schmitt. Stimulation of marine productivity with waste heat and mechanical power. J. Cons. Int. Explor. Mer, 33(1):20–29.

1970

With R. F. Devereux, M. W. Evans, R. F. Kosic, and R. A. Schwartzlose. Telemetering of oceanographic data for the North Pacific study. Telemetry J., 5(2):19–23, 36.
With R. A. Schwartzlose. The operational results from the North Pacific study. In: *Proceedings of the Sixth Annual Meeting, Marine Technology Society,* Washington, D.C., June 29–July 1, vol. 1, pp. 551–60.
Editor. Symposium on population and fisheries. Calif. Coop. Oceanic Fish. Invest. Conf., Avalon, Catalina Island, California,

December 1968. Calif. Coop. Oceanic Fish. Invest. Rep., 14:21–70.

With R. M. Born, D. M. Brown, R. A. Schwartzlose, and M. H. Sessions. Deep-moored instrument station design and performance, 1967–1970. Scripps Institution of Oceanography, SIO Reference no. 70-19.

1971

With M. R. Clarke. Other resources of the deep sea. In: *Deep Oceans*, ed. P. J. Herring and M. R. Clarke, pp. 270–76. London: Arthur Barker, Ltd.

With W. R. Schmitt. Enhancement of marine protein production. In: *Fertility of the Sea*, ed. J. D. Costlow, vol. 2, pp. 455–62. London: Gordon & Breach.

With D. M. Brown and M. H. Sessions. Continuous temperature-depth profiling deep-moored buoy system. Deep-Sea Res., 18:845–49.

Engineering problems in monitoring the ocean. (Abstract.) In: *The Ocean World*, ed. M. Uda, pp. 123–24. (Proceedings of the Joint Oceanographic Assembly, Tokyo, September 1970.) Tokyo: Japan Society for the Promotion of Science.

With A. Fleminger and J. K. Miller. Distributional atlas of zooplankton biomass in the California Current region: Winter 1955–1959. Calif. Coop. Oceanic Fish. Invest. Atlas, 14:i–xxiv; 1–122.

1972

With R. R. Hessler and E. L. Mills. Giant amphipod from the abyssal Pacific Ocean. Science, 175(4022):636–37.

Unstructured marine food webs and "pollutant analogues." Fish. Bull., 70(3):1053–59.

With H. Bradner. Overpressures due to earthquakes project. Final technical report to Advanced Research Project Agency (ARPA), December 15, 1968–December 31, 1972. Scripps Institution of Oceanography, SIO Reference no. 72-18, AOEL Report no. 72.

1973

The ocean margins. (Seminar, University of Washington, Seattle, February 21, 1968.) In: *Ocean Resources and Public Policy*, ed.

T. S. English, pp. 76–93. Seattle: University of Washington Press.
With R. J. Seymour. The ocean as a power resource. Int. J. Environ. Stud., 4:201–5.
With G. L. Wick. Optimized tactics for open-water marine predators. J. Mar. Biol. Assoc. India, Spec. Publ., May:193–99.
Potential trophic biomasses and trace-substance concentrations in unstructured marine food webs. Mar. Biol., 22:97–104.
With D. R. Young, J. N. Johnson, and A. Soutar. Mercury concentrations in dated varved marine sediments collected off Southern California. Nature, 244(5415):273–75.

1974

With G. L. Wick. Tungus event revisited. Nature, 247(5437):139.
With A. Soutar. Abundance of pelagic fish during the 19th and 20th centuries as recorded in anaerobic sediment off the Californias. Fish. Bull., 72(2):257–74.
With R. J. Seymour. Tethered float breakwaters. In: *Proceedings of the Floating Breakwaters Conference,* Newport, Rhode Island, April, ed. T. Kowalski, pp. 55–72. University of Rhode Island Marine Technical Report Series no. 24. (Also, in: University of California Institute of Marine Resources, IMR Reference no. 74-9, Sea Grant Publ. no. 30.)
With S. A. Tont and G. L. Wick. Deep scattering layers: Vertical migration as a tactic for finding food. Deep-Sea Res., 21:651–56.
With A. Fleminger and J. G. Wyllie. Zooplankton biomass measurements from CalCOFI cruises of July 1955 to 1959 and remarks on comparison with results from October, January and April cruises of 1955 to 1959. Calif. Coop. Oceanic Fish. Invest. Atlas, 21:i–xx; 1–118.

1975

With H. Bradner. A tentative hazard chart for submarines in earthquake zones. Naval Res. Rev., 28(1):21–25.
With J. W. Stork, D. B. Goldstein, and G. L. Wick. Effect of vorticity pollution by motor vehicles on tornadoes. Nature, 253 (5489): 254–55.
With W. R. Schmitt and C. K. Stidd. Ice ages and northern forests.

In: *Climate of the Arctic,* ed. G. Weller and S. A. Bowling, pp. 117–19. (Proceedings of the Twenty-Fourth Alaska Science Conference, August 1973.) College: Geophysical Institute, University of Alaska.

With R. A. Schwartzlose. Biological applications of underwater photography. Oceanus, 18(3):24–30.

With R. A. Schwartzlose. Active animals of the deep-sea floor. Sci. Am., 233(4):84–91.

With S. L. Costa. Anisotropic sand transport in tidal inlets. In: *Proceedings, Symposium on Modeling Techniques,* pp. 254–73. New York: American Society of Civil Engineers.

With G. L. Wick. Salinity power. Report based on a study group convened by the University of California Institute of Marine Resources and Oregon State University, San Francisco, September 1974. IMR Reference no. 75-9.

Assessment of man's impact on marine biological resources. In: *Marine Pollution and Marine Waste Disposal,* ed. E. Pearson and E. Frangipane, pp. 329–40. (Proceedings of the Second International Study Congress on Marine Waste Disposal, Sanremo, Italy, December 1973.) London: Pergamon Press.

Southern California Coastal Water Research Project findings. In: *Marine Pollution and Marine Waste Disposal,* ed. E. Pearson and E. Frangipane, pp. 463–71. (Proceedings of the Second International Study Congress on Marine Waste Disposal, Sanremo, Italy, December 1973.) London: Pergamon Press.

1976

Sanity and other factors in aquatic resource development. (Plenary, address.) In: *Mankind's Future in the Pacific,* ed. R. F. Scagel, pp. 72–85. (Plenary and special lectures of the Thirteenth Pacific Science Congress, Vancouver, B.C., August 1975.) Vancouver: University of British Columbia Press.

With J. W. Stork and G. L. Wick. Tornado forum. Isaacs, Stork & Wick reply to Kessler, Morton, Smith, McIntyre, Manton, Lilly, Darkow & Court. Nature, 260(5550):457–61.

Reproductive products in marine food webs. Bull. South. Calif. Acad. Sci. (Carl L. Hubbs Honorary Issue), 75(2):220–23.

With D. Castel and G. L. Wick. Utilization of the energy in ocean waves. Ocean Eng., 3:175–87.

The sea, the marine mystique, and the challenge to the scientific paradigm. In: *Literature and the Sea,* ed. R. Astro, pp. 25–30. (Proceedings of a conference at the Marine Science Center, Newport, Oregon, May.) Oregon State University Sea Grant College Program, Publ. no. ORESU-W-76-001.

Some ideas and frustrations about fishery science. (Presented at a symposium of the California Cooperative Oceanic Fisheries Investigations Conference on Fishery Science, "Fact, Fiction, and Dogma," San Clemente, California, November 1973.) Calif. Coop. Oceanic Fish. Invest. Rep., 18:34–43.

With G. Wick. Salinity power. In: *Symposia of Expo '75,* pp. 153–65; in Japanese, pp. 320–33. (Official Report: Symposium Section, Japan Association for the International Ocean Exposition, Okinawa, 1975.)

1977

With P. F. Tooby and G. L. Wick. The motion of a small sphere in a rotating velocity field: A possible mechanism for suspending particles in turbulence. J. Geophys. Res., 82(15):2096–100.

The life of the open sea. Nature (ocean sciences supplement), 267(5614):778–80.

With S. L. Costa. The modification of sand transport in tidal inlets. In: *Coastal Sediments '77,* pp. 946–65. (Proceedings of the Fifth Symposium of Waterway, Port, Coastal and Ocean Divisions, American Society of Civil Engineers, Charleston, South Carolina, November 2–4.)

Threshold of the future, pp. 58–59; The new resource, pp. 96–97; and Power from the sea, pp. 98–99. In: *The Mitchell Beazley Atlas of the Oceans,* ed. M. Bramwell. London: Mitchell Beazley Ltd. (Reprinted in 1979 as *The Rand McNally Atlas of the Oceans.* Skokie, Ill.: Rand McNally & Co. 208 pp.)

1978

With G. L. Wick. Salt domes: Is there more energy available from their salt than from their oil? Science, 199(4336):1436–37.

With V. M. V. Vidal, F. V. Vidal, and D. R. Young. Coastal submarine hydrothermal activity off northern Baja California. J. Geophys. Res., 83(B4):1757–74.

Power from the sea—forms and prospects. In: *Proceedings of the*

Spring Meeting/STAR Symposium, Society of Naval Architects and Marine Engineers, New London, Connecticut, April, pp. 5-1–5-14.

With S. Loeb and M. R. Bloch. Salinity power, potential and processes, especially membrane processes. In: *Advances in Oceanography* (papers presented in general symposia at the Joint Oceanographic Assembly, September 13–24, 1976, Edinburgh, Scotland), ed. H. Charnock and G. Deacon, pp. 267–88. New York: Plenum Press.

With G. L. Wick. Utilization of the energy from salinity gradients. In: *Proceedings of the ERDA Wave and Salinity-Gradient Energy Conversion Workshop,* University of Delaware, May 1976, ed. R. Cohen and M. E. McCormick. ERDA Report no. C00-2946-1, Conf. 760564. (Also in: University of California IMR Reference no. 78-2 [revision of 76-9].)

With G. L. Wick and W. R. Schmitt. Utilization of the energy from ocean waves. In: *Proceedings of the ERDA Wave and Salinity-Gradient Energy Conversion Workshop,* University of Delaware, May 1976, ed. R. Cohen and M. E. McCormick. ERDA Report no. C00-2946-1, Conf. 760564. (Also in: IMR Reference no. 78-3 [revision of 76-10].)

1979

With M. Olsson and G. L. Wick. Salinity gradient power: Utilizing vapor pressure differences. Science, 206(4417):452–54.

1980

With W. R. Schmitt. Ocean energy: Forms and prospects. Science, 207(4428):265–73.

Challenges of a wet planet. Paper presented at Technology and Ocean Space Conference, Oregon State University Sea Grant Program, April 29, 1978. (Edited version published in Chemtech, 10[3]:141–43.)

1981

With V. M. V. Vidal and F. V. Vidal. Coastal submarine hydrothermal activity off northern Baja California. 2. Evolutionary history and isotope geochemistry. J. Geophys. Res., 86(B10):9451–68.

BESSEL KOK

November 7, 1918–April 27, 1979

BY J. MYERS

THE DECADE 1955–1965 was a period of revolution in our thinking about the process of photosynthesis. A key event was the realization that the process, long assumed to require only one photoreaction, actually required two. A key figure in the revolution was Bessel Kok.

In the following years Bessel and his collaborators—in work that bore the stamp of greatness—filled in much of the framework for the Z-scheme model of the energetics of photosynthesis. A predictable result was the recognition that followed. There was a Kettering Research Award in 1963 given by the Charles F. Kettering Foundation and the National Academy of Sciences. There were two awards from the American Society of Plant Physiologists: the Charles F. Kettering Award in 1972 and the Stephen Hales Award in 1978. And there was election to the National Academy of Sciences in 1974.

In composing this memoir for Bessel Kok I shall use freely the thoughts of collaborators, family, and friends, which are recognized only partially in the acknowledgment at the end. I was for almost thirty years a distant colleague, a sometime confidant, a scientific admirer, and a friend—all of which accounts for the highly personal tone of this account. But it would be difficult for anyone to write otherwise because Bessel was a very personal person.

Bessel Kok was born November 7, 1918, in the village of Hardinxveld, The Netherlands. His father, Johannes Evert Kok, was the principal of a local school; he is remembered as a talented man who cast himself in the image of a professor, a puritan Calvinist who lived at the hand of the Bible. His mother, Cornelia Grondys-Kok, is remembered as "the image of Bessel in female form." Bessel was the oldest in a family of six children. He remembered his childhood as happy, although it was interspersed with the many frustrations that must have arisen for an inventive and energetic boy encumbered by a conservative father.

Bessel's own statement about his education was that he "never studied" and that he coasted through his high school and college years. Nevertheless, he assimilated a broad background in science and developed the self-discipline he needed thereafter. His college years began at the University of Leiden in 1934; they led to the undergraduate degree of Candidate of Natural Philosophy in 1938 and the advanced degree of Doctor of Natural Philosophy in 1941. An even more significant event occurred in 1938 when Bessel met Cornelia Hendrika Vogelesang at a Christian Student's Club. Cornelia—or Nell, as she became known to all—had been born and raised in Tandjung Pinang, Indonesia. Her memory of meeting Bessel is one of instantly recognizing him as her future husband.

In 1941 Bessel began work toward a Ph.D. in biophysics at the University of Utrecht. In that era the road toward a degree was tortuous and at times must have seemed impossible. Following the German occupation in 1940, young men were conscripted for labor camps in Germany. But for all it was a time of struggling merely to survive. To provide some protection against conscription, Nell and Bessel were married in 1943. And although she was seldom successful, Nell did her best to hide Bessel. He, on the other hand, was more inclined to trust to his luck and the weak support of a passport with a falsely increased statement of age. Bessel had become assistant manager of a distilling company, Johan Koster. He also improvised a small distillery at home to produce gin from rye and beets; the gin was readily bartered for food. Their first child, Lily, was born in March of 1945, two months before the end of the war. Nell remembers it as the "worst time" for an impoverished and starving people.

With the end of the German occupation, Bessel was free to turn his efforts from survival to science. The firm of Johan Koster provided him both with employment and some direct support of the research for his dissertation, which was presented early in 1948. In the foreword of the dissertation, Bessel recognizes with thanks his professors Bungenberg de Jong and Baas Becking at Leiden. Professor Koningsberger is named as the *Hooggeachte Promotor,* but it is also made clear that E. C. Wassink was the real supervisor. Hence, Bessel's "scientific genealogy" traces to the Biophysical Research Group under the direction of A. J. Kluyver and J. M. W. Milatz.

Bessel's dissertation was a study of the quantum yield of photosynthesis in the alga *Chlorella*. It is not now, and was not then, a very exciting document. One difficulty was that the subject itself, which had been hot in the early 1940s, was only smoldering in 1948. A second difficulty was that a quantum yield, usually expressed as the reciprocal or quantum number (quanta absorbed per oxygen molecules evolved), is actually no more than a number. Its validity hinges only on the nitty-gritty details of measurement.

It must be a source of amazement to much of the scientific world that the quantum yield of photosynthesis should have engendered so many man-hours of work and yet so much controversy. Certainly one of the many aspects of an explanation of this circumstance is historical. In 1923 Otto Warburg had reported a minimum quantum number of 4.3, naturally interpreted as 4. In its time this was an heroic accomplishment. Warburg had invented a manometric method for the measurement of gas exchange. And he had introduced a convenient plant material, the alga *Chlorella*. There were several additional features of experimental protocol that turned out to be important. The first was the use of optically dense cell suspensions that absorbed virtually all the light. Hence quanta absorbed from a monochromatic light beam could be counted simply as incident quanta. The second feature was an assumption that oxygen evolution of photosynthesis was properly evaluated from pressure changes observed in short light periods minus those observed in alternating short dark periods.

Considering the theoretical significance of the quantum number, it is remarkable that Warburg's value went unchallenged for some fifteen years. By the early 1940s, however, other measurements had been made. The number 4 was in doubt as being too low, and the special experimental protocol was being questioned.

Bessel's choice of experimental conditions shows his insight and understanding of the problem. First, he maintained conditions of steady-state photosynthesis and measured oxygen evolution over a long time period (an hour). Second, to ensure steady-state conditions in all cells, he used optically thin suspensions. (Otherwise, cells in a shaken suspension would alternate between periods of light and virtual darkness.) This required mastery of the technology of the Ulbricht sphere, a device for measuring fractional absorption by a light-scattering cell suspension. A third important choice was that for each cell preparation he measured rates of oxygen evolution at several different light intensities. Then the slope of the expected linear plot of oxygen per second versus absorbed quanta per second would give the quantum yield. The quantum numbers obtained from forty-two sets of measurements fell within the range 6.5 to 10.0. Bessel deduced that 7.5 was "the most favorable value."

In addition to finding that the quantum number was high (7 to 10) rather than low (4 to 5), Bessel discovered a related phenomenon. The curve for the oxygen rate versus the quantum rate had two linear segments with slopes in the approximate ratio of 2:1 and converging near the compensation point where photosynthesis just balances respiration. The phenomenon, which has come to be called the Kok effect, is commonly thought of as resulting from a "suppression of respiration." It provides a possible explanation for low quantum numbers (as 4 to 5) observed at very low light intensities below the compensation point.

In 1949, Bessel joined the Solar Energy Research Group of the Organization for Applied Scientific Research (T.N.O.) under E. C. Wassink at the Agricultural University in Wageningen. This was an excellent match for his needs. As he later wrote on an employment record, it provided for "full time research, freedom, adequate services." A major mission was the mass culture of algae, a subject that Bessel followed, albeit sporadically, for the rest of his life. An immediate question was the maximum efficiency of *Chlorella* in producing total cell material, the efficiency for growth. Bessel's result was an efficiency of about 20 percent (equivalent to a quantum number of about 10), which still stands as a benchmark. Simply growing algae, however, was too bland for Bessel's taste. Most of his efforts went into attendant basic problems.

There is an ultimate limitation on the yield of algae that can be achieved under sunlight illumination. The problem is that photosynthesis and growth become rate limited at a light intensity far less than that of midday sunlight. Those of us concerned with mass culture naturally sought ways to circumvent the limitation. Of several possibilities the most interesting was to take advantage of the intermittent light effect of photosynthesis. With sufficient turbulence in a dense culture, individual algal cells move rapidly into and out of the illuminated front surface and thereby receive high light only in flashes. It was well known that short flashes could be used with higher efficiency, but the time parameters of the effect were not known. Bessel set out to study photosynthesis in flashing light.

Bessel spent much of 1951–1952 on leave from Wageningen and as a fellow of the Carnegie Institution in the Department of Plant Biology at Stanford under Stacy French. The family—now with two children, Lily and young Bessel—lived in the old barracks-like buildings that later became the Stanford Research Institute. I first met them there and was attracted by the happy self-sufficiency of a family learning the ways of a strange land. Bessel's part of the laboratory became a shambles of equipment-building, and he was frustrated by the slow progress of a machinist who was constructing a sector for light chopping. His work at Stanford was reported in a chapter of the 1953 Carnegie monograph on algal culture, and it provided at least a partial answer: any reasonable turbulence could be expected to give some gains in the yield of an algal culture under sunlight. Large gains, requiring very short flashes, probably would be impractical because of the power cost for the necessary turbulence.

On his return from Stanford, Bessel began extending his work with flashing light to an attack on the kinetics surrounding the photochemical events in photosynthesis. His remarkable experimental talents now came into play. He used a high-intensity projection beam that could be chopped and/or attenuated; there were two coaxial sectors that allowed independent variation of both the light and the dark periods.

As a side effort, he had developed—almost to ultimate limits—the measurement of gas exchange by volumetry. Now he could choose a very small reaction vessel (<5 mm diameter) coupled to a volumeter arrangement that measured oxygen evolution with high sensitivity. The broad scope of the experiments provided an unequivocal answer to a twenty-year controversy about the reality of the "photosynthetic unit." The oxygen yield from short flashes confirmed the earlier finding of R. Emerson and W. A. Arnold: a maximum flash yield independent of temperature and equivalent to about one O_2 per 2,000 chlorophylls. Lengthening the flashes gave a temperature-dependent flash yield approaching the rate observed in continuous saturating light. Bessel again went beyond the immediate and obvious objective in order to obtain an explanation of earlier and apparently conflicting results.

In 1955 Bessel again visited the United States for two meetings: a Gatlinburg conference on photosynthesis followed by a world symposium on applied solar energy at Tucson and Phoenix. E. C. Wassink also was in attendance. It was evident to all, however, that Bessel had attained the status of an independent and innovative scientist.

The sectors of Bessel's flashing light apparatus must never have cooled down for very long. Within a year after the measurement of oxygen flash yields, the apparatus was redesigned. Now the reaction vessel was a cuvette that was cross-illuminated by a weak measuring beam from a monochromator. Any small changes in the transmission of an algal or chloroplast suspension could be observed by a photocell. Were there absorption changes that might reveal photochemical intermediates formed during a short flash and removed during the following dark period? There were. Actually there were several absorption changes observable across the spectrum. Bessel zeroed in on one of these, a reversible absorption change at 700 nm that he speculated might be the "eventual final photoreceptor of photosynthesis." At this point the tribute of Lou Duysens is appropriate: "The long working hours and inexhaustible inventivity and drive necessary to get such an apparatus working successfully in a relatively short time, and to carry out and analyze a large number of experiments, were amply rewarded. . . .Bessel discovered the far-red absorption changes associated with the reaction center P700 of system 1."[1]

By 1957 Bessel's accomplishments had become highly visible. He had outgrown his position at Wageningen, and no appropriate position in The Netherlands was open. Like many Dutch scientists before him, Bessel had become available for export. A position as director of a new institute in West Germany was offered; Bessel and Nell visited and together concluded that they should reject the offer. One major consideration was that the rigidity and formal protocol of the establishment was incompatible with their own life-style. Among other inquiries was one from the Research Institute for Advanced Studies (RIAS) in Baltimore. By 1958 the Kok family—now with three children—had found a new home in northwest Baltimore, not far from the converted mansion that housed the RIAS laboratories.

RIAS was then about two years old and not well known even in the United States. It was a subsidiary of the Martin Company, a corporate investment as an institute for basic science. In the course of a European trip, its director, Welcome Bender, had stopped to see Bessel in Wageningen, and his recruitment was that simple. Bessel elected to accept a position as a "staff scientist" in an unproven, industrially supported institute. There were no trappings to the position—

---

[1] L. N. M. Duysens, "In Memory of Bessel Kok," in *Proceedings, Fifth International Congress on Photosynthesis*, ed. G. Akoyunoglou (Philadelphia: Balaban International Science Services, 1981), pp. xix–xx.

not even the conventional one of academic rank—but only the promise of logistic support and freedom of choice in research.

Bessel had joined a small group labelled "Bioscience" and with a common bond of interest in photosynthesis. Within the year he had become the de facto leader of the group. No one worked harder, sprouted ideas faster, or drank more martinis at Friday afternoon parties. Welcome Bender managed the whole institute with the light touch of one who understood the needs of basic research. I was one of many visitors who joined in the excitement of the place. In later years other corporate managers were less supportive, but by that time Bessel and his group had achieved a position of strength.

In a former wine cellar Bessel assembled an improved version of his machine, which now could be called a split-beam phosphoroscope. A new sector program allowed measurements just before and just after the flash and was especially useful in studying the absorbance changes near 700 nm. Now the characteristics of the "700 pigment" were revealed: it was repeatedly bleached, even by rather weak flashes of far-red light, and its absorption regained in each subsequent dark period. Of course the measuring light (as at 700 nm) was itself a "far-red." If the measuring beam was made brighter, there was nothing left for far-red flashes to bleach. But now a new behavior appeared: if the flashes were red (instead of far-red), then each flash restored absorption of the "700 pigment." Here were reciprocal effects of red and far-red light like those described by Robert Emerson for the quantum yield of oxygen evolution.

At this stage Bessel acquired a young collaborator: George Hoch, a biochemist. The collaboration doubled the number of techniques of measurement but far more than doubled the imaginative interaction of two minds bouncing ideas back and forth. The first fruit of their effort came in a joint paper in a 1960 symposium entitled "Light and Life." In that paper they opened the modern era of thinking about photosynthesis by the first explicit statement that there must be two photochemical reactions "the first sensitized by chlorophyll a and a direct photochemical bleaching of P700; the second sensitized by accessory pigment, acting indirectly via mediation of dark steps, and restoring P700." The hypothesis was rephrased in other ways, presented as a diagram, and considered in terms of other related phenomena. Bessel and George had come with the ultimate excitement of science: they had discovered and understood an important truth that no one else had yet seen. But the reception of their paper was a disappointment. From the record of discussion one would judge that they had dropped an egg instead of a bomb. They had made the tactical error of presenting too many data, too many kinds of experiments. Most of the questions centered on experimental details that now appear trivial.

Unfortunately, publication of the symposium proceedings was delayed for over a year. By that time important publications from the laboratories of Lou Duysens and Robin Hill had derived independently the two-light-reaction hypothesis from other data. And the Hill-Bendall model became the convenient Z-scheme.

By 1960 the "black box" of photosynthesis had been opened up, and its bits and pieces were strewn about. The following decade was a time of fitting the pieces together. Now Bessel's work moved into high gear. It was remarkable in terms of the number of papers published and the variety of subjects addressed. It was even more remarkable in the number and diversity of collaborators: some came as senior scientists, some as postdoctoral students, and some as technicians; some even came from the ranks of high school students employed by the lab each summer. In the midst of this rather frantic pace, two particular events should be recorded. In 1963 Bessel and Andre Jagendorf served as coorganizers for a photosynthesis conference held at Airlie House in Virginia. In spite of the burden of new information let loose by the two-light-reaction hypothesis, that meeting is remembered as a very light-hearted conference.[2] And in 1964 Nell and Bessel became citizens of the United States.

Another event that became memorable was the extended visit of Anne and Pierre Joliot in 1967. This was something more than collaboration; rather, it was a convergence of the conceptual and instrumental developments of two laboratories. The Joliots had developed the art and technology of the polarographic measurement of oxygen at a platinum electrode. They brought this tool with them and sharpened it still further to measure reduction of a low-potential viologen dye by the reducing side of the photosynthetic mechanism. Together with techniques already available, there were now multiple windows through which to view interaction between the two photoreactions. The resulting joint papers were magnificent in the simplicity and clarity they brought to a complex subject.

On his return to France, Pierre Joliot engaged the activation phenomenon for oxygen evolution that he had discovered years before. After several minutes of darkness there was a delay in oxygen evolution during the first seconds of light. Now he observed the oxygen yields from short electronic flashes given in sequence after a dark period. Flash yields (Y) showed an interesting oscillation with a period of four: Y_1 was zero, Y_2 was small, and Y_3 was maximum and almost twice the steady-state yield to which the system damped out after several cycles. The pattern of oscillation

---

[2] A. Jagendorf, "In Memory of Bessel Kok," in *Proceedings, Fifth International Congress on Photosynthesis*, ed. G. Akoyunoglou (Philadelphia: Balaban International Science Services, 1981), pp. xxi–xxiii.

obviously contained information about the cryptic events of oxygen evolution. Pierre was led to a double two-step model that released two oxygen atoms in sequence. Bessel, now working independently, repeated the measurements and observed the oscillations, though with some small differences: Y_2 was very small and Y_3 was often much more than twice the steady-state yield. Though small, the differences were real, and they were incompatible with Pierre's model. They led Bessel to a flurry of effort that taxed the stamina of his younger colleagues. He assembled their elegant experiments to create a simple linear model that accumulated 1-2-3-4 charges to produce a molecule of oxygen. With a characteristic touch, Bessel called his model the "oxygen clock." In retrospect it appears that rather small technical improvements led Bessel to a model that was simpler and apparently more nearly correct than that which Pierre had derived. The history of research on photosynthesis records some acrimonious debates and personal animosities that arose under less stressful conditions. It is a tribute to both men that, in spite of the clash of their scientific results, they continued to be close personal friends, communicated their current findings to each other, and became joint authors of a review paper.

Following the oxygen clock there were obvious problems of proton release that—like oxygen—could be digitized by flash illumination. And quietly pursued in the background was continuing development of mass spectrometric measurements applied first to the interactions between photosynthesis and respiration and later to an extraterrestrial life detection system. It would take a rather detailed catalog—which in fact is provided by the bibliography—to do justice to the work of Bessel and his many collaborators.

Bessel Kok died in Baltimore on April 27, 1979, after a prolonged battle against lymphoma. He is survived by his wife, Cornelia Hendrika—Nell—a quietly resourceful lady who once hid him from labor camp conscription, later helped him reach out for his ambitions, and shared his love of family. She lives in the home into which the Koks first moved in 1958. Also surviving is a daughter, now Cornelie Angeline Forbush; two sons, Johannes Allart Bessel and Allart Alexander Bessel; and three grandchildren.

Among Bessel's scientific family of colleagues and friends there are many memories. From that legacy, at least a few recollections that provide special insight should be set down in writing:

- He appreciated a good hypothesis deeply and had the strength of character not to let an ugly fact stand in the way.
- He had a knack for discerning the "nuggets" of a problem.
- He was extraordinarily open-minded to any new concept or experiment, even if it came from a younger or unknown scientist and even if it was a contradiction to his own ideas.
- He could make you a better scientist just by asking questions.
- He had a basic belief that if he could measure anything with ten times greater sensitivity than had been achieved before, he was bound to discover something new.
- He had learned to smile while criticizing.
- He was always searching, either for a simpler hypothesis or for a better joke.

An appropriate conclusion to this memoir is taken from one of the several tributes[3] to Bessel that have been written.

---

[3] G. Cheniae and J. Myers, "Bessel Kok (1918–1979): A Tribute," in *Photosynthesis I: Energy Conversion in Plants and Bacteria*, ed. Govindjee (New York: Academic Press, 1982), pp. xxi–xxiii. Reprinted by permission. See footnotes 1 and 2 for two other tributes. A fourth is L. N. M. Duysens and C. J. P. Spruit, "In Memoriam Bessel Kok (1918–1979)," Vakbl. Biol., 59 (1979):210.

Bessel's scientific accomplishments reveal too little of a unique character that had many facets. Some may have seen only the outer veneer as a brusque and, at times, even boorish personality. Some may have felt his patience and his sensitivity to all people, whatever their walk in life. Some may have seen his intolerance of the trappings or of the pomp and ceremony of science. Some have enjoyed him as a witty and boisterous drinking companion.

Bessel was an uncommonly dedicated man, dedicated to his family, to his science, and to the joys of life. He pursued each endeavor with unrelenting fervor and passion and with enormous mental and physical stamina. He wore only a thin cloak of inhibitions, happily shared warmth and encouragement, but also gave sharp and sometimes brutal criticisms. His standards for his own work were uncompromisingly high, and he expected as much from others. Many of us earned his criticisms, some experienced his praise and encouragement, but all of us learned from Bessel.

On behalf of . . . many we salute and toast you, Bessel, for your scientific accomplishments, for your free spirit, and for all the fond personal remembrances you gave us.

I AM INDEBTED to Nell Kok who shared with me the story of her life with Bessel. I am indebted to Richard Radmer who assembled the bibliography and provided data from files of the Martin Marietta Laboratory. And I am grateful to many others of the Kok circle who shared their thoughts and recollections, notably, Welcome Bender, Leonard Bongers, George Cheniae, Lou Duysens, George Hoch, Andre Jagendorf, Anne and Pierre Joliot, Olga Owens, and Pete Zill.

BIBLIOGRAPHY

1940

With H. G. Bungenberg de Jong and D. R. Kreger. Tissues of prismatic cells containing biocolloids. I. Proc. K. Ned. Akad. Wet., 43:512–21.

With H. G. Bungenberg de Jong. Tissues of prismatic celloidin cells containing biocolloids. II. Coacervation of gum-arabic by toluidin-blue and the phenomena accompanying the dissolution of the coacervate. Proc. K. Ned. Akad. Wet., 43:728–31.

1942

With H. P. Wolvekamp, G. P. Baerends, and W. F. H. M. Mommaerts. O_2 and CO_2-binding properties of the blood of the cuttlefish (*Sepia officinalis*) and common squid (*Loligo vulgaris*). Arch. Neerl. Physiol., 26:203–11.

With H. G. Bungenberg de Jong. Tissues of prismatic cells containing biocolloids. IV. Morphological changes of the complex coacervate gelatin + gum arabic in consequence of a pH change of the medium flowing along the membrane. Proc. K. Ned. Akad. Wet., 45:51–58.

With H. B. Bungenberg de Jong. Tissues of prismatic cells containing biocolloids. V. Morphological changes of the complex coacervate gelatine-gum arabic owing to the addition of salts resp. non-electrolytes to the liquid flowing past the membrane. Proc. K. Ned. Akad. Wet., 45:67–75.

With H. G. Bungenberg de Jong. Tissues of prismatic celloidin cells containing biocolloids. VII. Stagnation effects. Proc. K. Ned. Akad. Wet., 45:204–5.

1948

A critical consideration of the quantum yield of *Chlorella* photosynthesis. Ph.D. diss., University of Utrecht. (Also in: Enzymologia, 13:1–56.)

1949

On the interrelation of respiration and photosynthesis in green plants. Biochim. Biophys. Acta, 3:625–31.

1951

Photo-induced interactions in metabolism of green plant cells. Symp. Soc. Exp. Biol., 5:211–21.

1952

On the efficiency of *Chlorella* growth. Acta Bot. Neerl., 1:445–67.
Photosynthesis in flashing light. Carnegie Inst. Washington Yearb., 51:138–39.
Efficiency of photosynthesis. Carnegie Inst. Washington Yearb., 51:148–50.

1953

With E. C. Wassink and J. L. P. van Oorschot. The efficiency of light–energy conversion in *Chlorella* cultures as compared with higher plants. In: *Algal Culture from Laboratory to Pilot Plant*, ed. J. S. Burlew. Carnegie Inst. Washington Publ., 600:55–62.
Experiments on photosynthesis by *Chlorella* in flashing light. In: *Algal Culture from Laboratory to Pilot Plant*, ed. J. S. Burlew. Carnegie Inst. Washington Publ., 600:63–75.
With G. W. Veltkamp and W. P. Gelderman. On differential mano- and volumetric methods. Biochim. Biophys. Acta, 11:7–16.

1954

Kinetic studies of photosynthesis using a recording volumeter of extreme sensitivity. Congr. Int. Bot. Rapp. Commun. (8th), pp. 9–10.
With J. L. P. van Oorschot. Improved yields in algal mass cultures. Acta Bot. Neerl., 3:533–46.

1955

Some sensitive and recording volumeters. Biochim. Biophys. Acta, 16:35–44.

1956

With C. J. P. Spruit. High initial rates of gas exchange in respiration and photosynthesis of *Chlorella*. Biochim. Biophys. Acta, 19:212–23.
With C. J. P. Spruit. Simultaneous observations of oxygen and carbon dioxide exchange during non-steady state photosynthesis. Biochim. Biophys. Acta, 19:417–24.

On the inhibition of photosynthesis by intense light. Biochim. Biophys. Acta, 21:234–44.
Licht und Pflanzen. Strahlentherapie, 101:563–68.
With J. A. Businger. Kinetics of photosynthesis and photoinhibition. Nature, 177:135–36.
On the reversible absorption change at 705 m in photosynthetic organisms. Biochim. Biophys. Acta, 22:399–401.

1957

Absorption changes induced by the photochemical reaction of photosynthesis. Nature, 179:583–84.
Light induced absorption changes in photosynthetic organisms. Acta Bot. Neerl., 6:316–36.
Changes of absorption spectrum induced by illumination and their bearing on the nature of the photoreceptor of photosynthesis. In: *Proceedings of the Second Photobiology Congress,* Turin, Italy, pp. 369–83. Turin: Edizioni Minerva Medica.
With C. J. P. Spruit and J. A. Businger. Report on some results at Wageningen. In: *Research in Photosynthesis,* ed. H. Gaffron, A. H. Brown, C. S. French, R. Livingston, E. I. Rabinowitch, B. L. Strehler, and N. E. Tolbert, pp. 353–65. New York: Interscience.

1958

Enige voorbeelden van het gebruik van tracers in het fotosynthese-onderzoek. Landbouwkd. Tijdschr., 70:334–43.

1959

Light induced absorption changes in photosynthetic organisms. II. A split-beam difference spectrophotometer. Plant Physiol., 34:184–92.
With J. M. Olson. Is oxidized bacteriochlorophyll an intermediate in bacterial photosynthesis? Biochim. Biophys. Acta, 32:278–80.

1960

Efficiency of photosynthesis. In: *Encyclopedia of Plant Physiology,* ed. W. Ruhland, vol. 5, pp. 566–633. Berlin: Springer-Verlag.
With W. Gott. Activation spectra of 700 mµ absorption changes in photosynthesis. Plant Physiol., 35:802–8.

1961

With G. Hoch. Spectral changes in photosynthesis. In: *Light and Life*, ed. W. D. McElroy and B. Glass, pp. 397–416. Baltimore: Johns Hopkins Press.

Partial purification and determination of oxidation reduction potential of the photosynthetic chlorophyll complex absorbing at 700 mμ. Biochim. Biophys. Acta, 48:527–33.

With G. Hoch. Photosynthesis. Annu. Rev. Plant Physiol., 12:155–94.

With M. Gibbs and C. C. Black. Factors affecting CO_2 fixation by chloroplasts. Biochim. Biophys. Acta, 52:474–77.

With L. H. Bongers. Radiation tolerances in photosynthesis and consequences of excesses. In: *Medical and Biological Aspects of the Energies of Space*, pp. 299–322. New York: Columbia University Press.

1962

With H. Beinert and G. Hoch. The light induced electron paramagnetic resonance signal of photocatalyst P700. Biochem. Biophys. Res. Commun., 7:209–12.

With H. Beinert. Light induced EPR signal of photocatalyst P700. II. Two light effects. Biochem. Biophys. Res. Commun., 9:349–54.

Light conversion in photosynthesis. In: *Biologistics for Space Systems Symposium*, pp. 83–104. AMRL-TDR-62-116. Dayton, Ohio: Wright Patterson AFB.

1963

With G. Hoch. A mass spectrometer inlet system for sampling gases dissolved in liquid phases. Arch. Biochem. Biophys., 101:160–70.

With G. Hoch and O. V. H. Owens. Photosynthesis and respiration. Arch. Biochem. Biophys., 101:171–80.

With G. Hoch and B. Cooper. Sensitization of chloroplast reactions. I. Sensitization of reduction and oxidation of cytochrome c by chloroplasts. Plant Physiol., 38:274–79.

With B. Cooper and L. Yang. Electron transport in chloroplast reactions. In: *Studies on Microalgae and Photosynthetic Bacteria*, pp.

373–96. (Special issue, Plant Cell Physiol.) Tokyo: University of Tokyo Press.

Significance of P700 as an intermediate in photosynthesis. In: *Proceedings of the Fifth International Congress of Biochemistry*, vol. 6, pp. 73–81.

Photosynthetic electron transport. In: *Photosynthetic Mechanisms in Green Plants*. NAS-NRC Publ., 1145:35–44.

Fluorescence studies. In: *Photosynthetic Mechanisms in Green Plants*. NAS-NRC Publ., 1145:45–55.

With H. Beinert. Relationship between light induced EPR signal and pigment P700. In: *Photosynthetic Mechanisms in Green Plants*. NAS-NRC Publ., 1145:131–37.

With G. Hoch. The photoreactions of photosynthesis. In: *La Photosynthèse*. Colloq. Int. CNRS, 119:93–107.

With G. Hoch and O. V. H. Owens. Oxygen metabolism in *Anacystis nidulans*. In: *La Photosynthèse*. Colloq. Int. CNRS, 119:261–72.

1964

With H. J. Rurainski and E. A. Harmon. Photo-oxidation of cytochromes *c*, *f*, and plastocyanin by detergent treated chloroplasts. Plant Physiol., 39:513–20.

With L. Bongers. Life support systems for space missions. Dev. Ind. Microbiol., 5:183–95.

With H. Beinert. An attempt at quantitation of the sharp light-induced electron paramagnetic resonance signal in photosynthetic materials. Biochim. Biophys. Acta, 88:278–88.

1965

With H. J. Rurainski. Plastocyanin photo-oxidation by detergent-treated chloroplasts. Biochim. Biophys. Acta, 94:588–90.

With E. B. Gassner and H. J. Rurainski. Photoinhibition of chloroplast reactions. Photochem. Photobiol., 4:215–27.

Photosynthesis: The path of energy. In: *Plant Biochemistry*, ed. J. E. Varner and J. Bonner, pp. 903–60. New York: Academic Press.

With H. J. Rurainski and O. V. H. Owens. The reducing power generated in photoact I of photosynthesis. Biochim. Biophys. Acta, 109:347–56.

With E. A. Datko. Reducing power generated in the second photoact of photosynthesis. Plant Physiol., 40:1171–77.

1966

Concentration and normal potential of primary photo-oxidants and reductants in photosynthesis. In: *Currents in Photosynthesis,* ed. J. P. Thomas and J. C. Goedheer, pp. 383–92. Rotterdam: Ad. Donker.

With L. W. Jones. Photoinhibition of chloroplast reactions. I. Kinetics and action spectra. Plant Physiol., 41:1037–43.

With L. W. Jones. Photoinhibition of chloroplast reactions. II. Multiple effects. Plant Physiol., 41:1044–49.

With S. Malkin. Fluorescence induction studies in isolated chloroplasts. I. Number of components involved in the reaction and quantum yields. Biochim. Biophys. Acta, 126:413–32.

With G. M. Cheniae. Kinetics and intermediates of the oxygen evolution step in photosynthesis. In: *Current Topics in Bioenergetics,* ed. D. R. Sanadi, vol. 1, pp. 1–44. New York: Academic Press.

With H. J. Rurainski. Long-wave absorption and emission bands in chloroplast fragments. Biochim. Biophys. Acta, 126:584–87.

The rate-limiting reaction in photosynthesis. In: *Conference on Bioregenerative Systems.* NASA Spec. Publ., 165:111–15.

With S. Malkin, O. Owens, and B. Forbush. Observations on the reducing side of the O_2-evolving photoact. In: *Energy Conversion by the Photosynthetic Apparatus.* Brookhaven Symp. Biol., 19:446–59.

1967

With J. E. Varner. Extraterrestrial life detection based on oxygen isotope exchange reactions. Science, 155:1110–12.

With J. E. Varner. Extraterrestrial life detection by means of isotopic oxygen exchange. Life Sci. Space Res., 5:206–16.

Photosynthesis—physical aspects. In: *Harvesting the Sun—Photosynthesis in Plant Life,* ed. A. San Pietro, F. A. Greer, and T. J. Army, pp. 29–48. New York: Academic Press.

1968

With P. Joliot and A. Joliot. Analysis of the interactions between the two photosystems in isolated chloroplasts. Biochim. Biophys. Acta, 153:635–52.

With B. Forbush. Reaction between the primary and secondary

acceptors of photosystems of photosynthesis. Biochim. Biophys. Acta, 162:243–53.

1969

Photosynthesis. In: *The Physiology of Plant Growth and Development,* ed. M. B. Wilkins, pp. 335–79. New York: McGraw-Hill.
With P. Joliot and M. P. McGloin. Electron transfer between the photoacts. In: *Progress in Photosynthesis Research,* ed. H. Metzner, pp. 1042–46. Tübingen: International Union of Biological Sciences.
With C. Sybesma. Photosynthetic electron transport induced by flashing light in the purple photosynthetic bacterium *Rhodospirillum rubrum.* Biochim. Biophys. Acta, 180:410–13.

1970

With B. Forbush and M. McGloin. Cooperation of charges in photosynthetic oxygen evolution. I. A linear four-step mechanism. Photochem. Photobiol., 11:457–75.
With T. V. Marsho. Interaction between electron transport components in chloroplasts. Biochim. Biophys. Acta, 223:240–50.

1971

With T. V. Marsho. Detection and isolation of P700. In: *Methods in Enzymology,* vol. 23, *Photosynthesis,* Part A, ed. A. San Pietro, pp. 515–22. New York: Academic Press.
With R. Radmer. A unified procedure for the detection of life on Mars. Science, 174:233–39.
With B. Forbush and M. P. McGloin. Cooperation of charges in photosynthetic oxygen evolution. II. Damping of flash yield oscillation, deactivation. Photochem. Photobiol., 14:307–21.

1972

With K. L. Zankel. Estimation of pool sizes and kinetic constants. In: *Methods in Enzymology,* vol. 24, *Photosynthesis and Nitrogen Fixation,* Part B, pp. 218–38. New York: Academic Press.
With W. W. Doschek. Photon trapping in photosystem II of photosynthesis—the fluorescence rise curve in the presence of DCMU. Biophys. J., 12:832–38.
With R. Radmer. An integrated multi-purpose biology instrument

utilizing a single detector, the mass spectrometer. Life Sci. Space Res., 10:211–25.
Efficiency of photosynthesis. In: *Horizons of Bioenergetics*, ed. A. San Pietro and H. Gest, pp. 153–70. New York: Academic Press.

1973

O_2 evolution in photosynthesis. In: *Proceedings of the Second International Symposium on Oxidases and Related Redox Systems*, ed. T. E. King, H. S. Mason, and M. Morrison, pp. 701–13. Baltimore: University Park Press.
With R. Radmer. A kinetic analysis of the oxidizing and reducing sides of the O_2-evolving system of photosynthesis. Biochim. Biophys. Acta, 314:28–41.
Photosynthesis. In: *Proceedings of the Workshop on Bio-Solar Conversion*, Bethesda, Maryland, pp. 22–30. Washington, D.C.: National Science Foundation.

1974

With T. V. Marsho. Photosynthetic regulation by cations in spinach chloroplasts. Biochim. Biophys. Acta, 333:353–65.
With R. Radmer. Kinetic observation of the system II electron pool isolated by mercuric ion. Biochim. Biophys. Acta, 357:177–80.
With C. F. Fowler. Proton evolution associated with the photooxidation of water in photosynthesis. Biochim. Biophys. Acta, 357:308–18.
With R. Radmer and C. F. Fowler. Electron transport in photosystem II. In: *Proceedings of the Third International Congress on Photosynthesis Research*, ed. M. Avron, pp. 485–96. Amsterdam: Elsevier.

1975

With P. Joliot. Oxygen evolution in photosynthesis. In: *Bioenergetics of Photosynthesis*, ed. Govindjee, pp. 387–412. New York: Academic Press.
With R. Radmer. Energy capture in photosynthesis. Annu. Rev. Biochem., 44:409–33.
Prospects of photosynthetic energy production. Sci. Technol., 35:519–26.

With J. P. Martin, R. D. Johnson, and R. Radmer. Unified Mars life detection system. J. Astronaut. Sci., 23:99–119.

1976

Photosynthesis: The path of energy. In: *Plant Biochemistry*, 3d ed., ed. J. Bonner and J. E. Varner, pp. 845–85. New York: Academic Press.
Prospects of photosynthetic energy production. In: *The Current State of Knowledge of Photochemical Formation of Fuel*, ed. N. N. Lichtin, pp. 133–39. Boston University Press.
With R. Radmer. Energy requirements of a biosphere. In: *Chemical Evolution of the Giant Planets*, ed. C. Ponnamperuma, pp. 183–97. New York: Academic Press.
With R. Radmer. Mechanisms in photosynthesis. In: *Chemical Mechanisms in Bioenergetics*, ed. D. R. Sanadi, pp. 172–220. American Chemical Society Monograph no. 172. Washington, D.C.
With C. F. Fowler. Determination of H^+/e^- ratios in chloroplasts with flashing light. Biochim. Biophys. Acta, 423:510–23.
With R. Radmer and J. P. Martin. System for biological and soil chemical tests on a planetary lander. J. Spacecr. Rockets, 13:719–26.
With R. Radmer. Photoreduction of O_2 primes and replaces CO_2 assimilation. Plant Physiol., 58:336–40.
With H. Hardt. Stabilization by glutaraldehyde of high-rate electron transport in isolated chloroplasts. Biochim. Biophys. Acta, 449:125–35.

1977

With R. Radmer. Light conversion efficiency in photosynthesis. In: *Encyclopedia of Plant Physiology*, n.s., ed. A. Trebst and M. Avron, vol. 5, pp. 125–35. Berlin: Springer-Verlag.
With R. Radmer. Photosynthesis: Limited yields, unlimited dreams. Bioscience, 27:599–605.
With B. Velthuys. Present status of the O_2 evolution model. In: *Research in Photobiology*, ed. A. Castellani, pp. 111–19. New York: Plenum Publishing Co.
With H. Hardt. Plastocyanin as the possible site of photosynthetic electron transport inhibition by glutaraldehyde. Plant Physiol., 60:225–29.

With B. Velthuys. Observations on the O_2 evolution system. In: *Proceedings of the Fourth International Congress on Photosynthesis*, ed. D. O. Hall, J. Coombs, and T. W. Goodwin, pp. 397–407. London: The Biochemical Society.

1978

With B. Velthuys. Photosynthetic oxygen evolution from hydrogen peroxide. Biochim. Biophys. Acta, 502:211–21.
With R. Radmer and O. Ollinger. Kinetics and apparent K_m of oxygen cycle under conditions of limiting carbon dioxide fixation. Plant Physiol., 61:915–17.
With H. Hardt. Comparison of photosynthetic activities of spinach chloroplasts with those of mesophyll and corn bundle sheath tissue. Plant Physiol., 62:59–63.
With J. H. Goldbeck. Further studies of the membrane-bound iron-sulfur proteins and P700 in a photosystem I subchloroplast particle. Arch. Biochem. Biophys., 188:233–42.
With J. H. Goldbeck and B. R. Velthuys. Evidence that the intermediate electron acceptor, A_2, in photosystem I is a bound iron-sulfur protein. Biochim. Biophys. Acta, 504:226–30.
With C. Waslien, J. Myers, and W. Oswald. Photosynthetic single-cell protein. In: *Protein Resources and Technology: Status and Research Needs*, ed. M. Milner, N. S. Scrimshaw, and D. I. C. Wang, pp. 522–42. Westport, Conn.: AVI Publishing Co.

1979

With J. H. Goldbeck. Redox titration of the electron acceptor Q and the plastoquinone pool in photosystem II. Biochim. Biophys. Acta, 547:347–60.
With R. Radmer. Rate–temperature curves as an unambiguous indicator of biological activity in soil. Appl. Environ. Microbiol., 38:224–28.

OTTO KRAYER
October 22, 1899–March 18, 1982

BY AVRAM GOLDSTEIN

Sie können eigentlich nur Solche brauchen, die sich brauchen lassen.
Schopenhauer. Neue Paralipomena §676,
Handschriftlicher Nachlass, Vol. 4 (Leipzig: P. Reclam, 1930).

For the style is the man, and where a man's treasure is there his heart, and his brain, and his writing, will be also.
A. Quiller-Couch, On The Art Of Writing
(London: G. P. Putnam's Sons, 1916).

IN your letter of 15 June you state that you feel the barring of Jewish scientists is an injustice, and that your feelings about this injustice prevent you from accepting a position offered to you.

You are of course personally free to feel any way you like about the way the government acts. It is not acceptable, however, for you to make the practice of your teaching profession dependent upon those feelings. You would in that case not be able in the future to hold any chair in a German university.

Pending final decision on the basis of section 4 of the Law on the Restoration of the Professional Civil Service, I herewith forbid you, effective immediately, from entering any government academic institution, and from using any State libraries or scientific facilities.

THIS REMARKABLE LETTER, dated 20 June 1933, and here reproduced in its entirety, was from the Prussian Minister for Science, Art, and National Education. The recipient, Otto Krayer, who died 18 March 1982, at the age of eighty-two, will be remembered for many things—his outstanding research contributions to cardiovascular pharmacology, his intensely enthusiastic teaching style, his very high standards of scientific publication and editorship, his guidance and support of the many young scientists who came under his influence and went on to significant careers in pharmacology or physiology. Krayer's unique contribution, however, was the example he set in ethical behavior—behavior that in his thirty-fifth year and in the flowering of a promising career brought upon him the full retribution of the Nazi hierarchy.

Robert Jungk, in his book *Brighter Than A Thousand Suns, A Personal History of the Atomic Scientists*,[1] writes about those days in early 1933 in Göttingen: "Only a single one of Göttingen's natural scientists had the courage to protest openly against the dismissal of the Jewish savants. This was the physiologist Krayer. He did not allow himself to be intimidated either by his own dismissal, which was then ordered by the new Prussian Minister of Education, Stuckart, or by the threat of being debarred from employment for the rest of his life."

Yet rare though it was for a non-Jewish German intellectual to jeopardize his own future for the sake of a moral principle, "protest openly" is certainly not accurate. That was not Krayer's style. Never a political activist—nor an organizer or preacher for causes—Krayer would have been the last to condemn his colleagues who, with various rationalizations,

---

[1] Robert Jungk, *Brighter Than A Thousand Suns, A Personal History of the Atomic Scientists* (New York: Harcourt, Brace and Company, 1958), p. 36.

accepted the evil situation as beyond their control. Krayer believed, very simply, that a person had to do what their conscience said was right, that in such matters it was not a question of weighing consequences. His letter of 15 June 1933, which so infuriated the Nazi bureaucrat, is poignant testimony to this belief. He explains why he cannot accept the proffered appointment to the chair of pharmacology at Düsseldorf—the chair from which the Jewish incumbent Philipp Ellinger had just been removed:

> ... the primary reason for my reluctance is that I feel the exclusion of Jewish scientists to be an injustice, the necessity of which I cannot understand, since it has been justified by reasons that lie outside the domain of science.
>
> This feeling of injustice is an ethical phenomenon. It is innate to the structure of my personality, and not something imposed from the outside. Under these circumstances, assuming such a position as the one in Düsseldorf would impose a great mental burden on me—a burden that would make it difficult to take up my duties as a teacher with joy and a sense of dedication, without which I cannot teach properly.
>
> I place a high value on the role of university teacher, and I myself would want the privilege of engaging in this activity to be given only to men who, apart from their research capabilities, also have special human qualities. Had I not expressed to you the misgivings that made me hesitate to accept your offer immediately, I would have compromised one of these essential human qualities, that of honesty.
>
> It seems to me, therefore, that the argument that in the interests of the task at hand I must defer my personal misgivings, is an empty one. I would not place even a lesser task in the hands of someone who cannot remain true to himself. Moreover, it is clear to me how great is the responsibility that you have to carry—a responsibility that gives you the right to expect honesty.
>
> The work to which I have heretofore dedicated all my strength, with the goal of applying my scientific knowledge and research expertise to effective university teaching, means so much to me that I could not compromise it with the least bit of dishonesty.
>
> I therefore prefer to forego this appointment, though it is suited to my inclinations and capabilities, rather than having to betray my convic-

tions; or that by remaining silent I would encourage an opinion about me that does not correspond with the facts.

A moral dilemma arises when the policies of a legitimately constituted authority are morally unacceptable. Resistance to a tyranny that can make no claim to a popular mandate is difficult and risky enough. But Hitler's regime had all the trappings of legitimacy, it had come to power in a constitutional manner, and its support went deep and wide among the German people, not excluding the university faculties and students. Noncompliance, under such circumstances, requires the courage of one's convictions to an extraordinary degree. One's support has to come principally from one's own conscience, while one's peers, by and large, tend to distance themselves, in order to avert unpleasant repercussions and to avoid confronting their own consciences.

The events that faced Krayer with a moral choice were unusual, from a historical perspective, but they were not unique. Fanaticism—political, religious, tribal, racial, intellectual, nationalistic—has periodically infected one or another part of the earth's population since civilization began. No country and no time is immune, and so the moral dilemma is an ever-recurring theme. During the agony of Vietnam, American academics could witness the same cautious neutrality on the part of most of their colleagues, at least until it became acceptable and popular to speak one's outrage. Apparently the simple ability to distinguish right from wrong and to act accordingly was incompatible with the scholarly temperament. "Not to decide is to decide," wrote the American theologian Harvey Cox. Most found it easiest "not to decide."

The surgeon Rudolf Nissen, writing of the German university faculties in 1933, has this to say:

> Another example of rare, almost isolated conduct amidst the crowd of opportunists was given by the Berlin Professor Extraordinarius, Otto

Krayer. His pupil, M. Reiter, has these wonderful words for this conduct: "The world is not particularly rich with people who prefer to jeopardize their career rather than sanction it with alien injustice. Nothing is more characteristic of Krayer's personality than his repeated refusal in 1933 to take over the chair in Düsseldorf, whose former holder, Philipp Ellinger, was driven from it on account of his race. The Professor Extraordinarius in Berlin, who was 34 at the time, did something that those in power felt was an open revolt and that many of his colleagues felt was at least inopportune and disturbing in the repercussions it had for them."[2]

Finally Nissen remarks: "It is unfortunate that such courageous and manly individual actions in the universities were not collected and made available to the public by officials who occupied themselves with the history of the Nazi period." He concludes by quoting Shakespeare (*The Winter's Tale*, act 1, scene 2) on the importance of publicly recognizing such actions: "One good deed, dying tongueless, slaughters a thousand waiting upon that."

Krayer's own laconic account of this landmark event in his life is found in an autobiographical sketch he wrote after his retirement for the *International Biographical Archives and Dictionary of Central European Emigrés, 1933–45*:

> In the Spring of 1933, while engaged in collaborative studies with Prof. H. Rein in the Department of Physiology, University of Göttingen, I was asked by the Department of Education of the State of Prussia to take over the Chair of Pharmacology in the Medical Academy of Düsseldorf. The vacancy had been created by the dismissal of the Jewish incumbent Prof. Philipp Ellinger. Refusal to fill the vacancy because of my stated disagreement with the unjust policies of the government led to my immediate suspension by the Prussian Minister of Education from my academic positions. Moreover, I was forbidden to enter any university premises including University and State libraries. Returning from Göttingen to Berlin, where I could make use of private libraries, I was able to continue literary work in progress. I was especially anxious to complete and edit and to supervise the printing of Volume 2 of *P. Trendelenburg: Die Hormone*, a task

---

[2] Rudolf Nissen, *Helle Blätter—dunkle Blätter: Erinnerungen eines Chirurgen* (Stuttgart: Deutsche Verlags-Anstalt, 1969), pp. 140–44.

which had been entrusted to me by my teacher shortly before his death in 1931.

Later in 1933 Krayer's academic privileges at the University of Berlin were restored. However, he obtained a leave of absence and accepted an invitation to join the Department of Pharmacology at University College, London, with support from the Rockefeller Foundation, and on the last day of 1933 he departed Germany. There followed an intense and productive nine months of research in collaboration with E. B. Verney, who had been Starling's pupil. The substance of the investigations with Verney is recounted in a later section of this memoir. Krayer's former Berlin associate W. Feldberg, himself a recent refugee from the Nazis, was also in London. And dominating the scene was H. H. Dale, the foremost pharmacologist of the day.

In the autumn of 1934 Krayer was called to head the Department of Pharmacology at the American University of Beirut. His research and teaching accomplishments there are described later. Officially representing the American University of Beirut at the Tercentenary Celebration of Harvard University in 1936, he was asked to stay on for a few months as a lecturer in pharmacology at the Harvard Medical School. Then in 1937 an invitation was extended for Krayer to join the faculty as associate professor of pharmacology. He accepted and two years later became Reid Hunt's successor as head of the department, a position he held until his retirement in 1966.

A little-known event of his early days in Boston sheds further light on the idealism that was a strong motivating force in Krayer's life. The Nobel peace prize had just been awarded to the German writer and journalist Carl von Ossietzky, a pacifist of international renown, who had exposed the secret rearming of Germany and who had been (and was until his death) incarcerated by the Nazi regime. Hitler's response to the award of the prize was a decree forbidding Germans to accept any Nobel prize in the future. At the regular meeting of the German Chemical Society on May 8, 1937, the president of the Society, Professor Stock, addressed himself to the honor bestowed upon von Ossietzky: "Every true German," he said, "must regard as a slap in the face this insulting abuse ... an abuse dictated by political hatred. It is understandable that both the government and the people are indignant over this, and want nothing more to do with Nobel prizes ... the crime of the Norwegian parliament's committee will be regretted deeply by Science."[3]

Krayer's immediate reaction was the following brief note to the society's office: "The remarks of President A. Stock concerning the award of the Nobel peace prize, which are printed on page 121 of the Proceedings of the German Chemical Society of 9 June 1937 oblige me to request that you strike my name from the list of members of the German Chemical Society."

Professor Stock, in reply, could only imagine that he had been misunderstood. "I was only reflecting the feelings of every German scientist," he wrote, "in being upset by such a conscious provocation ... by the honoring of a person who—even before the time of Hitler!—had been branded a traitor; and in deploring that the scientific Nobel prizes had to suffer from this circumstance.... Perhaps you will be so kind as to write me a word of clarification."

Krayer's response will ring a familiar note for all who, as students or colleagues, came under his influence. It recalls the curious blend of careful reasoning and objective presentation of facts on the one hand, coupled with extraordinary

---

[3] A. Stock, "Opening Remark," *Berichte der Deutschen Chemischen Gesellschaft,* 70(1937):121.

emotional intensity on the other, that colored many of his formal lectures and informal discourses.

Dear Mr. President: I am happy to communicate to you the reason for my protest against your remarks. However, it is not my intention to enter into a discussion about the political expression "traitor". That this expression does not necessarily have a precise ethical value must be obvious to everyone who has experienced how easily the meaning can be changed by various political trends that appear especially strongly and clearly at times of upheaval in the structure of a State.

What made me write my letter of 3 September was the urge to express the view that not every German and—as I am convinced—not every German scientist shares your feelings of being upset by the award of the recent Nobel peace prize.

The reason for this conviction is what I have read over the last ten years of the writings of Carl von Ossietzky and have learned from other sources about him. I have had no occasion to meet this man personally. But whoever, over the past decade in Germany, has followed the course of his career in an unprejudiced way would—even if he were a political opponent—not be able to ignore the fact of the man's extraordinary personality.

Here is a man who, in a hard life full of work and an abundance of general human and political experience, has developed a world outlook and has deduced from it the principles of his life philosophy, who has made the profession of political writer his mission in life, and who is ready to dedicate to this profession not only all the strength of his spirit but also his whole personality. An unyielding character who, whenever the obligation of sincerity necessitates, openly uses his right of free speech to express his opinion. A man who is not motivated by the lust for power and fame but who is forced to speak by the persuasion of the rightness of his beliefs, and who fights unafraid for that persuasion with the force of his arguments. Carl von Ossietzky has proven the sincerity of his mind and his selflessness by again refusing (he had already been amnestied once) to evade responsibility for his convictions. To back up his words with deeds was a necessity of life for him although he must have known that he could not expect any justice from his political enemies.

The reason for such a judgment as you, Mr. President, have formulated, must be sought in an ethical evaluation of the man. I do not find sufficient basis for your interpretation, and I am not of the opinion that the scientific Nobel prizes have lost any of their value or significance by the honoring of Carl von Ossietzky. It is to the credit of the Nobel organization that it honored the ethical qualities of this man; that is my conviction. What can promote peace between nations if not the deeds of such men, who are motivated by a pure and deep consciousness of their responsibility to a higher human order than is represented by the nation into which we [*sic!*] are born?

A final incident is noteworthy, again for the light it sheds on the ethical standards by which Krayer consistently guided all his actions. In 1965 the Academic Council of the Medical Academy of Düsseldorf voted to confer honorary membership on Krayer. Writing about this decision, the rector of the University explained as follows:

> They would like thereby to show their appreciation of the stand you took when, on grounds of conscience, you refused the call to the chair of pharmacology and toxicology in Düsseldorf in 1933, which would have been your first opportunity to be head of your own institute. At the same time the Academic Council wishes to acknowledge the fact that even after your emigration, and despite the unpleasantness you experienced in Düsseldorf, you nevertheless maintained and furthered your contacts with German science. Not the least, we would also like by our decision to acknowledge your scientific accomplishments, which relate to us in a special way through a traditional field of research at our Academy, namely, heart and circulation research.

Krayer's immediate response was to accept the honorary membership with pleasure. But as time passed, he evidently became increasingly uneasy. Somehow a mutually suitable date for the presentation ceremony in Düsseldorf could not be arranged. Finally, on January 26, 1966, Krayer sent what must have been a very difficult letter to write, as we can surmise from the three different preliminary handwritten drafts that are preserved, each full of deletions and alternative wordings. Addressing the rector of the University of Düsseldorf, Krayer wrote:

> In the course of the correspondence with you concerning the time of my visit to Düsseldorf, I have thought more deeply about the honor you are planning for me. I have come to the conclusion that the right thing for me to do is not to accept the honorary membership of the Medical Academy of Düsseldorf.
>
> Despite my happiness at your first letter, which reached me during my trip to Japan, I had certain reservations from the beginning. It is now clear to me that the original ethical position I took in 1933 does not permit of any external reward. I must ask you, therefore, to nullify the decision of the Scientific Council of the Medical Academy. I regret that I took so long to express my convictions clearly.

Krayer closes with the hope that his decision will not cause bad feelings to mar his personal relationships with colleagues at Düsseldorf.

The reference, in the rector's original letter, to Krayer's maintaining and furthering contacts with German science will be cryptic to those unfamiliar with an episode that followed shortly on the close of World War II. With Central Europe literally in ashes, its universities and research institutes in ruins, and its people starving, the Unitarian Service Committee organized a medical mission to Czechoslovakia with Harvard cardiologist Paul Dudley White as director and Krayer as an active participant. During that trip Krayer became fully aware of the devastation of the German universities through personal visits with university colleagues. It must have been then that he formulated a plan for rendering special material and moral assistance to the German academic communities. On his return to Harvard, he founded, and served as secretary-treasurer of, a Committee to Help German University Scientists. By 1948 a medical mission to Germany had been organized by the Unitarian Service Committee, with Krayer as its chairman. This effort was supported by the Department of State and by the U.S. occupation authorities. The visits to the universities of Frankfurt, Berlin, Göttingen, München, Tübingen, Freiburg, and Heidelberg brought a sense of concern and collegial friendship to supplement the material aid already being furnished by various groups in the United States.

RESEARCH CONTRIBUTIONS

Krayer's first research, published in 1926, the same year he received his M.D. degree at Freiburg, concerned the pharmacologic properties of apocodeine, an opiate alkaloid closely related to apomorphine. In this work he first experienced the importance of employing only pure compounds in pharmacologic investigations—a recurrent theme in his later writings. Here he showed that apocodeine obtained from one manufacturer was pure and gave reliable and reproducible results, while impure mixtures behaved differently in important respects. Two investigations followed dealing with the pharmacologic and pharmacokinetic aspects of thyroid hormone action (1928a,b), no doubt inspired by the endocrinologic interests of his mentor Paul Trendelenburg. By 1929, however, he seems to have found his metier. In that year he published the first of two investigations into the cardiovascular toxicity of Neosalvarsan, an organic arsenical then in wide use for the treatment of syphilis. Thus was initiated a lifelong commitment to the study of the circulatory system.

Over a period of four decades, Krayer published seventy-six original research articles (not counting abstracts and textbook chapters), all but one in the field of cardiovascular physiology and pharmacology; the exception was a brief note concerning pumpkin seeds as a chemotherapy for tapeworm infestation, a byproduct of his brief stay at the American University of Beirut. Nearly all his research employed a single technique—the dog heart-lung preparation (HLP)—technically a very difficult setup of which he was the acknowledged world-class master.

From the purely statistical and descriptive aspects of Krayer's research career, there is much to be learned. By standards presently in vogue, one might judge a lifetime output of seventy-six original papers to be surprisingly scanty. Closer scrutiny, however, reveals several features decidedly no longer fashionable today. Of the total output, for example, one-third were sole-author papers; and Krayer was first author on another one-third. To those who knew him, these numbers merely express what we saw every day in the "heart-lung room"—a scientist with hands-on involvement in every phase of his research and a devotion to thoroughness that precluded the publication of incomplete or indecisive experimental results.

Nor did Krayer follow the traditional German procedure (now so common elsewhere, too) of making the department or institute head a pro forma coauthor of all papers by junior colleagues. Here numbers and names are instructive. In the last decade of his career at Harvard, for example, Krayer himself was first author on three papers and coauthor on ten others. In the same period, ninety-one additional investigations in the field of cardiovascular pharmacology were published by those working under his tutelage, and none of those carry his name. To Krayer, evidently, coauthorship implied direct responsibility for important aspects of the experimental work. He was always generous with suggestions, technical assistance, and criticism, but he would not put his own name to research unless he had been a direct participant. I consider it more remarkable now than I realized at the time that although at the beginning I was only a medical student engaged in part-time research in his department, it was taken as a matter of course that I would coauthor work for which Krayer had prime responsibility and would be sole author when he had not been involved directly. This was for me a refreshing contrast to my one previous (and more typical) experience of publication, a short didactic clinical article I conceived and wrote without assistance, which my clinical instructor then submitted for publication with his own name added as first author!

Another interesting number is the mean length of Krayer's papers—11.2 pages—and the fact that one-quarter of them exceeded 14 pages. This, of course, was in the spirit of the times—and not only in the German literature so notorious for prolixity. If research was worth doing well, it was worth publishing well and fully. One's pride as a scientist simply ruled out the publication of incomplete or uncertain or fragmentary data. Modern biomedical science suffers from the "bit-by-bit" syndrome, wherein a staccato series of short papers report findings that may be raw, superficial, undigested, unconvincing, unexplored, and uninterpreted. Krayer's style, the very opposite, was to make each paper a complete *Arbeit*, every detail honed as nearly as possible to perfection. In an obituary on Otto Loewi (1962b), he wrote the following laudatory sentence, which is also an apt description of his own attitude: "He felt that any work worth publishing deserved as much care in the preparation of the manuscript as in the conduct of the experimental work."

Krayer held the belief that the aim of pharmacologic investigation is to elucidate mechanisms of drug action, that phenomenologic observations by themselves are only stepping stones to this ultimate goal. It follows automatically from this position that one's efforts have to be focused on a single problem and preferably on the perfection and use of a single methodology. The history of every field of science tells us that technique is the key to progress. Given the available knowledge base and technology, Krayer's adaptation of the Starling heart-lung preparation (HLP) to pharmacologic investigations represented a major achievement. The HLP was a new and powerful tool, with which a lifetime of research on cardiovascular drugs could be carried out.

A fundamental problem in pharmacology is the multiplicity of the actions of most drugs. Even a drug that acted with absolute specificity on a single receptor would usually find that receptor in numerous organs throughout the body. And in reality most drugs have overlapping selectivities for more than a single type of receptor deployed in more than one organ system. Thus even the direct actions of a drug are often too complex to analyze in the whole animal. To this difficulty must be added the confounding effects of indirect (secondary) actions, such as physiologic reflexes or other adaptive responses to a primary drug action. This problem is especially serious for cardiovascular drugs since the heart and circulation are under continuous reflex regulation. Consider, for example, a compound that increases the heart rate. Does it do so by a direct agonistic effect on receptors mediating cardioacceleration at the pacemaker? By antagonist effect on receptors mediating cardiac slowing? By causing the local release of a cardioaccelerator neurotransmitter? By releasing a cardioaccelerator hormone from a distant tissue into the circulation? By stimulating chemoreceptors, leading to reflex decrease of vagal activity or increase of sympathetic tone? By causing a pharmacologic action remote from the heart (e.g., a decrease in blood pressure through relaxation of arteriolar tone) that leads to a reflex cardioacceleration?

In the HLP the heart and lungs remain in situ, but the entire output of the left ventricle (except for the coronary circulation) is routed through an external circuit. There the peripheral resistance is under the experimenter's control, and the height of the blood reservoir determines the pressure at which the right atrium fills. Oxygenation is provided in a quasi-normal manner by a respiration pump. The innervation can be left intact, or specific kinds of partial or complete denervation can be carried out. Effects of drugs on the heart rate (chronotropic effects), force of contraction (inotropic effect), atrio-ventricular conduction (dromotropic effect), and other metrics can be studied. Thus the preparation offers a means to isolate sites and mechanisms of action of cardiovascular or cardiotoxic drugs free of multisite and reflex effects.

Krayer's first use of the HLP was during his Berlin period in the studies of Neosalvarsan toxicity (1929, 1930a). He discovered that the toxic agent was an oxidation product of the drug, and he showed that the effect was a direct one on the vascular beds of all the important organs. His succinct summary establishes the style that was to become his hallmark. Analyzing the evidence that the oxidation product causes a dose-related reduction of blood flow through the heart, lungs, kidneys, and liver, he concludes: "The increase in vascular resistance in these organs is to be attributed to changes in the vessels themselves. These changes are the cause of the far-reaching disturbances of hemodynamics, they are not the result of hemodynamic changes elsewhere."

Finding confusion among clinicians concerning the pharmacotherapy of heart failure, Krayer developed precise quantitative measures in the HLP, whereby cardioactive drugs could be characterized (1930b; 1931a,b,d; 1932b,c; 1933e). It was in his paper, "Versuche am insuffizienten Herzen" (1931d), that Krayer developed—extending the concepts laid down by his teacher P. Trendelenburg—a standard procedure for using the HLP to study drug effects on the failing heart. The competent heart increases its output in response to elevation of the venous reservoir without any significant increase in right atrial pressure—that is, the additional inflow leads responsively to an increased stroke volume. A large dose of a barbiturate reliably produced failure of a desired degree, which could be measured quantitatively as an impaired ability of the heart to respond this way. This ability, after impairment by barbiturates, was enhanced by digitalis glycosides even in the denervated heart, that is, in the absence of any change in the heart rate. Later (1948b) this phenomenon was observed with other drugs known for their central depressant effects, and it occurred at concentrations that would have been in the lethal range for the whole animal.

The important advance in this paper was the demonstration of a method for determining quantitatively the limits of cardiac sufficiency in response to specific measured changes in right atrial pressure. Later a specific "competence index" was developed to express the heart's response numerically (1948b). This method allowed a clear distinction to be made between drugs that primarily affected heart rate and those (like digitalis) that truly improved the work capacity of the impaired cardiac muscle. The paper concludes: "A cardiac drug, in the most rigorous meaning of the term, must restore the ability of the failing heart to put out a greater volume per beat and thereby—and not simply by a rate increase—restore the limits of its sufficiency." Thus the study of the actions of cardioactive drugs could be pursued "under controlled conditions of heart failure."

Krayer's mastery of the HLP led to a very fruitful collaboration with W. Feldberg in the Department of Physiology at Berlin. Loewi's demonstration of chemical neurotransmission in 1921 had ushered in a new era for physiology and pharmacology. By the early 1930s, evidence indicated strongly that the *Vagus-Stoff* was acetylcholine, which could be identified in the leech muscle treated with the specific cholinesterase inhibitor physostigmine. The early experiments had been carried out with frogs. In the classical paper by Feldberg and Krayer (1933c), intact dogs and cats were used at the outset to show that an "acetylcholine-like substance" is released into the coronary circulation of mammals on electrical stimulation of the vagus. But here was also the perfect opportunity to apply the HLP. The authors explain: "In order to make sure that as few extracardiac influences as possible modify the effect of stimulating the vagus, we considered it necessary also to demonstrate the *Vagus-Stoff* in the HLP." The same results were obtained in the HLP as in intact animals (Figure 1). Unless physostigmine was added both to the coronary circulation and to the bioassay preparation, and unless the vagus was stimulated, no "acetylcholine-like substance" was detectable. In a subsequent refinement of this experiment, Krayer (with Verney), soon after his emigration to London, showed that the vagus did not have to be stimulated artificially but could be stimulated reflexly by an induced increase in blood pressure (1934b). These ingenious experiments were carried out with an innervated HLP, the head (with no vascular connection to the heart) being perfused from a donor dog.

Krayer's interest in the veratrum alkaloids, which dominated his research interests from 1942 on, was stimulated, according to his own account (1962b), by his learning through a medical student's report that these substances were being used to lower blood pressure in eclampsia at the nearby Boston Lying-in Hospital. Crude extracts of the European *Veratrum album* (white false hellebore), the North American *Veratrum viride* (green false hellebore) (Figure 2), and the Central and South American *Veratrum sabadilla* (*Schoenocaulon officinale*) already enjoyed something of a reputation as beneficial in the management of heart disease. All parts of these plants—and also of the North American *Zygadenus* family—contain the cardioactive principles.

As long ago as 1818, Meissner and also Pelletier and Cavendou isolated veratrine, a potent alkaloidal mixture from sabadilla seeds. While still at Berlin, and recalling his earlier experience with apocodeine, Krayer had remarked on the futility of sophisticated pharmacologic studies with crude extracts. At that time he wrote: "Only when pure substances

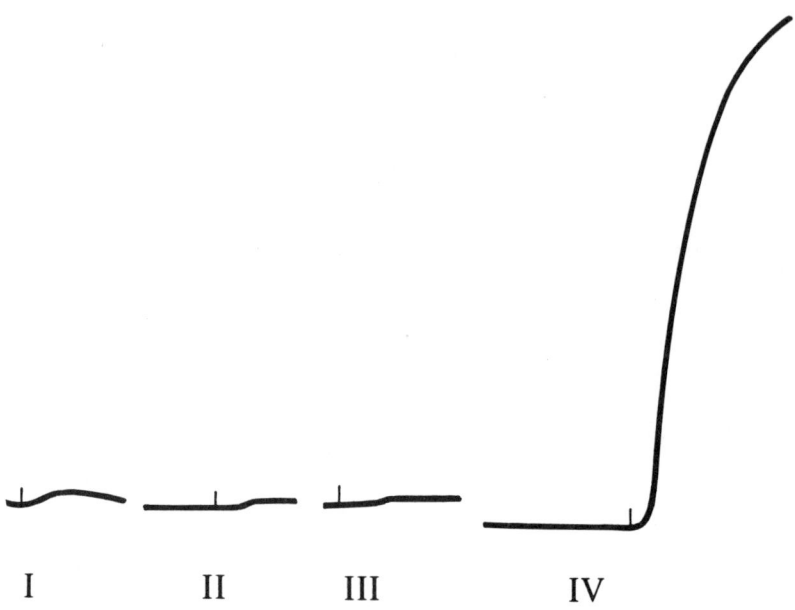

I II III IV

FIGURE 1 The first demonstration of acetylcholine release in a mammalian organism. Blood from the coronary sinus of a dog was tested on the eserinized leech muscle. Before injection of the cholinesterase inhibitor physostigmine, the blood had no effect on the leech muscle (I). Nor was there any effect of blood collected during electrical stimulation of the vagus (II), even though a transient cardiac arrest was produced. After the dog was injected with physostigmine and atropine, the blood was still without effect (III); but now vagal stimulation released an "acetylcholine-like substance" into the coronary blood (IV). [From Feldberg and Krayer, 1933b]. (Technical limitations made it necessary to reproduce this kymograph tracing and that in Figure 4 as black-on-white records rather than the original white-on-black.)

are available will it make sense to determine, by means of a thorough pharmacologic analysis, the conditions under which a favorable effect on the heart and an improvement of the circulation can be achieved" (1933d). Thus the initial experiments with a crude "veratrine" mixture (1942a) were immediately followed by studies on pure alkaloids. Krayer

FIGURE 2 *Veratrum viride*, popularly known as Indian pokeweed. This North American wild plant and related species that grow in Central and South America and Europe contain the cardioactive steroidal alkaloids in their roots, stems, and leaves.

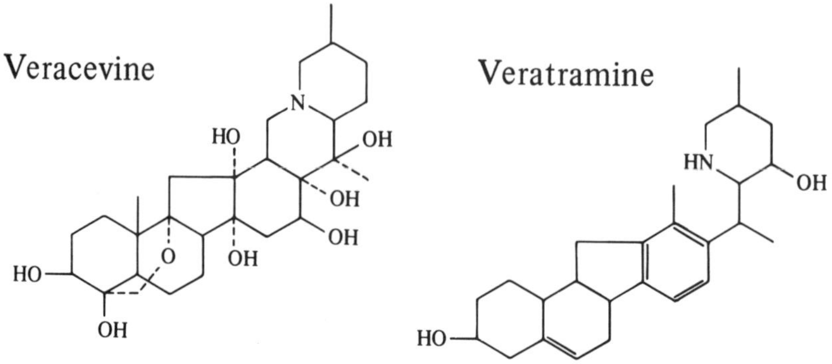

Veracevine **Veratramine**

FIGURE 3 Typical structures of the two families of veratrum alkaloids. *Left:* Veracevine, the base of the ester alkaloid veratridine, which contains one mole of veratric acid (3,4-dimethoxybenzoic acid). Other ester alkaloids such as protoveratrine are mono-, di-, or tri-esters of various organic acids. *Right:* Veratramine, a typical secondary amine alkaloid, which occurs naturally as a glycoside with a single mole of glucose.

sought and received help from chemists, beginning in 1941 and continuing for the next twenty-five years. At the Department of Chemistry at Harvard, there were R. P. Linstead and D. Todd, later S. M. Kupchan, and then in his own department F. C. Uhle. Much help came also from W. A. Jacobs and L. Craig at the Rockefeller Institute and also from chemists at Eli Lilly and Company and Winthrop Chemical Company.

There are two major groups of veratrum alkaloids, the tertiary amine esters and the secondary amines (Figure 3), and their pharmacologic actions are entirely different. The special virtues of the HLP proved wonderfully suited to the investigation of these compounds, and Krayer studied them for the rest of his research career. Most of our present knowledge about the pharmacology of this group of naturally occurring cardioactive substances is due to that sustained effort by Krayer and his colleagues over the years.

The tertiary amine esters, such as protoveratrine A and veratridine, each contain a polycyclic polyhydroxylated amine (e.g., veracevine, as in Figure 3) and one or more organic acids. Much as with acetylcholine, the ester linkage proved to be essential to the full pharmacologic activity. The "veratrine effect" was well known in skeletal muscle—a repetitive discharge after a single stimulus, now recognized to be a consequence of the opening of sodium channels by the drug. The hypotensive effect is a reflex action caused by stimulation of chemoreceptors in the heart, lungs, and carotid sinus (the Bezold-Jarisch effect). The hypotension is accompanied by bradycardia, also of reflex origin, and is mediated by a vagal mechanism, as could be demonstrated by comparison of the innervated and denervated HLP (1943b,d; 1944b,c).

With the discovery of the reflex mechanism of action of the ester alkaloids, Krayer characteristically immersed himself in a scholarly investigation of the very early work of von Bezold and the later studies of Jarisch. Eventually he published a historical review with forty-nine citations, "The History of the Bezold-Jarisch Effect" (1961a), as a tribute to Professor Jarisch on the occasion of his seventieth birthday. One of the conclusions was that the name of this reflex, hitherto known as the Bezold effect, should more appropriately also bear the name of Jarisch.

Krayer's studies with the tertiary amine polyesters, especially protoveratrine A, led him to explore their therapeutic utility in human hypertension. With E. Meilman, a clinician at nearby Beth Israel Hospital, he carried out systematic studies on dosage, toxicity, and duration of action (1950b; 1952e; 1977). Protoveratrine A was chosen from among a number of candidate compounds for its favorable therapeutic ratio and long duration of action when given by the oral route. In contrast to veratridine, its action was more selective for sensory nerves than for skeletal muscle. Also favorable was a positive inotropic action in the failing heart, as demonstrated by an increased work capacity in the HLP, later confirmed in patients. The positive inotropic action of veratridine or protoveratrine is of theoretical interest because of its similarity to the effect of the digitalis glycosides. Inhibition of the sodium pump (sodium-potassium ATPase) by the latter and opening of sodium channels by the former could both, through their different mechanisms, cause a net increase in sodium influx.

The basic pharmacology of the tertiary ester veratrum alkaloids is summarized in an exhaustive review by Krayer and Acheson (1946b). Protoveratrine A had some usefulness for a time in the treatment of malignant hypertension, hypertensive encephalopathy, and eclampsia (1949h, 1958a). Since it effectively lowered the "set point" for reflex control of the blood pressure without disturbing the adaptive reflexes themselves, it did not (for example) cause postural hypotension such as is common with the autonomic ganglionic blocking agents. Unfortunately, nausea and vomiting were common side effects (also from stimulation of vagal afferents), and in time a whole armamentarium of more effective antihypertensive drugs was developed. Thus protoveratrine A was eventually superseded, but it undoubtedly played a seminal role by pointing the way to a practical pharmacotherapy of hypertension.

The secondary amine alkaloids and their glycosides proved to have an entirely different pharmacology from the tertiary amine esters despite the close similarity of chemical structure. These compounds, of which veratramine (Figure 3) is the best studied, are also hypotensive in their action, but their most interesting effect proved to be a cardiodeceleration by a direct effect on the cardiac pacemaker (1949d,f,g). There were two main lines of evidence. First, the effect was not blocked by atropine, which abolishes the action of acetylcholine released by the vagus. Second, in the denervated HLP infused continuously with epinephrine, the steady-state marked increase in heart rate is promptly abolished by small doses of veratramine. At the same time the positive inotropic action of epinephrine remains unchanged. Thus this experiment sharply separates the cellular mechanisms that mediate the chronotropic and inotropic effects of the catecholamines (Figure 4). The novelty lay in the fact that although antagonists to the pressor action of epinephrine had been discovered, no antagonist to the cardioaccelerator effect was known.

Most of the thirty-seven papers in the series entitled "Studies on Veratrum Alkaloids" dealt with these secondary amines and their glycosides. Related steroid alkaloids with similar pharmacologic effect were found among the compounds isolated from plants of the *Zygadenus* and *Solanum* families. The aglycones and glycosides were found to be equipotent. Investigations of the structure–activity relationships, which included a group of novel steroids synthesized from pregnenolone by F. C. Uhle in Krayer's department, revealed that high potency required the N atom to be in a piperidine ring.

The selectivity of veratramine and its congeners for the pacemaker tissue intrigued Krayer. Not only did veratramine lack the positive inotropic actions of epinephrine, it also lacked all the other characteristic cardiovascular effects of the catecholamines. It did not constrict the peripheral arterioles and therefore lacked pressor action. It did not dilate the coronary vessels. It did not share the depressant effects of epinephrine upon the functional refractory period and A-V propagation time within the heart. Krayer wrote: "When a group of substances exhibits a high degree of selectivity of action, it should attract the investigative curiosity of the phar-

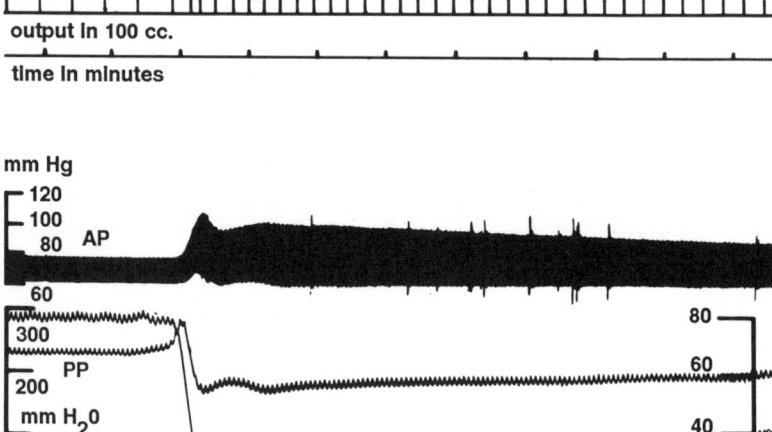

FIGURE 4 Dissociation, by means of veratramine, of the chronotropic and inotropic actions of epinephrine. The record is from a dog HLP in failure, treated with veratramine during the previous two hours. Epinephrine (10 micrograms) was administered at the broad marker signal on the bottom line. Within a minute, epinephrine increases the cardiac output (top line), thus lowering the elevated right atrial pressure and pulmonary pressure; it also increases the systolic arterial pressure—all without any increase of heart rate. *Symbols:* AP, arterial pressure; PP (lower curve on left, middle curve on right), pulmonary pressure; RAP (middle curve on left, lower curve on right), right atrial pressure; bottom horizontal row of figures, heart rate per minute. [From Krayer, 1949d]. (See parenthetic note under Figure 1 legend.)

macologist. The search for selective activity and the analysis of its nature is the central theme of his scientific pursuit" (1952d).

As Krayer learned later (1958d), the direct action of the secondary amine alkaloids on the pacemaker was not a blockade (at the receptor level) of the accelerator action of the catecholamines. Thus, veratramine was not a true forerunner of the beta-adrenergic receptor blocking agents, which have proved to be so useful therapeutically. Krayer's work, however, was the first demonstration that a cardioselective antagonism of a noradrenergic physiological effect at the sino-atrial node was possible.

Often, as plant alkaloids of various families became available in pure form, Krayer would test their effects in the HLP. Thus it was that in 1955 he began to examine the action of reserpine, a pure alkaloid from *Rauwolfia*. The *Rauwolfia* alkaloids had long been used in India for their tranquilizing effects, and the early 1950s had seen intensive interest in their therapeutic potential in Europe and the United States. Reserpine had been introduced into psychiatric practice as a tranquilizer and also for its antihypertensive effect. Because reserpine was regarded as primarily a psychopharmacologic agent, those interested in its mechanism of action naturally turned to the brain; even the hypotensive effect was presumed to be centrally mediated. It had already been shown, first in Brodie's and then in Marthe Vogt's laboratory that reserpine depletes the brain of its serotonin stores, and this same approach was being extended to brain catecholamines in several laboratories.

The immediate stimulus for Krayer's interest was a letter in the *New England Journal of Medicine* reporting heart failure in patients treated with reserpine. Krayer seized the opportunity to exploit the unique value of the HLP for distinguishing direct peripheral actions of drugs from those requiring intact innervation, and he was soon able to sort out the components of reserpine's actions. The alkaloid produced an immediate cardioacceleration that was similar in all respects to that of an infusion of norepinephrine. Matti Paasonen, a visiting scientist from Finland, measured tissue and blood catecholamine levels and found that the norepinephrine content of the heart fell sharply—that is, reserpine depleted the cardiac stores. In the HLP from reserpine-pretreated dogs, reserpine failed to produce the characteristic cardioacceleration. Moreover, serotonin infusions had no effect on the heart rate, showing that serotonin release (which also occurs) does not participate in the cardioaccelerator action. An additional finding of interest, revealing an independent effect of reserpine, was that in the HLP under the rate-increasing effect of a catecholamine infusion, reserpine reduced the heart rate in an atropine-resistant manner reminiscent of veratramine. All these effects occurred also in the denervated HLP, permitting the conclusion that ". . . reserpine exerts an action upon the heart in the absence of connections with the central nervous system" (1958b). Curiously (although it was not realized until later), the release of catecholamines in amounts sufficient to produce effects of their own was a peculiar property of the HLP, not evident in most organs or in whole animals. These important studies were published originally in 1957 in three abstracts—in *Federation Proceedings* (1957a), *Acta Physiologica Scandinavica* (1957b), and the *Journal of Physiology* (1957c).

In summary, Krayer had shown that reserpine depletes biogenic amine transmitters from peripheral as well central stores by a direct action. Thus the reserpine effect was a general phenomenon, not limited to the central nervous system, and this was pointed out explicitly in one of the 1957 abstracts. As so often happens, however, the same discovery was made almost simultaneously in several laboratories. Carlsson's group in Sweden was studying the depletion of catecholamines in peripheral as well as central tissues. A short paper from this group,[4] which was submitted for publication October 20, 1956, reported on the depletion of catecholamines from rabbit heart by reserpine. They also showed that

---

[4] A. Bertler, A. Carlsson, and E. Rosengren, "Release by Reserpine of Catechol Amines from Rabbits Hearts," *Naturwissenschaften*, 43(1956):521.

reserpine-treated adrenalectomized cats given carbachol to stimulate sympathetic ganglia and atropine to block the muscarinic actions of carbachol had no blood pressure rise, as they would normally have done as a result of norepinephrine release at the sympathetic nerve terminals in arteriolar walls. Moreover, electrical stimulation of the splanchnic nerves was without its usual hypertensive effect in these animals.

On March 22, 1957, Brodie et al. (National Institutes of Health) submitted a paper under the title "Possible Interrelationship Between Release of Brain Norepinephrine and Serotonin by Reserpine."[5] The paper also included a report of the depletion of norepinephrine from rabbit heart even after high cervical section of the spinal cord, showing that the depleting action of reserpine was direct and not centrally mediated.

The British pharmacologist J. H. Burn (Oxford) visited Krayer in 1957. In a letter dated May 7 of that year, expressing thanks for hospitality, Burn wrote: ". . . I enjoyed seeing the results with reserpine in the heart-lung preparation." More than a year later, on June 3, 1958, Burn and Rand submitted for publication "The Action of Sympathomimetic Amines in Animals Treated with Reserpine."[6] This major contribution established very thoroughly that reserpine depletes the stores of norepinephrine in arterial walls. In addition, several bioassay preparations from reserpine-treated animals were used to demonstrate that some sympathomimetic amines (e.g., tyramine and other noncatechol phenylethylamine derivatives) only act when the tissue catecholamine stores are intact, and therefore presumably owe their

[5] B. B. Brodie, J. S. Olin, R. G. Kuntzman, et al., "Possible Interrelationship Between Release of Brain Norepinephrine and Serotonin by Reserpine," *Science,* 125(1957):1293–94.

[6] J. H. Burn and M. J. Rand, "The Action of Sympathomimetic Amines in Animals Treated with Reserpine," *Journal of Physiology (London),* 144(1958):314–36.

own actions to the release of catecholamines. In addition, it was reported that tissues from reserpine-treated animals were supersensitive to catecholamines and that both the insensitivity to tyramine and the supersensitivity to catecholamines could be reversed by an infusion of norepinephrine that repletes the stores. Further significant conclusions were that a continuous slow release of norepinephrine from arteriolar stores probably plays a role in maintaining the normal vascular tone and also that circulating catecholamines from the adrenal gland probably participate in maintaining the stores at their proper level. This paper had an immediate and lasting impact in physiologic and pharmacologic circles; it is still regarded as a landmark contribution.

The full-length 1958 papers from Krayer's group (1958b,d,e,f) had not appeared in print when the manuscript by Burn and Rand was submitted for publication. Curiously, however, none of Krayer's three 1957 abstracts is cited, nor is any "personal communication" acknowledged. We know from his intimate associates that Krayer felt miffed; he may even have thought that Burn made improper use of what was learned during the May 1957 visit. A letter from Burn to Krayer dated October 11, 1958, is interesting in this respect. Edith Bülbring, one of Burn's colleagues at Oxford and a longtime friend of Krayer (they were colleagues in the Berlin days), had just returned from a visit to Boston. Burn writes: "A remark of Edith's since her return prompts me to write to you about my interest in reserpine, and how it began." There follows a detailed historical account and then the following passage: "I know that you showed me the action of reserpine on the rate of the heart-lung preparation in 1957, but it passed from my mind and played no part in my thoughts. I had forgotten what you showed me until I read your papers a month or two ago."

In one of the papers on reserpine that was published

from Krayer's laboratory in 1958, Innes and Krayer (1958d) compared the negative chronotropic effects of reserpine and veratramine. Using the HLP from reserpine-treated catecholamine-depleted dogs, they showed that the action of veratramine was unchanged and therefore that it did not act by antagonizing sympathomimetic amines. Until then such an adrenergic blocking mechanism could not be ruled out. It had earlier been shown that when the heart rate was elevated to a high steady-state level by an infusion of epinephrine or norepinephrine, veratramine lowered it dramatically. In the absence of added catecholamines, it also reduced the heart rate, but the normal heart rate might have been under the tonic accelerator action of a slow release of endogenous norepinephrine. Only by substantially eliminating the catecholamine stores could the direct depressant effect of veratramine on the atrial pacemaker be proved.

In another paper Innes, Krayer, and Waud (1958e) examined ten *Rauwolfia* alkaloids and showed that, whereas they all displayed a direct depressant effect on both the heart rate and atrio-ventricular transmission, only half of them were catecholamine depleters. Waud, Kottegoda, and Krayer (1958f) studied dosage and time-course details of the depleting effect of reserpine. Their method was to pretreat the dog with various doses of reserpine 24 hours prior to a challenge dose on the HLP or, alternatively, to pretreat with a standard dose at different times prior to the challenge. In this clever method the attenuation of the heart-rate increase caused by the challenge dose serves as a measure of the degree of catecholamine depletion by reserpine. They found a very slow onset of action of reserpine, peaking at 24 to 72 hours, and a good correlation with norepinephrine content (determined by bioassay on the cat blood pressure) throughout the time course. The threshold single dose was found to be a remarkably low 30 micrograms per kilogram.

In 1960 Waud and Krayer published a study that is a model of the application of sophisticated statistical methodology to a complex pharmacologic problem—a so-called "split-split-plot design." Epinephrine was compared with norepinephrine and shown to be equipotent. The HLP was found to become progressively less sensitive (as an experiment continued) to the cardiovascular effects of both catecholamines. Finally, reserpine pretreatment did not influence the effects of norepinephrine or epinephrine on the heart rate. This last conclusion was contrary to the findings of Burn and Rand. Burn, in a letter to Krayer, took issue, asserting that the method of catecholamine infusion could not have detected the reserpine-induced supersensitivity inasmuch as the infusion itself would quickly replete the stores. Waud and Krayer themselves acknowledge in their discussion: "The use of single doses might also contribute to the discrepancy." Inasmuch as their paper cites Burn and Rand, who showed that an infusion of norepinephrine abolishes the supersensitivity, it is surprising that Waud and Krayer did not compare single doses with infusions in their own experiments.

Papers in 1962 (Krayer, Alper, and Paasonen), 1966 (Krayer, Mosimann, and Silver), and 1972 (Krayer, Weiner, and Mosimann) completed the studies on catecholamine depletion. Guanidine derivatives had been found to share this action with reserpine, guanethidine having been studied principally in this respect. Krayer compared guanethidine with reserpine in the HLP; here he found that the catecholamine-depleted preparation was sensitized to both the chronotropic and inotropic effects of norepinephrine. Further studies employed a very simple compound, methylguanidine, which is 250 times less potent than guanethidine but has the same pharmacologic effects. By now, fluorimetric methods of catecholamine assay had been introduced, and these made possible precise, direct measurements in the coronary sinus blood. Methylguanidine always produced a higher level of norepinephrine in coronary sinus blood than in arterial blood that had passed through the pulmonary circulation, showing that the elevated norepinephrine was indeed derived primarily from cardiac stores.

Krayer's studies on reserpine never had the historical scientific impact they deserved. The reasons are evident in retrospect. His focus on the HLP tended to limit his "audience." Moreover, his steadfast refusal to draw a conclusion that went beyond his own data meant that the broad significance of the reserpine findings did not "leap off the page." It is true that the field quickly became competitive, whereas Krayer's discovery of catecholamine depletion was probably unique in 1955. Painstaking thoroughness about every aspect of experimentation and the preparation of manuscripts accounted for the passage of two years until the first brief meeting abstracts appeared, and three years until the first full-length papers were published. More than sixty HLP preparations were used for Krayer and Fuentes (1958b), about thirty-seven for Paasonen and Krayer (1958c), twenty-five for Innes and Krayer (1958d), and forty-four for Waud, Kottegoda, and Krayer (1958f).

Finally, it was not Krayer's style to promote his own work by aggressive public pronouncements, nor to engage in "priority battles." Certainly, he would never have voiced his concern in public over matters of scientific priority, and he disdained secrecy in the laboratory, always welcoming visitors and freely discussing work in progress with them. Not only the intensely competitive environment that developed around reserpine but also the passionate disputes over the relative importance of norepinephrine depletion and serotonin depletion disgusted him, and probably accounted for his withdrawal from further research on the reserpine problem. In retrospect there is no doubt that his studies, limited as they were, nevertheless represented an important contribution to the biochemical pharmacology of the catecholamines, with implications for physiology and pharmacology that reached far beyond the cardiovascular system.

Krayer's mastery of the HLP as an experimental tool placed him virtually in a class by himself. His department, at the peak of its activity from the late 1950s until his retirement in 1966, was certainly one of the world's leading centers for the training of cardiovascular physiologists and pharmacologists of the traditional kind. Yet it was the end of an era. Young physiologists and pharmacologists were turning increasingly to the methods of biophysics, biochemistry, and molecular biology to solve fundamental questions about physiologic mechanisms and their alteration by drugs. Krayer has to be seen, in historical context, as one of the last and one of the greatest in the long tradition of physiologic pharmacologists.

He was not only a master of the HLP, he was also a master of kymography. In an obituary memoir, P. B. Dews, long a member of Krayer's department, wrote: "Krayer brought kymography to its highest level as an art." We who experienced the transition from crude mechanical recording devices to electronic ones (polygraphs) can perhaps understand better than our younger colleagues the significance of kymography practiced as an art. To produce experimental records of the quality evident already in Krayer's Berlin publications of 1929–1933 implied an attention to detail affecting all aspects of an experiment. Thus kymography was a kind of window on the experimenter's methodology through which one could form some judgment of the overall quality of the work. The published experimental records let us appreciate the fastidious attention to detail that was his credo. Close inspection of any figure from his publications (e.g., Figure 4) must elicit admiration even from users of modern electronic recording devices. He had a stubborn pride in his ability to tame a difficult preparation and make it serve sophisticated purposes. He enjoyed the directness and truthfulness of the kymograph, and he was ever suspicious of the "black boxes" between input and output in modern experimental procedures. Above all, he took pleasure in squeezing the maximum of quantitative data out of so gross and intrinsically crude a bioassay system (cf. Waud and Krayer, 1960).

His perfectionism about scientific publication included a strong insistence on the correct use of words. His philosophy about this is expressed, in part, in a publication summarizing many of his studies on drugs affecting the heart rate (1963a). He alludes to Engelmann, a turn-of-the-century physiologist who coined the term "chronotropic," and he discusses a widespread confusion between direct and indirect chronotropic effects. He writes as follows:

> The creation of new words for new or old concepts is a continuous process in the biological—as in other—sciences. Men like T. W. Engelmann, and in our own time for example, H. H. Dale, who combine this creative ability with a deep biological knowledge and clarity of thought, are rare. As I have sought to demonstrate, the progress of science makes old concepts inadequate. It is therefore not surprising that scientific vocabulary should lose its precision through misuse of old terms and through poor choice of either old or new terms for new concepts. The time is ripe now for a systematic attempt, in physiology and pharmacology, to preserve the significance and beauty of our scientific language. The academic scientist has a dual obligation–not only to make advances in our understanding but also to create the appropriate new language to describe those advances.

PERSONAL HISTORY

Otto (Hermann) Krayer was born October 22, 1899, the second child and first son of Hermann and Frieda Berta (Wolfsperger) Krayer, in the village of Köndringen (Baden), Germany. The Krayers, like most of the villagers, were churchgoing Protestants. They were relatively well off, at least by the standards of this farming community of about one thousand inhabitants. They ran an inn (the Zum Rebstock) and a butcher shop, and they farmed. The father served as treasurer of the village. Before and after school there were chores for the children to do in the fields, vineyards, barnyard, and home. The boy developed a feeling of closeness to the land and to nature—a feeling he often expressed in later years. And though he lived most of his life in Boston and then in Tucson, Krayer always considered the little village at the edge of the Black Forest as home. The local dialect—Alemannic, virtually incomprehensible outside southern Germany and Switzerland—rolled easily off his tongue, and tales are told of his experimental dogs being castigated in that language at moments of exasperation. His attachment to Köndringen was lifelong. His mother lived to a very old age, and Krayer visited her in the old homestead on many occasions. He often said that among all the honors accorded him, the one that meant most was that of honorary citizenship of Köndringen, bestowed in 1957.

Young Krayer's intellectual gifts attracted the attention of the local schoolmaster and of the minister, who persuaded the parents to continue the boy's education. Thus he attended the six-year middle school in the nearby town of Emmendingen. This was followed by another three years of schooling in order to qualify for university matriculation, and he began these in the nearby city of Freiburg. However, World War I was in progress, and his education was interrupted when he turned eighteen: He was conscripted on June 19, 1917, and after half a year of infantry training was sent to the Western Front. A combat wound shortly before the armistice sent him to hospital and then, while still convalescing, he completed the educational requirements for university entrance. Finally, in the autumn of 1919, he enrolled as a medical student at the University of Freiburg.

The course that mainly captured Krayer's interest at the outset was gross anatomy. He discovered real joy in the use of manual skills for dissection—no doubt a foretaste of the pleasure he would experience in setting up hundreds of heart-lung preparations during his career. Years later he wrote about these early dissection experiences: "The beauty of the forms and the relation between form and function became a source of great satisfaction."

In the autumn of 1920, following the German student tradition of moving from university to university, Krayer transferred to the University of München. Here the professor of histology, Siegfried Mollier, made a lasting impression. "Every one of his lectures," Krayer recalled, "was a feast for the mind and the eye. His joy, uttered in a word of approval when he recognized in the drawing of a microscopic structure that the student had caught its beauty, made the course in microscopic anatomy a memorable, intellectually and spiritually enriching experience."

For his clinical studies Krayer returned, in 1922, to Freiburg. His love of the outdoors took him on long walks through the countryside, in the foothills of the Black Forest and along the little river Elz. Here was rooted his lifelong love of botany; he always made a point of knowing all the native plants and flowers of whatever region he was living in. In the winters he was fond of skiing, and he was expert enough to win a student ski competition. The prize, donated by the pharmacologist Walther Straub, is said to have been a single U.S. dollar—a princely sum in those days of rampant inflation in Germany. And here on the ski slopes near Freiburg he enjoyed the companionship of a classmate, Erna Ruth Philipp, who was (much later) to become his wife.

He found the didactic courses in medicine and surgery uninspiring, the more so as there was hardly any contact with patients. Seeking more intellectual stimulation, he undertook his first experimental research at this time—a project in the comparative morphology of amphibian kidneys, under the direction of Wilhelm von Möllendorf. Krayer would collect the specimens himself in the field—often near his native village—and make microscopic measurements on glomeruli and proximal tubules after vital staining with trypan blue.

Enthusiasm for research led Krayer next to pharmacology professor Paul Trendelenburg, whose personality and lectures had made a strong impact on him. After completing his formal course-work and passing the university and state examinations at the end of 1924, Krayer spent the first half of 1925 full time in Trendelenburg's department. In the second half of 1925 he fulfilled internship requirements in internal medicine. Finally, in 1926, he received the M.D. degree for his dissertation research on apocodeine, and he formally began his career in pharmacology as *Assistent* under Trendelenburg.

Krayer's deep commitment to teaching must have had its roots in this Freiburg period. His task was to prepare the lecture demonstrations. These were the students' only opportunities to observe the effects of drugs on animals; there were no facilities for routine laboratory teaching of medical students. It is interesting, in the light of Krayer's later strong belief in the importance of practical laboratory work in pharmacology for medical students, that in 1927 he embarked on what was then a radical innovation—a small, elective experimental laboratory course. Seven years later, in a letter requesting a leave of absence to study laboratory teaching, American style, at the American University of Beirut, he wrote as follows: "This form of instruction has outstanding advantages, provided it is carried out with the necessary earnestness and the number of students is not too great . . . as compared with a method that is based almost entirely on the textbook and spoken word, i.e., on knowledge divorced from experience."

Trendelenburg's interests lay in endocrinology, and at that time he was completing the first volume of a major treatise, *Die Hormone. Ihre Physiologie und Pharmakologie*. Krayer naturally began investigations in that field. He undertook a study of the relation between thyroid function and the autonomic nervous system and published some results (1928a). However, the aspect of endocrinology that dealt with the adrenal medullary hormone epinephrine turned Krayer's interests to the circulatory system. Soon he began to assemble equipment for the heart-lung preparation, which had been introduced by E. H. Starling. Attendance at the International Physiology Congress at Stockholm in 1926 gave Krayer the opportunity to meet some of the leading cardiovascular physiologists and pharmacologists of the day—Starling himself, J. H. Burn, and G. Liljestrand. Among the many visitors to the Freiburg department was H. B. van Dyke, who later became professor of pharmacology at Peiping Union Medical College and then at Columbia University, and who became a lifelong friend.

When Trendelenburg assumed the chair of pharmacology at Berlin in 1927, Krayer went with him. There he advanced rapidly through the academic ranks, from *Assistent* to *Oberassistent* to *Privatdozent*. He had by now turned his research interests fully to the circulatory system; the two mandatory lectures to qualify for the appointment as *Privatdozent* were on coronary blood flow (for the faculty) and on the analysis of the circulatory actions of drugs (for the public).

Trendelenburg became seriously ill in 1930, and Krayer had to assume full academic responsibility for the department. Then, with his chief's death in 1931, Krayer was made acting head; the following year—at the age of thirty-two—he was promoted to Professor Extraordinarius of Pharmacology and Toxicology. Now research had to be put aside while he dealt with the heavy teaching load: the required course in pharmacotherapy, an elective laboratory course, and special elective courses on cardiovascular pharmacology and industrial toxicology. The system of oral examinations for all medical students required his personal participation in more than 500 of these per year. He was also required to assist the courts with forensic toxicologic analyses and even ad hoc experimental studies. In addition, it was necessary to supervise the planning for a new building for the Department of Pharmacology.

Trendelenburg had left two literary legacies—his uncompleted second volume on the hormones and a textbook on the principles of therapeutics, the second edition of which had appeared in 1929. Krayer inherited both. The third edition of the textbook was brought to publication in 1931, but the more demanding task of completing the second volume of *Die Hormone* had to be deferred until the spring of 1932, when W. Heubner was appointed head of the department. Research could then also be resumed, and it was at this time that the important collaborative study with W. Feldberg was initiated. A leave of absence in April 1933 allowed Krayer to join H. Rein, the new professor of physiology at Göttingen, to pursue collaborative experiments with the HLP. But these plans were abruptly terminated in June by the events described at the opening of this memoir.

Returning to Berlin, Krayer found ways (despite the ban on his use of state libraries) to obtain the necessary books and journals needed to complete *Die Hormone*. One of those who assisted him at this difficult time was Dr. Erna Ruth Philipp, who had been a fellow medical student at Freiburg and eventually was to become Krayer's wife. In August Krayer received Verney's invitation to University College and in November an offer from van Dyke at Peiping. The Nazi authorities reinstated him in September, whereupon he requested and was granted a one-year leave of absence for study abroad. On December 31, 1933, with a fellowship from the Rockefeller Foundation, he left Berlin for London.

In Verney's laboratory Krayer plunged into research with the dog heart-lung-kidney preparation as his tool. The aim was to obtain quantitative information about the effects of antidiuretic hormone on kidney function. Using intact dogs equipped with indwelling ureteral catheters, he developed a method of standardizing the hormone. But Krayer's most significant work in the first half of 1934 was the demonstration with Verney (1934b, 1935b) that a physiologic indirect stimulus—a vagal reflex—would release acetylcholine into the coronary circulation. This added considerably to the force of the earlier proof (with Feldberg) that direct stimulation of the vagus released acetylcholine.

Within a few months Krayer was approached about the possibility of assuming direction of the Department of Pharmacology at the American University of Beirut. At the same time he was a leading candidate for the chair of pharmacology at Zurich. By the end of the summer he had accepted the Beirut position, technically a visiting professorship, and here his former associate in Freiburg and Berlin, Dr. Erna Ruth Philipp, joined him as his literary assistant. Because the class was small and newly built facilities were available, he was able to realize his dream of teaching pharmacology primarily as a laboratory course. Among the students who were attracted to his department for research experiences, at least two were inspired to pursue careers in pharmacology. These were Alfred Farah, who later joined Krayer at Harvard and then became department head at Syracuse; and George Fawaz, who eventually became professor of pharmacology and head of the department at Beirut. Glimpses into Krayer's personal life in Beirut are afforded by Fawaz, who describes a vigorous outdoor regimen of hiking and climbing and trips on horse-back—experiences that led to a deep attachment to the scenery of the region. Mount Sannin near Beirut especially captured Krayer's imagination, as did the alpine beauty of Mount Lebanon and its famous cedars. And in winter there was skiing. "Krayer on skis," according to Fawaz, "was an entirely different person: jolly, and uninhibited as a child." Explaining why Krayer gained the respect and love of all members of the University community, Fawaz writes:

> The explanation is simple: he was considerate and modest and demanded very little for himself and his own comfort. His ego never played a role in his decisions. His main concern was his work, which he performed conscientiously; he then sought to serve his students and friends. . . . However, his natural docility abandoned him when he was lecturing or demonstrating an experiment. Then he was transformed into an evangelist, full of zeal.

Although he carried on some research during the three-year stay in Beirut, including a study on pumpkin seeds as anthelmintics (1937), his chief preoccupation was teaching and revising the fourth edition of the Trendelenburg textbook of pharmacotherapy (1938). His sojourn in Lebanon left deep and lasting impressions of the natural beauty of that semiarid region remarkable for its mixture of populations and cultures. "The country is, to my taste, of an exceptional beauty," he wrote to his successor J. O. Pinkston. The circumstances of Krayer's seemingly impulsive decision, thirty-five years later, to spend the latter part of his life in Tucson—much to the surprise of former students and associates who had tried to attract him, after his retirement, to their own geographic areas—suggest that the desert beauty, the stark mountains, the climate with its rainy and dry seasons, and the ethnic diversity of Arizona evoked again all his strong positive feelings about the Beirut experience.

In 1936 Krayer was sent to Harvard's tercentenary celebrations as the official representative of the American University. Whether this was part of a grand design to move him to Harvard, or whether it was just a fortunate turn of events, is unclear. We do know that Krayer had made the acquaintance of Walter B. Cannon at the International Physiology Congress in the summer of 1935 in Moscow. Cannon was professor of physiology at Harvard Medical School and one of the world's foremost physiologists. And Cannon was the moving spirit in arranging a three-month appointment for Krayer as a lecturer in pharmacology for September, October, and November 1936. In 1937, shortly after his return to Beirut, the invitation was proffered to become, in effect, the successor to Reid Hunt, who had retired a year earlier as head of the Department of Pharmacology. We shall probably never know the details of the internal academic politics behind this curiously ambivalent appointment as associate professor without tenure and acting head of the department. Perhaps it was only shrewd Yankee trading practice to offer as little as possible; this is the interpretation put forward by Peter Dews in his obituary article. I think it was probably more than that, in view of Krayer's difficulties with the medical school administration over the next fourteen years. We can only speculate.

Those were the days—now happily gone—when ethnic and national and cultural diversity were counted as liabilities rather than as assets to an institution. The faculty and student body of Harvard Medical School were overwhelmingly white Anglo-Saxon Protestant males (indeed, women were excluded as a matter of explicit formal policy). And here was this rather intense foreigner, not exactly fitting the "old Harvard" mold. Acceptance was probably made no easier by Krayer's European mannerisms, an excessive formality (by American standards), and a stern—even moody—temperament. No easygoing, back-slapping, "old boy" camaraderie here; one could not imagine him cheering at a football game, playing a rubber of bridge or a round of golf, telling (or laughing at) a dirty joke. With close friends, however, the stern demeanor vanished, and he engaged readily in relaxed and good-natured banter or even teasing. His absolute rectitude must have repelled some, even while it attracted others. We know, furthermore, that prominent American pharmacologists communicated to the Harvard administration their displeasure that no qualified American had been found to fill the prestigious post.

When Krayer arrived, the department was a shambles. The only other faculty member was occupied nearly full time with administrative chores in the dean's office, equipment and facilities were primitive, and the school provided only a miniscule budget. Krayer became increasingly disillusioned with the situation and especially with the lack of support from the medical school administration. Six months after his arrival he was offered the chair of pharmacology at Peiping, which had been vacated when van Dyke moved to Columbia. Krayer was strongly inclined to accept, and on June 23, 1938, he actually informed Dean C. S. Burwell that he planned to accept the Peiping offer effective September 1939. What happened next may well be unique in the history of Harvard Medical School. In January 1939 the entire medical school class of 1941, who were in the midst of their pharmacology course, and many of the class of 1940, who had been taught pharmacology the previous year, petitioned Krayer to stay and delivered a copy of their petition to the dean. The document, with 152 signatures appended, reads as follows:

> We, the undersigned, have heard with regret of your plans to leave the Harvard Medical School. Students naturally form opinions of their teachers. As your students we wish to express our admiration for your teaching, our gratitude for all your efforts on our behalf, and our hope that, should

future developments make it possible, you might stay here to give coming classes something of what you have given us.

Forty-five years later, this episode was recalled vividly by one of its participants, Curtis Prout, as follows: "All of us signed it with great enthusiasm. . . . The morning following this action, when we had delivered one copy to Dean Burwell and put the other under his (i.e., Krayer's) door in Vanderbilt Hall, he gave his lecture as usual; it was technical, almost dry but precise and a gem. At the conclusion of the lecture, he started to walk out of the amphitheatre but just before he got to the door, he stopped, turned around, looked up, and he said, 'I have received your petition. Thank you very much.' and quickly made his exit. We gave him a round of applause." For all who knew and admired Krayer, this description of his restrained and dignified reaction to so extraordinary an event will ring absolutely true. At all events, the move to China was cancelled, and Krayer was given tenure (as associate professor) and made head of the department. At this time, too, he married Erna Ruth Philipp and moved into the comfortable house in West Newton in which so many students and young colleagues and their families were to be entertained.

Another vignette, from the spring of 1939, epitomizes Krayer's readiness to do—instantly and without weighing consequences—whatever was needed when a worthy person or cause required help. The government of the Spanish Republic, led by the physiologist Juan Negrin, had been overthrown in a bloody civil war. Military support of the insurgents under Franco by Nazi Germany and Fascist Italy, and of the leftist government of the Republic by the Soviet Union, had made Spain a controversial political cause célèbre in the United States. The safe course, in university life as elsewhere, was to distance oneself from political controversy and to keep quiet.

Rafael Mendez (later a distinguished scientist at the National Institute of Cardiology in Mexico and recently appointed general coordinator of the National Institutes of Health there) arrived in the United States as a political refugee in April 1939. A young pharmacologist still early in his career, Mendez had been drawn into government service by Negrin, first as financial attaché in Paris and Washington responsible for procuring military hardware, later as undersecretary of the interior in charge of information and internal security, and finally as the Spanish consul at Perpignan in southern France with the sad task of directing the mass emigration of the defeated loyalists from Spain to France. Mendez had met Krayer only twice: once while a visitor in Trendelenburg's department in 1929 and once for a few hours in London in 1934.

Mendez tells how, after arriving in the United States, he wrote to several universities and pharmaceutical companies asking for a job, and received "many kind replies but no offerings." Then Walter B. Cannon (who was an ardent supporter of the Spanish Republic) learned that Mendez was in New York. "The next day," Mendez writes, "Krayer showed up at the modest hotel in which I was staying with my wife and four-month-old son, and two weeks later he received me hospitably in Boston appointing me Instructor and Research Associate. . . . Krayer took care of me as a loving father. . . ."

From December 7, 1941, Krayer found himself in the awkward position of "enemy alien." Among the inconveniences he had to endure was a restriction of his travel to a 25-mile radius of Boston, so he could not attend the annual meetings of pharmacologists and physiologists at the "Federation" in Atlantic City every spring. Nevertheless, the war years saw increasing productivity of his own research and the foundations laid for the very strong department that was ultimately to develop. Krayer's first Ph.D. student, Albert Wollenberger (now a professor at the Academy of Sciences of the

German Democratic Republic in Berlin), received his degree in 1946. Junior faculty in this early period (1941–1944) included George H. Acheson, Edwin B. Astwood, H. Stanley Bennett, Ralph W. Brauer, Sydney Ellis, Dale G. Friend, Bertrand E. Lowenstein, Harriet M. Maling, Rafael Mendez, Gordon K. Moe, Richard Tyslowitz, Willard P. Vander Laan, Jr., and Earl H. Wood. With the help of these colleagues—and later of Alfred E. Farah, Arthur J. Linenthal, Douglas S. Riggs, and the author—Krayer was able to implement a full-fledged laboratory course in pharmacology for all the medical students, on a larger scale than he had done in Beirut. With a class of 125 each year, this was a major logistic undertaking, carried out by the capable and loyal *Diener* Mr. George, with Mary Root as the first of a succession of graduate students assigned to this important task.

The day began with a pharmacology lecture to the whole class. And what Harvard graduate of those early years does not recall with nostalgic delight the quaint Germanisms like "Make dark, Mr. Chorge!" or "If you administer alcohol to a typewriter. . . ."? Following the lecture, one-quarter of the students, in rotation on successive days, trooped upstairs to the old barn-like student laboratory on the top floor of Building E. It may not be fully realized the extent to which the concepts and even the specific experiments carried out in this laboratory course at Harvard spread to other medical schools by word of mouth, by dissemination of the laboratory preparation manual, and by Krayer's people leaving to join (or establish) other departments. Thus by the middle 1960s the Krayer influence had made itself felt in pharmacology courses throughout the United States. Subsequently, to Krayer's dismay, laboratory teaching was abandoned in school after school, as faculty members succumbed to pressure from student activists, who saw this and the rest of basic science as largely "irrelevant."

The immediate postwar years saw Krayer in the role of

organizer—of relief efforts for the German university students and professors, and later as a member of the Unitarian Service Committee Medical Mission to Czechoslovakia (directed by Harvard cardiologist Paul Dudley White). In 1948 Krayer served as chairman of the medical mission to Germany under the same auspices. His precisely crafted, thoughtful, 21-page typewritten report makes interesting reading even today. The question was what should and could be done most effectively to help the reconstruction (intellectual, moral, and physical) of the German universities and of German biomedical science. Krayer's faith in young people was a constant theme of his life, and here it dominated his response to the catastrophe that had befallen his homeland. He wrote:

> Of the "lost" generation, grown up under Hitler and supposedly poisoned beyond hope by the Nazi teaching, not much if anything can be seen. This generation is not lost. On the contrary, many of these young people now in the first years of their university education became skeptical of the Nazi doctrine long before its fallacies and disastrous features began to dawn upon the older generations. If they find response and encouragement at home and abroad as well as appropriate and wise guidance, these young men and women will be the best guarantee for a "better" Germany.

The report made a series of concrete recommendations: study tours abroad for professors who had not been active Nazis, fellowships for younger scientists, reconstruction of libraries, provision of equipment and supplies to selected institutions, establishment of blood banks and plasma fractionation laboratories, and production facilities for antibiotics. But most important, in Krayer's view, was the maintenance and extension of the personal contacts that could help bring the German intellectuals back into the civilized world system.

> The greatest accomplishment of the Mission seems to me to be that for the first time since cultural and political ties between Germany and the

rest of the democratic western world were ruptured ten to fifteen years ago a large group of university members not connected with government and not having political motives have met with their counterparts in German universities on a basis of equality in the scientific field and with the aim and good will to establish friendly relations. . . . have shown the German colleagues that the possibility exists of ending their isolation from the rest of the world. . . .

An interesting side event of these years was the formation of the ill-fated Pharmacotherapy Committee at Harvard. President James B. Conant himself was a prime mover in this program for integrating research and teaching in pharmacology and therapy, with the hope of attracting major corporate and individual donors. Krayer saw in it an opportunity to develop an adequately large single department of pharmacology and pharmacotherapy. In this he anticipated later developments elsewhere, when clinical pharmacology programs with strong roots in basic science became popular. Krayer's memoranda concerning this committee reflect his long-standing interest in the clinical applications of pharmacology and his view that good therapists require a very solid training in basic pharmacology.

Internal disagreements frustrated the committee's work under the chairmanship of Professor of Medicine W. B. Castle. Krayer's failure to concur with plans that struck him as opportunistically donor oriented but scientifically unsound must have irked powerful committee members; his lack of suitability for the role of "team player" surely also made trouble. Abruptly, without consulting Krayer or the other members, Conant dissolved the committee. Not surprisingly, by 1947 we find Krayer again considering a move—this time to Basel—and with both Burwell and Conant actually urging him to leave. As matters developed, however, the Basel chair was given to an internal candidate, and Krayer remained.

The turn in his political fortunes at Harvard came dramatically with the retirement of Burwell, and a few years later, of Conant. George Packer Berry, who was to bring distinction to the Harvard Medical School in many ways, became dean in 1949. He immediately recognized what had been obvious to so many as a rank injustice unworthy of Harvard, and he moved to correct it. So in 1951, after fourteen years as associate professor, Krayer was finally promoted to full professorship. The years of the Berry deanship were flourishing ones for the Department of Pharmacology. Budgets at last grew, plans for reconstruction and expanded space took shape, and a swelling stream of students, trainees, junior faculty, and visiting scientists filled the department. Krayer's relationship with Berry became exceedingly close, and Krayer played an increasingly important part in the affairs of the school, to be recognized before long as one of the wise senior statesmen in the Longwood Avenue basic sciences "quadrangle." His public vindication (if it may be called that) came with his election to the National Academy of Sciences in 1964.

Krayer's style in discourse with his peers could be bluntly honest. An excerpt from his remarks at a meeting of the Preclinical Council sheds light on this tendency to speak the unvarnished truth:

> The task is to build a strong faculty around the HMS quadrangle. We are not, in my opinion, an exceptional group. There are probably half a dozen medical schools in the country who measure up to us or are stronger. . . . We cannot allow to let the reputation of HMS rest with past glory. . . . Let us not be concerned overly much with the problem of personality. . . . Certainly we are not assembled here to form a group of congenial people who have the foremost task of getting along superbly with each other.

Krayer's view of pharmacology was a broad one. Although his own research was wholly devoted to understanding drug action at the physiologic level—on the functions of organs and organ systems—he nonetheless recognized and fully supported the most modern developments. He encouraged the new lines of experimentation by the young people in his department. I was one of the early beneficiaries of this enthusiasm for the newly developing fields of biochemical and molecular pharmacology. S. Ellis, F. L. Plachte, O. H. Straus, and I were able to apply enzymologic methods to studying the pharmacokinetics of cholinesterase inhibitors in dogs and in patients with myasthenia gravis (1943e; 1944a; 1949b), and in the course of those studies to discover some new principles about enzyme-substrate-inhibitor interactions. Krayer's interest was in learning how to quantitate the concept of "eserinization"—the blockade of the destruction of acetylcholine by inhibition of cholinesterases—in order to lay a basis for more rational treatment of myasthenic patients.

In like manner he foresaw the importance of behavioral pharmacology very early. He brought P. B. Dews into the department to establish a laboratory of behavioral pharmacology at a time when the pioneering techniques being developed across the river by B. F. Skinner had not yet been applied anywhere to studying the behavioral effects of drugs.

His plan and outlines for the ideal department he hoped to build reveal his belief that the strength of pharmacology lies in its cross-disciplinary breadth. To understand fully the action of a drug—usually through the joint efforts of several investigators—requires that the effects on whole organisms and their organ systems be related to the *relevant* biochemical and biophysical actions on cells and subcellular elements. He often ridiculed the reductionism that sometimes led to proposed mechanisms of drug action based on some test tube phenomenon at a concentration vastly higher than could ever be attained in vivo.

By 1960 the department had moved into new quarters, financed in part with funds provided by the National Institutes of Health in recognition of the national importance of this center for research and training in pharmacology. And in 1966, just before his retirement, Krayer's department was ranked first among all pharmacology departments in the nation by the American Council on Education.

Seeing the great future of neurobiology on the horizon, and recognizing quality wherever he saw it, Krayer had played the key role in bringing S. W. Kuffler and his colleagues from Johns Hopkins to Harvard. Putting the interests of the medical school ahead of the long-term needs of his own department, Krayer had set aside space for a laboratory of neurophysiology—"temporarily," as such arrangements are often planned to be at the outset. This statesmanlike action certainly brought glory to the Harvard Medical School (including, as it turned out, a Nobel prize), but there are those who argue (and Krayer discovered) that altruism can be a losing proposition amidst the intramural competitions of modern university life.

In the subsequent few years until his retirement, Krayer had to watch, painfully and helplessly, as the stage was set for the dismantling of the strong department he had built. The search for his successor was delayed repeatedly by fruitless philosophical debates about the role of pharmacology; meanwhile, other department heads made plans for possible uses to which one or another part of the pharmacology space could be put. Berry's retirement (in 1965) and Robert H. Ebert's accession to the deanship left pharmacology without an effective advocate. In January 1966, only seven months before his mandatory retirement, Krayer framed a letter of resignation, as a gesture of protest, and was only restrained from sending it by the insistence of his close colleagues that nothing could be accomplished that way. It is ironic, after his unquestioned research and teaching achievements and his worldwide recognition for having built what was probably, on balance, the most important department of pharmacology in the world, that Krayer felt compelled to say to a group of his younger associates at this time: "Frankly, I am impressed more by what I missed or bungled than by what I recognized and resolved."

On August 31, 1966, having reached the mandatory age, Krayer retired to the red brick house in West Newton, and for the next five years he never once returned to Harvard Medical School. Here, under the great apple tree, and in the carefully tended garden with its medicinal plants (especially *Digitalis* and *Veratrum*), was where so many generations of medical students and young scientists had gathered for tea or to drink Rhine wine, and to experience Krayer's sincere interest in their welfare and their educational and scientific progress. Whenever small children were brought to these gatherings, Krayer's stern exterior dissolved. Toddlers would climb onto his lap, and older children took him by the hand. Ullrich Trendelenburg, the son of Krayer's chief at Freiburg and Berlin—a longtime Krayer associate and now professor of pharmacology at Würzburg—recalls this remarkable affinity for children, which he himself experienced as a small child. Trendelenburg writes:

> "Onkel Krayer" was very popular with us. He invariably wore a dark suit, and he was very quiet. Nothing of his considerable temper ever showed when he was with children. It was in 1948 when he visited. . . . he mentioned that lightning had struck his plane, my little nephew wanted to know why being struck by lightning was less dangerous for a plane than for a human being on the ground. Otto promptly turned his full attention to the child, and he gave a full (though slightly simplified) explanation; there was no attempt to "palm off" the inquisitive child. At that moment I realized that Otto had always been willing to give complete answers to our questions, quite in contrast to all those innumerable adults who were convinced that the child was unable to understand it in any case.

For the first six months after his retirement Krayer held the title of Special Consultant to the Dean, but Dean Ebert did not seek advice and by June the post was abruptly abolished. Continued proximity to events at Harvard depressed Krayer deeply. He and his wife began to travel, and in September 1971 they settled in Tucson. The Krayers found this part of the Southwest much to their liking—especially the mountains, where they enjoyed long walks and strenuous hikes. Krayer worked sporadically on a biographic and scientific history of the schools of Rudolf Buchheim (1820–1879) and Rudolf Boehm (1844–1926), pioneers of German pharmacology, but this work was never completed. Making the best of both climates, the Krayers spent winters in Tucson and summers in München. He held a visiting professorship at the University of Arizona School of Medicine and a similar appointment at the Technical University of München, where his former associate Melchior Reiter was professor of pharmacology.

Krayer's abiding devotion to young people (as though they were all surrogates for the children he himself never had) was expressed well in a letter written toward the end of his life. In it, Krayer thanks the faculty and staff at the Technical University of München for their good wishes on the occasion of his eightieth birthday:

> My dear young friends: Your good wishes, at the end of my 80th year, were a welcome present. You gave me the possibility—while I was living amongst you for some time—to get to know your academic work and, more than that, to share some part of your personal thoughts, joys, and sorrows. Contact and exchange of ideas with teachers, coworkers and students were especially close to my heart during the half century of my academic activity. Thanks to your confidence and your friendly inclinations towards me, I am allowed once more, so near to the end of my time, to experience some of the joy which is the source of a fruitful contact between the generations. I thank you for it.

In anticipation of Krayer's eightieth birthday, a celebration and two-day symposium were organized by Thomas F. Burks and his colleagues and held at Tucson in March 1978. There many of his younger associates gathered in a moving display of affection and admiration. The papers presented were later published in *Life Sciences* (22:1113–1372, 1978). At Harvard Medical School an Otto Krayer Lectureship had been established, and the Krayers journeyed to Boston to attend the first lecture, which was delivered on March 13, 1974, by the noted British physiologist Sir Bernard Katz. Subsequent Otto Krayer lecturers (through 1984) have been S. Ebashi, G. Burnstock, H. W. Kosterlitz, E. G. Krebs, J. R. Vane, H. Umezawa, J. W. Black, T. Lindahl, and Y. Nishizuka. In 1982 (posthumously), Harvard established the Otto Krayer Professorship of Pharmacology, the first incumbent of which was Krayer's successor as head of the department, Irving H. Goldberg.

No account of Krayer's life would be complete without noting his services to the American Society for Pharmacology and Experimental Therapeutics. His first major contribution, appropriately, was to serve for five years as associate editor of one of the Society's journals, *Pharmacological Reviews*. This was followed by another five years as editor-in-chief. The year 1957–1958 saw him in the role of president of the Society. He organized and conducted, with great dignity, the centennial celebration, at Johns Hopkins University, commemorating John Jacob Abel, the father of American pharmacology. Krayer worked tirelessly and successfully to acquire a physical home for the Society at Beaumont House in Bethesda, near the National Institutes of Health. He conceived and brought to fruition the Corporate Associates program, which brings financial support to pharmacology from the pharmaceutical and chemical industries. Posthumously, in 1984, the Society that Krayer had served so well instituted the Otto Krayer Award in Pharmacology.

In 1980, after nine years of shuttling between Tucson and München, a macroglobulinemia of long standing progressed and became complicated by other conditions, so that the regimen of twice-yearly travel proved too taxing. Toward the end of 1981 Krayer's health deteriorated rapidly, a prostatic cancer being superimposed on the blood dyscrasia. Repeated hemodialyses and hospitalizations became necessary, he grew progressively weaker and more uncomfortable, and finally, at his own request, he was discharged from hospital to die at home in the care of his wife on March 18, 1982.

With Otto Krayer's passing the world lost one of the great pharmacologists of his time. But to those fortunate enough to have come under his influence he was much more than that. He will be remembered for the uncompromising standards he set—in research, in teaching, in ethical behavior. "Throughout the years," wrote U. Trendelenburg, "he has been the favourite of my younger coworkers. He set them something that is very rare nowadays—an example." Over the course of his thirty years at Harvard, Krayer trained, collaborated with, and set an example for an extraordinary number of scientists, a great many of whom became leaders in pharmacology throughout the world themselves. The names of these people are just as much Krayer's "bibliography" as the compendium of his own publications, and therefore it is appropriate that they be listed here. Represented are scientists from 26 foreign countries on 5 continents, as well as students, staff, and visiting scientists from the United States.

M. Abe	M. A. Aliapoulios	E. Amundsen
G. H. Acheson	A. A. Alousi	R. T. Anselmi
R. Aiman	M. H. Alper	L. Aronow

R. B. Arora
E. B. Astwood
D. Atanackovic
V. Atanackovic
M. L. Bade
B. W. Baker
D. L. Bassett
T. Bayer
J. M. Benforado
H. S. Bennett
F. G. Bergmann
J. R. Blinks
J. L. Borowitz
R. W. Brauer
P. Braveny
F. N. Briggs
L. H. Briggs
W. S. Brimijoin
H. Büch
F. J. Bullock
W. R. Burack
E. A. Carr, Jr.
J. Chamberlain
A. Clark
J. S. Cohen
V. H. Cohn, Jr.
C. W. Cooper
G. L. Coppoc
P. J. Costa
J. R. Crout
H. Croxatto
P. C. Dandiya
G. S. Dawes
C. V. Deliwala
P. B. Dews
R. Di Nirjana
J. Dörner
B. Douglas
P. R. Draskoczy

A. J. Dunipace
S. Ellis
H. L. Ennis
V. Eybl
J. D. Falk
A. E. Farah
J. J. Fischer
W. E. Flacke
J. H. Fleisch
W. W. Fleming
J. M. Flynn
G. N. French
S. Friedman
D. G. Friend
M. E. Fuday
J. Fuentes
M.-P. I. Gabathuler
R. R. Garcia
J. M. Garfield
R. A. Gillis
A. Goldstein
B. Gomez (Alonso
 de la Sierra)
J. S. Gravenstein
P. K. Gujral
J. M. Hagen
P. B. Hagen
R. Hancock
L. S. Harris
K. Hashimoto
D. F. Hawkins
M. L. Heideman, Jr.
P. F. Hirsch
F. Hoffmann
B. Hofheinz
F. Honerjäger
F. A. Howard
A. M. Hughes
H. Ibayashi

A. Illanes
I. R. Innes
S. D. Iversen
O. Jardetzky
J. A. Jehl
B. R. Jewell
H. Jick
N. S. Johary
J. A. Johnson
G. R. Julian
R. Kadatz
A. J. Kaumann
R. T. Kelleher
A. D. Kenny
C. J. Kensler
D. Kessel
R. Kilpatrick
J. Koch-Weser
H. W. Kosterlitz
S. R. Kottegoda
K. Kramer
J. E. Krueger
S. M. Kupchan
S. Z. Langer
D. Lavie
F.-L. Lee
M. V. Leeding
T. H. Li
J. Liebman
A. J. Linenthal
W. K. Long
A. V. Lorenzo
B. E. Lowenstein
M. Lubin
U. C. Luft
G. K. MacLeod
W. A. Mahon
H. M. Maling
J. J. Mandoki

J. F. Marchand
G. Maresh
E. Marley
J. M. Marshall
M. L. Mashford
A. Matallana
H. M. Mazzone
R. J. McKay, Jr.
J. W. McKearney
D. E. McMillan
E. Meilman
C. Mendez
R. Mendez
M. D. Miller
B. A. Mitman
G. K. Moe
E. Moisset de
 Espanes
G. Montes
W. H. Morse
P. L. Munson
A. J. Muskus
 (Arevalo)
A. Nakamura
M. F. Narrod
P. Ofner
C. B. Olson
P. B. Ourisson
M. K. Paasonen
P. Pappas
A. F. Parlow
A. Pekkarinen
T.-C. Peng
S. A. Pereira
F. L. Plachte
R. Pluchino
S. B. Pluchino

L. T. Potter
M. Rabadija
S. Ramachandran
H. A. Ravin
H. W. Reas
M. Reiter
U. I. Richardson
D. S. Riggs
S. H. Robinson
B. H. Rogers
A. Roos
M. A. Root
C. O. Rutledge
H. J.-P. Ryser
J. K. Saelens
M. M. Saint-Paul
F. Sallmann
H. Schaer
I. Scheuling
J. Schmier
G. L. Schmir
H. R. Schröter
B. W. Searle
J. C. Seed
E. E. Seifen
G. W. G. Sharp
C. B. Smith
L. H. Smith
E. Sodi-Pallares
M. Speckert
J. B. Stanbury
J. D. Stoeckle
O. H. Straus
V. S. Subbu
C. R. Swaine
N. Taira
T. Tamai

K. Tanaka
A. H. Tashjian, Jr.
E. W. Thomas
P. J. Thomas
E. Thorogood
C. D. Thron
U. G. Trendelenburg
T.-H. Tsai
R. Tyslowitz
F. C. Uhle
W. Ulbricht
G. E. Vaillant
W. P. Vander Laan,
 Jr.
C. G. Van Dongen
M. van Leeuwen
E. F. Van Maanen
A. Vere
T. K. Wadhwani
M. B. Waller
A. B. Wasthed
J. M. Wattenberg
 (Sanpere)
D. R. Waud
N. Weiner
H. Wells
P. N. Witt
D. E. Wolfe
D. Wolff
A. Wollenberger
E. H. Wood
E. A. Wright
M. M. Wright
S. J. Yaffe
T. S. Yeoh
C. Yuan
B. Zimmermann

A few selected assessments by Krayer's trainees, coworkers, and academic colleagues may serve, collectively, as an appropriate epitaph with which to end this memoir.

P. B. Dews: "One of Krayer's great strengths was his absolute honesty and trustworthiness. When he advised a course of action, one could be quite sure that it represented his judgment of what was best for the individuals involved, untinged by what was best for Krayer. The complete loyalty to his colleagues and helpers engendered a reciprocal loyalty to himself. He was dedicated to the pursuit of excellence but did not believe this pursuit required a lack of consideration of others or ruthlessness. He confidently expected people to rise to excellence."

P. R. Draskoczy: "His integrity and high ethical standards combined with a special place in his heart for those who were suffering or deprived made him both strong and compassionate."

D. S. Riggs: ". . . a man of unflinching conscience and shining integrity, he set his associates—young and old—an example which none of us will ever forget."

A. C. Barger: "He was one of the few teachers in the medical school that I worshipped—for his superb pedagogic skills, his warm human qualities, and his willingness to fight for principles."

B. D. Davis: "Otto was for me the personification of academic integrity and dignity, and I often thought of his high standards of behavior as I watched the deterioration of standards that has been creeping into medical research in recent years."

J. R. Blinks: "He was, without doubt, the finest human being I have ever known."

I AM GRATEFUL to Mrs. Otto Krayer for making numerous source materials available to me and for helpful discussions about past events. Mr. Richard J. Wolfe, archivist at the Countway Library of Harvard Medical School, facilitated my access to Krayer's Harvard files. All original documents upon which this memoir was based can now be found at the Countway Library.

Ullrich Trendelenburg, Melchior Reiter, and Peter B. Dews furnished much useful information both in personal communications and in their published obituary notices, which are listed at the end of these acknowledgments.

Many colleagues in the United States and abroad were helpful to me in large ways and small. Wilhelm Feldberg, G. Kuschinsky, and Marthe Vogt provided information and reminiscences about the Berlin years; and George Fawaz contributed material about the Lebanon period. For recollections of the early Harvard years, A. Baird Hastings and Eugene M. Landis graciously allowed me to impose on their time. My own memories were supplemented by those of Rafael Mendez and Douglas S. Riggs. Others who were helpful included George H. Acheson, John R. Blinks, Alfred E. Farah, Werner E. Flacke, William W. Fleming, Louis S. Harris, Werner F. Mosimann, Paul L. Munson, Matti K. Paasonen, Douglas R. Waud, and Norman Weiner. Some of those mentioned above commented on a draft of the manuscript and pointed out errors, but of course they have no responsibility for the final product. I am grateful to all my colleagues who helped so generously.

German texts of letters or articles have been translated freely here; the reader should consult the original documents for exact wordings. I had help with some of the translations, for which I thank Malcolm Brown, Louisa Laube, and Jean-Pierre von Wartburg.

Finally, for her invaluable and expert assistance at all stages of this project, I am indebted to my secretary, Sharon Fields.

TESTIMONIAL AND OBITUARY ARTICLES

Otto Krayer zum 65. Geburtstag. 1965. Gewidmete Arbeiten erschienen, in *Naunyn-Schmiedebergs Archiv für experimentelle Pathologie und Pharmakologie*, Berlin, Heidelberg, and New York: Springer-Verlag. (Reprinted from 248:1–560; 249:1–528; 250:59–71.)

M. Reiter. 1964. "Otto Krayer zum 65. Geburtstag," *Die Medizinische Welt*, 48:2604–5.

U. Trendelenburg. 1964. "Zum 65. Geburtstag von Professor Dr. Dr.h.c. Otto Krayer," *Arzneimittelforschung*, 14:1171–72.

U. Trendelenburg. 1978. "Remembrances. Otto Krayer," *Life Sciences*, 22:1113–14.

M. Reiter and U. Trendelenburg. 1982. "In memoriam. Otto Krayer," *Naunyn-Schmiedebergs Archives of Pharmacology*, 320:1–2.

H. Rašková. 1982. "Otto Krayer 1899–1982," *Physiologia Bohemoslovaca*, 32:468–69.

P. B. Dews. 1983. "Otto Krayer: 1899–1982," *Trends in Pharmacological Sciences*, 4:143–46.

U. Trendelenburg. 1983. "Otto Krayer: 1899–1982," *The Pharmacologist*, 25:31–32.

P. B. Dews. 1983. "Otto Krayer 1899–1982," *Harvard Medical Alumni Bulletin*, 571:60–61.

HONORS AND DISTINCTIONS

DEGREES AND HONORARY DEGREES

1926 M.D., University of Freiburg
1942 M.A. (Honorary), Harvard University
1957 M.D. (Honorary), University of Freiburg
1962 M.D. (Honorary), University of Göttingen
1973 M.D. (Honorary), Technical University of München

PROFESSIONAL APPOINTMENTS

1926 Assistant in Pharmacology, University of Freiburg (with P. Trendelenburg)
1928 Senior Assistant in Pharmacology, University of Berlin (with P. Trendelenburg)
1929 *Privatdozent* for Pharmacology and Toxicology, University of Berlin
1930 Acting Head, Department of Pharmacology and Toxicology, University of Berlin
1932 Professor Extraordinarius of Pharmacology and Toxicology (with W. Heubner), University of Berlin
1934 Rockefeller Fellow, University College, London (with E. B. Verney)
1934 Visiting Professor and Head, Department of Pharmacology, American University of Beirut
1936 Lecturer in Pharmacology, Harvard Medical School
1937 Associate Professor of Pharmacology, Harvard Medical School
1939 Associate Professor of Comparative Pharmacology and Head, Department of Pharmacology, Harvard Medical School
1951 Professor of Pharmacology, Harvard Medical School
1954 Charles Wilder Professor of Pharmacology, Harvard Medical School
1964 Gustavus Adolphus Pfeiffer Professor of Pharmacology, Harvard Medical School
1966 Gustavus Adolphus Pfeiffer Professor of Pharmacology, Emeritus, Harvard Medical School

MEMBERSHIPS

Deutsche Pharmakologische Gesellschaft (1927)
Deutsche Chemische Gesellschaft (1933, resigned 1937)
American Society for Pharmacology and Experimental Therapeutics (1938); President (1957–1958); Chairman, Board of Publications Trustees (1960–1962)
New York Academy of Sciences (1943); Fellow (1951); Life Member (1975)
American Association for the Advancement of Science (1944)
Society for Experimental Biology and Medicine (1944)
American Academy of Arts and Sciences (1949)
Pharmacological Society of Canada (1957)
National Academy of Sciences (1964)

HONORARY MEMBERSHIPS

Alpha Omega Alpha, Harvard Medical School (1943)
Society for Pharmacology and Therapeutics of the Argentinian Medical Association (1947)
Czechoslovakian Medical Society of J. E. Purkinje (1948)
Deutsche Pharmakologische Gesellschaft (1952)
British Pharmacological Society (1956)
Finnish Pharmacological Society (1961)
Deutsche Akademie der Naturforscher Leopoldina (1962)
Swiss Academy of Medical Sciences (1964)
Japanese Pharmacological Society (1972)

PROFESSIONAL AND PUBLIC SERVICE

Associate Editor, *Ergebnisse der Physiologie, biologischen Chemie und experimentellen Pharmakologie* (1933–1935, 1939–1976)
Treasurer, Boston Committee to Help German Scientists (1946–1948)
Member, Unitarian Medical Mission to Czechoslovakia (1946)
Chairman, Unitarian Medical Mission to Germany (1948)
Associate Editor, *Pharmacological Reviews* (1948–1953)
Member, Pharmacology Study Section, U.S. Public Health Service (1950–1954)
Consultant, Eli Lilly & Co. (1950–1956)
Editor-in-chief, *Pharmacological Reviews* (1953–1959)

Member, Scientific Advisory Committee, Massachusetts General Hospital (1959–1961)
Member, U.S. National Committee for the International Union of Physiological Sciences (1959–1965)
Special Consultant to the Dean, Harvard Medical School (1967)
Member, Editorial Board, *Annual Review of Pharmacology* (1967–1972)

AWARDS AND HONORS

Order of the White Lion, Class IV, Republic of Czechoslovakia (1946)
Medal for Service to the University, Charles University, Prague (1946)
Commemorative Plaque, Czechoslovakian Medical Society (1946)
Honorary Citizen of Köndringen (1957)
Torald Sollmann Award of the American Society for Pharmacology and Experimental Therapeutics (1961)
Schmiedeberg Plakette of the German Pharmacological Society (1964)
Festschrift (65th Birthday), *Naunyn-Schmiedebergs Archiv für experimentelle Pathologie und Pharmakologie*, volumes 248–250 (1964)
Otto Krayer Lectureship at Harvard Medical School (established, 1966)
Research Achievement Award, American Heart Association (1969)
Otto Krayer Professorship of Pharmacology, Harvard Medical School (established posthumously, 1982)

LECTURESHIPS

Mayo Foundation Lecturer, Rochester, Minnesota (1947, 1952)
University Lecturer, Aberdeen, Scotland (1955)
Litchfield Lecturer, University of Oxford, England (1955)
Special Lecturer, University College, London, England (1955)
Fahr Lecturer, University of Minnesota (1956)
University Lecturer, Helsinki, Finland (1961)
A. N. Richards Lecturer, Physiological Society of Philadelphia (1962)
Visiting Lecturer, Tohoku Medical Society, Sendai, Japan (1965)

Visiting Centennial Professor of Pharmacology, Howard University Medical School (1966)
Visiting Professor of Pharmacology, Stanford University (1968)
Visiting Professor, Department of Pharmacology, Technical University of München (1972–1980)
Visiting Professor, Department of Pharmacology, College of Medicine, University of Arizona (1972–1980)

BIBLIOGRAPHY

1926

O. Krayer. Die pharmakologischen Eigerschaften des reinen Apokodeins. Arch. Exp. Pathol. Pharmakol., 111:60–67.

1928

a. O. Krayer and G. Sato. Schilddrüsenwirkung und autonomes Nervensystem. Arch. Exp. Pathol. Pharmakol., 128:67–81.
b. O. Krayer. Über Verteilung und Ausscheidung des Jodes nach Zufuhr von Schilddrüsenstoffen. Arch. Exp. Pathol. Pharmakol., 128:116–25.

1929

O. Krayer. Die akute Kreislaufwirkung des Neosalvarsans. I. Mitteilung: Die Analyse der Kreislaufwirkung. Arch. Exp. Pathol. Pharmakol., 146:20–43.

1930

a. O. Krayer. Die akute Kreislaufwirkung des Neosalvarsans. II. Mitteilung: Über die Ursache der Kreislaufwirkung. Arch. Exp. Pathol. Pharmakol., 153:50–66.
b. O. Krayer. Über die Beziehung zwischen Pulsfrequenz, Minutenvolumen und Venendruck am isolierten Saügetierherzen. Verh. Dtsch. Pharmakol. Ges., 157:90–91.

1931

a. O. Krayer. Die Theorie der Digitaliswirkung. Verh. Dtsch. Ges. Kreislaufforsch., IV. Tagung, 163–90.
b. O. Krayer. Die Physiologie der Coronardurchblutung. Verh. Dtsch. Ges. Inn. Med., XLIII. Kongress Wiesbaden, 237–47.
c. O. Krayer. Paul Trendelenburg. Arch. Exp. Pathol. Pharmakol., 162:III–IX. (Obituary.)
d. O. Krayer. Versuche am insuffizienten Herzen. Arch. Exp. Pathol. Pharmakol., 162:1–28.
e. O. Krayer and A. Rühl. Über die Wirkung einer reinen Gefässerweiterung auf den Gesamtkreislauf. Arch. Exp. Pathol. Pharmakol., 162:70–85.

f. O. Krayer. Der toxikologische Nachweis des Coniins. Arch. Exp. Pathol. Pharmakol., 162:342–72.
g. O. Krayer and W. Koll. Coniinähnliche Eigenschaften einiger Aminbasen. Arch. Exp. Pathol. Pharmakol., 162:373–84.
h. P. Trendelenburg's Grundlagen der allgemeinen und speziellen Arzneiverordnung, 3d ed. rev. O. Krayer. Berlin: Springer.

1932

a. O. Krayer. Über die Behandlung von Kreislaufstörungen mit Organ- und Muskelextrakten. Bemerkungen zur Pharmakologie. Dtsch. Med. Wochenschr., 58:123–24.
b. O. Krayer and E. Schütz. Mechanische Leistung und Aktionsstrom des Warmblüterherzens. Verh. Dtsch. Pharmakol. Ges., XI. Tagung, 99–100.
c. O. Krayer and E. Schütz. Mechanische Leistung und einphasisches Elektrogramm am Herz-Lungen-Präparat des Hundes. Z. Biol., 92:453–61.

1933

a. O. Krayer. Ist die Integrität der sympathischen Schilddrüseninnervation notwendig für die thyreotrope Wirkung des Hypophysenvorderlappens? Arch. Exp. Pathol. Pharmakol., 171:473–79.
b. W. Feldberg and O. Krayer. Nachweis einer bei Vagusreiz freiwerdenden azetylcholinähnlichen Substanz am Warmblüterherzen. Verh. Dtsch. Ges. Kreislaufforsch, VI. Tagung, 81–83.
c. W. Feldberg and O. Krayer. Das Auftreten eines azetylcholinartigen Stoffes im Herzvenenblut von Warmblütern bei Reizung der Nervi vagi. Arch. Exp. Pathol. Pharmakol., 172:170–93.
d. O. Krayer. Zur Kreislaufwirkung der Leberpräparate des Handels. Dtsch. Med. Wochenschr., 59:576–78.
e. O. Krayer. Zur Pharmakotherapie der Herzinsuffizienz. Erkrankungen des Herzmuskels und der Herzklappen, pp. 84–94. Dresden and Leipzig: Steinkopff.

1934

a. F. Grabe, O. Krayer, and K. Seelkopf. Beitrag zur Aufklärung der kreislaufwirksamen (adrenalinähnlichen) Stoffe in Leberextrakten. Klin. Wochenschr., 13:1381–83.

1934

b. O. Krayer and E. B. Verney. Veränderung des Acetylcholingehaltes im Blute der Coronarvenen unter dem Einfluss einer Blutdrucksteigerung durch Adrenalin. Klin. Wochenschr., 13:1250–51.

c. *Die Hormone. Ihre Physiologie und Pharmakologie,* by Paul Trendelenburg, vol. 2, ed. O. Krayer. Berlin: Springer.

1935

a. O. Krayer. Beitrag zur Aufklärung der Natur der kreislaufwirksamen Stoffe in als Heilmittel verwandten Leberextrakten. Institut de Recherches Physiologiques de Moscou. Problèmes de Biologie et de Médecine Volume Jubilaire dédié au Prof. Lina Stern, pp. 179–83.

b. O. Krayer and E. B. Verney. Reflektorische Beeinflussung des Gehaltes an Acetylcholin im Blute der Coronarvenen. Arch. Exp. Pathol. Pharmakol., 180:75–92.

1937

O. Krayer. Kürbissamen als Bandwurmmittel. Klin. Wochenschr., 16:1651–52.

1938

P. *Trendelenburg's Grundlagen der allgemeinen und speziellen Arzneiverordnung,* 4th ed. rev. O. Krayer. Berlin: Springer.

1941

a. D. G. Friend and O. Krayer. The estimation by a manometric method of the activity of cholinesterase in lymph. J. Pharmacol. Exp. Ther., 71:246–52.

b. D. G. Friend and O. Krayer. The elimination of prostigmine. J. Pharmacol. Exp. Ther., 72:15.

1942

a. O. Krayer and R. Mendez. Studies on veratrum alkaloids. I. The action of veratrine upon the isolated mammalian heart. J. Pharmacol. Exp. Ther., 74:350–64.

b. R. P. Linstead and O. Krayer. Effect of l-ascorbic acid on the isolated frog heart. Science, 95:332–33.

c. O. Krayer, R. Mendez, E. Moisset de Espanes, and R. P. Linstead. Pharmacology and chemistry of substances with cardiac activity. I. Effect of unsaturated lactones on the isolated frog heart. J. Pharmacol. Exp. Ther., 74:372–80.
d. O. H. Lowry, O. Krayer, A. B. Hastings, and R. P. Tucker. Effect of anoxemia on myocardium of the isolated heart of the dog. Proc. Soc. Exp. Biol. N.Y., 49:670–74.
e. E. B. Astwood, J. M. Flynn, and O. Krayer. Effect of continuous intravenous infusion of glucose in normal dogs. J. Clin. Invest., 21:621.
f. O. Krayer. The effect of veratrum alkaloids on circulatory reflexes. Fed. Proc. Fed. Am. Soc. Exp. Biol., 1:156.

1943

a. O. Krayer, R. P. Linstead, and D. Todd. Pharmacology and chemistry of substances with cardiac activity. II. Effect of l-ascorbic acid and some related compounds and of hydrogen peroxide on the isolated frog heart. J. Pharmacol. Exp. Ther., 77:113–22.
b. G. K. Moe and O. Krayer. Studies on veratrum alkaloids. II. The action of veratridine and cevine upon the isolated mammalian heart. J. Pharmacol. Exp. Ther., 77:220–28.
c. O. Krayer. Action of l-ascorbic acid upon the isolated frog heart. Proc. Soc. Exp. Biol. N.Y., 53:51–52.
d. O. Krayer, E. H. Wood, and G. Montes. Studies on veratrum alkaloids. IV. The sites of the heart rate lowering action of veratridine. J. Pharmacol. Exp. Ther., 79:215–24.
e. S. Ellis, O. Krayer, and F. L. Plachte. Studies on physostigmine and related substances. III. Breakdown products of physostigmine; their inhibitory effect on cholinesterase and their pharmacological action. J. Pharmacol. Exp. Ther., 79:309–19.

1944

a. O. Krayer, A. Goldstein, and F. L. Plachte. Studies on physostigmine and related substances. I. Quantitative relation between dosage of physostigmine and inhibition of cholinesterase activity in the blood serum of dogs. J. Pharmacol. Exp. Ther., 80:8–30.
b. G. K. Moe, D. L. Bassett, and O. Krayer. Studies on veratrum

alkaloids. V. The effect of veratridine and cevine upon the circulation in anesthetized dogs, with particular reference to femoral arterial flow. J. Pharmacol. Exp. Ther., 80:272–84.
c. O. Krayer, G. K. Moe, and R. Mendez. Studies on veratrum alkaloids. VI. Protoveratrine: Its comparative toxicity and its circulatory action. J. Pharmacol. Exp. Ther., 82:167–86.
d. O. Krayer. A difference in cardiodecelerator action between digitoxin and digitoxigenin. Proc. Soc. Exp. Biol. N.Y., 57:167–69.

1946

a. H. M. Maling and O. Krayer. The action of erythrophleum alkaloids upon the isolated mammalian heart. J. Pharmacol. Exp. Ther., 86:66–78.
b. O. Krayer and G. H. Acheson. The pharmacology of the veratrum alkaloids. Physiol. Rev., 26:383–446.
c. A. Farah and O. Krayer. The action of dimethylaminoethanol upon the heart-lung preparation of the dog. Fed. Proc. Fed. Am. Soc. Exp. Biol., 5:177–78.
d. O. Krayer, A. Farah, and F. C. Uhle. Pharmacology and chemistry of substances with cardiac activity. IV. Effect of methylaminoethanol, dimethylaminoethanol, and related substances on the isolated mammalian heart. J. Pharmacol. Exp. Ther., 88:277–86.

1947

O. Krayer, J. C. Aub, I. T. Nathanson, and P. C. Zamecnik. The influence of antitoxin upon the action of *Clostridium oedematiens* toxin in the heart-lung preparation of the dog. J. Clin. Invest., 26:411–15.

1948

a. O. Krayer and A. Farah. Action of cysteine and of dimercaptopropanol in heart failure caused by sodium bismuth tartrate. Fed. Proc. Fed. Am. Soc. Exp. Biol., 7:235.
b. A. Wollenberger and O. Krayer. Experimental heart failure caused by central nervous system depressants and local anesthetics. J. Pharmacol. Exp. Ther., 94:439–43.

1949

a. O. Krayer, S. B. Wolbach, J. H. Mueller, and G. B. Wislocki. Reid Hunt. Harv. Med. Alumni Bull., 23:39–42. (Obituary.)
b. A. Goldstein, O. Krayer, M. A. Root, G. H. Acheson, and M. E. Doherty. Plasma neostigmine levels and cholinesterase inhibition in dogs and myasthenic patients. J. Pharmacol. Exp. Ther., 96:56–85.
c. O. Krayer. Veratramine, an antagonist to the cardioaccelerator action of epinephrine. Proc. Soc. Exp. Biol. N.Y., 70:631–32.
d. O. Krayer. Studies on veratrum alkaloids. VIII. Veratramine, an antagonist to the cardioaccelerator action of epinephrine. J. Pharmacol. Exp. Ther., 96:422–37.
e. E. Meilman and O. Krayer. Clinical studies on the pure veratrum alkaloids: Protoveratrine and veratridine. Forty-first Annual Meeting, American Society for Clinical Investigation, Atlantic City, May 2. J. Clin. Invest., 28:798.
f. O. Krayer. Studies on veratrum alkaloids. IX. The inhibition by veratrosine of the cardioaccelerator action of epinephrine and of norepinephrine. J. Pharmacol. Exp. Ther., 97:256–65.
g. O. Krayer and E. F. Van Maanen. Studies on veratrum alkaloids. X. The inhibition by veratramine of the positive chronotropic effect of accelerans stimulation and of norepinephrine. J. Pharmacol. Exp. Ther., 97:301–7.
h. O. Krayer. The pharmacological basis for the use of veratrum alkaloids in the treatment of hypertension. Proc. Rudolf Virchow Med. Soc. City N.Y., 8:126–27.

1950

a. *Lectures—Unitarian Service Committee Medical Mission to Germany, July 2–September 3, 1948*, ed. O. Krayer. Berlin: Springer.
b. E. Meilman and O. Krayer. Clinical studies on veratrum alkaloids. I. The action of protoveratrine and veratridine in hypertension. Circulation, 1:204–13.
c. O. Krayer. A quantitative comparison of the antiaccelerator action of veratramine and jervine. J. Pharmacol. Exp. Ther., 98:19.
d. K. Kramer, U. Luft, and O. Krayer. Action of epinephrine and veratramine upon heart rate and oxygen consumption in the

heart-lung preparation of the dog. Fed. Proc. Fed. Am. Soc. Exp. Biol., 9:292.
e. M. Reiter and O. Krayer. Jervine and pseudojervine, antagonists to the cardioaccelerator action of epinephrine and of accelerans stimulation. J. Pharmacol. Exp. Ther., 98:27.
f. O. Krayer and M. Reiter. Studies on veratrum alkaloids. XI. Jervine and pseudojervine, antagonists to the cardioaccelerator action of epinephrine and of accelerans stimulation. Arch. Int. Pharmacodyn. Ther., 81:409–26.
g. O. Krayer. Studies on veratrum alkaloids. XII. A quantitative comparison of the antiaccelerator cardiac action of veratramine, veratrosine, jervine and pseudojervine. J. Pharmacol. Exp. Ther., 98:427–36.
h. O. Krayer. Solanum alkaloids with antiaccelerator cardiac activity. Fed. Proc. Fed. Am. Soc. Exp. Biol., 9:292.
i. O. Krayer and L. H. Briggs. Studies on solanum alkaloids. I. The antiaccelerator cardiac action of β-dihydrosolasodine and tetrahydrosolasodine. Br. J. Pharmacol., 5:118–24.
j. O. Krayer and L. H. Briggs. Studies on solanum alkaloids. II. The antiaccelerator cardiac action of solasodine and some of its derivatives. Br. J. Pharmacol., 5:517–25.
k. O. Krayer. The antiaccelerator cardiac action of quinine and quinidine. J. Pharmacol. Exp. Ther., 100:146–50.
l. O. Krayer. Untersuchungen über die Kreislaufwirkung der Veratrumalkaloide. Arch. Exp. Pathol. Pharmakol., 209:405–20.

1951

a. J. J. Mandoki, C. Mendez, R. R. Garcia, and O. Krayer. The action of veratramine and epinephrine on the functional refractory period of A-V conduction. J. Pharmacol. Exp. Ther., 101:25.
b. O. Krayer. Quinine-like action of veratramine upon the single twitch and upon the "veratrine response" of the sartorius muscle of the frog. Fed. Proc. Fed. Am. Soc. Exp. Biol., 10:316.
c. O. Krayer, F. C. Uhle, and P. Ourisson. Studies on veratrum alkaloids. XIV. The antiaccelerator cardiac action of derivatives of veratramine and jervine and of synthetic steroid secondary

alkamines obtained from pregnenolone and from sapogenins. J. Pharmacol. Exp. Ther., 102:261–68.
d. O. Krayer and H. W. George. Studies on veratrum alkaloids. XV. The quinine-like effect of veratramine upon the single twitch and upon the "veratrine response" of the sartorius muscle of the frog. J. Pharmacol. Exp. Ther., 103:249–58.
e. O. Krayer, J. J. Mandoki, and C. Mendez. Studies on veratrum alkaloids. XVI. The action of epinephrine and of veratramine on the functional refractory period of the auriculo-ventricular transmission in the heart-lung preparation of the dog. J. Pharmacol. Exp. Ther., 103:412–19.

1952

a. O. Krayer, B. H. Rogers, S. M. Kupchan, and C. V. Deliwala. Pharmacological and chemical relation between the veratrum alkaloids and the zygadenus alkaloids. Fed. Proc. Fed. Am. Soc. Exp. Biol., 11:364.
b. R. B. Arora, E. Meilman, and O. Krayer. Action of veratramine and of sympathomimetic amines upon the automaticity of the atrio-ventricular node. Fed. Proc. Fed. Am. Soc. Exp. Biol., 11:318.
c. P. Ourisson and O. Krayer. Antagonistic action to the cardio-accelerator effect of ephedrine, synephrine, isuprel, tuamine and oenethyl. Fed. Proc. Fed. Am. Soc. Exp. Biol., 11:381.
d. O. Krayer. Antiaccelerator cardiac agents. J. M. Sinai Hosp. N.Y., 19:53–69.
e. E. Meilman and O. Krayer. Clinical studies on veratrum alkaloids. II. The dose-response relations of protoveratrine in hypertension. Circulation, 6:212–21.
f. R. B. Arora and O. Krayer. The antiveratrinic action of the cardiac glycosides and of bufotoxin. J. Pharmacol. Exp. Ther., 106:371–72.
g. *P. Trendelenburg's Grundlagen der allgemeinen und speziellen Arzneiverordnung*, 7th ed., rev. O. Krayer and M. Kiese. Berlin, Göttingen, and Heidelberg: Springer.

1953

a. O. Krayer, S. M. Kupchan, C. V. Deliwala, and B. H. Rogers. Untersuchungen über die Veratrumalkaloide. XVIII. Die

chemischen und pharmakologischen Beziehungen zwischen den Zygadenusalkaloiden und den Veratrumalkaloiden. Arch. Exp. Pathol. Pharmakol., 219:371–85.
b. O. Krayer. The history of the Bezold-Jarisch effect. Presented at a symposium, Reflexes from the Cardiac and Pulmonary Areas. Nineteenth International Physiology Congress, Montreal.

1954

a. H. W. Kosterlitz, O. Krayer, and A. Matallana. The effect of moderately large doses of veratramine and veratrosine on the rhythm of the acutely denervated heart of the cat. J. Physiol. (London), 124:40P.
b. O. Krayer and P. Ourisson. Studies on veratrum alkaloids. XIX. The action of veratramine upon cardioacceleration caused by ephedrine, tyramine, phenylephrine and isopropylarterenol. J. Pharmacol. Exp. Ther., 112:341–55.
c. O. Krayer. Veratrum alkaloids. In: *Pharmacology in Medicine*, ed. V. A. Drill, pp. 1–10. New York: McGraw-Hill.

1955

a. O. Krayer and J. M. Benforado. Die Schlagfrequenz des akut denervierten Herzens im Herz-Lungen-Präparat des Hundes mit einem Hinweis auf die frequenzbeschleunigende Wirkung des Adrenalins. Pflüg. Arch. Ges. Physiol., 260:177–87.
b. O. Krayer, R. B. Arora, and E. Meilman. Studies on veratrum alkaloids. XXI. The action of veratramine upon impulse generation in the dog heart. J. Pharmacol. Exp. Ther., 113:446–59.
c. H. W. Kosterlitz, O. Krayer, and A. Matallana. Studies on veratrum alkaloids. XXII. Periodic activity of the sino-auricular node of the denervated cat heart caused by veratramine. J. Pharmacol. Exp. Ther., 113:460–69.
d. S. Ellis and O. Krayer. Properties of a toxin from the salivary gland of the shrew, *Blarina brevicauda*. J. Pharmacol. Exp. Ther., 114:127–37.

1956

a. O. Krayer and J. Fuentes. Chronotropic cardiac action of reserpine. Fed. Proc. Fed. Am. Soc. Exp. Biol., 15:1462.

b. F. C. Uhle, B. A. Mitman, and O. Krayer. Synthetic esters of dimethylaminoethanol exhibiting positive inotropic cardiac activity. J. Pharmacol. Exp. Ther., 116:444–49.
c. I. R. Innes, H. W. Kosterlitz, and O. Krayer. Studies on veratrum alkaloids. XXIV. The inhibition by veratramine and veratrosine of the cardioaccelerator effect of electrical stimulation of the accelerator nerves. J. Pharmacol. Exp. Ther., 117:317–21.

1957

a. M. K. Paasonen and O. Krayer. Effect of reserpine upon the mammalian heart. Fed. Proc. Fed. Am. Soc. Exp. Biol., 16:326–27.
b. O. Krayer and M. K. Paasonen. Direct cardiac action of reserpine. Acta Physiol. Scand., 42:88–89.
c. I. R. Innes and O. Krayer. Depletion of the cardiac catecholamines by reserpine. J. Physiol. (London), 139:18P.

1958

a. O. Krayer. Veratrum alkaloids. In: *Pharmacology in Medicine*, 2d ed., ed. V. A. Drill, pp. 515–24. New York: McGraw-Hill.
b. O. Krayer and J. Fuentes. Changes in heart rate caused by direct cardiac action of reserpine. J. Pharmacol. Exp. Ther., 123:145–52.
c. M. K. Paasonen and O. Krayer. The release of norepinephrine from the mammalian heart by reserpine. J. Pharmacol. Exp. Ther., 123:153–60.
d. I. R. Innes and O. Krayer. Studies on veratrum alkaloids. XXVII. The negative chronotropic action of veratramine and reserpine in the heart depleted of catecholamines. J. Pharmacol. Exp. Ther., 124:245–51.
e. I. R. Innes, O. Krayer, and D. R. Waud. The action of *Rauwolfia* alkaloids on the heart rate and on the functional refractory period of atrio-ventricular transmission in the heart-lung preparation of the dog. J. Pharmacol. Exp. Ther., 124:324–32.
f. D. R. Waud, S. R. Kottegoda, and O. Krayer. Threshold dose and time course of norepinephrine depletion of the mammalian heart by reserpine. J. Pharmacol. Exp. Ther., 124:340–46.

1959

M. K. Paasonen and O. Krayer. The content of noradrenaline and adrenaline in the rat heart after administration of *Rauwolfia* alkaloids. Experientia, 15:75–76.

1960

D. R. Waud and O. Krayer. The rate-increasing effect of epinephrine and norepinephrine and its modification by experimental time in the isolated heart of normal and reserpine-pretreated dogs. J. Pharmacol. Exp. Ther., 128:352–57.

1961

a. O. Krayer. The history of the Bezold-Jarisch effect. Arch. Exp. Pathol. Pharmakol., 240:361–68.
b. O. Krayer, E. B. Astwood, D. R. Waud, and M. H. Alper. Rate-increasing action of corticotropin and of α-intermedin in the isolated mammalian heart. Proc. Natl. Acad. Sci. USA, 47:1227–36.

1962

a. O. Krayer, M. H. Alper, and M. K. Paasonen. Action of guanethidine and reserpine upon the isolated mammalian heart. J. Pharmacol. Exp. Ther., 135:164–73.
b. O. Krayer, B. D. Davis, and S. W. Kuffler. Obituary—Otto Loewi. Pharmacologist, 4:47–49.
c. O. Krayer. Accidents in the pursuit of knowledge. (Sollmann Award oration.) Pharmacologist, 4:68–76.

1963

a. O. Krayer. Über chronotrope Herzwirkung. Klin. Wochenschr., 41:272–76.
b. M. H. Alper, W. Flacke, and O. Krayer. Pharmacology of reserpine and its implications for anesthesia. Anesthesiology, 24:524–42.

1964

D. F. Hawkins, F. C. Uhle, and O. Krayer. Studies on veratrum alkaloids. XXXVII. Chronotropic cardiac action and toxicity of

N-alkyl derivatives of veratramine. J. Pharmacol. Exp. Ther., 145:275–85.

1965

O. Krayer, W. Mosimann, and G. Schroder. Positive chronotropic cardiac effect of methyl guanidine. Fed. Proc. Fed. Am. Soc. Exp. Biol., 24:487.

1966

O. Krayer, W. Mosimann, and G. Silver. Rate-increasing action of methylguanidine upon the isolated mammalian heart. J. Pharmacol. Exp. Ther., 154:73–82.

1972

O. Krayer, N. Weiner, and W. Mosimann. Blood norepinephrine levels during responses of the heart-lung preparation to methylguanidine. J. Pharmacol. Exp. Ther., 181:108–15.

1977

O. Krayer and E. Meilman. Veratrum alkaloids with antihypertensive activity. In: *Handbook of Experimental Pharmacology*, Heffter-Heubner, new ser., ed. G. V. R. Born, O. Eichler, A. Farah, H. Herken, and A. D. Welch, pp. 547–70. Berlin, Heidelberg, and New York: Springer-Verlag.

REBECCA CRAIGHILL LANCEFIELD
January 5, 1895–March 3, 1981

BY MACLYN McCARTY

REBECCA CRAIGHILL LANCEFIELD was born on January 5, 1895, in Fort Wadsworth, New York, where her father, Col. William E. Craighill, was stationed as an officer in the U.S. Army Engineer Corps. As a member of an Army family, she lived in many different communities during her early years. After graduating from Wellesley College, however, and spending one year teaching in a girls school in Vermont, she returned to New York City. Except for a year's sojourn at the University of Oregon, she spent the remainder of her life there.

Her first move toward a career in science apparently came at Wellesley. Stimulated by her roommate's course in zoology, she dropped her notion of majoring in French and English and concentrated her efforts on biology. By the time she graduated in 1916, she was eager to begin graduate training. But she was forced to compromise: funds were short because of the death of her father, and her mother needed her help in supporting her five sisters. She saved enough from her earnings as a teacher during the following year to enable her to accept a scholarship with graduate tuition at Teachers' College of Columbia University. Fortunately, although this scholarship (established by the Daughters of the Cincinnati for daughters of Army and Navy officers) specified Teachers'

College, it was not necessary for her to take her courses there. Thus she spent the year in Hans Zinsser's Department of Bacteriology at the College of Physicians and Surgeons of Columbia University. Here she was able to broaden substantially her knowledge and experience in the branch of biology that interested her most.

There were a series of notable events in Rebecca Craighill's life in the spring of 1918. She received her master's degree from Columbia University and shortly thereafter was married to Donald Lancefield, a fellow graduate student at Columbia who was in the famous Department of Genetics under T. H. Morgan. Even more significant from the point of view of her future career in research, her application for a position at the Rockefeller Institute for Medical Research was accepted. That June she became a technical assistant to O. T. Avery and A. R. Dochez.

The timing of her arrival at the Rockefeller Hospital was of considerable importance in shaping the course of her life's work. Until late in 1917, Avery and Dochez had concentrated their efforts on studies of the pneumococcus. At that time, however, they traveled to Texas as consultants to the Surgeon General of the Army to investigate an outbreak of serious streptococcal infections that had been superimposed on a measles epidemic in a number of military installations there. Returning to New York with a collection of streptococcal strains that had been isolated during the visit, they set about trying to determine whether, as in pneumococcus, there were separate and distinct types of streptococci involved in the epidemic rather than a single unvarying pathogen. Their approach was to use the serological procedures that had proved successful in delineating pneumococcal types: the agglutination reaction and the protection of mice with specific antisera.

Their progress in these efforts was reported at a conference on *Streptococcus hemolyticus* that was held at the Princeton laboratories of the Rockefeller Institute on June 1, 1918. The discussions at the conference dealt with various aspects of the problem of streptococcal infections, but much attention was focused on the recently isolated strains. Avery prefaced his comments with this statement: "It is rather difficult from a study of the strains that we have isolated to tell whether they are all alike, whether they constitute one or several types." Dochez later enlarged on this point, describing the difficulties they had encountered with agglutination reactions as well as with mouse protection experiments. He concluded: "Up to now, however, we have been unable to obtain immune serum which affords any considerable degree of protection for white mice against experimental infection. We are still working along this line and it is possible that the proper combination of immune serum and test animal may be obtained."

It was to assist in this effort that Rebecca Lancefield was brought into the laboratory soon after. And although she had had no real opportunity before to display her special talents, it was clearly a case of bringing the right person to the right place at the right time. Within a year they had together identified four distinct serological types—as determined both by agglutination and mouse protection—that served to classify 70 percent of the 125 strains studied. The paper describing these results was submitted for publication on June 1, 1919, one year to the day after the conference. There can be little doubt that Rebecca Lancefield's native talent for solving this type of problem, perhaps accelerated in its development under the tutelage of two established masters, was a prime factor in the success of these studies. That she contributed much more than simply technical help was tacitly acknowledged by the inclusion of her name as a coauthor of the paper, a type of recognition seldom accorded to technical assistants in those days. It was a major publication, running to some thirty-four pages and replete with tables that documented the findings in great detail. In addition to being the first account of specific types among the hemolytic streptococci, it also represented a record of the first encounter between these microorganisms and the investigator who was destined over the next five decades to become the master of their diversity.

At this point, however, the work with these streptococcal strains ended temporarily. The war was over and with it the Army support for the studies. Dochez went to Johns Hopkins; Avery returned to his first love, the pneumococcus; and Lancefield moved back to Columbia where she worked as a research assistant on problems of *Drosophila* genetics. Nevertheless, the streptococcal strains were not all simply discarded. Some of them remain today in the Lancefield collection as reference type strains of group A streptococci, still identified by the same letter and number designation that was assigned on their isolation in 1917.

In 1922, after her year at the University of Oregon, during which she and her husband Donald both taught, Lancefield came back to the Rockefeller Hospital for good. Mrs. L. (as she came to be affectionately known to her colleagues) was now associated with the rheumatic fever service of Dr. Homer Swift rather than with the pneumonia service. She was also enrolled again as a graduate student at Columbia, and most of the laboratory work for her Ph.D. thesis was carried out at Rockefeller on a problem concerned with the so-called "green" or viridans streptococci. These streptococci were erroneously suspected of having something to do with rheumatic fever; her studies, published in her thesis and in two papers in the *Journal of Experimental Medicine,* helped to dispel this notion. The viridans streptococci are an extraordinarily heterogeneous and protean group of microorganisms. It must have been of some relief to her—and of considerable importance to science—that she was able before too long to resume her studies of hemolytic streptococci.

It is important to realize that the relationship of hemolytic streptococci to human disease was not well characterized in the period immediately following World War I. They were looked upon as important primarily as secondary invaders in such situations as puerperal fever, wound infections, and pneumonia that followed measles or influenza, as in the Army camp epidemics. The great prevalence of primary streptococcal sore throat did not appear to be clearly recognized, and the key role of streptococci in scarlet fever was yet to be discovered. There was even less of a clue with regard to their implication in the pathogenesis of rheumatic fever and glomerulonephritis. Thus Lancefield's early studies were initiated before the present picture of streptococcal disease had been formulated. The results that she obtained had much to do with originating and crystallizing these concepts and with providing a basis for understanding the clinical and epidemiological patterns of disease caused by these organisms.

Although Lancefield was no longer directly associated with Avery, their laboratories were in close proximity, and she continued to look to him for advice and counsel in the development of her research. As a great admirer of his scientific insights and approaches, she was well prepared to bring to her studies of the streptococci the same points of view that he had used so successfully in the case of pneumococci. Consequently, she considered the laborious and detailed serological analysis of the large family of streptococci as being primarily an essential means to a more significant end: that of determining the chemical nature and biological significance of the antigenic substances responsible for the serological reactions. The systematic classification that emerged from her serological grouping and typing of streptococci was not in her mind the ultimate goal of her research. Rather, it was a needed step in identifying the most significant antigens and determining their role in the disease-producing capacity of the microorganisms.

In the mid-1920s she succeeded in obtaining two antigens in soluble form from hemolytic streptococci: one that was type specific and responsible for the distinction between the strains from the epidemic in 1918 and another that was species specific and present in all of the human strains that she examined. She soon encountered a surprising result in attempting to determine the nature of the type-specific antigen. Avery and Heidelberger had earlier established that the type-specific antigens of the pneumococcus were polysaccharides present in the capsule of the organism; subsequently, other pathogenic bacteria had been found to be similarly equipped with capsular polysaccharides that determined type specificity. Lancefield thus anticipated a similar situation in streptococci, but after careful studies was forced to conclude that this was not the case. Her soluble, type-specific antigen of streptococcus was clearly a protein, which she later designated as M-protein on the basis of the association of the antigen with the matt colony form of the organism when grown on an agar medium. The M-protein appeared to serve essentially the same function in determining the virulence of hemolytic streptococci that the capsular polysaccharide did in the pneumococcus.

Her soluble species-specific antigen did, however, prove to be carbohydrate in nature and was designated the C-carbohydrate. (The continuing close relationship with the Avery laboratory is illustrated by the fact that when Avery and his colleagues shortly thereafter found an analogous species-specific carbohydrate in pneumococcus, it was also called C-carbohydrate or C-substance.) The great importance of the streptococcal C-carbohydrate, however, proved to be in the sorting out of the many different varieties of hemolytic streptococci that exist in nature. As she received more strains from numerous sources, it became apparent to Lancefield that her species-specific antigen was really group specific. It was common to strains isolated from strep throat and certain other human diseases, but a group of strains from bovine mastitis had a quite different group-specific carbohydrate and those from horses with strangles still a third. A continuation of this process established that there are several distinct serological groups of hemolytic streptococci in nature. Their differentiation proved of great importance in the study of streptococcal disease.

Lancefield designated the human strains that had been the object of her initial studies as group A and assigned letters of the alphabet to the others in sequence. Group A streptococci are responsible for most of the serious streptococcal infections of man, and it is infection with this group of organisms that leads to the poststreptococcal sequelae, rheumatic fever and glomerulonephritis. But the other groups of streptococci, regardless of their normal habitat, also occur in man and may be associated with disease. Group B streptococci, for example, which were initially encountered in cattle, are not uncommon in man and today are receiving much attention as the cause of septicemia and meningitis of the newborn. Lancefield carried out extensive studies of group B streptococci that laid the necessary groundwork for the present efforts to deal with this pediatric problem. In contrast to the situation in group A with its M-protein, she found that the type-specific antigens of group B streptococci are capsular polysaccharides, fully analogous to the pneumococcal polysaccharides. In working out the interrelationships between the several prevalent types of group B streptococci, she showed that specific antibodies to the capsular polysaccharide were highly protective against experimental infections. Many years later she returned to work on group B streptococci and initiated studies on their complex biochemical and antigenic structure that continue to be pursued in numerous laboratories throughout the world.

In company with many other experimentalists, Rebecca Lancefield's enthusiasm for working at the laboratory bench did not extend to the painful process of writing up the work for publication. She worked for nearly four years on the hemolytic streptococci without publishing any of her findings, but she quickly remedied the situation with a flurry of seven papers, all appearing in the *Journal of Experimental Medicine* in 1928. These papers included the first description of her M-protein and C-carbohydrate, with details of their chemical and immunological properties, and some information on their relationship to the bacterial cell. Her continuing work built on this base of new knowledge and led to the differentiation of serological groups of streptococci and delineation of the biological significance of the type-specific M-protein.

An interesting episode in the further sorting out of streptococcal diversity relates to Lancefield's exchanges with Fred Griffith, the noted British microbiologist. Griffith, after his famous work on the discovery of the transformation of pneumococcal types, had turned to studies of hemolytic streptococci. His technical approach differed significantly from that of Lancefield: he depended primarily on slide agglutination for serological differentiation of his strains, and she used a precipitin technique that depended on the property of her soluble antigens to give visible precipitates when mixed with antisera. Both workers used extensive adsorption of their antisera with heterologous strains to eliminate cross-reactions. Griffith examined a large number of human strains by his procedure and published his first extensive description of types of streptococci early in 1935.

On January 22, 1935, Lancefield wrote to Griffith requesting a reprint of his paper, and she included the following comment: "I have just read your paper in the current Journal of Hygiene with the greatest interest. I should not have supposed it possible to classify the majority of strains of *S. pyogenes* into so small a number of types as 27. It certainly makes a much more workable situation in this group if one can do that." Her interest had obviously been captured, and two months later she wrote requesting his cultures and samples of his antisera "to compare the types that I have encountered with yours." This began a long series of exchanges of strains, sera, and data that was prematurely terminated by Griffith's tragic death in the London Blitz in 1940.

The two workers had great respect for one another—even though they did not see eye to eye on methodology and were never converted to each other's approaches. There was much in common between the types defined by the two different techniques, and Lancefield adopted the numbers that Griffith had assigned to his types in order to achieve uniformity. In a few cases discrepancies arose because Griffith was not grouping his strains on the basis of C-carbohydrate, and strains that did not belong to group A were included among his types. Another source of discrepancy led Lancefield to the discovery of a second surface protein antigen of group A streptococci, which she designated as T-antigen. T-antigen could take part in slide agglutination and thus be detected by Griffith, but it was not present in the soluble M-protein extracts. Subsequently, Lancefield and her colleagues were able to show that T-antigen—unlike M protein—has no relation to virulence and, further, that the same or closely related T-antigen may be present on different M types. In the end, M types became the standard classification for bacteriological, clinical, and epidemiological studies, even though T typing by slide agglutination remains an adjunct technique applicable to a number of situations in which M-protein is absent or difficult to detect.

As it turned out, the doubts that Lancefield expressed to Griffith about being able "to classify the majority of strains of *S. pyogenes* into so small a number of types as 27" proved to be well founded. The total number of recognized types has been added to by laboratories all over the world and is now well over sixty. She herself had little interest in the business of identifying new types, preferring to devote her energies to the biological properties of the organism and their bearing on disease-producing capacity. The most dramatic illustration of the fruits of this approach is the unfolding of the story of the central role of M-protein in streptococcal infections. This surface antigen not only determines the type specificity of the numerous strains of group A streptococci but also serves to protect the organism from host defenses. When M-protein is present, the white blood cells appear to be unable to engulf and destroy the organisms; in the presence of specific antibody, however, this protective effect of M-protein is neutralized and the white cells can do their job. These facts led to the concept that immunity to streptococcal disease is primarily type specific and that recovery from infection with one type does little to provide protection against the numerous other types of group A organisms. This served to explain why repeated strep throats were so common in childhood and why rheumatic fever is a notoriously recurrent disease. Thus her work on this antigen provided the basis for a better understanding of the epidemiology of the disease and a more rational approach to its control.

The work that she and her colleagues pursued during World War II continued with the sorting out of the various antigens, especially the relationships between M- and T-antigens. At the same time she supervised the large-scale production of the grouping and typing sera that were provided to the military services for the first intensive studies of the epidemiology of streptococcal disease using the powerful tools that she had developed. In the postwar years she resumed her efforts to purify and characterize the properties of the important antigens. She carried out extensive studies of representative M- and T-antigens, a new surface protein that she designated as R-antigen, and the polysaccharide antigens of group B streptococci. In addition, in an illuminating study of the persistence of type-specific antibodies in man following group A streptococcal infections, she showed that lasting immunity to the M-antigen is commonly encountered.

Over the course of her work a vast number of streptococcal strains were sent to her; most of these are still preserved in the lyophilized state in her collection of some thousands of different strains. They were sent to her for identification, for a confirmation of identity, or because of some special feature of the situation in which they were obtained. They all received attention and analysis, resulting in a few dozen volumes of loose-leaf notebooks, in sturdy hard-cover binders, in which the data on each strain are recorded. Much of this information is written in her own hand, and it took some experience to be able to decipher her notes. But with persistence one could usually learn what he wanted to know about the strain in question. An equally large set of notebooks dealing with her research projects also exists, and these are even more difficult to decipher. (On occasion she even had trouble herself when trying to review experiments carried out two or three decades earlier.)

Rebecca Lancefield's devotion to her streptococcal studies was just as durable and persistent as the type-specific antibodies that she had described, and she maintained her laboratory activity until a few months before her death. In June 1979, sixty years after her arrival at the Rockefeller Hospital to work with Avery and Dochez, she was still coming in regularly, driving her own car back and forth from Douglaston, Queens, as she had since before the war. Although the annoying infirmities of age began to make it impossible for her to maintain her customary schedule, she did not abandon the effort until Thanksgiving Day, 1980, when she fell at home and broke her hip. She never regained full mobility, and she died on March 3, 1981.

Many of her colleagues feel that there was an inexplicable delay in general recognition and appreciation of her great scientific contributions. There is certainly some truth in this, but it must also be noted that among microbiologists she had long ago attained international stature as the outstanding authority on streptococci. Both the national and international organizations devoted to streptococcal problems have renamed their groups "The Lancefield Society," the former while she was still active. As further evidence of her recognition within the general field, she was elected president of the Society of American Bacteriologists in 1943 and of the American Association of Immunologists in 1961. Even though they may have been somewhat delayed in arriving, a number of other honors also came to her. She received the T. Duckett Jones Award of the Helen Hay Whitney Foundation in 1960, the American Heart Association Achievement Award in 1964, and the Medal of the New York Academy of Medicine in 1973. Rockefeller University recognized her contributions and long service to the institution with an honorary D.Sc. in 1973; her alma mater Wellesley College followed suit with a similar honor on the occasion of the sixtieth anniversary of her graduation in 1976.

She was elected to the National Academy of Sciences in 1970. Regrettably, this came too late for the Lancefields to enjoy the fellowship of the annual meetings with their longtime friends, the A. H. Sturtevants. "Sturt" and his wife,

Phoebe, had regaled them for years with tales of the Academy meetings during their shared summer holidays at Woods Hole. Rebecca attended a few meetings, but I am sure that she missed the special flavor that might have been contributed by the presence of her friends. She always spent the summer at Woods Hole, a place that was second in her heart only to her laboratory. For the most part she did not engage in laboratory work or writing there, the stay being reserved for renewal and recreation. In fact, a major aim was to escape the hot, humid weather of a New York City summer, which she detested; and in any event, throughout her early decades at Rockefeller it was impractical to try to do bacteriological or immunological work where neither the laboratories nor the animal quarters were air conditioned. She found Woods Hole ideal for relaxation, tennis, and especially swimming, an activity that she pursued to her final summer.

The description of Lancefield's scientific contributions gives an incomplete picture of her life in the laboratory. As single-minded as she was in the pursuit of her research goals, she could always find time to provide advice and assistance to other workers, both within and outside the laboratory. A visitor with an interest in streptococcal problems would leave with a thorough indoctrination and with most of his questions answered—as well as with a collection of cultures of reference streptococcal strains and samples of the relevant antisera. Streptococcal strains and antisera, together with directions for their use, were freely supplied to laboratories all over the world. The younger associates and postdoctoral fellows in our group found that she was not only ready to help whenever needed but that she expected to participate fully in all of the activities of the laboratory, including the parties and informal get-togethers. The pre-Thanksgiving eggnog party that she initiated is still carried on today, using her recipe.

Since I became the head of the rheumatic fever service after Dr. Swift's retirement in 1946, my own direct association with Rebecca Lancefield extended over more than half of her career at Rockefeller. Many of her major contributions had been completed and the groundwork already laid for others by this time, but I had ample opportunity to observe her working methods at first hand and to collaborate with her in more than one research project. Out of this came some insight into the qualities that were responsible for her success as an investigator. Because of her intuitive recognition of the great complexity of hemolytic streptococci, she was fully aware of the inherent danger of drawing premature conclusions from limited data. Accordingly, she could never be satisfied with the results obtained with one or two strains exhibiting a given characteristic after analysis with one or two antisera. It was always necessary to examine all available strains with each of many antisera, a procedure that greatly increased the burden of the analysis because of the diversity of the organisms and the heterogeneity of the antibody response of different rabbits to the multiple antigens involved. Such careful investigations, however, prevented her from drawing misleading and oversimplistic conclusions, and her meticulous approach is responsible, I believe, for the great durability and reproducibility of her published findings.

Rebecca Lancefield never developed very much sympathy for the modern feminist's point of view on women in science. She was not enthusiastic about honors that recognized her as the "first woman" to do this or that and preferred those that came without reference to her sex. She had no illusions about the difficulties of having both a scientific career and a family, but she felt that with determination and hard work it was possible without special treatment. In the case of her own small family, her efforts to provide a rewarding home life along with her scientific pursuits were notably successful, even though there must have been problems at times in adapting. She commuted by car from Douglaston, Long Island, for over forty years, which by itself was something of a triumph, considering bad weather, gasoline shortages, and the like.

Donald Lancefield survived Rebecca by only a few months. Their daughter, Jane Hersey, did not follow her parents into a career in biology and received her education in the classics. She has not managed to avoid science altogether, however; for some time, she served as a book review editor for *The American Scientist*. She and her husband, George Hersey, have two sons, Donald and James.

MUCH OF THE MATERIAL on which I drew for this memoir came from my own files. I am indebted, however, to the Rockefeller University Archives for the opportunity to reread some of Rebecca Lancefield's correspondence and for access to the annual reports to the Board of Scientific Directors of the Rockefeller Institute, which were helpful in piecing together the early history of her work.

SELECTED BIBLIOGRAPHY

1919

With O. T. Avery and A. R. Dochez. Studies on the biology of streptococcus. I. Antigenic relationship between strains of streptococcus haemolyticus. J. Exp. Med., 30:179–213.

1921

With C. W. Metz. Non-disjunction and the chromosome relationship of *Drosophila willistoni*. Proc. Natl. Acad. Sci. USA, 7:225–29.

1922

With C. W. Metz. The sex-linked group of mutant characters in *Drosophila willistoni*. Am. Nat., 36:211–41.

1924

Antigenic relationships of the nucleo-proteins from the Gram-positive cocci. Proc. Soc. Exp. Biol. Med., 22:109–11.

1925

The immunological relationships of streptococcus viridans and certain of its chemical fractions. I. Serological reactions obtained with antibacterial sera. J. Exp. Med., 42:377–95.

The immunological relationships of streptococcus viridans and certain of its chemical fractions. II. Serological reactions obtained with antinucleoprotein sera. J. Exp. Med., 42:397–412.

1928

The antigenic complex of *Streptococcus haemolyticus*. I. Demonstration of a type-specific substance in extracts of *Streptococcus haemolyticus*. J. Exp. Med., 47:91–103; II. Chemical and immunological properties of the protein fractions, 469–80; III. Chemical and immunological properties of the species-specific substance, 481–91; IV. Anaphylaxis with two non-type specific fractions, 843–55; V. Anaphylaxis with the type-specific substance, 857–75.

With E. W. Todd. Variants of hemolytic streptococci; their relation

to type-specific substance, virulence, and toxin. J. Exp. Med., 48:751–67.
With E. W. Todd. Antigenic differences between matt hemolytic streptococci and their glossy variants. J. Exp. Med., 48:769–90.

1933

A serological differentiation of human and other groups of hemolytic streptococci. J. Exp. Med., 57:571–95.

1934

A serological differentiation of specific types of bovine hemolytic streptococci. J. Exp. Med., 59:441–58.
Loss of the properties of hemolysin and pigment formation without change in immunological specificity in a strain of *Streptococcus haemolyticus*. J. Exp. Med., 59:459–69.

1935

With K. Goodner and H. F. Swift. The serological classification of hemolytic streptococci in relation to epidemiological problems. Am. J. Med. Sci., 190:445–53.
With R. Hare. The serological differentiation of pathogenic and nonpathogenic strains of hemolytic streptococci from parturient women. J. Exp. Med., 61:335–49.

1938

Two serological types of group B hemolytic streptococci with related, but not identical, type-specific substances. J. Exp. Med., 67:25–40.
A micro precipitin-technic for classifying hemolytic streptococci, and improved methods for producing antisera. Proc. Soc. Exp. Biol. Med., 38:473–78.

1939

With G. K. Hirst. Antigenic properties of the type-specific substance derived from group A hemolytic streptococci. J. Exp. Med., 69:425–45.

1940

Type-specific antigens, M and T, of matt and glossy variants of group A hemolytic streptococci. J. Exp. Med., 71:521–37.

The significance of M and T antigens in the cross reactions between certain types of group A hemolytic streptococci. J. Exp. Med., 71:539–50.

1941

Specific relationship of cell composition to biological activity of hemolytic streptococci. Harvey Lect., 36:251–90.

1943

With H. F. Swift and A. T. Wilson. Typing group A hemolytic streptococci by M precipitin reactions in capillary pipettes. J. Exp. Med., 78:127–33.

Studies on the antigenic composition of group A hemolytic streptococci. I. Effects of proteolytic enzymes on streptococcal cells. J. Exp. Med., 78:465–76.

1944

With W. A. Stewart. Studies on the antigenic composition of group A hemolytic streptococci. II. The occurrence of strains of a given type containing M but no T antigen. J. Exp. Med., 79:79–88.

With R. F. Watson. Studies on the antigenic composition of group A hemolytic streptococci. III. Types with serologically identical M but distinct T antigens: Types 10 and 12. J. Exp. Med., 79:89–98.

With W. A. Stewart, A. T. Wilson, and H. F. Swift. Studies on the antigenic composition of group A hemolytic streptococci. IV. Related T but distinct M antigens in types 15, 17, 19, 30, and in types 4, 24, 26, 28, 29, 46. Identification by slide agglutination. J. Exp. Med., 79:99–114.

1946

With V. P. Dole. The properties of T antigens extracted from group A hemolytic streptococci. J. Exp. Med., 84:449–70.

1952

With G. E. Perlmann. Preparation and properties of type-specific M antigen isolated from a group A, type 1, hemolytic streptococcus. J. Exp. Med., 96:72–82.

With G. E. Perlmann. Preparation and properties of a protein (R antigen) occurring in streptococci of group A, type 28, and in certain streptococci of other serological groups. J. Exp. Med., 96:83–97.

1954

Cellular constituents of group A streptococci concerned in antigenicity and virulence. In: *Streptococcal Infections*, ed. M. McCarty, pp. 3–18. New York: Columbia University Press.

1955

With M. McCarty. Variation in the group specific carbohydrate of group A streptococci. I. Immunochemical studies on the carbohydrates of various strains. J. Exp. Med., 102:11–28.

1957

Differentiation of group A streptococci with a common R antigen into three serological types, with special reference to the bactericidal test. J. Exp. Med., 106:525–44.

1958

Occurrence of R antigen specific for group A type 3 streptococci. J. Exp. Med., 108:329–41.

1959

Persistence of type-specific antibodies in man following infection with group A streptococci. J. Exp. Med., 110:271–92.

1960

With E. W. Hook and R. R. Wagner. An epizootic in Swiss mice caused by a group A streptococcus, newly designated type 50. Am. J. Hyg., 72:111–19.

1962

Current knowledge of type-specific M antigens of group A streptococci. J. Immunol., 89:307–13.

1964

With E. H. Freimer. Type-specific polysaccharide antigens of group B streptococci. J. Hyg., 64:191–202.

1971

With J. Rotta, R. M. Krause, W. Everly, and H. Lackland. New approaches for the laboratory recognition of M types of group A streptococci. J. Exp. Med., 134:1298–315.

1975

With M. McCarty and W. Everly. Multiple mouse-protective antibodies directed against group B streptococci. Special reference to antibodies effective against protein antigens. J. Exp. Med., 142:165–79.

1977

With S. D. Elliott and M. McCarty. Teichoic acids of group D streptococci with special reference to strains from pig meningitis (Streptococcus suis). J. Exp. Med., 145:490–99.

1979

With J. Y. Tai and E. C. Gotschlich. Isolation of type-specific polysaccharide antigen from group B type Ib streptococci. J. Exp. Med., 149:58–66.

HAROLD DWIGHT LASSWELL

February 13, 1902–December 18, 1978

BY GABRIEL A. ALMOND

HAROLD D. LASSWELL ranks among the half dozen creative innovators in the social sciences in the twentieth century. Few would question that he was the most original and productive political scientist of his time. While still in his twenties and early thirties, he planned and carried out a research program demonstrating the importance of personality, social structure, and culture in the explanation of political phenomena. In the course of that work he employed an array of methodologies that included clinical and other kinds of interviewing, content analysis, para-experimental techniques, and statistical measurement. It is noteworthy that two decades were to elapse before this kind of research program and methodology became the common property of a discipline that until then had been dominated by historical, legal, and philosophical methods.

Lasswell was born in 1902 in Donnellson, Illinois (population ca. 300). His father was a Presbyterian clergyman, his mother, a teacher; an older brother died in childhood. His early family life was spent in small towns in Illinois and Indiana as his father moved from one pulpit to another, and it stressed intellectual and religious values. Although the regional milieu of his childhood and adolescence might suggest that Lasswell was raised in an intellectual backwater, in fact it was an unusually rich environment. He was especially influenced in adolescence by a physician uncle who was familiar with the works of Freud; by an English teacher in the Decatur, Illinois, high school he attended who introduced him to Karl Marx and Havelock Ellis; and by a brilliant young teacher of high school civics, William Cornell Casey, who later became a professor of sociology at Barnard College in Columbia University. He excelled in high school, edited the school newspaper, gave the valedictory address at graduation, and was awarded a scholarship to the University of Chicago after winning a competitive examination in modern history and English.

When Lasswell entered the University of Chicago in 1918—at age sixteen—the university was in the third decade of its remarkable growth. At a time when sociology as a curriculum did not yet exist at most universities, Chicago had a major department that was staffed by such gifted theorists and researchers as W. I. Thomas, Albion W. Small, and Robert Park. Its philosophy department was dominated by realists and empiricists such as James Tufts and George Herbert Mead. Its economics department, in which Lasswell majored, included Jacob Viner, John M. Clark, Harry Alvin Millis, and Chester Wright. Its political science department was soon to begin its dramatic rise, but in Lasswell's undergraduate years the department was in transition with Henry Pratt Judson soon to retire, and Charles Edward Merriam in the wings. Lasswell was a member of a graduate cohort that included Robert Redfield, Louis Wirth, and Herbert Blumer.

His graduate years in the Department of Political Science at Chicago coincided with the publication of Merriam's manifesto, *The Present State of the Study of Politics,* in 1921 and with Merriam's and Gosnell's survey study of nonvoting in Chicago (1924). In *The Present State,* Merriam proposed that two steps be taken to make the study of politics more scientific: (1) the exploration of the psychological and sociological bases of political behavior, and (2) the introduction of quantification in the analysis of political phenomena. The nonvoting study was a demonstration of the uses of social–psychological hypotheses and quantitative methods in the explanation of political phenomena. It was a survey of the "political motives" of some 6,000 nonvoters in the Chicago mayoral election of 1923; individuals to be surveyed were selected by a "quota control" sampling procedure that was intended to match the census demographic distributions. In the immediate aftermath of this study and during Lasswell's graduate student days, Harold Foote Gosnell (then a first-term assistant professor of political science) conducted the first experimental study in political science—and what may very well have been the first experimental study in the social sciences outside of psychology. This was a survey of the effects on voting of a nonpartisan mail canvass in Chicago that was intended to get out the vote in the national and local elections of 1924 and 1925. The experimental technique Gosnell devised was quite rigorous: there were carefully matched experimental and control groups, different stimuli were employed, and the results were analyzed with the most sophisticated statistical techniques then available. Reflecting the programmatic and comparative vision of these researches, follow-up studies of voting turnout were made by Gosnell in Britain, France, Germany, Belgium, and Switzerland.

While Harold Gosnell was chosen by Merriam to develop the statistical component of his early 1920s vision, it was Harold Lasswell who was encouraged to develop the clinical, psychological, and sociological components. As a young graduate student, Lasswell published an article in 1923 entitled "Chicago's Old First Ward,"[1] and in collaboration with Mer-

---

[1] *National Municipal Review,* 12:127–31.

riam he published another in 1924 on public opinion and public utility regulation.²

Merriam threw out two challenges to the brilliant and ambitious young political scientist. The first came out of Merriam's wartime experience as chief American propagandist in Rome; the second arose from Merriam's interest in the characteristics of political leaders and the uses of the study of the abnormal and the psychopathological in explaining normal and typical behavior. Merriam's first interest—the importance of morale, propaganda, and civic training in the explanation of political behavior—led to Lasswell's 1927 doctoral dissertation, *Propaganda Technique in the World War,* and ultimately to his invention of systematic content analysis and its uses in World War II. Merriam's second interest—the psychological and personality aspects of leadership and the uses of the abnormal in the explanation of the normal—led to a series of articles by Lasswell on political psychology and personality in politics, culminating in his *Psychopathology and Politics.*

Lasswell's doctoral dissertation on propaganda in the 1914–1918 war was a systematic effort to place World War I propaganda experience in the context of a theory of politics. Although there was something of antiwar muckraking in its tone, it also had the marks of rigorous scholarship: careful operational definitions, specification of the techniques of propaganda, and the conditions that limit or facilitate their effectiveness. Lasswell had done field research in Europe for this study, interviewing scholars and governmental officials regarding aspects of the propaganda experience and the Great War. He also anticipated his later invention of content analysis in a simple quantitative study—"Prussian School-

---

² "Current Public Opinion and the Public Service Commissions," in: *Public Utility Regulation,* ed. M. L. Cooke (New York: Ronald Press, 1924).

books and International Amity"—which was carried out in connection with his dissertation. (In the study Lasswell counted and evaluated the significance of the references to national superiority, military glory, foreign inferiority, military heroes, and the like in textbooks approved by the Prussian Ministry of Education after the establishment of the Weimar Republic.)[3]

Lasswell was appointed assistant professor of political science at Chicago in 1926 and soon embarked on researches in political psychology. Papers that he published from 1925 to 1929 showed him to be engaged in a search of the literature concerned with political psychology and political personality. One paper published in the *American Journal of Psychiatry* in 1929 recommended that psychiatrists keep adequate personality records and make them available to bona fide researchers; another published in the *American Political Science Review* the same year argued the case for the use of data on mentally ill persons with some involvement in politics as one approach to the analysis of the relationship between personality and politics. This literature search and his concern with the improvement of psychiatric recordkeeping were incidental to the preparation and publication of Lasswell's extraordinary book, *Psychopathology and Politics,* which appeared in 1930 when he was twenty-eight.

Lasswell's work in preparing the book was extensive. He had been granted a postdoctoral fellowship by the Social Science Research Council for 1927–1928 and spent most of that year in Berlin undergoing psychoanalysis at the hands of Theodor Reik, a student of Freud. There is a report that he made a presentation at a Freud seminar urging that psychiatric records be kept in order to facilitate research. He also

[3] "Prussian Schoolbooks and International Amity," *Journal of Social Forces,* 3(1925):718–22.

discussed these ideas with leading psychiatrists in Vienna and Berlin. In late 1928 and 1929 he consulted with the psychiatric directors of the most important mental institutions on the eastern seaboard, tapping their memories of cases of politician patients. With their permission he examined psychiatric records at St. Elizabeth's in Washington, D.C.; Sheppard and Enoch Pratt Hospital near Baltimore; Pennsylvania State Hospital in Philadelphia; Bloomingdale Hospital of White Plains, New York; and Boston Psychopathic Hospital. He also gave depth psychiatric interviews to a number of "normal" volunteers.

Psychopathology and Politics was the first relatively systematic, empirical study of the psychological aspects of political behavior, and it coincided with the very beginnings of the culture and personality movement in anthropology and psychiatry. Lasswell was already in communication with anthropologist Edward Sapir, then a colleague at the University of Chicago, as well as with the New York psychiatrist Harry Stack Sullivan. The three of them began to plan an ambitious program of culture and personality research in the middle and late 1920s. Margaret Mead's *Coming of Age in Samoa* appeared two years before *Psychopathology and Politics,* and Ruth Benedict's *Patterns of Culture* appeared four years later. The first publication of the authoritarian personality research of the Frankfurt School—*Studien über Autorität und Familie*—appeared in 1936, and the *Authoritarian Personality* of Adorno, Frenkel-Brunswick, Daniel Levinson, and Nevitt Sanford only appeared in 1950.

Chapters 6 through 9 of *Psychopathology and Politics* report Lasswell's case materials. These are not and are not represented as being findings or scientific explanations of political behavior. They are presented as clinically supported hypotheses regarding the personality-etiological bases of recruitment to different kinds of political roles and attitudes. Thus

Lasswell draws on clinical material and his own depth interviews to suggest why some individuals become agitators and others become administrators. Similarly he illuminates the relationship between personality variables and ideological propensities such as ultrapatriotism, internationalism, pacifism, socialism, and anarchism.

The rest of the book deals with methodological and theoretical issues. Among the methodological issues he treats are the uses of life histories in political science; the uses of the study of the deviant or the abnormal for the understanding of the normal; the dimensions used in typologies of politicians, the prolonged, "depth," or psychoanalytic interview as a mode of research in the psychological bases of social behavior; and the technique of free association as a method of getting data on politically relevant feelings and attitudes. He also presents a general theory of political behavior derived from a review of the various propositions of the psychoanalytic movement. This proposition, presented in the form of an equation, reduces political behavior—in the sense of choice of political roles and ideologies—to displacements of private, essentially "oedipal" and "libidinal" motives as rationalized in terms of political ideas and issues. It is a matter of some contention among Lasswell students as to whether this equation was literally intended or was a rhetorical exaggeration to draw attention to the importance of psychological motivation in the explanation of political phenomena. Supporting the reductionist position is the fact that the Freudian movement at this time took a similarly reductionist stand in the explanation of social, political, and aesthetic phenomena. Supporting the rhetorical interpretation is the fact that in this as in later work, Lasswell interprets unconscious oedipal and libidinal tendencies as powerful constraints on rational, object-oriented behavior, constraints that can be mitigated by psychotherapy. This was to be a theme of Lasswell's entire intellectual career; that professional political science had the obligation of discovering or inventing a "politics of prevention" of war and other evils; that there was a "commonwealth of human dignity" to which it ought to aspire; and that both of these required substantial psychotherapeutic inputs.

This dualism and ambivalence of reductionism and therapeutic optimism in some sense characterized the three principle influences on Lasswell's thought; the Presbyterianism of his family and childhood background, which deals with the question of how good may be wrested from an intractable evil; the Marxist-sociological background, which deals with the necessarily revolutionary confrontation of the traditional and reactionary with progressive forces; and the Freudian-psychoanalytic background, which deals with the confrontation of neurosis with psychotherapy. Lasswell's later contributions to political psychology took the constraint rather than the reductionist perspective. It is of interest that in an "Afterthoughts" he wrote for the 1960 edition of *Psychopathology and Politics,* he makes no reference to his equation; instead he tells us that at the time of writing the book he already shared in a revisionist ego-psychology trend, a movement in psychoanalysis that affirmed the importance of rational and cognitive processes.

In addition to the empirical and methodological parts, *Psychopathology and Politics* included a theoretical or metamethodological part. Chapters 12 and 13—"The Personality System and Its Substantive Reactions" and "The State as a Manifold of Events"—presented Lasswell's framework of politically relevant variables and a strategy of political explanation, which moves from intrapsychic processes and their etiology, to interpersonal and social processes, to domestic and international political processes, and back again. Personality, economy, society, and politics are considered and dealt with as interacting systems.

What Lasswell presented as a theoretical framework and set of hypotheses in *Psychopathology and Politics* became his research program during the decade of the 1930s. Consider the intellectual balls he was juggling during these years.

For the psychiatrists whom he had been urging to keep records of their interviews in the interest of scientific research, he set up a model laboratory in his own offices in the Social Science Research Building at the University of Chicago. Advised and encouraged by psychiatrists Harry Stack Sullivan of Sheppard and Enoch Pratt Hospital and William A. White of St. Elizabeth's, he devised a procedure under which skin conductivity, pulse rate, respiration, and body movements of experimental subjects were measured as the spoken word was recorded. Three articles describing this procedure and reporting preliminary results appeared in psychoanalytic journals in 1935, 1936, and 1937. Unfortunately these research records were destroyed in 1938 in an accident that befell the vans moving Lasswell's effects to Washington on his departure from Chicago. This project, if not the first, was certainly one of the earliest efforts to link physiological, autonomic, and behavioral variables with communications and personality processes.

If this laboratory research was an effort to implement the methodological message of *Psychopathology and Politics*, then *World Politics and Personal Insecurity* (1934) was an elaboration of the theoretical perspectives spelled out in the final chapters of *Psychopathology and Politics*. Lasswell called his approach to political explanation *configurative analysis*. In configurative analysis the political process is defined as conflict over the definition and distribution of the dominant social values—income, deference, and safety—by and among elites. In his first paragraph he proposes the formula long associated with his name: "Politics is the study of who gets what, when, and how." Political science research hence requires the analysis of the social origins, skills, personal traits, attitudes, values, and assets of world elites, and their changes over time. Proper understanding of political processes calls for a combination of equilibrium and developmental analysis and the adoption of contemplative and manipulative attitudes toward political change. Equilibrium analysis emphasizes the systemic, the recurrent, the stable interaction of economic, social, political, and personality variables; developmental analysis stresses the dynamic, the dialectical and transformative aspects of social change. The contemplative attitude contributes to the discovery of "regularities," "laws," principles of social behavior. The manipulative attitude subjects these regularities to the test of imagination, tracing the consequences of changes in conditions and policies, extrapolating trends, and the like. What Lasswell had in mind by the manipulative attitude is not fully clear in these passages. From the beginning he had a commitment to a moral and consequential political science, but his earlier work focused on politics and power. In his early schematization of political values as income, deference, and safety, he describes them rather casually as illustrative and representative values—not a complete set of political goals. He did not begin to deal explicitly with the political value and public policy realm until his association with Myres McDougal and the Yale School of Law in the late 1930s.

The bulk of *World Politics and Personal Insecurity* illustrates his method and approach. In chapters 2 through 6, conflicts among and within nations are related to human aggressive propensities, as well as the structural conditions of international relations, and domestic societies. The consequences of economic and class structure, cultural diffusion, and the media of communication, are the topics of chapters 7, 8, and 9. In chapter 10, politics, culture, and personality are related in an interesting discussion of trends in American society: he treats the possibilities of the emergence of right-wing extremism and fascism and the approach of political psychiatry in a politics of prevention. A final chapter deals—in sociological and psychoanalytic terms—with the prospects of peace and social justice.

A briefer book, *Politics: Who Gets What, When, and How,* was published in 1936; it presented much of what was argued in *World Politics* but in a more succinct and more schematic form. If Lasswell has written a textbook, then this is it. It defined politics as the struggle among elite groups over such representative values as income, deference, and safety. The actors in these conflictual processes are groups organized around skill, class, personality, and attitude characteristics; they employ in different ways and with different effects the political instrumentalities of symbol manipulation, material rewards and sanctions, violence, and institutional practices.

These three books, which were written over a six-year period, constitute Lasswell's most important contributions to political theory. In this same productive decade of the 1930s, Lasswell was involved in two other major enterprises. He consolidated his earlier interest in propaganda research by collaborating with R. D. Casey and B. L. Smith in the preparation of an annotated bibliography of some 4,500 items. It was published in 1935 as a book—*Propaganda and Promotional Activities: An Annotated Bibliography*—with an introduction on the theory of propaganda by Lasswell. Later editions continued to guide and codify the field of communications and public opinion research. In an effort to implement the research program laid out in *World Politics,* Lasswell and a number of his graduate students carried out a field study of propaganda and political agitators and organizers among the unemployed in the city of Chicago during the depression and New Deal years. A book coauthored with Dorothy Blumenstock Jones reported these findings in 1939.

The first phase in Lasswell's career came to an end in

1938. He left the University of Chicago to join forces with psychiatrist Harry Stack Sullivan and Yale anthropologist Edward Sapir, under the auspices of the William Alanson White Psychiatric Foundation. There was both "push" and "pull" behind these plans to leave. Under the presidency of Robert Maynard Hutchins, the hospitality of the University of Chicago to the empirical social sciences had notably cooled. Merriam's department came under criticism on grounds of "number crunching" and "psychologizing," as well as internal recruitment. Hutchins's conception of political science was humanistic, deductive, even Aquinian. Although Lasswell had tenure—as did Gosnell—both men left the University: Lasswell in 1938 for Washington, D.C., and the William Alanson White Psychiatric Foundation; Gosnell a few years later, also to the capital but for government service. Merriam himself was approaching retirement and was unable to defend his younger men.

The "pull" of the eastern seaboard on Lasswell had an earlier origin. During the mid-1920s when he was preparing for his study of psychopathology and politics, Lasswell encountered the maverick psychiatrist Harry Stack Sullivan during his visits at eastern psychiatric hospitals. He also made the acquaintance of Dr. William Alanson White, the director of St. Elizabeth's, who was strongly interested in research and in collaboration with the social sciences. (Lasswell, because of his association with Merriam, was in a position to facilitate access for Dr. White to the early organizational meetings of the Social Science Research Council, then being held in Hanover, New Hampshire.) During these same years, Sullivan had come to know the cultural anthropologist Edward Sapir, then a colleague of Lasswell's at the University of Chicago. The three men, although of different ages—Sapir was born in 1884, Sullivan in 1892, and Lasswell in 1902—were attracted to one another out of the strongest interest in culture–personality themes. They dreamed of a research institute that would combine the study of culture, society, and personality and contribute to a better and happier world. The research institute never came to fruition, but these encounters surely influenced Lasswell's program at the University of Chicago, Sapir's Institute of Human Relations at Yale, and Sullivan's William Alanson White Psychiatric Foundation in Washington, D.C.

In 1938, however, it appeared that these plans for a social science-cum-psychiatry institute in either New York or Washington with Sapir, Sullivan, and Lasswell as the full-time core research faculty were about to mature. In April 1938 the trustees of the William Alanson White Foundation decided to seek funds to support a full-time permanent research staff in psychiatry and the social sciences. And the three men were ready to move: Lasswell was pessimistic about prospects at Chicago, Sapir was acutely uncomfortable at Yale, and Sullivan looked forward to creative research collaboration under the most favorable of auspices.

It was in this mood of high hopes that in the spring of 1938 Harold Lasswell packed and shipped his files and belongings in two moving vans—which were fated to collide and burn on a lonely Indiana highway. But this was only the beginning of misadventure and tragedy. The fund-raising plans were unsuccessful, and relations between Sullivan and Lasswell deteriorated. Sapir died in early 1939.

Lasswell thus began the second phase of his career at age thirty-six, in Washington, D.C., with uncertain prospects. He improvised for a while, giving educational radio broadcasts on "Human Nature in Action" over NBC and consulting to foundations. Beginning in the academic year 1938–39 he taught seminars as a visiting lecturer in association with Myres McDougal at the Yale School of Law; he was appointed professor of law there in 1946. As the international crisis deepened, he became involved in research programs at the Library of Congress and the Department of Justice. The Library of Congress at Lasswell's recommendation established a war communications research project, drawing on his experience with World War I propaganda. And the Department of Justice set up a special war policies unit to help administer the Foreign Agents Registration Act and the Sedition Act. Both of these tasks involved content analysis of the media of communication: on the world scale, as the propaganda war heated up in 1939 and 1940, and on the domestic organizational scale, as Nazis and fascists infiltrated foreign language groups and media in the United States. Lasswell gave expert testimony in a number of trials under this legislation; he was also instrumental in the effort to have quantitative content analysis admitted as evidence in the federal courts.

During the war years he played an active role as a consultant to the Office of Facts and Figures and its successor organization, the Office of War Information; the Office of Strategic Services; the Foreign Broadcast Monitoring Service of the Federal Communications Commission; and the Army's Psychological Warfare Branch. For the social sciences these various research divisions of the government departments constituted advanced training centers for young social scientists. Leading scholars such as Lasswell, Lazarsfeld, Samuel Stouffer, and Carl Hovland trained groups of specialists in survey research, experimental small group research, propaganda and content analysis, and the like.

The methodological and substantive payoffs of Lasswell's wartime research are reported in *The Language of Politics; Studies in Quantitative Semantics* (1949), which was jointly edited with one of Lasswell's most brilliant students, Nathan Leites. This volume places mass communications content in the context of domestic and international politics, offers solutions for the principal methodological problems of quantitative content analysis, and reports on a number of successful uses of content analysis, both as a judicial tool and as a technique of intelligence gathering.

It had been Lasswell's ambition during World War II to set up what he termed a "world attention survey": a continual quantitative analysis of the content of the principle print and broadcast media of the major nations—friend, neutral, and enemy. It was a project of immense proportions and was set aside in the war years in favor of a much more modest program of propaganda analysis located in the Office of War Information and the Federal Communications Commission. But in the aftermath of the war and working with wartime collaborators—particularly sociologist Daniel Lerner and political scientist Ithiel Pool—Lasswell pursued these research themes. Based now as a professor in the Yale School of Law, in collaboration with Lerner, Pool, and others at the Hoover Institute and Library at Stanford, he undertook a series of comparative studies of elites and political symbols. Several volumes reporting the findings of these researches appeared in the 1950s. But one of the most important products of these Stanford years was *The Policy Sciences,* a state-of-the-art analysis of social science methodology as of the early 1950s that Lasswell coedited with Daniel Lerner, with coauthors Ernest R. Hilgard, and others.

The third phase of Lasswell's career began in 1946 when he joined the Yale Law School faculty as a professor of law. He had been teaching part-time at Yale in association with Myres McDougal since 1938, and was a visiting research associate in the Institute of International Studies during the war years. His permanent location in New Haven in 1946 made possible a fruitful collaboration between Lasswell and McDougal in teaching, research, and contributions to legal and political theory, a collaboration that continued for the next several decades. In a major monographic contribution to the *Yale Law Journal* of March 1943, Lasswell and McDougal recommended the fundamental reform of law school curricula. The monograph argued that lawyers were the principal policymakers in modern democratic societies and that traditional law school curricula failed to provide training for the variety of policymaking roles lawyers were called upon to perform. In this seminal article, Lasswell and McDougal sought to remedy these shortcomings. They formulated a curricular philosophy based on the assumption that law had to be understood as a process of authoritative decision by which the members of a community clarify and secure their common interests. They then elaborated a sequence of seminars and courses that would effectively implement this philosophy. Prominent in this and later collaborations with McDougal and other law school colleagues were two theoretical innovations—components of an "institutional and value map"—that are properly associated with Lasswell's Yale career. The first innovation was a functional scheme for the analysis of decision-making. This became in its final form a seven-phase process beginning with intelligence, in the sense of knowledge, and proceeding to promotion, prescription, invocation, application, termination, and evaluation. The second innovation was a classification of goals or base values that included power, wealth, respect, well-being, affection, skill, rectitude, and enlightenment. These two theoretical schemes enabled the legal scholar to locate his research in the policy process and to specify its substantive value aspects. The theoretical categories served to place in context the various legal and other studies that Lasswell carried on in the next decades.

One of Lasswell's most influential contributions in legal studies was *Power and Personality* (1948) in which he presented a series of case histories of judges to demonstrate the connection between personality characteristics and patterns of legal decision-making. Other Lasswell contributions to legal research and analysis are contained in such volumes as *Studies in World Public Order* (with Myres McDougal, 1960); *In Defense of Public Order: The Emerging Field of Sanction Law* (with Richard Arens, 1961); *Law and Public Order in Space* (with Myres McDougal and Ivan A. Vlasic, 1963); and *Human Rights and World Public Order: The Basic Policies of an International Law of Human Dignity* (with McDougal and Lung-chu Chen, 1980). A final volume, entitled *Jurisprudence for a Free Society: Studies in Law, Science, and Policy* and coauthored with McDougal, is still to appear.

Lasswell became Ford Professor of Law and Social Science Emeritus at Yale in 1970. The last seven years of his life were spent in New Haven, where he continued his research interests, and in New York City, where he was affiliated with the Policy Sciences Center that he had helped to found in the 1940s.

Quantitatively Lasswell's productivity was enormous. He wrote, coauthored, edited, and coedited some sixty books. He also contributed more than 300 articles to a wide range of journals: political science, sociological, psychiatric and psychological, legal, journalism, and public opinion. His publications also include several hundred reviews and comments. Among the important works that have not yet been mentioned are *Power and Society* (with Abraham Kaplan, 1950); *Democratic Character* (1951); *The Decision Process: Seven Categories of Functional Analysis* (1956); *The Future of Political Science* (1963); *The Sharing of Power in a Psychiatric Hospital* (with Robert Rubenstein, 1966); *Peasants, Power, and Applied Social Change: Vicos as a Model* (with Henry F. Dobyns and Paul L. Doughty, 1971); and *The Signature of Power: Buildings, Communication and Policy* (with Merritt B. Fox, 1979).

These titles suggest the enormous range of Lasswell's interests, which he maintained throughout his life. *Power and Society*, which was written in collaboration with the philosopher Abraham Kaplan, was a propositional inventory and conceptual handbook for political science. Among its noteworthy contents was the elaborated version of Lasswell's classification of base values (see above). Lasswell's monograph, *Democratic Character*, was an important addendum to a 1951 reprint of his *Psychopathology and Politics* and *Politics: Who Gets What, When, and How*, neither of which dealt with the psychological aspects of democracy. This monograph sought first to define the value orientations that would be supportive of democratic institutions and then to spell out "democratic" personality characteristics and the social and family conditions that were likely to produce them. His monograph on the decision process (1956) spelled out more clearly his theoretical framework for the phases of policymaking and implementation discussed above.

In *The Future of Political Science* (1963), evocative of earlier visions of a world in which social science research has reached high influence, he draws on two social science research projects in which he was engaged in the 1960s. The first of these was an anthropological study of a hacienda in Peru. In this effort Lasswell collaborated with Allan Holmberg of Cornell and later produced a book (with Dobyns and Doughty) entitled *Peasants, Power, and Applied Social Change: Vicos as a Model* (1971). The experiment involved giving increasing initiative in decision-making to the peasants in the hacienda and attempting to measure the consequences of these and other experimental inputs of modernization and democratization. The second, done collaboratively with Robert Rubenstein, was a study of an experiment at the Yale Psychiatric Institute involving the participation of patients with staff and psychiatrists in decision-making on the ward. The research was concerned with the effects of this participation on the effectiveness of the ward and on the therapeutic goals of the institute. (A book documenting the study appeared in 1966 under the title, *The Sharing of Power in a Psychiatric Hospital*.) *The Future of Political Science* proposes that the political science profession develop the capacity to administer comprehensive surveys of world political change in order to advise effectively in the avoidance of war and other social evils. Such a survey would be informed by Lasswell's decision-process and goal-value conceptualizations. He also describes the kind of professional education that would be required to administer this kind of research program and cultivate the creativity essential for effective intervention.

Finally, in a book published after his death, *The Signature of Power: Buildings, Communication and Policy* (1979), Lasswell explores the relations between the architecture of public buildings, their public functions, and the surrounding political culture. Using photographs of public buildings and monuments from all over the world to illustrate his points, he demonstrates that the functions of buildings—civil or military, judicial, legislative, and bureaucratic—influence their structures. These structures in turn are influenced by national cultures, which produce their own structural variations.

Lasswell received many honors in the course of his career. He served as president of the American Political Science Association in 1956 and of the American Society of International Law from 1966 to 1968. He received honorary degrees from the University of Chicago, Columbia University, the University of Illinois, and the Jewish Theological Seminary. He was actively associated as officer, board member, or consultant to the Committee for Economic Development, the Commission on the Freedom of the Press, the Rand Corporation, the American Association for the Advancement of Science, and many other organizations. He was a fellow of the American Academy of Arts and Sciences and was inducted into the National Academy of Sciences in 1974.

Harold Lasswell suffered a massive stroke on December 24, 1977, from which he never recovered. He died of pneumonia in his apartment in New York City on December 18, 1978.

I WISH TO ACKNOWLEDGE the help I have received from a number of sources: from Dwaine Marvick's "Introduction" to his anthology, *Harold Lasswell on Political Sociology* (1977); from the various contributions to Harold Lasswell's festschrift, *Politics, Personality, and Social Science in the Twentieth Century* (ed. Arnold Rogow, 1969); the memorial volume, *Harold Dwight Lasswell 1902–1978,* which was published by the Yale Law School under the editorship of Myres McDougal; and Helen Swick Perry's *Psychiatrist of America: The Life of Harry Stack Sullivan* (1982), which contains information on the early collaboration of Lasswell with Sapir and Sullivan; and from personal communications and accounts provided by William T. R. Fox, Bruce L. Smith, Andrew R. Willard, Rodney Muth, and Myres McDougal.

SELECTED BIBLIOGRAPHY

1925

Two forgotten studies in political psychology. Am. Political Sci. Rev., 19:707–17.

1927

Propaganda Technique in the World War. (Ph.D. dissertation.) New York: A. A. Knopf; London: Kegan Paul.
Types of political personalities. Proc. Am. Sociological Soc., 22:159–69.

1929

Personality studies. In: *Chicago: An Experiment in Social Science Research*, ed. T. V. Smith and L. D. White, pp. 177–93. Chicago: University of Chicago Press.
Problem of adequate personality records: A proposal. Am. J. Psychiatry, 7:1057–66.
The study of the ill as a method of research into political personalities. Am. Political Sci. Rev., 23:996–1001.

1930

Psychopathology and Politics. Chicago: University of Chicago Press.
Personality system and its substitutive reactions. J. Abnorm. Psychol., 24:433–40.
Psychoanalytic interviews as a method of research on personalities. Childs Emotions, February:136–57.
The scientific study of human biography. Sci. Mon., 30:79–80.
Self-analysis and judicial thinking. Int. J. Ethics, 40:354–62.

1931

The measurement of public opinion. Am. Political Sci. Rev., 25:311–26.

1932

Triple-appeal principle: A contribution of psychoanalysis to political and social science. Am. J. Sociology, 37:523–38.

1935

With R. D. Casey and B. L. Smith. *Propaganda and Promotional Activities: An Annotated Bibliography.* Minneapolis: University of Minnesota Press.

World Politics and Personal Insecurity. New York: McGraw-Hill.

Verbal references and physiological changes during the psychoanalytic interview: A preliminary communication. Psychoanal. Rev., 22:10–24.

1936

Politics: Who Gets What, When, How. New York: Whittlesey House, McGraw-Hill.

Certain prognostic changes during trial (psychoanalytic) interviews. Psychoanal. Rev., 23:241–47.

1937

A method of interlapping observation in the study of personality in culture. J. Abnorm. Psychol., 32:240–43.

1938

What psychiatrists and political scientists can learn from one another. Psychiatry, 1:33–39.

1939

With Dorothy Blumenstock Jones. *World Revolutionary Propaganda: A Chicago Study.* New York: A. A. Knopf.

1941

The garrison state. Am. J. Sociology, 46:455–68.

1943

With Myres McDougal. Legal education and public policy: Professional training in the public interest. Yale Law J., 52:533–61.

1945

World Politics Faces Economics. New York: McGraw-Hill.

Interrelations of world organization and society. Yale Law J., 55:889–909.

1948

The Analysis of Political Behaviour: An Empirical Approach. London: Routledge and Kegan Paul, Ltd.
Power and Personality. New York: W. W. Norton.

1949

With Nathan Leites, eds. *Language of Politics: Studies in Quantitative Semantics.* New York: George Stewart.

1950

With Abraham Kaplan. *Power and Society.* New Haven, Conn.: Yale University Press.
National Security and Individual Freedom. New York: McGraw-Hill.

1951

With Daniel Lerner, eds. *The Policy Sciences: Recent Developments in Scope and Method.* Stanford, Calif.: Stanford University Press.
Democratic character. In: *The Political Writings of Harold D. Lasswell,* pp. 465–525. Glencoe, Ill.: The Free Press.

1952

With Daniel Lerner and C. Easton Rothwell. *The Comparative Study of Elites.* Hoover Institute Studies. Stanford, Calif.: Stanford University Press.
With Daniel Lerner and Ithiel de Sola Pool. *The Comparative Study of Symbols.* Hoover Institute Studies. Stanford, Calif.: Stanford University Press.

1956

The Decision Process: Seven Categories of Functional Analysis. College Park: University of Maryland Press.
The political science of science: An inquiry into the possible reconciliation of mastery and freedom. Am. Political Sci. Rev., 50:961–79.

1959

Political constitution and character. Psychoanal. Rev., 46:3–18.
The qualitative and quantitative in political and legal analysis. *Dae-*

dalus: Journal of the American Academy of Arts and Sciences, 88:633–45.

With Myres McDougal. The identification and appraisal of diverse systems of public order. Am. J. Int. Law, 53:1–29.

1960

With Myres McDougal. *Studies in World Public Order.* New Haven, Conn.: Yale University Press.

With L. Z. Freedman. The common frontiers of psychiatry and law. Am. J. Psychiatry, 117:490–98.

1961

With Richard Arens. *In Defense of Public Order: The Emerging Field of Sanction Law.* New York: Columbia University Press.

With L. Z. Freedman. Cooperation for research in psychiatry and law. Am. J. Psychiatry, 117:692–94.

1963

The Future of Political Science. New York: Atherton Press.

With Myres McDougal and Ivan A. Vlasic. *Law and Public Order in Space.* New Haven, Conn.: Yale University Press.

With Arnold A. Rogow. *Power, Corruption, and Rectitude.* Englewood Cliffs, N.J.: Prentice-Hall, Inc.

1964

With Bruce M. Russett, Hayward R. Alker, Jr., and Karl W. Deutsch. *World Handbook of Political and Social Indicators.* New Haven, Conn., and London: Yale University Press.

1965

With Daniel Lerner, eds. *World Revolutionary Elites: Studies in Coercive Ideological Movements.* Cambridge, Mass.: MIT Press.

1966

With Robert Rubenstein. *The Sharing of Power in a Psychiatric Hospital.* New Haven, Conn.: Yale University Press.

1967

With Myres McDougal and James C. Miller. *The Interpretation of Agreements and World Public Order: Principles of Content and Procedure.* New Haven, Conn.: Yale University Press.

1968

With Myres McDougal and W. Michael Reisman. Theories about international law: Prologue to a configurative jurisprudence. Virginia J. Int. Law, 8:188–299.

1969

With Satish Arora. *Political Communication: The Public Language of Political Elites in India and the United States.* New York: Holt, Rinehart & Winston.

With Allan Holmberg. Toward a general theory of directed value accumulation and institutional development. In: *Political and Administrative Development,* ed. Ralph Braibanti, pp. 354–99. Durham, N.C.: Duke University Press.

1971

With Henry F. Dobyns and Paul L. Doughty. *Peasants, Power, and Applied Social Change: Vicos as a Model.* Beverly Hills, Calif.: Sage Publications.

1975

With Warren F. Ilchman, John D. Montgomery, and Myron Weiner. *Policy Sciences and Population.* Lexington, Mass.: D.C. Heath and Company.

1979

With Merritt B. Fox. *The Signature of Power: Buildings, Communication and Policy.* New Brunswick, N.J.: Transaction Books.

1980

With Myres McDougal and Lung-chu Chen. *Human Rights and World Public Order: The Basic Policies of an International Law of Human Dignity.* New Haven, Conn.: Yale University Press.

With Daniel Lerner and Hans Speier, eds. *Propaganda and Communication in World History.* 3 vols. Honolulu: The University Press of Hawaii.

JAY LAURENCE LUSH
January 3, 1896–May 1, 1982

BY ARTHUR B. CHAPMAN

JAY LAURENCE LUSH made the following autobiographical statement in 1967[1]:

I was born in a log house on a farm in southwestern Iowa [Shambaugh], the second of six children. . . . My father was born in Canada. His parents were brought as children from southern England. My mother's father came from northern Ireland, but her mother was of old American stock, Scotch and Scotch-Irish in origin.

In our home we read many books of the kinds which were still considered classics around 1900 to 1910. Although money was scarce, we always had enough to eat, plenty to read, and clothing enough to keep warm. I went to an ungraded country school and entered a high school in Kansas at the age of 11. At Kansas State Agricultural College (now Kansas State University) I majored in animal husbandry. Mathematics was easy but not intriguing. History, physical geography, geology and parts of chemistry and biology were most interesting. I was active in debating. About 1914 I got my first intriguing glimpses of genetics. Also I encountered several interesting, friendly and challenging professors, mostly in biology or some of its applications.

After receiving the B.S. degree in 1916, I taught agriculture and chemistry in a Kansas High School for a year; then returned to KSU for my Master's degree and an apprenticeship in agricultural research. My first contribution to science was an article printed in the *Journal of Heredity* 12:57–71 in 1921. This was what I then thought was worth publishing from my Master's degree.

I spent nine months in the Air Force immediately after receiving the

---

[1] Autobiographical statement, National Academy of Sciences, 1967.

M.S. degree and I was commissioned as a Second Lieutenant in the reserve in February of 1919. I installed the Smith-Hughes program of agricultural instruction in another Kansas High School in the early part of 1919. I went to the University of Wisconsin in June of 1919 to do more graduate study in genetics.

Immediately after finishing my Ph.D. work there [1922], I went to the Texas Agricultural Experiment Station at College Station, Texas.

An important bit of Lush's personal history for the following year—1923—was his marriage to Adaline Lincoln. Mrs. Lush, a second cousin once removed of Abraham Lincoln, is a truly remarkable person. She graduated from high school at the age of thirteen and from the University of Arkansas at sixteen; she then earned a master's degree at the University of Chicago at age seventeen. In an award speech given when Lush was being honored at the Poultry Breeders Roundtable meeting in 1969, the speaker, Arthur Heisdorf, made this remark about Mrs. Lush: "I think she is the person who has been the secret catalyst [who] has sparked Dr. Lush onto the accomplishments he has made." To this tribute should be added how important a role she has taken as a gracious hostess and "foster mother" to countless students. She also found time—and had the ability—to teach French, German, Italian, Latin, and Spanish to private pupils; to conduct a number of trips to Europe; and to be active in a number of organizations. She was named Iowa Mother of the Year in 1963. Dr. and Mrs. Lush have a daughter, Mary Elizabeth Hausrath, a son, David Alan, and seven surviving grandchildren.

Lush's history, as recounted by him in 1967, continues below:

For more than eight years I did research in animal husbandry [in Texas]. Most of that pertained to animal breeding, but some of it was in other areas of animal production. The necessities of the research drew me further into biometry. In January of 1930 I came to Iowa State University (then Iowa State College) as Professor in the Department of Animal Husbandry to do research and teaching in Animal Breeding.... All of my work has hinged around finding ways to apply genetics more efficiently in improving animals and plants. For these purposes I used many biometrical tools developed by others and for myself made a few minor innovations in those. Most of my discoveries were small ones, usually growing out of some actual problem in application. These are put together in some 200 research papers and in my textbook, *Animal Breeding Plans* [1937] which has sold more than 22,000 copies. It is currently being printed in its fourth language [Spanish; earlier in Polish, Portugese, and Rumanian]. Perhaps the most important single paper was one in the *American Naturalist* in 1947 entitled "Family merit and individual merit as bases for selection."

In 1972 a symposium[2] was held in his honor. All the papers presented except one by Lush himself, "Teaching Animal Breeding and Training Graduate Students" (1973), were by Lush's former students or one-time colleagues at Iowa State University. These papers reflect the high esteem in which Lush was held—as research worker, teacher, and human being—by those who knew him best. The deep insight and extensive coverage given by these papers to Lush's life and contributions to his chosen field have led me to quote extensively from them in this biographical memoir.

A former student, R. R. Shrode, introduced the symposium and captured the essence of Lush's contributions:

> In effect, the field of Animal Breeding is a program of intellectual "linebreeding" to Lush.
>
> It is with tremendous professional respect and personal affection for our honoree that we dedicate this Symposium to our friend and teacher, Jay L. Lush, who has contributed more than any other individual, directly and indirectly through his many students, toward the continuing evolution of Animal Breeding from an art into a science.[3]

---

[2] The Animal Breeding and Genetics Symposium in honor of Dr. Jay L. Lush, sponsored jointly by the American Society of Animal Science, American Dairy Science Association, and Poultry Science Association, Virginia Polytechnic Institute and State University, Blacksburg, Virginia, July 29, 1972 (1973). Copies of the symposium proceedings may be obtained from Business Office, American Society of Animal Science, 309 West Clark St., Champaign, Illinois 61820.

[3] R. R. Shrode, "Introduction—Why We Are Here," in *Proceedings of the Animal Breeding and Genetics Symposium in Honor of Dr. Jay L. Lush,* American Society of

An Iowa State University colleague, A. E. Freeman, phrased it this way:

> As problems arose and could be defined in a mathematical or statistical sense, he and his students found answers to them in a way useful to improving domestic animals. The emphasis on breeding plans did not preclude interest and work on problems of a more theoretical nature. He clearly contributed to problems of almost purely theoretical interest, at least at the time; but it is safe to say that most of this work was started by seeing an actual problem arise that generated the germ of an idea for the theoretical work.... Dr. Lush's special interest in animal breeding was definitely aroused in 1914 by the teaching and enthusiasm of E. N. Wentworth [see Lush's obituary for Wentworth (1962) and his response during the dedication of the Jay L. Lush Auditorium at Iowa State (1974)] who was later his major professor for the M.S. degree [at Kansas State Agricultural College]....
>
> [Lush] continued his graduate training at the University of Wisconsin under the direction of Dr. L. J. Cole. Though it may now seem a bit strange, Dr. Lush was a physiologist. His Ph.D. thesis was "The possibility of sex control by artificial insemination with centrifuged spermatozoa" (Lush, 1925). He didn't succeed in this venture, but neither has anyone since. His interest in measurement and use of statistical tools was clear in this work. The data were arrayed by expected sources of variability, correlation coefficients were computed and probable errors were used to help determine if associations were real. Also, he fit normal curves to distributions of sperm head length measurements and tested these for goodness of fit. So, even as a physiologist, Dr. Lush's interest in measurement and statistics was evident.[4]

G. E. Dickerson, a former colleague at Iowa State University, referred in his symposium paper to the influence Sewall Wright's work had on Lush's biological and statistical thinking:

Animal Science, American Dairy Science Association, and Poultry Science Association, Blacksburg, Virginia, July 29, 1972 (1973), p. iii.

[4] A. Freeman, "Genetic Statistics in Animal Breeding," in *Proceedings of the Animal Breeding and Genetics Symposium in Honor of Dr. Jay L. Lush*, American Society of Animal Science, American Dairy Science Association, and Poultry Science Association, Blacksburg, Virginia, July 29, 1972 (1973), pp. 1, 2, 3.

How packed with meaning this subject [Inbreeding and Heterosis in Animals] is for animal breeders! And how greatly our understanding of the potential usefulness of inbreeding and heterosis in animal improvement has expanded during the last four decades as a result of the research, writing and teaching of Dr. Jay Laurence Lush! While Dr. Lush was busy at Texas A&M from 1922 to 1930 publishing studies of inheritance and performance evaluation, he must also have been studying Sewall Wright's interpretations of the U.S.D.A. inbreeding and crossbreeding work with guinea pigs (1922).[5] This seems clear from his 1927 paper clarifying the limitations of "percentage of blood" in describing genetic likeness, particularly among collateral relatives and from the subsequent series with his students and collaborators on the amount and kind of inbreeding, occurring during breed development in cattle, sheep and swine (1932 to 1939, 1946), using the technique of Wright and McPhee (1925)[6] for sampling random lines of ancestry.

When Dr. Lush arrived at Iowa State in 1930, earlier experiments with full-sib inbreeding in swine at Iowa and elsewhere had been discontinued due to loss of fertility. However, Wright's theoretical analyses and some results with guinea pigs (1921,[7] 1922[8]) had indicated that selection might be able to offset unfavorable effects of milder inbreeding and that inbreeding was a powerful tool for creating genetic diversity among lines.

This led Dr. Lush to initiate an experiment in 1930 comparing intense and mild linebreeding in pigs, with concurrent individual and progeny test selection. During this same period (1933), Lush's famous bulletin on linebreeding was published. It eloquently stated the case for subdivision of breeds into many lines, each mildly linebred to carefully selected ancestors, with continuous elimination of the poorer ones and recombining of better ones, closely paralleling Wright's (1931)[9] ideas on optimum population structure for evolution.[10]

---

[5] S. Wright, "The Effects of Inbreeding and Crossbreeding on Guinea Pigs," *U.S. Department of Agriculture Bulletin*, 1090(parts 1 and 2, 1922); 1121 (part 3, 1922).

[6] S. Wright and H. C. McPhee, "Approximate Method of Calculating Coefficients of Inbreeding and Relationship from Livestock Pedigrees," *J. Agric. Res. (Washington, D.C.)*, 31(1925):377–83.

[7] S. Wright, "Systems of Mating," *Genetics*, 6(1921):111–78.

[8] S. Wright, "Effects of Inbreeding and Crossbreeding," 1090.

[9] S. Wright, "Evolution in Mendelian Populations," *Genetics*, 16(1931):97–159.

[10] G. E. Dickerson, "Inbreeding and Heterosis in Animals," in *Proceedings of the Animal Breeding and Genetics Symposium in Honor of Dr. Jay L. Lush*, American Society of Animal Science, American Dairy Science Association, and Poultry Science Association, Blacksburg, Virginia, July 29, 1972 (1973), pp. 54–77.

Freeman also pointed to Sewall Wright's influence on Lush's thinking: "Lush commuted [in 1931] to the University of Chicago to audit Sewall Wright's course in Statistical Genetics and other Zoological courses there. The influence of this training and these visits with Dr. Wright on Dr. Lush's teaching and research is evident."[11] Lush said, at the Poultry Breeders Roundtable in 1969: "Those were by far the most fruitful ten weeks I ever had."

R. A. Fisher's work was also called on frequently by Lush, as Freeman states: "Before about 1930, the primary statistical tools used in animal breeding were correlation and regression methods. R. A. Fisher lectured at Iowa State through the summers of 1931 and 1936. Fisher's work greatly advanced the knowledge and use of statistics. Dr. Lush was unique in combining the work of both Fisher and Wright to solve animal breeding problems."[12]

In what specific areas of animal breeding were Lush's contributions made? Freeman notes the following:

> Many of his early papers explored husbandry problems; others considered the mode of inheritance of qualitative traits; some were concerned with measurement and description of economically important traits; and others are clearly a start of current-day animal breeding theory. In the early years, the first three types of papers were more numerous than the last type. Of course, this changed. As Dr. Lush was confronted with questions that stemmed from practical problems, he tried to answer them from the existing knowledge in classical genetics, plant breeding or allied theory. If existing knowledge did not yield an acceptable answer, he used statistical methods to better describe problems or relations existing between traits, then put this statistical description into a form usable by the breeder.... Many of Dr. Lush's publications from 1926 to 1930 could be described as developing and using more accurate ways to measure quantitative traits.[13]

Lush undertook studies using records collected on swine, dairy cattle, beef cattle, sheep, goats, poultry, and honeybees.

[11] Freeman, "Genetic Statistics," p. 4, 5.
[12] Ibid., p. 5.
[13] Ibid., p. 3, 4.

In 1930 he also initiated an experiment on "closed-herd" selection in dairy cattle as well as the one on selection and inbreeding in swine. Both of these long-term experiments provided data for many M.S. and Ph.D. theses and resulted in major contributions to the field of animal breeding.

R. W. Touchberry, another former student, gives a detailed discussion in his symposium paper[14] of "some of the pertinent points in a few of what I [Touchberry] consider to be his [Lush's] most important papers." For those who are familiar with the terminology of genetics, statistics, and animal breeding, Touchberry's paper provides a summary of many of Lush's contributions to the field. I will attempt to give the essence of these contributions.

There is one paper (Lush, 1947) that serves well as a prototype for many of his papers. It is also the one that Lush considered his "most important single paper." It can be used to illustrate his way of thinking about a problem and how that approach leads to a solution.

The study began, as did so many of Lush's projects, with a practical problem: "how much attention ought to be paid to the merits and defects of litter mates when choosing boars and gilts to use for breeding." The problem developed into the more general one of asking how much a population mean would be changed by selecting on individual performance alone versus selecting on family merit alone versus selecting on a combination of the two.

How did Lush approach this and similar problems? He started with the fundamental principles of genetics; then, by invoking a deductive argument, he gave them effect through the use of the tools of population genetics (discontinuous classes, qualitative differences) and biometrical genetics (con-

[14] R. W. Touchberry, "The Life and Contributions of Dr. Jay Laurence Lush," in *Proceedings of the Animal Breeding and Genetics Symposium in Honor of Dr. Jay L. Lush*, American Society of Animal Science, American Dairy Science Association, and Poultry Science Association, Blacksburg, Virginia, July 29, 1972 (1973), p. 89.

tinuous distributions, quantitative or measurement differences). In this *American Naturalist* paper, Lush points out: "The process of selection consists only of predicting the breeding value [genetic make-up or transmitting ability for the trait under consideration] of each individual which is being considered and then keeping it or culling it on the basis of that prediction. If the same fraction of the population must be saved but there is a choice of bases on which selection may be made, then the difference in results depends only on how accurately each individual's breeding value can be predicted from each of these bases."[15]

In comparing the three bases of selection in this paper, Figure 1 is used as a graphic way of looking at the interrelationships between the variables. The arrows in this diagram lead from "cause" to "effect," and the value attached to each one is defined as a path coefficient (standard partial regression coefficient) by Sewall Wright, who developed this procedure.[16] The bidirectional arrows refer to simple correlations between the variables. In this diagram P_i stands for the phenotype (observed measured value) of an individual, i; Y, the average phenotype of a family; G_i, the breeding value of an individual (average effects of the genes it contains—Fisher's "expected value"[17]); W, the factors other than G_i that affect each P_i in a family the same way but may differ from family to family; U_i, the factors other than G_i that affect P_i but that are no more alike for members of the same family than they are for individuals that belong to different families;

---

[15] J. L. Lush, "Family Merit and Individual Merit as Bases for Selection," *American Naturalist*, 81(1947):243–44.

[16] S. Wright, "On the Nature of Size Factors," *Genetics*, 3(1918):367–74; "Correlation and Causation," *Journal of Agricultural Research (Washington, D.C.)*, 20(1921):557–85; "The Method of Path Coefficients," *Annals of Mathematical Statistics*, 5(1934):161–215.

[17] R. A. Fisher, *The Genetical Theory of Natural Selection* (New York: Oxford University Press, 1930).

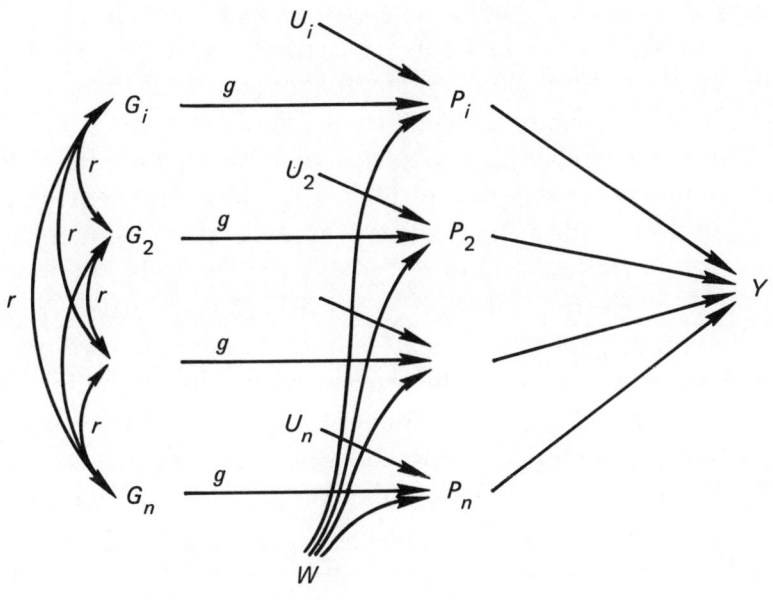

$$r_{GP} = g$$

$$r_{GY} = g\frac{1 + (n-1)r}{\sqrt{n[1 + (n-1)t]}}$$

$$r_{PY} = \sqrt{\frac{1 + (n-1)t}{n}}$$

$$t = r_{PP} = g^2 r + r^2_{WP}$$

FIGURE 1 Path coefficient diagram of biometrical relations involved in mass, family, and combination selection.
Source: J. L. Lush, "Family Merit and Individual Merit as Bases for Selection," part I, *American Naturalist*, 81(1947):246.

and r, the correlation between the breeding values of members of a family (Wright's relationship coefficient[18]).

The algebra to which this approach leads has been spelled out by Wright (see note 16) in a form that relates correlation coefficients to their path coefficient components. Some of the pertinent correlations—in terms of path coefficients—are given below the diagram in Figure 1. The correlations (r_{GP}, r_{GY}, and r_{GI}) reflect the relative progress expected under the three methods of selection, "where I is the index or most probable breeding value of an individual, as estimated from the optimum linear combination of attention to its own phenotype and attention to the average phenotype of the family to which it belongs." The phenotypic correlation between members of a family is denoted by t.

As an example of the use that can be made of these correlations in terms of their path coefficient components, let's look at the make-up of r_{GP} and r_{GY}. If selection is practiced on family average (Y) alone, the progress made would be expected to be $1+(n-1)r/\sqrt{n[1+(n-1)t]}$ times as rapid as mass selection (selection on individual performance); that is, $r_{GY} = g[1+(n-1)r]/\sqrt{n[1+(n-1)t]}$ versus $r_{GP} = g$, where g = the path of influence from G to P or the square root of heritability (the portion of the phenotypic variance due to genetic differences between individuals), and n = the number of individuals in the family. By inserting the values for g, n, r, and t that apply in a particular case, the difference in predictive value for transmitting ability from Y and P becomes evident.

As a graphic representation of the relative effectiveness of the three methods of selection, Lush (1947) gives the following diagram (Figure 2) for a case where n = 21. The progress from mass selection is represented by a level plane

---

[18] S. Wright, "Coefficients of Inbreeding and Relationship," *American Naturalist*, 56(1922):330–38.

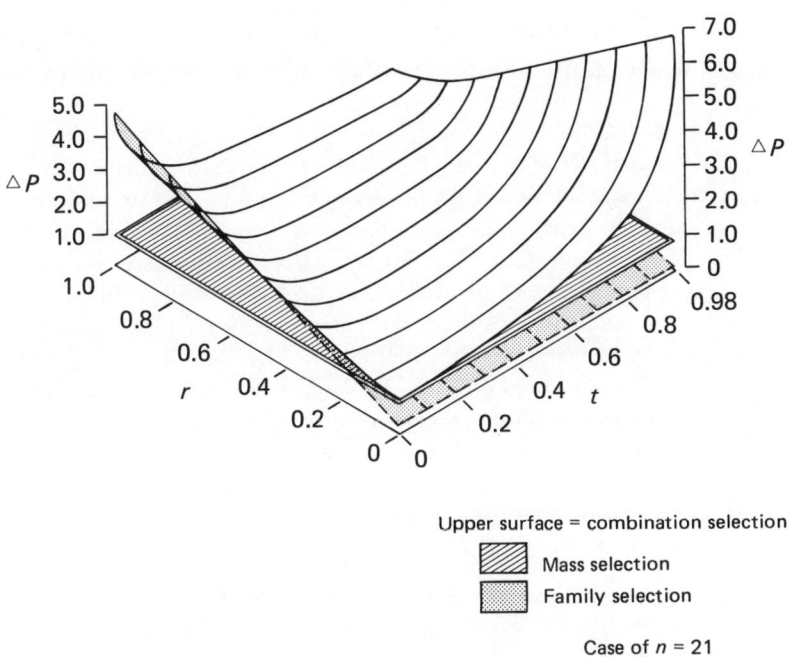

FIGURE 2 Relative effectiveness of the three methods of selection at all combinations of r and t when families contain 21 individuals.
Source: J. L. Lush, "Family Merit and Individual Merit as Bases for Selection," part I, *American Naturalist*, 81(1947):256.

at height 1.0 above the base and where all combinations of r and t are given.

The above gives the basic approach used in this paper and many others by Lush, but the full substance of this study goes much further. Readers of Lush's papers were usually made aware (as they are in this one) of the danger of accepting conclusions without taking into account the role played by chance, the frequent need for making simplifying (possibly oversimplifying) assumptions in order to grapple with a problem, and the errors likely to be made by semantic arguments that are not supported by experimental evidence or by quantitatively evaluated deductive arguments.

As an illustration of one of the caveats stemming from the above in the paper under discussion, he points to this possibility:

> If the actual effects of a gene substitution upon P are sometimes larger and sometimes smaller than the average effect of that gene substitution in that population, depending upon what other genes are present, the differences between the actual and average effects are termed epistatic or dominance deviations. These give rise to "special" breeding values. That is, they cause some matings to produce better offspring and some to produce poorer ones than would be expected if one knew the kind of offspring those same parents would produce if mated to a representative sample of the whole population. Most of the dominance and epistatic deviations from the additive scheme are included in U, but a small part are in W.

He also points to the need to keep in mind other factors: the fiducial limits of the estimates; the role that mutations might play; the effect of selection in the same or in a different direction within the population; the need for experiments to check on the theory involved in this work; and "the naive view, repeatedly disproven but still often inferred to be axiomatic, that family, breed, and race are unimportant, or even unreal, unless the families, breeds, or races are so distinct that they do not overlap at all." Lush showed statistically that "family selection is most superior to mass selection when family members resemble each other least; i.e., when the families overlap widely in their phenotypes and t is therefore low!"

As is usual in Lush's papers, he not only answers the specific questions asked but expands the answer to encompass much more. In this case he states the solution in terms of interclass correlations and then translates the solution into analysis of variance and intraclass correlations in the hope that the "biometrical relations may be clearer." These translations have undoubtedly helped students understand the equivalent meanings of two important ways of stating the solution statistically.

Furthermore, he provides, in regression form, the equations for predicting breeding value of the individual based on its own phenotype and its family average. He discusses under what conditions negative attention is paid to family average and the effect inbreeding would have on the results. Family selection for "all-or-none" characteristics, as well as characteristics distributed continuously, is clearly discussed. A number of other qualifications and special conditions are also mentioned. And finally, the implications of these conclusions for man are given consideration. This is a paper in which the conclusions and interpretations make a contribution to genetics, to animal and plant breeding, to statistics, and to sociology and anthropology. Many of his other papers also have a significant bearing on problems in several fields.

The other papers summarized by Touchberry,[19] which follow the same pattern as the one just discussed, made major contributions to animal breeding by clarifying problems involving progeny tests, individual performance, pedigree information, heritability, selection, and the role played by chance.

Some of the sources of information used by Lush in his research were the records from private farms enrolled in the Iowa Cow Testing Association, on animals registered in the breed associations and on poultry of the Kimber Poultry Farm. These provided an insight into the genetic and environmental sources of variation in economically important traits under commercial conditions. Lush was also associated with an Atomic Energy Commission research project on the genetic effects of ionizing radiation in swine.

Lush's view on teaching is given in the paper "Teaching Animal Breeding and Training Graduate Students," which he presented at the symposium in his honor in 1973. His introductory remarks in this paper reflect an attitude of his that was clearly evident to his students in his teaching.

[19] Touchberry, "Life and Contributions," pp. 89–104.

Immediately on completing my Ph.D. degree, I did research for more than 8 years, with almost no interruption for teaching. I'm glad it happened that way. If I had taught the same course as much as three times in succession, using the available texts and my graduate notes and all the rest of what I thought I knew, I would surely have come to believe those things myself so firmly that the errors among them could scarcely have been corrected by any amount of subsequent experience.

As it was, the cattle and sheep and goats talked back to me. Having no papers to grade or class rolls to call, I listened. Usually the animals were saying something like: "Most of the things you think you know may be true in principle but you have many of them out of all proportion to their actual importance. When you draw a conclusion, you often overlook circumstances which, if you considered them properly, would upset your recommendations badly." Trying to solve these apparent inconsistencies drove me, whether I wished it or not, in the direction of measuring more accurately the factors in the problems. I was always needing to be surer of how the various factors interacted in any whole operation we might be considering.[20]

Lush had a penchant for those apposite sayings that are so helpful to students trying to think through what is meant by some of the more esoteric concepts of genetics, statistics, and animal breeding. In my symposium paper,[21] I have quoted a number of these. One that I found myself using quite frequently in my teaching because of the effect it had had on me is one that he used because "Some of us think we have seen signs that many populations [being selected] do not actually change [as] rapidly [as we think they should]: Heritability may not be as high as we think. Selection may not have been as intense as we think. Perhaps the rate of

---

[20] J. L. Lush, "Teaching Animal Breeding and Training Graduate Students," in *Proceedings of the Animal Breeding and Genetics Symposium in Honor of Dr. Jay L. Lush*, American Society of Animal Science, American Dairy Science Association, and Poultry Science Association, Blacksburg, Virginia, July 29, 1972 (1973), p. 78.

[21] A. B. Chapman, "Selection Theory and Experimental Results," in *Proceedings of the Animal Breeding and Genetics Symposium in Honor of Dr. Jay L. Lush*, American Society of Animal Science, American Dairy Science Association, and Poultry Science Association, Blacksburg, Virginia, July 29, 1972 (1973), pp. 42–53.

progress actually is substantially as much as it should be." Dr. Lush then points out that "we ought to think of the old adage that when one is asked to explain how it is that witches can turn milk blue, the first thing is to find out is whether witches really can turn milk blue!"[22]

His success as a teacher and director of graduate students (26 who earned the M.S. and 124 a Ph.D. under his direction) is admirably presented in Touchberry's symposium paper, which he concludes by saying:

> As an advisor of graduate students, Dr. Lush was highly respected and admired. He was firm without being threatening and he got his points and message across without raising his voice or using profanity. He was a warm and friendly person with a tremendous respect and tolerance for students.[23]

Lush's influence on animal breeding around the world has been enhanced greatly by the wide distribution of his classical book *Animal Breeding Plans* (1937). His equally authoritative mimeographed notes, "The Genetics of Populations" (1948), have also played a major role in the thinking of animal breeders who were lucky enough to have them.

He played a major role in establishing and was an active participant in the regional laboratories for animal breeding research—joint ventures of cooperating states and the U.S. Department of Agriculture. He was also instrumental in the formation and guidance of the National Poultry Breeders' Roundtable, an organization of commercial poultrymen and academic staff that meets annually to discuss research in genetics and in animal and plant breeding. The meeting in 1969 (Eighteenth Annual Session, May 7–8) was held in his honor.

[22] J. L. Lush, "Summary (Symposium on Selection, Chicago, November 1949)," *Journal of Animal Science*, 10(1951):18–21.
[23] Touchberry, "Life and Contributions," p. 104.

Lush acted in an advisory capacity to these and many other organizations, both foreign and domestic. (He traveled extensively abroad and served as an advisor on animal breeding in a number of countries.) As a result, he was responsible for a profound change in the approaches to animal breeding research and practice in many countries.

Lush received a number of honors and awards, one of which was to dedicate to him the Iowa State University Auditorium in 1973. His remarks on this occasion (1974) illustrated his humility and include a typical "Lush" analogy: "I'm proud of this occasion, of course, although I am uncomfortably aware that others deserved the honor more. Also, I know that sheer luck had much to do with the things I did accomplish. In some ways they resemble the occurrence of an avalanche in the mountains. For an avalanche to occur at all requires some snow, of course, but the small event which actually triggers the avalanche might just as well have happened a hundred yards to the right or to the left, or it might as well have happened yesterday or not until day after tomorrow! An avalanche is contagious in that once it starts, it jars things loose for hundreds of yards around."

A fitting ending to this biographical memoir is the symposium statement of Touchberry: "He [Lush] has defined the problems of genetically changing farm animals in a logical, biological, quantitative and economic way. Further, he has shown how genetics and mathematics can help in solving problems of animal breeding. In doing this he has beneficially affected the lives of many. Thus, to me, it seems fitting to say that, rather than having followed a profession, he has, for the past 40 years, led a profession."[24]

---

[24] Ibid.

HONORS AND DISTINCTIONS

HONORARY DOCTORAL DEGREES

1957   Royal Agricultural College of Sweden
1957   Justus Liebig University, Giessen, Germany
1958   Royal Veterinary and Agricultural College of Denmark
1964   Michigan State University
1969   University of Illinois
1970   Kansas State University
1970   University of Wisconsin
1971   Swiss Federal Institute of Technology, Zurich
1975   Agricultural University of Norway

AWARDS

1946   Morrison Award of the American Society of Animal Science
1956   Honored Guest, American Society of Animal Science
1957   Charles F. Curtiss Distinguished Professor in Agriculture, Iowa State University
1958   Borden Award for research in dairy production, American Dairy Science Association
1960   Herman von Nathusius Medal of the German Society for Animal Breeding
1965   Armour Award for animal breeding and genetics, American Society of Animal Science
1965   Medal of the Mendel Centennial Association, Czechoslovakia
1966   Order of Merit in Science, Italy
1968   National Medal of Science

MEMBERSHIPS

1967   Member, National Academy of Sciences
1972   Member, Royal Society of Edinburgh
       Foreign member of the Academies of Science or Agriculture of Sweden, Norway, and Italy

BIBLIOGRAPHY

1921

Inheritance in swine. J. Hered., 12:57–71.

1922

An hereditary notch in the ears of Jersey cattle. J. Hered., 13:8–13.
The influence of age and individuality upon the yield of wool. Proc. Am. Soc. Anim. Prod., 1922:105–9.

1923

With E. N. Wentworth. Inheritance in swine. J. Agric. Res., 23:557–82.
With J. M. Jones and J. H. Jones. I. Fattening steers on cottonseed meal and hulls with and without corn. II. The influence of age on fattening steers. Tex. Stn. Bull. 309.
With J. M. Jones. The influence of individuality, age and season upon the weight of fleeces produced by range sheep. Tex. Stn. Bull. 311.

1924

Twinning in Brahma cattle. J. Hered., 15:25–27.
"Double ears" in Brahma cattle. J. Hered., 15:93–96.
With J. M. Jones. The influence of individuality, age and season upon the weights of fleeces produced by Angora goats under range conditions. Tex. Stn. Bull. 320.

1925

The possibility of sex control by artificial insemination with centrifuged spermatozoa. J. Agric. Res., 30:893–913.
With J. M. Jones. Methods of selecting wool samples in shrinkage studies. Proc. Am. Soc. Anim. Prod., 1925:115–17.

1926

Practical methods of estimating the proportions of fat and bone in cattle slaughtered in commercial packing plants. J. Agric. Res., 32:727–55.

Inheritance of horns, wattles, and color in grade Toggenburg goats. J. Hered., 17:72–91.
With W. H. Black. How much accuracy is gained by weighing cattle three days instead of one at the beginning and end of feeding experiments. Proc. Am. Soc. Anim. Prod., 1926:206–10.

1927

"Percentage of blood" and Mendelism. J. Hered., 18:351–67.
Practices and problems involved in crossbreeding cattle in the Coastal Plain of Texas. Proc. Am. Soc. Anim. Prod., 1927:58–61.
With J. M. Jones. A statistical interpretation of some Texas lamb feeding data. Proc. Am. Soc. Anim. Prod., 1927:167–70.

1928

Changes in body measurements of steers during intensive fattening. Tex. Stn. Bull. 385.
With F. W. Christensen, C. V. Wilson, and W. H. Black. The accuracy of cattle weights. J. Agric. Res., 36:551–80.

1929

With W. H. Black and A. T. Semple. The use of dressed beef appraisals in measuring the market desirability of beef cattle. J. Agric. Res., 39:147–62.
Atavism in Jersey cattle. J. Hered., 20:381–83.
Twins in Jersey cattle. J. Hered., 20:510–13.
With J. M. Jones. The inheritance of cryptorchidism. Proc. Am. Soc. Anim. Prod., 1929:57–61.

1930

"Duck-legged" cattle on Texas ranches. J. Hered., 21:84–90.
With J. M. Jones and W. H. Dameron. The inheritance of cryptorchidism in goats. Tex. Stn. Bull. 407.
With J. M. Jones, W. H. Dameron, and O. L. Carpenter. Normal growth of range cattle. Tex. Stn. Bull. 409.
With O. C. Copeland. A study of the accuracy of measurements of dairy cattle. J. Agric. Res., 41:37–49.
Earlessness in Karakul sheep. J. Hered., 21:107–12.
"Nervous" goats. J. Hered., 21:242–47.

How farm animals inherit. (Review of Christian Wriedt's *Heredity in Live Stock.*) J. Hered., 21:306–8.

1931

Interpreting the results of group feeding experiments. Proc. Am. Soc. Anim. Prod., 1930:44–55.
The number of daughters necessary to prove a sire. J. Dairy Sci., 14:209–20.
Predicting gains in feeder cattle and pigs. J. Agric. Res., 42:853–81.

1932

Genetic aspects of the record of performance work with swine. Proc. Am. Soc. Anim. Prod., 1931:51–62.
With M. D. Lacy. The ages of breeding cattle and the possibilities of using proven sires. Iowa Stn. Bull. 290.
With M. D. Lacy. How old are your bulls and cows and what difference does it make? (Abridged ed. Iowa Stn. Bull. 290.) Iowa Stn. Bull. 290A.
An empirical test of the approximate method of calculating coefficients of inbreeding and relationship from livestock pedigrees. J. Agric. Res., 456:565–69.
With A. B. Chapman. Twinning, sex-ratios, and genetic variability in birth weight in sheep. J. Hered., 23:473–78.
The relation of body shape of feeder steers to rate of gain, to dressing percent, and to value of dressed carcass. Tex. Stn. Bull. 471.
The amount and kind of inbreeding which has occurred in the development of breeds of livestock. In: *Proceedings of the Sixth International Congress of Genetics*, vol. 2, pp. 123–26. Menasha, Wisc.: Brooklyn Botanic Garden.
Mutton, and how it gets that way. (Review of John Hammond's *Growth and the Development of Mutton Qualities in the Sheep.*) J. Hered., 23:312–14.

1933

With W. F. Dickson. Inbreeding and the genetic history of the Rambouillet sheep in America. J. Hered., 24:19–33.

The use of statistical methods in animal husbandry. Proc. Am. Soc. Anim. Prod., 1932, 15–29.
Linebreeding. Iowa Agric. Exp. Stn. Bull. 301.
With P. B. Pearson. A linebreeding program for horse breeding. J. Hered., 24:185–91.
The bull index problem in the light of modern genetics. J. Dairy Sci., 16:501–22.

1934

With A. L. Anderson, C. C. Culbertson, and W. E. Hammond. The reliability of some measures of productiveness in brood sows. Proc. Am. Soc. Anim. Prod., 1933:282–87.
With Mogens Plum. Freshening ages of purebred cows in Iowa cow testing associations. J. Dairy Sci., 17:625–38.
With G. M. Harris and E. N. Shultz. Progress report on comparison of lactation and yearly records. J. Dairy Sci., 17:737–42.
With W. H. Black and A. T. Semple. Beef production and quality as influenced by crossing Brahman with Hereford and Shorthorn cattle. U.S. Dep. Agric. Tech. Bull. 417.
A herd of cattle bred for twenty years without new blood. J. Hered., 25:209–16.
With H. O. Hetzer and C. C. Culbertson. Factors affecting birth weights of swine. Genetics, 19:329–43.

1935

Progeny test and individual performance as indicators of an animal's breeding value. J. Dairy Sci., 18:1–19.
The inheritance of productivity in farm live stock. V. Discussion of preceding contributions. Emp. J. Exp. Agric., 3:25–30.

1936

With J. C. Holbert and O. S. Willham. Genetic history of the Holstein-Friesian cattle in the United States. J. Hered., 27:61–72.
Genetics and animal breeding. (Review of C. Kronacher's *Genetik und Tierzuchtung*.) J. Hered., 27:201–3.
Genetic aspects of the Danish system of progeny-testing swine. Iowa Agric. Exp. Stn. Res. Bull. 204.
With B. H. Thomas, C. C. Culbertson, and F. J. Beard. Variations

in the softness of lard produced in the record performance testing. Proc. Am. Soc. Anim. Prod., 1936:258–59.

1937

With Dorsa M. Yoder. A genetic history of the Brown Swiss cattle in the United States. J. Hered., 28:154–60.
Identical twins in cattle. (Review of C. Kronacher's *Neue Ergebnisse der Zwillingsforschung beim Rind.*) J. Hered., 28:415–18.
Animal Breeding Plans. Ames, Iowa: The Collegiate Press.
With A. E. Molln. The degree to which litter size is a constant characteristic of sows. Proc. Am. Soc. Anim. Prod., 1937:133–37.

1938

With Earl N. Shultz. Pedigree promise and progeny test among sires proved in Iowa Cow Testing Associations. J. Dairy Sci., 21:421–32.
Teaching animal breeding. Proc. Am. Soc. Anim. Prod., 1938:175–80.

1939

With P. S. Shearer and C. C. Culbertson. Crossbreeding hogs for pork production. Iowa Agric. Exp. Stn. Bull. 380.
With J. C. Berry. High records contrasted with unselected records and with average records as a basis for selecting cows. J. Dairy Sci., 22:607–17.
With A. L. Anderson. A genetic history of Poland-China swine. J. Hered., 30:149–56, 219–24.
President's address. Proc. Am. Soc. Anim. Prod., 1939:11–18.

1940

Intra-sire correlations or regressions of offspring on dam as a method of estimating heritability of characteristics. Proc. Am. Soc. Anim. Prod., 1940:293–301.
With D. M. Seath. "Nicking" in dairy cattle. J. Dairy Sci., 23:103–13.

1941

With H. W. Norton III and Floyd Arnold. Effects which selection of dams may have on sire indexes. J. Dairy Sci., 24:695–721.
With P. S. Shearer and C. C. Culbertson. Crossbreeding hogs? Farm Sci. Rep., January:8–11.
Applications of genetics to animal breeding. Proc. Iowa Acad. Sci., 48:65–72. (Also in Portuguese in: Ceres [Brazil], 6[1944]:44–51.)

1942

With L. N. Hazel. The efficiency of three methods of selection. J. Hered., 33:393–99.
With F. S. Straus. The heritability of butterfat production in dairy cattle. J. Dairy Sci., 25:975–82.
With A. E. Molln. Litter size and weight as permanent characteristics of sows. U.S. Dep. Agric. Tech. Bull. 836.
With H. H. Stonaker. Heritability of conformation in Poland-China swine as evaluated by scoring. J. Anim. Sci., 1:99–105.
With Leslie E. Johnson. Repeatability of type ratings in dairy cattle. J. Dairy Sci., 25:45–56.

1943

Animal Breeding Plans, 2d ed. Ames, Iowa: The Collegiate Press.

1944

The optimum emphasis on dam's records when proving dairy sires. J. Dairy Sci., 27:937–51.
Are better hogs coming? Farm Sci. Rep., April:3–6.

1945

Animal Breeding Plans, 3d ed. Ames, Iowa: The Collegiate Press.

1946

Chance as a cause of changes in gene frequency within pure breeds of livestock. Am. Nat., 80:318–42.
With G. E. Dickerson and C. C. Culbertson. Hybrid vigor in single crosses between inbred lines of Poland-China swine. J. Anim. Sci., 5:16–24.
With Roberto M. Miranda and C. C. Culbertson. Factors affecting

rate of gain and their relation to allotment of pigs for feeding trials. J. Anim. Sci., 5:243–50.
Out on first record? Iowa Farm Sci., January: 6–7.
With R. C. Cook. Genetics for the millions. (Review of Dunn and Dobzhansky's *Heredity, Race and Society*.) J. Hered., 38:299–305.

1947

With Robert R. Shrode. The genetics of cattle. Adv. Genet., 1:209–61.
With Raul Brequet, Jr. Heritability of amount of spotting in Holstein-Friesian cattle. J. Hered., 38:98–105.
Family merit and individual merit as bases for selection. Am. Nat., 81:241–61, 362–79.

1948

With G. G. Carneiro. Variations in yield of milk under the pen keeping system in Brazil. J. Dairy Sci., 31:203–11.
With W. F. Lamoreux and L. N. Hazel. The heritability of resistance to death in the fowl. Poult. Sci., 27(4):375–88.
The genetics of populations. Mimeo. 381 pp.

1949

Heritability of quantitative characters in farm animals. In: *Proceedings of the Eighth International Genetics Congress*, pp. 356–75. Lund: Berlingska Boktryckeriet.
Ernest W. Lindstrom, 1891–1948. J. Hered., 40(2):44–46.
The algebra of genetics. (Review of C. C. Li's *An Introduction to Population Genetics*.) J. Hered., 40:156.

1950

With R. W. Touchberry. The accuracy of linear body measurements of dairy cattle. J. Dairy Sci., 33(1):72–80.
Inheritance of susceptibility to mastitis. J. Dairy Sci., 33(2):121–25.
With R. H. Nelson. The effects of mild inbreeding on a herd of Holstein-Friesian cattle. J. Dairy Sci., 33:186–93.
With R. R. Shrode. Changes in milk production with age and milking frequency. J. Dairy Sci., 33(5):338–57.
Review of R. A. Fisher's "The Theory of Inbreeding." Am. J. Hum. Genet., 2(1):97–100.

With Martin Polhemus and Walter C. Rothenbuhler. Mating systems in honey bees. J. Hered., 41(6):151–55.
With L. N. Hazel. Computing inbreeding and relationship coefficients from punched cards. J. Hered., 41:301–6.

1951

Summary. (Symposium on selection, Chicago, November 1949.) J. Anim. Sci., 10:18–21.
The impact of genetics on animal breeding. A general invitation review and forecast. J. Anim. Sci., 10(2):311–21.
Inbreeding and outbreeding as practiced with poultry. In: *Proceedings of the Fourth Pacific Northwest Chicken and Turkey Breeders Roundtable*, pp. 11–18. Mimeographed.
Numbers of sires, dams and progeny required for reliable progeny testing. In: *Proceedings of the Fourth Pacific Northwest Chicken and Turkey Breeders Roundtable*, pp. 68–74. Mimeographed.

1952

With Walter R. Harvey. Genetic correlation between type and production in Jersey cattle. J. Dairy Sci., 35(3):199–213.
How dominance and gene interaction modify the effectiveness of breeding plans. In: *Proceedings of the First Poultry Breeders Roundtable*, pp. 15–25. Mimeographed.

1954

Breeding structure of populations. I. General considerations. In: *Statistics and Mathematics in Biology*, pp. 537–42. Ames: Iowa State College Press.
With J. E. Legates. A selection index for fat production in dairy cattle: Utilizing the fat yields of the cow and her close relatives. J. Dairy Sci., 37(6):744–53.
With G. G. Carneiro. Reproductive rates and growth of purebred Brown Swiss cattle in Brazil. J. Dairy Sci., 37:1145–57.
Rates of genetic changes in populations of farm animals. In: *Proceedings of the Ninth International Congress of Genetics*, vol. 6, Suppl., pp. 589–99. Florence: Ex. Officina Typographica Florentina.

1955

Estimates of heritability in breeding problems. In: *Breeding Beef Cattle Adapted to Unfavorable Environments*, King Ranch Centennial, pp. 113–26. Austin: University of Texas Press.
With Lon D. McGilliard. Proving sires and dams. J. Dairy Sci., 38:163–80.
With D. E. Madden and L. D. McGilliard. Relations between parts of lactations and producing ability of Holstein cows. J. Dairy Sci., 38(11):1264–71.
Gene action as related to physiological characteristics. In: *Proceedings of the Fourth Poultry Breeders Roundtable*, pp. 7–23. Mimeographed.
Statistics in investigations in animal production. J. Ind. Soc. Agric. Stat., 7:7–22.

1956

Dairy cattle genetics. J. Dairy Sci., 39(6):693–94.
With L. D. McGilliard. Changes in type classifications of dairy cattle. J. Dairy Sci., 39(7):1015–26.
Answer to query about repeatability of number at a birth. Biometrics, 12(1):84–88.
Theoretical consequences of breeding for the heterozygote. In: *Proceedings of the Fifth Poultry Breeders Roundtable*, pp. 3–26. Mimeographed.
Recent advances in animal breeding. In: *Proceedings of the Western Section, American Society of Animal Production*, pp. 20–21. Mimeographed.

1957

With David E. Anderson and Doyle Chambers. Studies on bovine ocular squamous carcinoma. II. Relationship between eyelid pigmentation and occurrence of cancer eye lesions. J. Anim. Sci., 16:739–46.
With David E. Anderson and Doyle Chambers. Studies on bovine ocular squamous carcinoma. III. Inheritance of eyelid pigmentation. J. Anim. Sci., 16:1007–16.
With C. E. Meadows. Twinning in dairy cattle and its relation to production. J. Dairy Sci., 40:1430–36.

1958

With C. M. von Krosigk. Effect of inbreeding on production in Holsteins. J. Dairy Sci., 41:105–13.

Practical applications of performance testing. The Shorthorn World, 43(11):44, 318–21.

Genetics in plant and animal breeding. (Translated title.) Tolvmandsbladet, 30(10):403–9.

With D. W. Blackmore and L. D. McGilliard. Genetic relations between body measurements at three ages in Holsteins. J. Dairy Sci., 41:1045–49.

With D. W. Blackmore and L. D. McGilliard. Relationships between body measurements, meat conformation, and milk production. J. Dairy Sci., 41:1050–56.

1959

With F. Pirchner. Genetic and environmental portions of the variation among herds in butterfat production. J. Dairy Sci., 42:115–22.

Making use of new knowledge about basic principles. In: *Proceedings of the Eighth Poultry Breeders Roundtable*, pp. 141–55. Mimeographed.

With Ivar Johansson. Zucht- und selektionsmethoden. In: *Handbuch der Tiersuchtung*, vol. 2, pp. 383–473.

1960

Improving dairy cattle by breeding. I. Current status and outlook. J. Dairy Sci., 43:702–6.

1961

With John D. Wheat. Accuracy of partial trapnest records. Poult. Sci., 40(2):399–406.

Mejoramiento Animal. Publicacion Tecnica no. 6. Buenos Aires: CAFADE.

Selection indexes for dairy cattle. Z. Tierz., 75(3):249–261.

Large farm animals. Germ Plasm Resour., 66:127–36.

Der Sinn und die Bedeutung des Erblichkeitsanteiles. In: *Vortrage des II Internationalen Ferienkurses u.s.w.*, Mariensee, Germany, pp. 171–99.

1962

With T. M. Sutherland. Effects of inbreeding on size and type in Holstein-Friesian cattle. J. Dairy Sci., 45(3):390–95.

Obituary: Edward N. Wentworth. Rec. Genet. Soc. Am., 31:20–21.

1964

With Hector A. Molinuevo. Reliability of first, second and third records for estimating the breeding value of dairy cows. J. Dairy Sci., 47(8):890–93.

1965

With Ben Bereskin. Genetic and environmental factors in dairy sire evaluation. III. Influence of environmental and other extraneous correlations among the daughters. J. Dairy Sci., 48:356–60.

1967

With D. J. Kelleher and A. E. Freeman. Importance of bull × herd-year-season interaction in milk production. J. Dairy Sci., 50:1703–7.

1968

Importance of family structure in the dairy cattle population. J. Dairy Sci., 51:296–306.

With R. M. Acharya. Genetic progress through selection in a closed herd of Indian cattle. J. Dairy Sci., 5:1059–64.

1969

Genetic unknowns in animal breeding a century after Mendel. Trans. Kans. Acad. Sci., 71:309.

Pushing back the frontier of animal breeding. In: *Proceedings of the Eighteenth Annual Session, National Poultry Breeders Roundtable*, pp. 93–111. Mimeographed.

1971

Research in animal production: Its accomplishments and present prospects. In: *Bulletin of the Swiss Association of Agricultural Graduates from the Eidgenossischen Technischen Hochschule* (ETH), Zurich, November, pp. 45–62.

1972

Early statistics at Iowa State University. In: *Statistical Papers in Honor of George W. Snedecor,* pp. 211–26. Ames: Iowa State University Press.

1973

Teaching animal breeding and training graduate students. In: *Proceedings of the Animal Breeding and Genetics Symposium in Honor of Dr. Jay L. Lush,* American Society of Animal Science, American Dairy Science Association, and Poultry Science Association, Blacksburg, Virginia, July 29, 1972, pp. 78–88.

1974

Dedication of the Jay L. Lush auditorium—response by Jay L. Lush. Iowa State J. Res., 48(4):281–84.

JOHN HOWARD MUELLER

June 13, 1891–February 16, 1954

BY A. M. PAPPENHEIMER, JR.

JOHN HOWARD MUELLER was born June 13, 1891, in Sheffield, Massachusetts, where his father was a Unitarian minister. After a few years, the family moved to Illinois, where young Howard received his secondary schooling. He then attended Illinois Wesleyn University, receiving his B.S. degree with honors in biology in 1912. Two years as an instructor of chemistry at the University of Louisville followed; he was awarded an M.S. degree in 1914.

While at Louisville he became interested in bacteriology and pathology, and in the summer of 1914 he attended a summer course in pathology at the College of Physicians and Surgeons, Columbia University. The instructors in this course encouraged him to remain as a graduate student at Columbia, which he did. He was awarded an Alonzo Clark Fellowship in Pathology and received his Ph.D. degree in 1916. He worked as assistant pathologist at the Presbyterian Hospital until war was declared in 1917; he then enlisted as a private and went overseas with the Presbyterian Hospital Unit to Etretat, France, where he actively participated in the work that demonstrated that "trench fever" (like typhus fever, a rickettsial disease) was transmitted by lice. It was doubtless during this period that he became interested in pathogenic bacteria and in their physiology and metabolism. His talents were recognized by the Army, and he was commissioned a lieutenant in the Sanitary Corps before the war ended.

On his return to civilian life in 1919, Mueller was appointed an instructor in the bacteriology department, chaired by Hans Zinsser, at the College of Physicians and Surgeons. There he began his studies on the cultural requirements of pathogenic bacteria. Papers I and II of this series appeared in 1922. In introducing the series, Mueller wrote:

> Perhaps the most important results to which success in such a piece of work might lead, are the applications of the findings to problems of more general biological importance, particularly to those of animal metabolism. For, whatever may prove to be the nature of these substances which cause growth of bacteria, they are largely or entirely components of animal tissue, and it is probable that they are either needed also by the animal body and supplied by plant or other sources, or else are synthesized by the animal itself to fill some metabolic requirement. When it is possible to catalogue the substances required by pathogenic bacteria for growth, it will probably be found that most of them are either required by, or important in, animal metabolism, and while many of them will surely be compounds at present familiar to the physiological chemist, it is equally probable that some will be new, or at least of hitherto unrecognized importance.

It was not long before his predictions were verified. He soon found that although he could use an acid hydrolysate of animal protein supplemented with tryptophane—instead of commercial "peptones"—as a base for growth of *Streptococcus hemolyticus,* the hydrolysate could not be replaced by a mixture of the then known amino acids. This led to the fractionation of casein hydrolysate and to the discovery of a new, ubiquitously distributed sulfur-containing amino acid: methionine. Mueller's 1923 paper in the *Journal of Biological Chemistry* reporting the isolation of the new amino acid from acid hydrolysates of casein and of ovalbumin and his determination of its elemental composition is an excellent example of the thoroughness that characterized all of his work. He made a good many derivatives and carried out the elementary analysis of each one himself. This led to the correct empirical formula: $C_5H_{11}NO_2S$. Only two likely structural formulae were possible. An organic chemist from Cambridge University suggested to him that the new amino acid might simply be the ethyl thioether of cysteine. Mueller proceeded to synthesize this thioether and proved that it was *not* identical with his new amino acid, the structure of which he stated remained to be determined.

In the same year as the discovery of methionine, Hans Zinsser was appointed chairman of the Department of Bacteriology and Immunology at the Harvard Medical School and asked Mueller to join him as an assistant professor. After arriving in Boston, Mueller was persuaded to abandon—temporarily—his studies on bacterial nutrition. Instead he joined Zinsser in the study of so-called "residue antigens" extracted from pneumococci, tubercle bacilli, yeast, and other microorganisms. These heat-stable, nonprotein antigens were independently shown to be polysaccharides by Avery and his coworkers, whose subsequent brilliant work revealed their role in the pathogenesis of pneumococcal lobar pneumonia and other bacterial diseases.

At about this time in England, W. E. Gye published a series of papers purporting to show that Rous chicken sarcoma filtrates contained two essential factors, both of which were required for tumour induction. The first was a substance specifically affecting certain chicken cells and thereby rendering them susceptible to transformation to malignancy by a virus. The same virus was supposedly present in many mammalian tumours, including human carcinomas. Because the implications of this work seemed so important at the time, Mueller attempted unsuccessfully to repeat Gye's experiments and spent several frustrating years working on this problem. In the end, Gye came to work in Mueller's laboratory, and in 1929 a joint paper appeared in the *Journal of Experimental Medicine*—but with two opposing sets of conclusions: one written by Gye, the other by Mueller. Subsequent events proved Mueller's interpretation of the data to be correct.

After these rather disappointing years, Mueller finally returned to the field that had always been his major interest since his early work leading to the discovery of methionine. Papers I and II of the series "Studies on the Culture Requirements of Bacteria" appeared in the *Journal of Bacteriology* in 1922; paper III did not appear until 1933! Nevertheless, in 1930 when Mueller began his classic studies on the nutrition of the diphtheria bacillus, bacterial cells were *still* regarded as lowly forms of life that had little, if any, relationship to the cells of higher animals and plants. Tissue extractives, inspissated serum, "peptones," etc., were regarded as essential for the cultivation of pathogenic microorganisms, and any notion of bacterial genetics was unheard of. It was not until 1929 that the first enzyme (urease) was crystallized and shown to be protein.

The decade that followed must be regarded as the most fruitful of Mueller's career. He selected the diphtheria bacillus as the organism for his intensive studies. From the very outset, he recognized the importance of being able to measure growth quantitatively. Spectrophotometers were not yet on the market, and Mueller decided to use the micro-Kjeldhal method for estimation of growth as bacterial nitrogen. Although this method was tedious, it was accurate. It also gave him a great advantage over others who were beginning to enter the field because it became possible to work out conditions for *maximal* yields of the bacteria and their products.

Within a few years the Mueller laboratory had identified

which amino acids were essential for growth of the diphtheria bacillus and had made the important observation that different strains of the same bacillus varied widely in their amino acid requirements. (For example, if a certain amino acid was not needed for growth of a given strain, that strain possessed the enzymes required for its biosynthesis.) Mueller then went on to isolate and identify what he called "accessory" factors. He isolated nicotinic acid from liver and showed that it or nicotinamide were essential growth factors for all strains of the diphtheria bacillus being tested. With S. Cohen he isolated a second factor from liver that proved to be β-alanine. He then showed that pantothenic acid would also satisfy the β-alanine requirement, and others found diphtherial strains that were dependent on pantothenic acid itself for growth. Soon afterward, both nicotinamide and pantothenic acid were shown to be part of the vitamin B complex required for animal nutrition. Finally, in paper X of the series that appeared in 1937, Mueller described the isolation and identification of pimelic acid from cow urine, which was required in trace amounts for growth. Later, after the discovery of biotin, pimelic acid was shown by du Vigneaud to be an intermediate in biotin biosynthesis.

Thus, by 1940 the prediction Mueller had made in 1922 had been fully realized, and the universality of biochemistry had become accepted by everyone. The importance of Mueller's research in helping to bring about this recognition should not be forgotten. It was his work on bacterial nutrition that paved the way for the rapid identification of coenzymes and for the elucidation of the pathways of intermediary metabolism and biosynthesis that took place in the 1940s and early 1950s. The work on nutrition of the diphtheria bacillus also had important practical applications in improving the yield and quality of the diphtheria toxin used in production of toxoid for human immunization. By 1941 the diphtherial studies were essentially complete, and Mueller turned his major attention to the tetanus bacillus and to production of its toxin. These studies were still in progress at the time of his death in 1954.

Hans Zinsser died in 1940 and shortly thereafter Howard Mueller was appointed to succeed him as head of the department. Mueller was one of those rare individuals who continued to work with his own hands even after becoming chairman of a large department at a major university. He was an early riser, and daybreak usually found him at the bench. Several hours later, soon after his devoted research associate and friend Pauline Miller had arrived, Mueller was ready to leave the laboratory for his office to pursue his administrative duties. He took his obligations toward the department, toward the teaching of medical students, and toward his clinical associates very seriously. He was interested in all aspects of infectious disease and felt that his own research should be medically oriented with ultimate practical applications. And indeed, in addition to its fundamental scientific importance, much of his work did have important practical application in immunization and in diagnosis.

Mueller was a man of great generosity who had impeccable integrity—particularly with regard to scientific accuracy—and an unusual capacity for brushing aside all that was irrelevant in order to get at the core of the matter. He had no use for the sham, the half-truth, or the pretentious. Those who knew him well were always impressed by his modesty—indeed, he used to refer to himself as only "a high school chemist." Yet as pointed out in the "Minute" on his life that was read to the faculty of medicine of Harvard University following his death: "Howard Mueller belongs among the scientific 'élite' as Kirtley Mather has recently defined them—that is among those who actively seek insight and meaning, whose minds are constantly on the alert to the possibility of new generalizations and new relationships as distinguished from those who merely know how to do that which they have been trained to do." No better example of his remarkable insight can be given than his reaction to the 1944 discovery by Avery, Macleod, and McCarty that the rough-to-smooth transformation could be induced by DNA. In his chapter on the chemistry and metabolism of bacteria, which was written in that same year for the *Annual Review of Biochemistry,* Mueller wrote (the italics are mine):

> In other words it appears that a polymer of a nucleic acid may be incorporated into a living, degraded cell, and will endow the cells with a property never previously possessed, namely, the ability to produce a capsule composed of a complex polysaccharide entirely different in structure from that produced by the smooth organism from which the degraded form was originally derived. When thus induced the function is permanent, and the nucleic acid itself is also reproduced in cell division. The importance of these observations can scarcely be overestimated and stimulates speculation concerning such matters as the chemical basis for specificity in nucleic acids, and the *genetic* implications presented by the ability to induce permanent *mutation* in a cell by the introduction of a chemical substance. Such speculation may well include considerations of the relation of this phenomenon to the sequence of events following the introduction of a filterable virus (or a bacteriophage particle) into a susceptible cell.

Mueller wrote those words at a time when recombination in bacteria was unknown, microbial genetics did not exist, and no one had previously spoken of mutations in connection with bacteria.

BIBLIOGRAPHY

1920–1921

Growth-determining substances in bacteriological culture media. Proc. Soc. Exp. Biol. Med., 18:225–28.

Observations on bacterial metabolism. Proc. Soc. Exp. Biol. Med., 18:14–17.

1921–1922

A new sulphur-containing amino acid isolated from casein. Proc. Soc. Exp. Biol. Med., 19:161–63.

1922

Studies on cultural requirements of bacteria. I. J. Bacteriol., 7:309–24.

Studies on cultural requirements in bacteria. II. J. Bacteriol., 7:325–38.

1923

A new sulfur-containing amino-acid isolated from the hydrolytic products of protein. J. Biol. Chem., 56:157–69.

A new sulfur-containing amino-acid isolated from the hydrolytic products of protein. II. Sulfur excretion after ingestion. J. Biol. Chem., 58:373–75.

1924

With J. Tomcsik. The chemical nature of residue antigen prepared from yeast. J. Exp. Med., 40:343–52.

With M. Wayman and H. Zinsser. A preliminary report on the chemical composition of residue antigen. Proc. Soc. Exp. Biol. Med., 21:241–43.

1925

With H. Zinsser. On the nature of bacterial allergies. J. Exp. Med., 41:159.

A chemical study of tuberculin. Proc. Soc. Exp. Biol. Med., 22:209–11.

With D. E. Smith and S. Litarczek. "Residue antigen" from a strain of Friedlander bacillus. Proc. Soc. Exp. Biol. Med., 22:373–74.

Chemical studies on tuberculin. Proc. Natl. Acad. Sci. USA, 11:23–25.

1926

Observations on Gye's work with the Rous sarcoma. Proc. Soc. Exp. Biol. Med., 23:704.
A chemical study of the specific elements of tuberculin. I. J. Exp. Med., 43:1–8.
A chemical study of the specific elements of tuberculin. II. The preparation of residue antigen from old tuberculin. J. Exp. Med., 43:9–12.

1927

The virus problem in transplantable tumors. (Abstract.) J. Bacteriol., 13:26.
An experimental study of Gye's cancer theory. J. Exp. Med., 45:243–62.

1928

With H. Zinsser. Antigenic properties of the bacterial cell and antibody reactions. In: *The Newer Knowledge of Bacteriology and Immunology*, ed. E. O. Jordan and I. S. Falk, pp. 721–32. Chicago: University of Chicago Press.
The effect of oxidation of filtrates on a chicken sarcoma (chicken tumor I-Rous). J. Exp. Med., 48:343–49.
The oxidative destruction of the agent of the chicken tumor I (Rous). Science, 68:88–89.

1929

With W. F. Gye. An experimental study of the etiology of chicken sarcoma I (Rous). J. Exp. Med., 49:195.

1931

With L. Whitman. An improved method for the detection of hemolytic streptococcus carriers. J. Bacteriol., 21:219–23.
The effect of alexin in virus–antivirus mixtures. J. Immunol., 20:17–23.

1932

With K. S. Klise. Agglutination of hemolytic streptococci. (Abstract.) J. Bacteriol., 23:83.
With K. S. Klise. Mass cultures of *Streptococcus hemolyticus* in broth. Proc. Soc. Exp. Biol. Med., 29:454–55.
With S. Sturgis. Prevention of blood coagulation by cysteine. Science, 75:140.
With K. S. Klise. A method for the agglutination of hemolytic streptococci. J. Immunol., 22:53–59.

1933

With K. S. Klise, E. F. Porter, and A. Graybiel. Studies on cultural requirements of bacteria. III. The diphtheria bacillus. J. Bacteriol., 25:509–19.
With K. S. Klise. An agglutinative classification of the hemolytic streptococci of scarlet fever. J. Infect. Dis., 52:139–45.

1934

Amino acids required by the diphtheria bacillus for growth. Proc. Soc. Exp. Biol. Med., 32:318–20.

1935

Studies on cultural requirements of bacteria. IV. Quantitative estimation of bacterial growth. J. Bacteriol., 29:383–87.
Studies on cultural requirements of bacteria. V. The diphtheria bacillus. J. Bacteriol., 29:515–30.
Studies on cultural requirements of bacteria. VI. The diphtheria bacillus. J. Bacteriol., 30:513–24.
With I. Kapnick. Studies on cultural requirements of bacteria. VII. Amino acid requirements for the Park-Williams no. 8 strain of diphtheria. J. Bacteriol., 30:525–34.
Methionine as an impurity in natural leucine preparations. Science, 81:50–51.

1936

Studies on cultural requirements of bacteria. VIII. Utilization of glutamic acid by the diphtheria bacillus. J. Bacteriol., 32:207–10.

1937

With Y. Subbarow. Studies on cultural requirements of bacteria. IX. Tissue extractives in the growth of the diphtheria bacillus. J. Bacteriol., 34:153–61.
Studies on cultural requirements of bacteria. X. Pimelic acid as a growth stimulant for *C. diphtheriae.* J. Bacteriol., 34:163–78.
With S. Cohen. Beta alanine as a growth accessory for the diphtheria bacillus. J. Bacteriol., 34:381–86.
Nicotinic acid as a growth accessory substance for the diphtheria bacillus. J. Bacteriol., 34:429–41.
Pimelic acid as a growth accessory for the diphtheria bacillus. J. Biol. Chem., 119:121–31.
Substitution of β-alanine, nicotinic acid, and pimelic acid for meat extract in growth of diphtheria bacillus. Proc. Soc. Exp. Biol. Med., 36:706–8.
Nicotinic acid as a growth accessory for the diphtheria bacillus. J. Biol. Chem., 120:219–24.
Pimelic acid as a growth accessory factor for a strain of the diphtheria bacillus. Science, 85:502.
With A. M. Pappenheimer, Jr., and S. Cohen. Production of potent diphtherial toxin on a medium of chemically defined composition. Proc. Soc. Exp. Biol. Med., 36:795–96.

1938

The replacement of meat infusion by known substances in the cultivation of *Corynebacterium diphtheriae.* (Abstract.) J. Bacteriol., 35:7–8.
A synthetic medium for the cultivation of *C. diphtheriae.* J. Bacteriol., 36:499–515.
The utilization of carnosine by the diphtheria bacillus. J. Biol. Chem., 123:421.
With A. Klotz. Pantothenic acid as a growth factor for the diphtheria bacillus. J. Am. Chem. Soc., 60:3086–87.

1939

Factors concerned in formation of toxin by the diphtheria bacillus. (Abstract.) In: *Third International Congress for Microbiology, Abstracts of Communications,* p. 203. International Association for Microbiology.

A simplified formula for diphtheria toxin broth. J. Immunol., 37:103–12.
An unidentified growth factor for certain strains of the diphtheria bacillus. Proc. Soc. Exp. Biol. Med., 40:632–33.

1940

Physical and chemical properties of filterable viruses. In: *Virus and Rickettsial Diseases with Especial Consideration of Their Public Health Significance*, pp. 65–88. Cambridge, Mass.: Harvard University Press.
With P. A. Miller. Tetanus toxin production on a simplified medium. Proc. Soc. Exp. Biol. Med., 43:389–90.
With J. C. Snyder. Nutritional factors concerned with colony development of *C. diphtheriae*. Proc. Soc. Exp. Biol. Med., 45:243.
With S. Cohen. Oleic acid in colony development of *C. diphtheriae*. Proc. Soc. Exp. Biol. Med., 45:244.
Hans Zinsser (1878–1940). J. Bacteriol., 40:747–53.
Nutrition of the diphtheria bacillus. Bacteriol. Rev., 4:97–134.

1941

With P. A. Miller. Production of diphtheric toxin of high potency (100 Lf) on a reproducible medium. J. Immunol., 40:21–32.
With E. R. Johnson. Acid hydrolysates of casein to replace peptone in the preparation of bacteriological media. J. Immunol., 40:33–38.
With P. A. Miller. A modification of Rosenthal's chromium-sulfuric acid method for anaerobic cultures. J. Bacteriol., 41:301–3.
With S. Cohen and J. C. Snyder. Factors concerned in the growth of *Cornyebacterium diphtheriae* from minute inocula. J. Bacteriol., 41:581–91.
With E. B. Schoenbach and J. F. Enders. The apparent effect of tyrothrycin on *Streptococcus hemolyticus* in the rhinopharynx of carriers. Science, 94:217–18.
The influence of iron on the production of diphtheria toxin. J. Immunol., 42:343.
With J. Hinton. A protein-free medium for primary isolation of the gonococcus and meningococcus. Proc. Soc. Exp. Biol. Med., 48:330–33.

1942

With O. F. Cox and M. McDermott. Delayed planting of gonococcus cultures: Preliminary report. Vener. Dis. Info., 23:226–27.
With J. Hinton and P. A. Miller. Growth requirements of *Neisseria*. (Abstract.) J. Bacteriol., 43:100.
With P. A. Miller. Growth requirements of *Clostridium tetani*. J. Bacteriol., 43:763–72.
With P. A. Miller. Folic acid in the growth of *Cl. tetani*. Proc. Soc. Exp. Biol. Med., 49:211–12.

1943

With R. E. Feeney and P. A. Miller. Growth requirements of *Clostridium tetani*. II. Factors exhausted by growth of the organism. J. Bacteriol., 46:559–62.
With R. E. Feeney and P. A. Miller. Growth requirements of *Clostridium tetani*. III. A "synthetic" medium. J. Bacteriol., 46:563–71.
With P. A. Miller. Large-scale production of tentanal toxin on a peptone-free medium. J. Immunol., 47:15–22.
The relation of the carrier to epidemic meningitis. Ann. Intern. Med., 18:974–77.
With L. R. Seidman and P. A. Miller. A comparison of antigenicities of hydrolysate and peptone tetanus toxoids in the guinea pig. J. Clin. Invest., 22:321–24.
With E. B. Schoenbach and J. J. Jezukawicz. Conversion of hydrolysate tetanus toxin to toxoid. J. Clin. Invest., 22:319–20.
With E. B. Schoenbach, J. J. Jezukawicz, and P. A. Miller. Production of tetanus toxin on peptone-free media. J. Clin. Invest., 22:315–18.
With L. R. Seidman and P. A. Miller. Antitoxin response in man to tetanus toxoids. J. Clin. Invest., 22:325–28.

1943–1944

Nutrition of the single cell: Its applications in medical bacteriology. Harvey Lect. Ser. 39:143–61.

1944

With R. G. Gould and L. W. Kane. On the growth requirements of *Neisseria gonorrhoeae*. J. Bacteriol., 47:287–92.

With O. F. Cox and M. A. Kinney. Methods of transporting gonococci to laboratories for cultural studies. Vener. Dis. Info., 25:207–9.

1945

The chemistry and metabolism of bacteria. Annu. Rev. Biochem., 14:733–48.
With P. A. Miller. Production of tetanal toxin. J. Immunol., 50:377–84.

1946

Graduate training in bacteriology. (Abstract.) J. Bacteriol., 51:630.
With P. A. Miller. A new tellurite plating medium and some comments on the laboratory "diagnosis" of diphtheria. J. Bacteriol., 51:743–50.
With H. L. Ley, Jr. On the isolation from agar of an inhibitor for *Neisseria gonorrhoeae*. J. Bacteriol., 52:453–60.

1947

With F. S. Cheever. Epidemic diarrheal disease of suckling mice; manifestations, epidemiology, and attempts to transmit disease. J. Exp. Med., 85:405–16.
With P. A. Miller. Factors influencing the production of tetanal toxin. J. Immunol., 56:143–47.

1948

With P. A. Miller. Factors affecting the production of tetanus toxin: Temperature. J. Bacteriol., 55:421–23.
With S. Lavin and L. E. Farr. Shaking device for multiple containers. Proc. Soc. Exp. Biol. Med., 68:99–100.
With F. S. Cheever. Epidemic diarrheal disease of suckling mice; effect of strain, litter, and season upon incidence of disease. J. Exp. Med., 88:309–16.
With P. A. Miller and E. M. Lerner. Factors influencing the production of tetanus toxin: Gaseous products of growth. J. Bacteriol., 56:97–98.
With P. A. Miller. Unidentified nutrients in tetanus toxin production. J. Bacteriol., 56:219–33.

1949

With P. A. Miller. Inhibition of tetanus toxin formation by D-serine. J. Am. Chem. Soc., 71:1865.

With P. A. Miller. Glutamine in the production of tetanus toxin. J. Biol. Chem., 181:39–41.

1950

The use of thick paper for chromatography. Science, 112:405–6.

With W. L. Aycock. Meningococcus carrier rates and meningitis incidence. Bacteriol. Rev., 14:115–60.

1951

With H. E. Umbarger. Isoleucine and valine metabolism of *Escherichia coli*. I. Growth studies on amino acid-deficient mutants. J. Biol. Chem., 189:277–85.

With R. M. Drew. A chemically defined medium suitable for the production of high titer diphtheriae toxin. J. Bacteriol., 62:549–59.

1954

With P. A. Miller. Variable factors influencing the production of tetanus toxin. J. Bacteriol., 67:271–77.

With N. H. Fisek and P. A. Miller. Muscle extractives in the production of tetanus toxin. J. Bacteriol., 67:329–34.

1955

With P. A. Miller. Separation from tryptic digests of casein of some acid-labile components essential in tetanus toxin formation. J. Bacteriol., 69:634–42.

Photograph by Fabian Bachrach

ROBERT FRANKLIN PITTS

October 24, 1908–June 6, 1977

BY ROBERT W. BERLINER AND
GERHARD H. GIEBISCH

THE SCIENTIFIC CONTRIBUTIONS of Robert Franklin Pitts have been a major force in molding the shape of renal physiology in the last half-century. There are few aspects of kidney function that he did not explore, and his work illuminated each element that came under his scrutiny. But his contributions to physiology were not limited to the study of the kidney. He produced important work in neurophysiology early in his career, making contributions that for many would be sufficient to lend prestige to the work of a lifetime, but that Bob Pitts was able to accomplish in only a few short years.

Robert F. Pitts was born in Indianapolis on October 24, 1908, the younger of the two children of John Franklin and Estelle Coffin Pitts. His sister Rebecca, three years his senior, has provided much of the information about the family background, childhood, and upbringing of her younger brother. Both parents were members of the Society of Friends and traced their ancestry back to the earliest days of Quakerism. They had known each other since childhood and were married in 1899, moving to Indianapolis the same year. According to Rebecca Pitts: "Because John Franklin Pitts had been a farmer's son, he was ill-equipped for city life, and for several years the young couple was very poor. In fact, throughout

Robert's childhood and youth our circumstances were, though not poverty stricken, certainly marked by severely necessary economies and occasional periods of real hardship. . . . Until Robert was about fourteen his social life was limited to membership in church youth groups. Our parents had strict notions about keeping us at home in the evenings. . . . Such an environment gives lessons in the old Puritan virtues of discipline and industry, economy and careful planning; and my brother learned them very well."

At Butler University, which he entered as an undergraduate a month before his seventeenth birthday, he did very well. According to his sister's account: "He was a member of Phi Delta Theta—a fraternity noted more for football, at least on the Butler campus, than for scholarship. But the Phi Delts were proud of his scholarship . . . and elected him president of the chapter. . . . Although he was never an athlete he was a good tennis player, and in his high school and college years spent many summer afternoons or early mornings on the court."

After receiving the Bachelor of Science degree from Butler at the age of twenty, Bob was awarded a fellowship in biology at Johns Hopkins University. It had been his intention, first expressed at the age of four (!) in admiration of the family doctor, to study medicine. It may be assumed that to obtain a Ph.D. in a basic science was, in view of his financial limitations, a practical step toward his long-term goal. In any case, having had a taste of research in pursuit of his first doctoral degree, it became clear to him that research rather than the practice of medicine was his real passion.

Bob joined the Department of Physiology at the New York University College of Medicine in 1932, fresh from his doctoral work in biology at Johns Hopkins. His dissertation work had dealt with physiological processes in amoebae; having obtained his Ph.D., however, he closed the book on that field and never returned to it. In the 1930s, the NYU Department of Physiology was the center of an intensive exploration of the function of the kidney. Leadership in renal physiology at that time was divided between the group under Homer Smith at NYU and that led by A. N. Richards at the University of Pennsylvania. The approaches of the two groups were quite separate and distinct. Richards and his associates were developing and applying the early and—by latter-day standards—primitive micropuncture techniques. Homer Smith always considered his greatest contribution to experimental physiology to have been the trained, intact, unanesthetized dog. Indeed, except for diversions into work with fish in the summers at the Mount Desert Island Biological Laboratory in Salisbury Cove, Maine, work in the NYU Department of Physiology stuck pretty closely to the intact dog (or occasionally man), and Bob Pitts's work was no exception. In fact, his preference for the intact animal (although not necessarily unanesthetized) was reflected in his experimental work throughout his career, even when most others had shifted, with greatly improved instruments and techniques, to the trail of A. N. Richards and micropuncture.

From 1932 to 1938, Bob Pitts was an active and productive member of the physiology department. His first paper from his new environment at NYU dealt with the relationship between the excretion of inorganic phosphate and the plasma phosphate level in the dog. The subject matter of this work is noteworthy because it was a later and more definitive study of phosphate reabsorption by the renal tubules that led to what most would consider to be Bob Pitts's most important single contribution to renal physiology: his work on acidification of the urine. During this first six-year period at NYU, Bob explored the renal mechanisms involved in the excretion of a number of substances: creatine, urea, xylose, hexamethenamine, ammonia, and phenol red. The work was a significant contribution to the state of the art at the time, although it did not lead to any major new fields of study or new ways of looking at renal function.

During this period, however, Bob found time to enroll as a medical student and, while continuing his work in the laboratory, managed to complete the work for the M.D. degree that he was awarded in 1938. It is clear, moreover, that his completion of medical school was not accomplished in an offhand way: he graduated at the head of his class and received a medal for his work in pathology, as well as the senior prizes in both medicine and surgery! Although he never chose to develop his obvious talent for clinical activities, his thorough grounding in medicine influenced all his subsequent efforts, and he never failed to orient his fundamental physiological work to clinically important problems and to call attention to the relevance of his findings to medicine.

Those whose exposure to biomedical science has been limited to the more recent era of relative affluence and availability of research funds may imagine that Pitts's coworkers and technicians kept things running in the lab with only periodic guidance from him, thus allowing him to continue his research in the laboratory while giving unstinted attention to the medical school curriculum. Nothing could be further from the truth. He did all of his own experiments and all of the analyses himself. It is also probable, although undocumented, that he washed his own glassware. Nevertheless, in that six-year period, he published twelve highly creditable papers, and he was the sole author of eleven of them.

Upon graduation from medical school, he chose to launch into a new field and, as a fellow of the Rockefeller Foundation, he spent a year at Northwestern University in the laboratory of Magoun and Ranson and the subsequent year in the Johnson Foundation laboratories at the University of Pennsylvania with Detlev Bronk. (Both of these were leading laboratories in what would now be called neuroscience.) Although many would hold that one year in a laboratory is hardly enough time to accomplish anything much, particularly in a new field, it is apparent that this rule did not apply in this instance. The immediate output of that brief period was eight papers; for seven of them, Pitts was the senior author. Moreover, he did not merely fall in step with projects already under way. He built his own electronic equipment and launched into a new field: the study of the medullary respiratory centers and related phenomena. The judgment of those familiar with the field appears to have been that these were important contributions to neurophysiology. Some six years later, when he had already established himself as the leading contributor to renal physiology, he was still the author of textbook chapters on the regulation of respiration. In fact, he held what must have been a unique distinction in writing, by invitation, a review entitled "Organization of the Respiratory Center" for *Physiological Reviews* and the chapter on the kidney in *Annual Reviews of Physiology*, both in the same year (1946).

In 1940 he returned as an assistant professor to the Department of Physiology at NYU. For two years he continued his studies on the control of respiration and then moved a short distance up the east side of Manhattan to join the Department of Physiology at Cornell University Medical College. It had been his intention to continue his work in neurophysiology, but the expense of establishing a new laboratory based on electronic equipment, and the difficulty in obtaining financial resources to do so, led him to abandon that plan. All that was needed for his work in renal physiology was a little glassware, some chemicals, and a few trained dogs; so he returned to the study of the kidney. The next four years in New York were a period of productivity that included what Bob himself considered to be some of his best work. It is easy to concur with his judgment without disparagement of the enormous value of his many contributions in subsequent years.

The first few papers that Bob Pitts produced after taking up his position at Cornell dealt with the mechanisms for the reabsorption of amino acids by the renal tubules. He then returned to work on the reabsorption of phosphate, which was described in a paper with Robert Alexander as coauthor: "The Renal Reabsorptive Mechanism for Inorganic Phosphate in Normal and Acidotic Dogs." The essence of this paper was that phosphate was reabsorbed with a saturable transport process and that the capacity of this transport process was not affected by changes in the acid-base status of the animal.

Many years later, in a 1971 paper entitled "Some Aphorisms on Research and Writing," Bob related how this study led to his work on the mechanism of urinary acidification. It seems that Bob presented the results of the study at the Cornell Research Society, where his statement that phosphate reabsorption was not increased by acidosis was challenged by one of his biochemist colleagues. This colleague stated that inasmuch as it was well known that the urine is rendered acid by the reabsorption of disodium phosphate, leaving behind the more acid member of the buffer pair, the reabsorption of phosphate must increase in acidosis when the excretion of acid in the urine is increased. Bob thought for several months about that conflict between theory and data, and he concluded that the phosphate reabsorption data were not wrong but that the mechanism postulated by his biochemical colleague probably was. In fact, Bob's mentor, Homer Smith, the theoretician and philosopher of renal physiology, had suggested a different mechanism some ten years earlier: namely, secretion of hydrogen ion by exchange for fixed cation. Neither hypothesis had ever been tested. Bob decided it was time to do so. The experiment that he designed to examine the alternatives was beautifully conceived to provide a definitive answer. According to Bob's account, and the story is confirmed by Robert Alexander, his collaborator and coauthor of the resulting paper, Bob wrote the entire paper—minus only the data—before they carried out the first experiment! Clearly, the results were all he could have hoped for, showing that hydrogen ion secreted by the renal tubules was indeed responsible for acidifying the urine. The paper, "The Nature of the Renal Tubular Mechanism for Acidifying the Urine" appeared in the *American Journal of Physiology* in 1945. It was considered to be absolutely definitive and a landmark of renal physiology. Bob's older sister tells us that their mother was fond of saying, "Plan your work, then work your plan." Bob had learned the lesson well.

The paper on acidification of the urine established Robert F. Pitts as the leading investigator in renal physiology, but it was only the beginning of a series of studies in which he explored a number of related aspects of renal function: the reabsorption of bicarbonate by the tubules, the factors governing the rate of excretion of titratable acid, and the renal tubular reabsorption of chloride. In addition, a paper with William Lotspeich, "The Role of Amino Acids in the Renal Tubular Secretion of Ammonia," introduced a subject that in later years was to be the focus of Bob Pitts's major line of study.

In 1946 Pitts left Cornell to assume the chairmanship of the Department of Physiology at Syracuse University (the school of medicine that subsequently became the State University of New York Upstate Medical Center). The move was accomplished without any apparent discontinuity in his research. With a new group of younger associates, the work on acidification and bicarbonate reabsorption was extended to the normal human, using the investigators as subjects. The interests of Bob and his series of younger associates were not, however, limited to acid secretion by the tubules and related phenomena; while he was at Syracuse, papers appeared dealing with the effects of adrenal hormones on electrolyte reabsorption and excretion and on the effects of mercurial diuretics. The latter were his first venture into the study of diuretics and their site and mechanisms of action, an area of investigation that was to be an important element of his work over the next decade.

In 1950 Pitts returned to Cornell as the chairman of the Department of Physiology, a position he held until 1973, shortly before his retirement from the university. Bob was a conscientious chairman and a devoted teacher. His lectures were carefully prepared and models of clarity. In addition, he placed great importance on the teaching efforts of the members of his department. He regularly attended *all* the lectures in the course in physiology throughout the period of his chairmanship and participated enthusiastically in the student laboratory exercises.

The stream of published reports of first-rate work was never interrupted during the period of his chairmanship. This was the case despite problems of illness, both of his wife and of himself, that began in the middle fifties and were to plague him through the remainder of his life. His wife was stricken with progressive, incapacitating neurological disease that caused her to be bedridden for many years, during which Bob devoted great personal effort to her care. And Bob himself was the victim of at least three ailments that might have led a less dedicated and determined man to give up. In 1958, when one of us was his companion on a mission to the Middle East for the Unitarian Service Committee, his pockets contained a medicine cabinet's assortment of prescribed medications. Nevertheless, through the years Bob not only continued his extraordinarily productive activities but also adhered to his practice of doing a great deal of the laboratory work himself. In fact, he not only did most of the laboratory work he also built much of his own apparatus, including an early flame photometer for the measurement of sodium and potassium, and later an amino-acid analyzer. Throughout his career he washed his own glassware and insisted that others follow his rigid protocol for achieving adequate chemical cleanliness. He later explained his participation in these activities by noting that "some of my best ideas have come to me when I'm performing some routine analytical chore."

His work explored many areas of renal physiology. He strayed from the kidney only slightly and for a brief period when he, along with Roy Swan and Gerhard Giebisch, defined the extrarenal buffering of acid and base loads. An excellent series of papers dealing with the site and mechanism of action of diuretics, particularly the mercurial diuretics that were then the therapeutic mainstay, appeared seriatim from 1950 to 1962. His studies of the potentiation of the diuretic effect by acidifying salts and of the relationship between structure and activity among the mercurial diuretics led him to conclude that the effect was probably on the transport of chloride and attributable to the intact molecule. This contrasted with the inference of others that dissociation of the mercury was necessary for the effect that was thought to be produced on the transport of the sodium ion. Studies nearly twenty years later with isolated tubules have shown that the Pitts interpretation was correct.

Except for a brief dalliance with the stop-flow method in some of his studies of diuretics, Bob stuck pretty much to the intact kidney, often using the intact dog. Even when his own department became one of the leading centers of micropuncture work, Bob Pitts steered clear of that method. In part, at least, he explained this decision in one of his "aphorisms on research" in the paper referred to earlier. "Pick an area in which there is no, or at least little current research activity," he advised. The reason: The investigator can develop his ideas without pressure to publish to establish priority. He followed his own precepts studiously, followed his own course unpressured by the work of others, and never published a trivial paper or a wrong one.

In the last dozen years of his work, Bob returned to the area that he had opened up in his studies of acidification of the urine and explored that other element in the regulation of acid-base balance, the excretion of ammonia. Almost everything beyond the initial identification of glutamine by Van Slyke and his associates that we know about the sources of ammonia and the renal processes involved in its excretion is based on the work of Bob Pitts.

In 1974 Bob Pitts accepted emeritus status at Cornell and moved to the University of Florida in Gainesville where he held the rank of Research Professor in Renal Medicine and Physiology. Unfortunately, his health, for a long time far from robust, deteriorated further, and he was able to add little to the list of his magnificent accomplishments before his death on June 6, 1977. It might be said that, in the last half-century, if Homer Smith was the high priest of renal physiology, then Bob Pitts was surely the builder of its temple.

AWARDS AND DISTINCTIONS

1948 American Society of Clinical Investigation
1956 National Academy of Sciences
1957 American Academy of Arts and Sciences
1959 President, American Physiological Society
1960 President, Harvey Society
1960 Borden Award in Medical Science
1962 New York University Medical Alumni Award
1963 First Homer W. Smith Award in Renal Physiology
1967 Honorary Master's Degree, Oxford, England
1970 American College of Physicians Award for Distinguished Contributions in Science as Related to Medicine
1972 Association of Chairmen of Departments of Physiology, First Annual Award for Distinguished Contributions to Physiology
1972 Honorary Fellowship Award, Cornell University Medical College Alumni Association

BIBLIOGRAPHY

1932

Effect of cyanide on respiration of the protozoan, *Colpidium campylum*. Proc. Soc. Exp. Biol. Med., 29:542

Constant temperature apparatus adapted for use on the microscope stage. Science, 76:626.

1933

The relation between rate of locomotion and form in *Amoeba proteus*. Biol. Bull., 64:418.

With S. O. Mast. The relation between inorganic salt concentration, hydrogen ion concentration and physiological processes in *Amoeba proteus*. I. Rate of locomotion, gel/sol ratio, and hydrogen ion concentration in balanced salt solutions. J. Cell. Comp. Physiol., 3:449.

The secretion of urine in the dog. Inorganic phosphate in relation to plasma phosphate level. Am. J. Physiol., 106:1.

1934

With S. O. Mast. The relation between inorganic salt concentration, hydrogen ion concentration and physiological processes in *Amoeba proteus*. II. Rate of locomotion, gel/sol ratio and hydrogen ion concentration in solutions of single salts. J. Cell. Comp. Physiol., 4:237. III. The interaction between salts (antagonism) in relation to hydrogen ion concentration and salt concentration. J. Cell. Comp. Physiol., 4:435.

The clearance of creatine in dogs and man. Am. J. Physiol., 109:532.

The clearance of creatine in the phlorizinized dog. Am. J. Physiol., 109:542.

Urinary composition in marine fish. J. Cell. Comp. Physiol., 4:389.

1935

The effect of protein and amino acid metabolism on the urea and xylose clearance. J. Nutr., 9:657.

1936

The clearance of hexamethenamine in the dog. Am. J. Physiol., 115:706.
The comparison of urea with urea + ammonia clearances in acidotic dogs. J. Clin. Invest., 15:571.
Excretion of creatine by the marine teleost, the red grouper. In: *Annual Report of the Tortugas Laboratory,* 1935–36, p. 99. Washington, D.C.: Carnegie Institution of Washington.

1938

The excretion of phenol red by the chicken. J. Cell. Comp. Physiol., 11:99.
With I. M. Koor. The excretion of urea by the chicken. J. Cell. Comp. Physiol., 11:117.

1939

The excretion of creatine by the dogfish, *Squalus acanthius*. J. Cell. Comp. Physiol., 19:151.
With H. W. Magoun and S. W. Ranson. Localization of the medullary respiratory centers in the cat. Am. J. Physiol., 126:673.
With H. W. Magoun and S. W. Ranson. Interrelations of the respiratory centers in the cat. Am. J. Physiol., 126:689.
With H. W. Magoun and S. W. Ranson. The origin of respiratory rhythmicity. Am. J. Physiol., 127:654.

1940

The respiratory center and its descending pathways. J. Comp. Neurol., 72:605.

1941

With M. G. Larrabee and D. W. Bronk. An analysis of hypothalamic cardiovascular control. Am. J. Physiol., 134:359.

1942

With D. W. Bronk. Excitability cycle of the hypothalamus-sympathetic neurone system. Am. J. Physiol., 135:504.
The function of components of the respiratory complex. J. Neurophysiol., 5:403.

1943

A renal reabsorptive mechanism in the dog common to glycine and creatine. Am. J. Physiol., 140:156.

The basis for repetitive activity in phrenic motorneurons. J. Neurophysiol., 6:439.

1944

A comparison of the renal reabsorptive processes for several amino acids. Am. J. Physiol., 140:535.

The effects of infusing glycin and of varying the dietary protein intake on renal hemodynamics in the dog. Am. J. Physiol., 142:355.

With R. S. Alexander. The renal reabsorptive mechanism for inorganic phosphate in normal and acidotic dogs. Am. J. Physiol., 142:648.

1945

With R. S. Alexander. The nature of the renal tubular mechanism for acidifying the urine. Am. J. Physiol., 144:239.

The renal regulation of acid-base balance with special reference to the mechanism for acidifying the urine. Science, 102:49.

1946

Organization of the neural mechanisms responsible for rhythmic respiration, pp. 896–912; Regulation of respiration, pp. 913–32. In: *Howell's Textbook of Physiology*, ed. J. F. Fulton.

Kidney. Annu. Rev. Physiol., 8:199.

Organization of the respiratory center. Physiol. Rev., 26:609.

With W. D. Lotspeich. Bicarbonate and the renal regulation of acid-base balance. Am. J. Physiol., 147:138.

With W. D. Lotspeich. Factors governing the rate of excretion of titratable acid in the dog. Am. J. Physiol., 147:481.

1947

With W. D. Lotspeich and R. C. Swan. The renal tubular reabsorption of chloride. Am. J. Physiol., 148:445.

With W. D. Lotspeich. Use of thiosulfate clearance as a measure of glomerular filtration rate in acidotic dogs. Proc. Soc. Exp. Biol. Med., 64:224.

With W. D. Lotspeich. The role of amino acids in the renal tubular secretion of ammonia. J. Biol. Chem., 168:611.
With J. L. Ayer and W. A. Schiess. Independence of phosphate reabsorption and glomerular filtration in the dog. Am. J. Physiol., 151:168.

1948

With W. D. Lotspeich, W. A. Schiess, and J. L. Ayer. The renal regulation of acid-base balance in man. I. The nature of the mechanism for acidifying the urine. J. Clin. Invest., 27:48.
With W. D. Lotspeich, W. A. Schiess, and J. L. Ayer. The renal regulation of acid-base balance in man. II. Factors affecting the excretion of titratable acid by the normal human subject. J. Clin. Invest., 27:57.
Renal excretion of acid. Fed. Proc. Fed. Am. Soc. Exp. Biol., 7:418.
With I. Jahan. Effect of parathyroid on renal tubular reabsorption of phosphate and calcium. Am. J. Physiol., 155:42.

1949

With J. L. Ayer and W. A. Schiess. The renal regulation of acid-base balance in man. III. The reabsorption and excretion of bicarbonate. J. Clin. Invest., 28:35.
With O. W. Sartorius and J. C. Roemmelt. The renal regulation of acid-base balance in man. IV. The nature of the renal compensations in ammonium chloride acidosis. J. Clin. Invest., 28:423.
With J. C. Roemmelt and O. W. Sartorius. Excretion and reabsorption of sodium and water in the adrenalectomized dog. Am. J. Physiol., 159:124.

1950

With J. J. Duggan. Studies on diuretics. I. The site of action of mercurial diuretics. J. Clin. Invest., 29:365.
With J. J. Duggan. Studies on diuretics. II. The relationship between glomerular filtration rate, proximal tubular absorption of sodium and diuretic efficacy of mercurials. J. Clin. Invest., 29:372.
With O. W. Sartorius. Mechanism of action and therapeutic use of diuretics. J. Pharmacol. Exp. Ther., 98:161.
Acid-base regulation by the kidneys. Am. J. Med., 9:356.

With M. J. Browne and M. W. Pitts. Alkaline phosphatase activity in kidneys of glomerular and aglomerular marine teleosts. Biol. Bull., 99:152.

1951

With W. S. Wiggins, C. H. Manry, and R. H. Lyons. The effect of salt loading and salt depletion on renal function and electrolyte excretion in man. Circulation, 3:275.
With D. D. Thompson and M. J. Barrett. Significance of glomerular perfusion in relation to variability of filtration rate. Am. J. Physiol., 167:546.
Effect of adrenal cortical hormones on renal function. In: *Adrenal Cortex, Transactions of the Third Conference,* ed. E. D. Ralli, p. 703. New York: Josiah Macy, Jr., Foundation.
With S. Kupfer and D. D. Thompson. The isolated kidney and its response to diuretic agents. Am. J. Physiol., 167:703.

1952

With K. E. Roberts. The influence of cortisone on renal function and electrolyte excretion in the adrenalectomized dog. Endocrinology, 50–51.
With D. R. Axelrod. Effects of hypoxia on renal tubular function. J. Appl. Physiol., 4:593.
With D. D. Thompson. Effects of alterations of renal arterial pressure on sodium and water excretion. Am. J. Physiol., 168:490.
With D. R. Axelrod. The relationship of plasma pH and anion pattern to mercurial diuresis. J. Clin. Invest., 31:171.
With D. R. Axelrod. Anoxia as a factor in resistance to mercurial diuretics. Am. J. Physiol., 169:350.
Modern concepts of acid-base regulation. Arch. Int. Med., 89:864.
With J. N. Capps, W. S. Wiggins, and D. R. Axelrod. The effect of mercurial diuretics on the excretion of water. Circulation, 6:82.
With O. W. Sartorius and D. Calhoon. The capacity of the adrenalectomized rat to secrete hydrogen and ammonium ions. Endocrinology, 51:444.

1953

With K. E. Roberts and M. G. Magida. Relationship between potassium and bicarbonate in blood and urine. Am. J. Physiol., 172:47.

With O. W. Sartorius and D. Calhoon. Studies on the interrelationships of the adrenal cortex and renal ammonia excretion by the rat. Endocrinology, 53:256.
With K. E. Roberts. The effects of cortisone and desoxycorticosterone on the renal tubular reabsorption of phosphate and the excretion of titratable acid and potassium in dogs. Endocrinology, 52:324.
Mechanisms for stabilizing the alkaline reserves of the body. Harvey Lect. Ser. 48.

1954

With P. J. Dorman and W. J. Sullivan. The renal response to acute respiratory acidosis. J. Clin. Invest., 33:82.
With G. Giebisch and H. D. Lauson. Renal excretion and volume of distribution of various dextrans. Am. J. Physiol., 178:168.
With R. C. Swan and H. Madisso. Measurement of extracellular fluid volume in nephrectomized dogs. J. Clin. Invest., 33:1147.
With P. J. Dorman and W. J. Sullivan. Factors determining carbon dioxide tension in urine. Am. J. Physiol., 179:181.
With G. Giebisch and L. Berger. The extrarenal response to acute acid-base disturbances of respiratory origin. J. Clin. Invest., 34:231.
With R. C. Swan. Neutralization of infused acid by nephrectomized dogs. J. Clin. Invest., 34:205.
Über active transport Mechanisem in den Tubuli der Niere. Klin. Wochenschr., 33:365.
With G. R. Fuller and M. B. MacLeod. The influence of the administration of potassium salts on the renal tubular reabsorption of bicarbonate. Am. J. Physiol., 182:111.
With R. C. Swan, D. R. Axelrod, and M. Seip. Distribution of sodium bicarbonate infused into nephrectomized dogs. J. Clin. Invest., 34:1795.
With G. Giebisch and M. B. MacLeod. The effects of adrenal steroids on renal tubular reabsorption of bicarbonate. Am. J. Physiol., 183:377.

1956

With R. R. M. Borghgraef. The distribution of chlormerodrin (Neohydrin) in tissues of the rat and dog. J. Clin. Invest., 35:31.
With R. L. Greif, S. J. Sullivan, and G. S. Jacobs. Distribution of

radiomercury administered as labeled chlormerodrin (Neohydrin) in the kidneys of rats and dogs. J. Clin. Invest., 35:38.
With B. K. Ochwadt. Effects of intravenous infusion of carbonic anhydrase on carbon dioxide tension of alkaline urine. Am. J. Physiol., 185:426.
With R. R. M. Borghgraef and R. H. Kessler. Plasma regression, distribution and excretion of radiomercury in relation to diuresis following the intravenous administration of Hg^{203} labeled chlormerodrin to the dog. J. Clin. Invest. 35:1055.
With B. K. Ochwadt. Disparity between the phenol red and the diodrast clearances in the dog. Am. J. Physiol., 187:318.

1957

With P. Poulos. An indirect flame photometric method for calcium in plasma and urine. J. Lab. Clin. Med., 49:300.
With R. H. Kessler and R. Lozano. Studies on structure diuretic activity relationships of organic compounds of mercury. J. Clin. Invest., 36:656.
With D. D. Thompson, F. Kavaler, and R. Lozano. An evaluation of the cell separation hypothesis of autoregulation of renal blood flow and filtration rate. I. Blood flow, filtration rate and PAH extraction as functions of arterial pressure in normal and anemic dogs. Am. J. Physiol., 191:494.
With R. H. Kessler and O. P. A. Heidenreich. An evaluation of the cell separation hypothesis of autoregulation of renal blood flow and filtration rate. II. Glucose titrations in normal and anemic dogs. Am. J. Physiol., 191:150.

1958

Some reflections on mechanisms of action of diuretics. Am. J. Med., 24:745.
With F. Kruck, R. Lozano, D. W. Taylor, O. P. A. Heidenreich, and R. H. Kessler. Studies on the mechanism of action of chlorothiazide. J. Pharmacol. Exp. Ther., 123:89.
With R. S. Gurd, R. H. Kessler, and K. Hierholzer. Localization of acidification of urine, potassium and ammonia secretion and phosphate reabsorption in the nephron of the dog. Am. J. Physiol., 194:125.
With R. H. Kessler, K. Hierholzer, and R. S. Gurd. Localization of

the diuretic action of chlormerodrin in the nephron of the dog. Am. J. Physiol., 194:540.

1959

With R. H. Kessler, K. Hierholzer, and R. S. Gurd. Localization of action of chlorothiazide in the nephron of the dog. Am. J. Physiol., 196:1346.
The Physiological Basis of Diuretic Therapy. Springfield, Ill.: Charles C Thomas.

1960

With K. Hierholzer, R. Cado, R. Gurd, and R. H. Kessler. Stop flow analysis of renal absorption and excretion of sulfate in the dog. Am. J. Physiol., 198:833.
With G. Giebisch and E. E. Windhager. Mechanism of urinary acidification. In: *Biology of Pyelonephritis*, p. 277. Boston: Little, Brown & Co.
The teacher and the ferment in education. (Past president's address to the American Physiological Society.) Physiologist, 3:20.

1961

With J. L. Brown and A. H. E. Samiy. Localization of aminonitrogen reabsorption in the nephron of the dog. Am. J. Physiol., 200:370.
With J. R. Cade, B. Shalhoub, and M. Canessa-Fischer. The effect of strophanthidin on the renal tubules of the dog. Am. J. Physiol., 200:373.
A comparison of the modes of action of certain diuretic agents. Prog. Cardiovasc. Dis., 3:537.
With W. A. Webber and J. L. Brown. Interactions of amino acids in renal tubular transport. Am. J. Physiol., 200:380.

1962

With S. Balagura. The excretion of ammonia injected into the renal artery. Am. J. Physiol., 203:11.

1963

With R. J. Shalhoub, W. Webber, S. Glabman, M. Ganessa-Fischer, J. Klein, and J. deHaas. Extraction of amino acids from and their addition to renal blood plasma. Am. J. Physiol., 204:181.

With J. deHaas and J. Klein. Relation of renal amino and amide extraction to ammonia production. Am. J. Physiol., 204:187.

With M. Canessa-Fischer, R. J. Shalhoub, S. Glabman, and J. deHaas. The effects of infusions of ammonia, amides and amino acids on the excretion of ammonia. Am. J. Physiol., 204:192.

Physiology of the Kidney and Body Fluids. Chicago: Yearbook Publishers.

1964

With G. Denis and H. Preuss. The pNH_3 of renal tubular cells. J. Clin. Invest., 43:571.

With S. Balagura. Renal handling of α-ketoglutarate by the dog. Am. J. Physiol., 207:483.

Renal production and excretion of ammonia. Am. J. Med., 36:720.

1965

With L. A. Pilkington and J. deHaas. N^{15} tracer studies on the origin of urinary ammonia in the acidotic dog with notes on the enzymatic synthesis of labeled glutamic acid and glutamine. J. Clin. Invest., 44:731.

With L. A. Pilkington and J. Welch. Relationship of pNH_3 of tubular cells to renal production of ammonia. Am. J. Physiol., 208:1100.

With L. A. Pilkington, R. Binder, and J. deHaas. Intrarenal distribution of blood flow. Am. J. Physiol., 208:1107.

With G. Fulgraff. A study of the kinetics of ammonia production and excretion in the acidotic dog. Am. J. Physiol., 209:1206.

1966

With L. A. Pilkington. The relation between plasma concentrations of glutamine and glycine and utilization of their nitrogens as sources of urinary ammonia. J. Clin. Invest., 45:86.

The renal metabolism of ammonia. Physiologist, 9:97.

1967

With W. J. Stone. Renal metabolism of alanine. J. Clin. Invest., 46:530.
With W. J. Stone. Pathways of ammonia metabolism in the intact functioning kidney of the dog. J. Clin. Invest., 46:1141.
With W. J. Stone and S. Balagura. Diffusion equilibrium for ammonia in the kidney of the acidotic dog. J. Clin. Invest., 46:1603.

1969

With M. L. Lyon. Species differences in renal glutamine synthesis in vivo. Am. J. Physiol., 216:117.
Renal excretion of ammonia. In: *Progress in Nephrology*, ed. G. Peters and F. Roch-Ramel, p. 75. Berlin: Springer-Verlag.

1970

With A. C. Damian. Rates of glutaminase I and glutamine synthetase reactions in rat kidney in vivo. Am. J. Physiol., 218:1249.
With A. C. Damian and M. B. MacLeod. Synthesis of serine by rat kidney in vivo and in vitro. Am. J. Physiol., 219:504.
Production and excretion of ammonia in relation to acid-base regulation. In: *Handbook of Physiology, Renal Physiology*, p. 455. Washington, D.C.: American Physiological Society.
With L. A. Pilkington and T. K. Young. Properties of renal lumen and antiluminal transport of plasma glutamine. Nephron, 17:51.

1971

The role of ammonia production and excretion in regulation of acid-base balance. N. Engl. J. Med., 284:32.
Metabolism of amino acids by the perfused rat kidney. Am. J. Physiol., 220:862.
Some aphorisms on research and writing. Yale J. Biol. Med., 43:331.

1972

With M. B. MacLeod. Synthesis of serine by the dog kidney in vivo. Am. J. Physiol., 222:394.
With L. A. Pilkington, M. B. MacLeod, and E. Leal-Pinto. Metab-

olism of glutamine by the intact functioning kidney of the dog. Studies in metabolic acidosis and alkalosis. J. Clin. Invest., 51:557.

Control of ammonia production and excretion. Kidney Int., 1:297.

1973

With E. Leal-Pinto, H. C. Park, V. F. King, and M. B. MacLeod. The metabolism of lactate by the intact functioning kidney of the dog. Am. J. Physiol., 224:1463.

Photographic Media Center
University of Wisconsin — Extension

JOHN ROBERT RAPER
October 3, 1911–May 21, 1974

BY KENNETH B. RAPER

PRIOR TO HIS UNTIMELY DEATH in 1974, John R. Raper was recognized as the foremost investigator of sexuality in the fungi. Beginning at the University of North Carolina in Chapel Hill and continuing at Harvard University, he gained wide recognition while still a graduate student for his imaginative researches on the hormonal control of sexuality in species of *Achlya,* a common genus of aquatic fungi. Further pioneering studies followed while he was a National Research Fellow at the California Institute of Technology and as a member of the botany staff at Indiana University; during World War II he was recruited as a radiation biologist for the Manhattan Project in Chicago and Oak Ridge. At the University of Chicago after the war, he further refined and extended his observations on the induction and regulation of sexual interactions in aquatic fungi by diffusible hormones that are produced in a sequential and invariant pattern. Then—as if sexuality in *Achlya* were too straightforward— he turned his attention to the more complicated phenomena in the higher fungi and chose as the primary object for experimentation a small wood-rotting basidiomycete, *Schizophyllum commune.* Following his return to Harvard in 1954, and for twenty years thereafter, John, his wife Carlene, and his students and associates were dedicated to understanding and revealing the bewildering intricacies of this complex system. They were singularly successful in this task, which led eventually to John's authoritative book, *Genetics of Sexuality in High Fungi*.

John R. Raper, the eighth child and seventh son of William Franklin and Julia Crouse Raper, was born on a farm near Welcome, North Carolina, on October 3, 1911. As the youngest in the family, he received special attention and consideration. But more was involved than his tender age: John was someone special, not just in our immediate household but in the community at large. He was handsome, he was smart, and he was talented. Whether he enjoyed performing before church and public school audiences, or whether he just accepted the role because it was expected of him, one cannot say. But perform he did, reciting in a singularly clear voice and singing with a tonal quality seldom heard in the rural community where we lived.

John was a lover of good music, a taste he acquired quite early and one that sustained him throughout his life. He grew up in a Moravian community where brass choirs were as much a part of special church services as were the "lovefeasts," featuring coffee and hot cross buns. Although the latter delighted all of us, the music must have held a special fascination for John, for he was playing the trumpet almost by the time he could hold a horn to his lips. His proficiency with the instrument increased steadily: by the time he was a student at the university in Chapel Hill—and first trumpet in the newly organized North Carolina Symphony—he was seriously considering music as a profession. Fortunately, he chose biology—not that he would have been a poor musician, but fortunately because otherwise he could not have made the important discoveries and contributions that marked his career in science.

Concerning his childhood and adolescence, John has written in part:

> My father had suffered a massive heart attack before my birth and I never knew him as a robust man. The hard work on the farm and largely the direction of its operations were thus left to my older brothers, each of whom in turn went away to high school (there being none locally), then college, and soon thereafter developed careers elsewhere. In the matter of education and independent development there was every possible encouragement from home save appreciable financial assistance. Born during the Civil War, my father was unable to secure the education and training he desired, and feeling that he had been trapped by circumstances, did what he could to insure that his children obtain the education he had been denied. Mother's attitude was somewhat different. Having grown up on a highly productive farm, her greatest wish was that one of her sons would take over the farm and operate it efficiently. No one of the seven accepted the challenge.
>
> Most of our social activities revolved around the public school and three churches, Friedberg and Enterprise, Moravian, and Mt. Olivet, Methodist, among which the family membership oscillated. Services were attended by the whole family, occasionally at all three on the same Sunday! Our home was bone dry and dancing and card playing were not encouraged. As the youngest member of this rather strict paternalistic family, I was always the object of much affection if not frivolity.
>
> My first four years of school were spent in a 3-room school with no pretensions beyond the elementary level. At this time, a new, consolidated school (for which my father was a leading organizer and donor of the building site) was opened, and my further education through high school was received there. Aside from two years in the fifth grade—for reasons never learned—secondary school was reasonably uneventful, and I graduated from high school in 2nd or 3rd place in a class of 11. I was not good in sports or in other extra-curricular activities, such as dramatics, for which some rudimentary opportunities were provided. I was reasonably proficient with the trumpet, but the school, with neither musical instruction nor performing groups, provided no outlet for musical expression. English grammar and literature were my preferred subjects, and French was enjoyable. Science instruction was very rudimentary and generated only mild interest.

About this time, cows became very prominent in my life. With the successive defection of my older brothers, there was no longer the labor force necessary to continue intensive tobacco farming, and a herd of miscellaneous cows became a major source of farm revenue. All through high school, usually with the help of a hired man, the care, feeding and milking of the cows was a constant preoccupation. Otherwise, I read avidly and widely and a reasonably good library at Winston Salem, some 10 miles distant, was routinely visited about once a week. It was there also that I discovered serious music *via* the record department of a furniture store in which an uncle worked; all available cash for some years went into classical recordings.

Poorly prepared, and under considerable stress, my first year at the University of North Carolina was quite difficult, and it was made more so by the necessity of working 30–40 hours per week. In the spring quarter, however, my first science course, Introductory Botany under Professor John N. Couch, kindled an intense interest such as I had not previously known. In the second year, more botany and introductory zoology sustained and heightened this interest, and the offer of a teaching assistantship in the Department of Botany for the following year was recognized as an opportunity to indulge more fully my newfound interest. Aside from a passing flurry of musical activity (see above), there has been no subsequent significant distraction from the pursuit of scientific interests. Major influences throughout this period in determining the selection of a particular field of specialization were the enthusiasm and dedication of three teachers with whom I early worked: John N. Couch and William C. Coker of the University of North Carolina and William H. Weston of Harvard. Kenneth Raper's influence was also considerable during my student days.

John's first contribution to science (1936) was an attempt to determine the pattern of sexual interaction between self-sterile strains of *Achlya bisexualis*, a heterothallic water mold, previously described by Coker. Approximately 500 new collections—mostly from streams and ponds near Chapel Hill— were examined; of these 500, 32 were self-sterile. Of the latter, 27 were identified as *A. bisexualis* and could be classified as female (8), male (7), and hermaphroditic-female (12). The last were of special interest because in the presence of strong males they behaved as true females.

In the autumn of 1936, John transferred to Harvard University and, as the recipient of an Austin Teaching Fellowship, resumed his researches on *A. bisexualis* under the guidance of Professor Weston. About a year later he isolated from the Charles River several cultures of a new and even more interesting *Achlya* that he described as *A. ambisexualis*. This specific name was chosen because some of the isolates possessed both male and female potential and could behave as either sex, depending on the stronger sexual character of a paired mate. For this and other reasons, increased attention was subsequently given to the latter species. It soon became clear that the mating process consisted of a number of well-defined steps or stages, that these occurred in an orderly and invariant sequence, and that each was associated with a visually evident developmental change in the paired culture. Additionally, because the stages appeared reciprocally in the two plants (thalli), and with these generally separated by some distance, it was reasonable to surmise that the successive changes observed in one plant were induced by diffusible substances, or hormones, produced by the other. Subsequent researches involving selected cultures and interspecific crosses amply confirmed this supposition; they also provided the first unequivocal proof of hormonal, or pheromonal (alternate term), control of sexual reproduction in lower plants. In fact, if one wished to demonstrate "courtship" in plants, no better example exists than that of the interacting male and female thalli of the water mold *Achlya*—which John so carefully described and so beautifully illustrated some forty years ago.

The sexual process in *Achlya* was shown to proceed in this manner. When strong male and female strains were implanted at some distance in an agar plate—or when they were grown on halved hemp seed floating in water—the terminal areas of the male hyphae began to branch profusely as the thalli approached each other. (The branches [antheridial] were quite thin, highly ramified, and at this first stage randomly distributed.) In the second stage, several hours later, the female hyphae nearest the activated male began to swell terminally or to produce short, lateral, club-shaped branches that in a few hours enlarged to form globose structures (oogonial initials). In the third stage the antheridial hyphae grew toward the oogonial initials and on reaching their surfaces became appressed against them. The fourth stage was again expressed by the antheridial hyphae. Soon after these applied themselves against the oogonial walls, protoplasm accumulated in their tips and transverse walls were laid down to delimit the male gametangia, or antheridia. The fifth stage followed soon thereafter and was marked by the appearance of crosswalls that delimited the swollen termini of the female hyphae and their club-shaped branches. The spherical structures thus formed were the oogonia, or female gametangia. Whereas elapsed time varied appreciably depending on cultural and environmental conditions, the entire process could be completed in thirty to thirty-six hours on agar—or in appreciably shorter periods when plants were cultivated in water. In either case the sequence was the same, and the intervals between stages were proportional. The reciprocating responses, and the markedly shorter time necessary for stage one to be expressed in water, strongly indicated that the formation of the antheridial branches was dependent upon some substances produced by the vegetative female plant; this in turn suggested that the female initiated the entire sexual process. These suppositions were then confirmed in different ways.

In one experiment male and female plants were separated by permeable membranes, either in the form of tubes or as sheets laid under the agar for some distance and then bent upward at 90 degrees. When the plants arrived at positions on opposite sides of the membranes, the male plant began to produce antheridial hyphae; six to eight hours later, oogonial initials were seen to emerge on the female plant, and as these matured the antheridial hyphae grew toward them and spread outward on the membrane nearest the oogonial initials. In another experiment, male and female plants were grown separately on halved hemp seeds in petri dishes. When these reached maturity, the water was drained off and fresh water was added and allowed to remain for twenty-four hours. Liquid from these vessels was then drawn through Seitz filters and added to plants of the opposite sex. Antheridial hyphae appeared on the male plants at seven hours and were very abundant at twelve hours. The response of female plants was less rapid but nonetheless positive. A perfusion experiment was the most dramatic of all. It was accomplished with a series of four connected micro-aquaria through which water flowed at a constant rate. The experiment was described in this way:

> In the first cell were placed two vegetatively mature female plants of *Achlya ambisexualis;* in the second, two male plants of that species; in the third, two females; and in the fourth, a single male. Beginning about 5–6 hours after the introduction of the plants, a few antheridial hyphae were formed on the male plants in cells 2 and 4, but no reaction was given by the female plants in cell 3.
>
> Accordingly this experiment was repeated, but two female plants of *A. bisexualis* were placed in the first cell, since, as previously found, the male of *A. ambisexualis* reacts more strongly to this than to female plants of the same species; the plants in the remaining three cells were selected as before. Approximately 3 hours after the introduction of the plants, the male in cell 2 was seen to be reacting strongly. Two hours later the male plant in cell 4 was reacting vigorously. Twelve to fourteen hours after the initiation of the female reaction in cell 2, oogonial initials began to appear scattered over the entire female mycelium in cell 3. Following the beginning of the male reaction, directional growth of antheridial hyphae in the vicinity of the siphon tip in cell 4 began to take place, and at the end of another day this directional growth was fairly pronounced.

From these and other studies John concluded that four major hormones, alternately produced by the female and male plants, were responsible for initiating and regulating the sexual process in *Achlya*. These were designated hormones A, B, C, and D; they were characterized as follows: hormone A, produced by the mycelium of the female plant, induces the formation of antheridial hyphae on the male; hormone B, produced by the antheridial hyphae of the male plant, induces the formation of oogonial initials on the female; hormone C, produced by the oogonial initials, attracts antheridial hyphae to themselves and promotes delimitation of antheridia; and hormone D, produced by the antheridia, causes delimitation of the oogonia and subsequent differentiation of oospheres. For technical reasons, fertilization and maturation of oospheres could not be followed.

Upon receiving his doctorate from Harvard, John was awarded a National Research Fellowship. He subsequently went to work with Professor A. J. Haagen-Smit at the California Institute of Technology, his avowed purpose being to isolate and, if possible, chemically characterize hormone A. In this he was partially successful. Much was learned about the properties of hormone A: "a final fraction, weighing 0.0002 g and still impure, contained 37 percent of the initial hormone-A activity of 1,440 liters of filtrate from female plants and induced antheridial hyphal formation when tested in a dilution of 1/10,000,000,000,000." For several reasons— economic and otherwise—the work could not be continued at that time, but a very small amount of hormone-A concentrate was retained for future study. Not until a quarter of a century later was hormone A finally isolated and characterized by Trevor McMorris and Alma Barksdale at the New York Botanical Garden. It was found to be a sterol and renamed *antheridiol*, the first steroid hormone found in plants. It is of more than passing interest that in the course of their work they reexamined a concentrate of hormone A that John had sealed in a vial in 1943; upon assay, they found that little of its activity had been lost. More recently, McMorris and coworkers have resolved hormone B into three steroidal compounds, which have been designated oogoniol-1, oogoniol-2, and oogoniol-3.

Work on *Achlya* continued when John was at Indiana University; it was resumed when he returned to Chicago after the war. There at the university important events transpired, and about one of these he tells this story:

> During my first year at the University of Chicago after the war years as a radiobiologist, work was continued on the hormonal action of hormone A and the physiology of antheridial induction in *Achlya*. For this work, there was available a pitifully small supply of hormone A of high purity and standardized activity, and this vial of standard was dear to my heart—it being used only in critical experiments and then only in 0.01 ml portions.
>
> Imagine my horror upon returning from a lecture to find my assistant, a fair-haired, first-year graduate student (Carlene Allen), on her hands and knees in the middle of the laboratory sucking up this precious liquid with a tiny pipette. She had dropped the bottle, which had broken, and had intuitively gone about the rational business of recovering what she could of the hormonal solution with the equipment at hand. In a mixture of shock at the obvious carelessness on the one hand and my admiration of her initiative in making the best of a totally unnecessary and bad situation on the other, I could only urge the completion of the task and enjoin her not to cry over spilt hormone. There was, of course, no possibility of precise comparison of the activity of the recovered hormone with the original, and it may well be that the quantitative aspects of the work with *Achlya* underwent a slight discontinuity as a result of the accident.
>
> Forgiveness, however, was apparently not too difficult. Perhaps my failure to erupt into the violent display of temper that had been suggested in earlier and far less serious situations convinced her that I might be human after all. In any event, a couple of years later we were married, but over the years I've come to appreciate the monicker of "Spilly" bestowed on her by her family at a very early age.

Following their marriage, Carlene continued to work with John in the laboratory and soon became a full partner in his researches. In the years after his death, she obtained her doctorate from Harvard University and developed an independent research career centered upon the genetics of higher fungi.

In the early 1950s, John's attention began to shift increasingly to a quite different area of experimental mycology: the analysis of tetrapolar sexuality in the Basidiomycetes. Hans Kniep, H. R. R. Buller, and others had outlined the broad picture of the genetic control system and the developmental sequence from spore to spore. Additionally, Haig Papazian, one of John's students, had expanded this work and discovered several unusual features, including the appearance of rare, new, mating types, presumably as a result of recombination; the existence of hemi-compatible heterokaryons; and the frequent occurrence of morphological mutations in certain of the heterokaryons. Intrigued by these discoveries and impelled by his deep interest in the sexuality of all fungi, John spent the remainder of his professional career probing every facet of the biology of the Basidiomycetes, particularly *Schizophyllum commune*. Among the problems he addressed were the analysis of the genetic fine structure of the incompatibility system, the biochemical mechanism of incompatibility in the Basidiomycetes, the genetics of fruiting, the mutational dissection of the morphogenetic sequences of heterokaryosis, and the physiological consequences of compatible and incompatible mycelial interactions. His efforts and those of an ever-expanding group of students and associates raised *S. commune* to prominence as the best-understood representative of the Basidiomycetes; his laboratory, then at Harvard University, became a mecca for research in experimental mycology of the higher fungi. Some highlights of the *Schizophyllum* research conducted there are briefly noted below.

John demonstrated in great detail the immensity of the

allelic alternatives of the incompatibility genes present in the worldwide population of *S. commune,* and he projected that no fewer than 20,000 resulting mating types had arisen during the evolution of the species. He proved the complex nature of both the A and B incompatibility mating type factors, and proposed a more refined picture of the requisites for sexual compatibility in terms of the α and β subloci that he had defined as mating genes for these factors.

He also provided evidence for the nature of each of these four incompatibility genes as regulators of development in the sexual cycle leading to mushroom production and sexual spore formation. He and his collaborators analyzed the complexity of these genes through mutational dissection. They demonstrated that single mutations in a mating-type gene could result in loss of allelic specificity and constitutive function of the relevant developmental pathway. This produced a homothallic, self-fertile mutant (a combination of two such mutations, one an *A* mating-type gene and one a *B* mating-type gene, converts the heterothallic mycelium to a homothallic mutant). He demonstrated further that secondary mutations in these mating-type loci resulted in a variety of regulatory alterations. These ranged from a near wild-type, nonparental allele capable of initiating a normal developmental pathway, through degrees of regulatory deficiencies of the pathway, to complete loss of function in which the genes are deleted. The latter have no allelic specificity and no capability of initiating sexual development. He and his associates also identified eighty loci, in all parts of the genome, which come to expression only when the development in the sexual cycle is initiated by the incompatibility genes. These loci were recognized in mutant form as modifiers of the normal course of development.

He assigned specific regulatory functions to each genetic factor—for example, nuclear migration by the two genes of the B factor, and clamp connection initiation by the two genes of the A factor. And he pushed our understanding of each of these processes to substantially higher levels of cytological and biochemical understanding. The hemi-compatible heterokaryons took their place along with the dikaryon and the homokaryon as well-defined developmental states with their own distinctive phenotypes and potentialities for exploitation in research.

John initiated the first series of attempts, using immunological as well as electrophoretic techniques, to identify the biochemical products of incompatibility interactions and thereby the physiological mechanisms of tetrapolar sexuality. His efforts to unravel the mating type system and its consequences led him into various related areas of the biology of *S. commune:* he investigated the inheritance of fruiting competence in dikaryotic strains and identified polygenic as well as single-gene controls over fruiting; he studied the origin and expression of morphological mutations that appeared within both homokaryotic and heterokaryotic mycelia and characterized a large number of these mutants; he devised techniques for dedikaryotization of established dikaryons; and he studied the kinetics of nuclear migration within hyphae and identified some of the physiological conditions underlying this process.

It was not just the sum of his work that was impressive but also the ingenuity and artistry of its style, design, and execution. He enjoyed utilizing the unique biological features of an organism to devise experiments for elucidating unsolved questions. He kept abreast of the latest advances in genetics, microbiology, and biochemistry and applied these toward the solution of problems relating to sexual development. He seized upon every seemingly irrelevant result in his search for clues and practical means for experimentation, and he carefully weighed each bit of information that accrued, recognizing in them valuable pieces of the larger puzzle. He probably knew that ultimate solutions would be unattainable within his lifetime, but he blazed a new and highly rewarding trail among eukaryotic, mycelial organisms—and he stimulated a great many others to follow his lead.

For three years during World War II, John's mycological researches were interrupted while he worked as an associate biologist in the Manhattan Project's Plutonium Division in Chicago and Oak Ridge, Tennessee. He was chosen for his reputation as an innovative scientist who was capable of pioneering in a totally new area of radiation biology. Investigations for the project centered on the effects of irradiating laboratory animals with beta and gamma rays, such tests commonly representing total body exposure to beta irradiation. Because limited information existed at the outset, the studies involved different isotopes; measurement of beta and gamma emissions; comparisons of type and geometry of radiation sources; fashioning of suitable exposure chambers; and standardizing terminology and methods of recording data so that dosage effects could be compared in different animals with regard to growth, health, and carcinogenesis. Without attempting to cite specific information concerning the tests, it was observed that when different animals were subjected to sublethal doses of total surface beta irradiation, some species (rats and mice) showed a significantly higher incidence of tumor formation than did others (rabbits and guinea pigs). And on the basis of absorbed energy, gamma rays were 1.75 times more effective than beta rays in producing lethality. Out of this exploratory work came a total of fifteen papers by John and his coworkers, published mostly as chapters in *Biological Effects of External Beta Radiation* (National Nuclear Energy Series, Div. IV, vol. 22E [1951]). Out of it also came a man chastened by the experience and frightened by the implications of what he had learned.

Not only was John imaginative in designing experiments, but he was innovative in improving culture methods and in fashioning needed instruments as well. While still in Chapel Hill he devised a method for freeing *Achlya* of the aerobic bacteria that always accompany it in nature. The method—which was simple and effective—consisted of allowing hyphae to grow downward through agar, pass under a vertical barrier, and grow back to the surface on the opposite side. Clean hyphal tips were then excised and recultivated. When work on *Schizophyllum* required the isolation of large numbers of single spores with no possibility of duality, John designed a small conical cutter (fashioned of stainless steel) that he mounted on a swinging arm attached to a metal collar fitted on a Leitz $6.3 \times$ microscope objective. The cutter, which was 1.0 mm in diameter, could be accurately positioned over the microscope field by means of centering screws; it was activated by a spring cable release. Viewing with 20 or $25 \times$ oculars, one could isolate spores almost as rapidly as they could be located, each atop a small agar plug waiting to be removed with a chisel-shaped needle. He was also coinventor of a cell press, which was similar to the French press but with much greater capacity. It was especially suitable for preparing large quantities of cell-free extracts in a well-preserved condition.

John was also a skilled photographer and master draftsman whose illustrations not only graced his own publications but those of other authors as well. For example, copies of delicately executed line drawings of *Achlya* appear on the covers of books by J. T. Bonner and by H. van den Ende. He was no less creative at home: in his basement workshop he fashioned many pieces of furniture—chairs, tables, chests, etc.—not to mention smaller pieces such as lamps, sconces, and decorative objects that he not only used but shared liberally with his less creative brothers, sister, and friends. John and his wife were especially fond of classical music, and he equipped his home with excellent facilities for playing records and tapes, of which he had a large and varied collection. He enjoyed good food, and he was adept in preparing special dishes that on occasion were served to house guests with obvious joy and pride. Thanksgiving at the John Rapers' was a warm tradition well remembered by several generations of students who couldn't make it home for the holiday. A bountiful dinner was always preceded by a walk around Thoreau's Walden Pond; it was followed by listening to music before an open fire.

John was a man of many talents who enjoyed life thoroughly and who enriched the lives of all the people who knew him—commonly serene, sometimes impulsive, occasionally quixotic, but never dull. In recognition of his outstanding accomplishments, John received many honors. He was awarded a Guggenheim fellowship and a Fulbright scholarship to carry on researches in Germany in 1960 and 1961, and he received the Award of Merit of the Botanical Society of America in 1969. He served as vice-president and president of the Mycological Society of America, and he was a fellow and secretary of the American Academy of Arts and Sciences. (As the holder of that office, he signed the letter of felicitation sent by that Academy on the occasion of the centennial of the National Academy of Sciences in 1963.) He was elected to the National Academy the following year. Active in university affairs, he was nearing the end of a four-year term as chairman of the Department of Biological Sciences of Harvard University at the time of his death.

John died on May 21, 1974, after a brief illness. Quite fittingly a memorial service was held in Harvard's Memorial Chapel that consisted primarily of choral music by J. S. Bach, Monteverdi, and Vittoria.

He is survived by his wife and coworker, Carlene; his son

Jonathan, a developmental neurobiologist and recipient of an appointment as research scientist at the Max Planck Institut für Virusforschung in Tübingen, Germany; his daughter Linda Carlene, a professional quilt artist; and, by a previous marriage, his son William, a high school teacher.

THE WRITER WISHES to express his appreciation to his brother John for having deposited with the Academy comments and reminiscences concerning his childhood and early adult life; to his wife, Dr. Carlene Raper, for his portrait and for her counsel and suggestions; and to Dr. T. J. Leonard for summarizing John's studies of sexuality in the higher Basidiomycetes.

BIBLIOGRAPHY

1936

Heterothallism and sterility in *Achlya* and observations on the cytology of *Achlya bisexualis*. J. Elisha Mitchell Sci. Soc., 52:274–89.

1937

A method of freeing fungi from bacterial contamination. Science, 85:342.

1939

Role of hormones in the sexual reaction of heterothallic *Achlyas*. Science, 89:321–22.
Sexual hormones in *Achlya*. I. Indicative evidence for a hormonal coordinating mechanism. Am. J. Bot., 26:639–50.

1940

Sexuality in *Achlya ambisexualis*. Mycologia, 32:710–27.
Sexual hormones in *Achlya*. II. Distance reactions, conclusive evidence for a hormonal coordinating mechanism. Am. J. Bot., 27:162–73.

1942

Sexual hormones in *Achlya*. III. Hormone A and the initial male reaction. Am. J. Bot., 29:159–66.
With A. J. Haagen-Smit. Sexual hormones in *Achlya*. IV. Properties of hormone A of *Achlya bisexualis*. J. Biol. Chem., 143:311–20.
Sexual hormones in *Achlya*. V. Hormone A', a male-secreted augmenter or activator of hormone A. Proc. Natl. Acad. Sci. USA, 28:509–16.

1947

Effects of total surface beta irradiation. Radiology, 49:314–24.

1950

Beta rays: Biological effects. In: *Medical Physics*, vol. 2, ed. Otto Glasser, pp. 66–71. Chicago, Ill.: The Year Book Publishers.

Sexual hormones in *Achlya*. VI. The hormones of the A-complex. Proc. Natl. Acad. Sci. USA, 36:524–33.

Sexual hormones in *Achlya*. VII. The hormonal mechanism in homothallic species. Bot. Gaz., 112:1–24.

1951

Sexual hormones in *Achlya*. Am. Sci., 39:110–20.

Chemical regulation of sexual processes in fungi. In: *Plant Growth Substances*, ed. F. Skoog, pp. 301–13. Madison: University of Wisconsin Press.

With R. E. Zirkle and K. K. Barnes. Techniques of external irradiation with beta rays. Natl. Nuclear Energy Ser. Div., IV-22E:1–41.

With J. E. Wirth and K. K. Barnes. Gross effects of beta irradiation on restricted surface of rabbits. Natl. Nuclear Energy Ser. Div., IV-22E:42–61.

With R. E. Zirkle and K. K. Barnes. Comparative lethal effects of external beta irradiation. Natl. Nuclear Energy Ser. Div., IV-22E:62–76.

With K. K. Barnes. Gross effects of total-surface beta irradiation. Natl. Nuclear Energy Ser. Div., IV-22E:77–109.

With K. K. Barnes. Rate of recovery from total-surface beta irradiation. Natl. Nuclear Energy Ser. Div., IV-22E:110–20.

With K. K. Barnes. Additivity of lethal effects of external beta and gamma irradiation (I). Natl. Nuclear Energy Ser. Div., IV-22E:121–29.

With K. K. Barnes. Additivity of lethal effects of external beta and gamma irradiation (II). Natl. Nuclear Energy Ser. Div., IV-22E:130–36.

With R. S. Snider. Histopathological effects of single doses of total-surface beta radiation on mice. Natl. Nuclear Energy Ser. Div., IV-22E:152–78.

With K. K. Barnes. Effects of external irradiation with beta rays on the peripheral blood of rabbits. Natl. Nuclear Energy Ser. Div., IV-22E:179–84.

With J. E. Wirth. Reactions of human skin to single doses of beta rays. Natl. Nuclear Energy Ser. Div., IV-22E:193–99.

With P. S. Henshaw and R. S. Snider. Delayed effects of single

exposures to external beta rays. Natl. Nuclear Energy Ser. Div., IV-22E:200–11.
With P. S. Henshaw and R. S. Snider. Effects of periodic total-surface beta irradiation. Natl. Nuclear Energy Ser. Div., IV-22E:212–26.

1952

Chemical regulation of sexual processes in the Thallophytes. Bot. Rev., 18:447–545.

1953

Tetrapolar sexuality. Q. Rev. Biol., 28:233–59.

1954

With J. P. San Antonio. Heterokaryotic mutagenesis in Hymmenomycetes. I. Heterokaryosis in *Schizophyllum commune*. Am. J. Bot., 41:69–86.
Life cycles, sexuality, and sexual mechanisms in the fungi. In: *Sex in Microorganisms*, pp. 42–81. Washington, D.C.: American Association for the Advancement of Science.

1955

Some problems of specificity in the sexuality of plants. In: *Biological Specificity and Growth*, ed. E. G. Butler, pp. 119–40. Princeton: Princeton University Press.
Heterokaryosis and sexuality in fungi. Trans. N.Y. Acad. Sci. (II), 17:627–35.

1956

With P. G. Miles and H. Lund. The identification of indigo as a pigment produced by a mutant culture of *Schizophyllum commune*. Arch. Biochem. Biophys., 62:1–5.
With P. G. Miles. Recovery of the component strains from dikaryotic mycelia. Mycologia, 48:484–94.

1957

Hormones and sexuality in lower plants. Symp. Soc. Exp. Biol., 11:143–65.

1958

With G. S. Krongelb and M. G. Baxter. The number and distribution of incompatibility factors in Schizophyllum. Am. Nat., 92:221–32.

With M. G. Baxter and R. B. Middleton. The genetic structure of the incompatibility factors in Schizophyllum commune. Proc. Natl. Acad. Sci. USA, 44:889–900.

With P. G. Miles. The genetics of Schizophyllum commune. Genetics, 43:530–46.

With J. P. San Antonio and P. G. Miles. The expression of mutations in common-A heterokaryons of Schizophyllum commune. Z. Vererbungsl., 89:540–58.

With G. S. Krongelb. Genetic and environmental aspects of fruiting in Schizophyllum commune Fr. Mycologia, 50:707–40.

With P. J. Snider. Nuclear migration in the Basidiomycete Schizophyllum commune. Am. J. Bot., 45:538–46.

1959

Sexual versatility and evolutionary processes in the fungi. Mycologia, 51:107–25.

Schizophyllum umbrinum Berkeley in culture. Mycologia, 51:474–76.

1960

The control of sex in fungi. Am. J. Bot., 47:794–808.

With M. G. Baxter and A. H. Ellingboe. The genetic structure of the incompatibility factors of Schizophyllum commune: The A-factor. Proc. Natl. Acad. Sci. USA, 46:833–42.

With Y. Parag. Genetic recombination in a common-B cross of Schizophyllum commune. Nature, 188:765–66.

Tetrapolarity in Schizophyllum fasciatum. Mycologia, 52:334–36.

1961

With S. Dick. Origin of expressed mutations in Schizophyllum commune. Nature, 189:81–82.

With K. Esser. Antigenic differences due to the incompatibility factors in Schizophyllum commune. Z. Vererbungsl., 92:439–44.

Incompabilität bei den Basidiomyceten Schizophyllum commune. Ber. Dtsch. Bot. Ges., 74:326–28.

Parasexual phenomena in Basidiomycetes. In: *Recent Advances in Botany,* pp. 379–83. Toronto: University of Toronto Press.

1962

With A. H. Ellingboe. Somatic recombination in *Schizophyllum commune.* Genetics, 47:85–98.
With A. H. Ellingboe. The Buller phenomenon in *Schizophyllum commune:* Internuclear selection in compatible dikaryotic-homokaryotic matings. Am. J. Bot., 49:545–49.
With M. T. Oettinger. Anomalous segregation of incompatibility factors in *Schizophyllum commune.* Rev. Biol. (Lisbon), 3:205–21.

1963

Patterns of sexuality in fungi. Mycologia, 55:79–92.
With E. A. Hyatt. Modified press for disruption of microorganisms. J. Bacteriol., 85:712–13.
Device for isolation of spores. J. Bacteriol., 86:342–44.
With G. N. Bistis. Heterothallism and sexuality in *Ascobolus stercorarius.* Am. J. Bot., 50:880–91.

1964

With K. Esser. The fungi. In: *The Cell,* ed. J. Brachet and A. E. Mirsky, vol. 6, pp. 139–244. New York: Academic Press.
With C. A. Raper. Mutations affecting heterokaryosis in *Schizophyllum commune.* Am. J. Bot., 51:503–12.

1965

With D. H. Boyd and C. A. Raper. Primary and secondary mutations at the incompatibility loci in *Schizophyllum.* Proc. Natl. Acad. Sci. USA, 53:1324–32.
With P. J. Snider. Nuclear ratios and complementation in common-A heterokaryons of *Schizophyllum commune.* Am. J. Bot., 52:547–52.
Introduction. In: *Incompatibility in Fungi,* ed. K. Esser and J. R. Raper, pp. 1–6. Berlin: Springer-Verlag.
With J. T. Mullins. Heterothallism in biflagellate aquatic fungi: Preliminary genetic analysis. Science, 150:1174–75.

1966

Life cycles, basic patterns of sexuality and sexual mechanisms. In: *The Fungi (II)*, ed. G. C. Ainsworth and A. S. Sussman, pp. 473–511. New York: Academic Press.

With Y. Koltin. *Schizophyllum commune:* New mutations in the *B* incompatibility factor. Science, 154:510–11.

Genetics of Sexuality in Higher Fungi. New York: Ronald Press.

With C. A. Raper. Mutations modifying sexual morphogenesis in *Schizophyllum.* Genetics, 54:1151–68.

1967

The role of specific secretions in the induction and development of sexual organs and in the determination of sexual affinity. In: *Handbuch der pflanzen Physiologie*, ed. H. F. Linskins, vol. 18, pp. 214–34. Heidelberg, Berlin, and New York: Springer-Verlag.

With Y. Koltin and G. Simchen. Genetic structure of the incompatibility factors of *Schizophyllum:* The *B* factor. Proc. Natl. Acad. Sci. USA, 57:55–62.

With Y. Koltin. The genetic structure of the incompatibility factors of *Schizophyllum commune:* Three functionally distinct classes of *B* factors. Proc. Natl. Acad. Sci. USA, 58:1220–26.

With Y. Koltin. The genetic structure of the incompatibility factors of *Schizophyllum commune:* The resolution of class III factors. Mol. Gen. Genet., 100:275–82.

1968

With M. Raudaskowski. Secondary mutations at the $B\beta$ locus of *Schizophyllum.* Heredity, 23:109–17.

With C. A. Raper. Genetic regulation of sexual morphogenesis in *Schizophyllum commune.* J. Elisha Mitchell Sci. Soc., 84:267–73.

On the evolution of fungi. In: *The Fungi (III)*, ed. G. C. Ainsworth and A. S. Sussman, pp. 677–93. New York: Academic Press.

With Y. Koltin. Dikaryosis: Genetic determination in *Schizophyllum.* Science, 160:85–86.

Steroid sexual hormones in a water mould. Proc. Sect. Sci. Isr. Acad. Sci. Humanit., 11:1–8.

1969

With C.-S. Wang. Protein specificity and sexual morphogenesis in *Schizophyllum commune.* J. Bacteriol., 99:291–97.
With T. J. Leonard. *Schizophyllum commune:* Gene controlling haploid fruiting. Science, 165:190.

1970

Chemical ecology among lower plants. In: *Perspectives in Chemical Ecology,* ed. E. Sondheimer, pp. 21–43. New York: Academic Press.
With A. S. Flexer. The road to diploidy with emphasis on a detour. In: *Organization and Control in Prokaryotic and Eukaryotic Cells,* ed. H. P. Charles and B. C. J. G. Knight, pp. 401–32. New York: Cambridge University Press.
With J. H. Perkins. Morphogenesis in *Schizophyllum commune.* III. A mutation that blocks initiation of fruiting. Mol. Gen. Genet., 106:151–54.
With C.-S. Wang. Isozyme patterns and sexual morphogenesis in *Schizophyllum.* Proc. Natl. Acad. Sci. USA, 66:882–89.

1971

Growth and reproduction of fungi. In: *Plant Physiology, A Treatise,* ed. F. C. Steward, vol. 6, pp. 167–230. New York and London: Academic Press.
With A. S. Flexer. Mating systems and evolution of Basidiomycetes. In: *Evolution in the Higher Basidiomycetes,* ed. R. H. Petersen, pp. 149–67. Knoxville: University of Tennessee.
With R. M. Hoffman. Genetic restriction of energy conservation in *Schizophyllum.* Science, 171:418–19.

1972

With R. M. Hoffman. Lowered respiratory response to adenosine diphosphate of mitochondria isolated from a mutant-*B* strain of *Schizophyllum commune.* J. Bacteriol., 110:780–81.
With C. A. Raper. Life cycle and prospects for interstrain breeding of *Agaricus bisporus.* Mushroom Sci., 8:1–9.
With C. A. Raper and R. E. Miller. 1972. Genetic analysis of the life cycle of *Agaricus bisporus.* Mycologia, 64:1088–117.

1973

With C. A. Raper. Incompatibility factors: Regulatory genes for sexual morphogenesis in higher fungi. In: *Basic Mechanisms in Plant Morphogenesis,* pp. 19–39. Brookhaven Symposia in Biology no. 25. Upton, N.Y.: Brookhaven National Laboratory.

With C. A. Raper. Mutational analysis of a regulatory gene for morphogenesis in *Schizophyllum.* Proc. Natl. Acad. Sci. USA, 70:1427–31.

1974

With A. S. Flexer. Heterothallism in Basidiomycetes. In: *Mycology Guidebook,* ed. R. B. Stevens, pp. 524–39. Seattle: University of Washington Press.

With R. M. Hoffman. *Schizophyllum.* In: *Handbook of Genetics,* vol. 1, ed. R. C. King, pp. 597–626. New York: Plenum Press.

With R. M. Hoffman. Genetic impairment of energy conservation in development of *Schizophyllum:* Efficient mitochondria in energy-starved cells. J. Gen. Microbiol., 82:67–75.

With R. C. Ullrich. Number and distribution of bipolar incompatibility factors in *Sistotrema brinkmannii.* Am. Nat., 108:507–18.

1975

With R. C. Ullrich. Primary homothallism—relation to heterothallism in the regulation of sexual morphogenesis in *Sistotrema.* Genetics, 80:311–21.

KARL SAX
November 2, 1892–October 8, 1973

BY CARL P. SWANSON AND NORMAN H. GILES

As I view my contribution to the writing of our time, it seems to me to consist of a double affirmative, saying first that an awareness and experience of Nature is necessary to Man if he is to have his humanity, and saying in the second place that that same awareness must have something of a religious quality, the Italian pieta, if you will.

Nature is a part of our humanity, and without some awareness and experience of that divine mystery man ceases to be man. When the Pleiades and the wind in the grass are no longer a part of the human spirit, a part of the very flesh and bone, man becomes, as it were, a kind of cosmic outlaw, having neither the completeness and the integrity of the animal nor the birthright of a true humanity.

THESE WORDS by Henry Beston from his now classic volume, *Outermost House*, strike us as uniquely applicable to Karl Sax. He would not have been found wanting—although he, most certainly, would have raised a quizzical eyebrow unless the term "religious quality" were stripped of any cloying mysticism. He grew up and throughout his life remained close to the soil, and he expressed in words and actions the dignity, integrity, inner strength, and outer optimism that are so often the legacy of such a birthright. He knew the wheatfields of southeastern Washington; he knew how to care for and to harvest that which he had sown; and he knew the wonder of growing things, whether these were plants or human beings. He acknowledged his birthright and was proud of it, and he shared it with those in both high and low places. His public career was a long and distinguished one, but to those who knew him privately as well, that record was but a partial measure of a great and warm human being.

Karl Sax was born of pioneer parents in Spokane, Washington, on November 2, 1892; he died in Media, Pennsylvania, on October 8, 1973, less than a month shy of his eighty-first birthday. His father, William L. Sax, was, at various times, schoolteacher, county superintendent of schools, farmer, businessman, and mayor of Colville, Washington. His mother, Minnie A. Sax (née Morgan), was an artist and amateur botanist. An exposure to plants and to the natural environment as well as the advantages of higher education were very much a part of his early background. Sax entered Washington State College in 1912 to major in agriculture, and it was here that he met Professor Edward Gaines, a wheat breeder in the Experiment Station. Gaines led him into research and undoubtedly encouraged him to continue his studies at the graduate level. As Sax once wrote, "Here I learned that one could have all of the pleasures of an agricultural career without the financial headaches by going into agricultural research work." This early experience with the problems and techniques of plant breeding expanded into a continuing and absorbing interest that was pursued throughout his life. Other later studies brought him national and international recognition, but they never fully replaced his need to be close to the soil and to growing things.

Sax graduated from Washington State College in 1916, the year in which his first scientific paper appeared. Prior to graduation he had married his cytology teacher, Dr. Hally Jolivette. In the fall of 1916, she accepted an instructorship at Wellesley College, and he entered the Bussey Institution Graduate School of Applied Biology of Harvard University to work under the direction of Professor E. M. East. He received an M.S. degree in 1917, but his graduate studies were interrupted by World War I. He entered the army as a private and was discharged as a second lieutenant in the Coast Artillery in 1918.

Sax's first academic position was as an instructor in genetics at the University of California, Berkeley, where he also undertook cytological studies in the genus *Crepis* under Professor E. B. Babcock. His stay in Berkeley was brief, however, as was his next move to the private Riverbank Laboratories in Geneva, Illinois, where he initiated his studies on wheat. In 1920 he accepted a position at the Maine Agricultural Experiment Station in Orono; here he completed his doctoral thesis on wheat hybrids, and the D.Sc. was awarded to him in 1922 by the Bussey Institution. One of his colleagues at Orono was John W. Gowen, and they collaborated on a number of occasions: the genetics, productivity, and root and bud selection of apples were their primary concerns. The wheat studies were pursued almost as an avocation, but Sax considered the papers dealing with wheat species and hybrids to be his most important contribution during these early years—in large part because they were among the first of the published works that opened up what was then the new science of cytotaxonomy in this country.

Sax remained at Orono until 1928 when he was appointed associate professor of plant cytology at the Arnold Arboretum and named to the faculty of the Bussey Institution Graduate School of Applied Biology, an affiliate of Harvard University concerned with teaching and research in agriculture and horticulture. Here he joined a faculty of distinguished biologists: W. M. Wheeler and C. T. Brues in entomology, W. E. Castle and E. M. East in genetics, Oakes Ames in economic botany, and I. W. Bailey in wood anatomy. The graduate student body must also have been a stimulating one because many of those who received their degrees from the Bussey Institution were to become worthy successors to their professors.

Sax was elevated to a full professorship in 1936, the same year in which the dissolution of the Bussey graduate school took place. (In the view of President Lowell, Harvard and applied biology were incompatible.) The dissolution, however, necessitated a move of office, laboratory, and students to the new Biological Laboratories in Cambridge; here he taught courses in cytology and, for a while, genetics—Sax took over teaching the latter on the death of Professor East in 1938. This move, on the other hand, did not terminate his association with the Arboretum and the Bussey. His cytotaxonomy studies continued, and many of his students lived in the Bussey buildings during the summer months of their graduate careers. For many of us this was during the latter years of the Great Depression and under the lengthening shadows of World War II; to make ends meet we were encouraged by him to grow our own vegetables and to raid the Arboretum for appropriate fruits.

With the retirement of E. D. Merrill, Sax was appointed acting director of the Arnold Arboretum in 1946; in 1947 he was named its third director. He held simultaneously the rather empty title of superintendent of the Bussey Institution. But both administrative appointments were abruptly terminated by Harvard University in 1954 as a result of his vigorous but losing opposition to the proposal that the general resources of the Arnold Arboretum—books, herbarium specimens, and funds—be transferred to Cambridge as part of a move for the consolidation of botany. Sax not only believed that the science of botany suffered when instruction at the Bussey was terminated, and that it would deteriorate further when interest in the Arboretum as a living center for horticultural studies was lessened; he also considered the action taken by the Harvard Corporation to be an outright breach of trust. To combat the transfer, he enlisted the aid of The Friends of the Arnold Arboretum and cooperated with them when the group filed suit in Massachusetts against the corporation. He contended that he, as director and as a matter of principle, could not be party to the divestiture of the Arboretum's resources without judicial review and legal approval. Sax remained as professor of biology in Cambridge until his retirement in 1959, but the controversy left its mark. The latter years were bitter ones: he was hurt by the alienation of some of his botanical colleagues and by the scientific decline of the Arboretum that had been for so long a significant part of his productive years.

About thirty graduate students took their advanced degrees with Sax, and another fourteen spent their postdoctoral years in his laboratory. He is remembered and revered with unabashed affection by these students; in his gruff but quiet way he embraced them all and brought them into his family. As he said, "My academic children seemed almost as much a part of our family as our three sons."

Karl Sax established a solid and enviable reputation both in this country and abroad. He was as well known to nurserymen as to his fellow cytologists, and this was reflected in his professional affiliations and in the honors bestowed on him. He was a member of the Genetics Society of America, serving as president in 1958; the Botanical Society of America—he received its certificate of merit in 1956; American Society of Horticultural Science; American Genetics Association; Population Association of America; Planned Parenthood League, serving as president of the Massachusetts chapter in 1958; American Academy of Social and Political Sciences; and the Radiation Research Society. He was elected to membership in the American Academy of Arts and Sciences (1941) and the National Academy of Sciences (1941), to honorary membership in Phi Beta Kappa (1941) and the Japanese Genetics Society (1956), and as foreign correspondent to the French Academy of Agriculture (1946). The Jackson Dawson Memorial Medal of the Massachusetts Horticultural Society was awarded to him in 1959, as was the Norman J. Coleman Award of the American Association of Nurserymen in 1961. He received an honorary doctoral degree from the University of Massachusetts in 1965, from his alma mater Washington State University in 1966, and from the University of Maine in 1971. He was equally pleased, however, to be named "Horticulturist of the Year" (1959) by the Student Horticultural Club of the University of Massachusetts, and to be grouped, by Katherine White in *The New Yorker,* with Charles Sargent and Ernest "Chinese" Wilson as "a distinguished plantsman."

Sax was a national lecturer on the academic circuit for the American Institute of Biological Sciences in 1957 and in 1962 for Sigma Xi. In 1951 he received the signal honor of being asked to deliver the Lowell Lectures in Boston, choosing as his topic world population problems.

The research and publication record of Karl Sax spanned a period of fifty-five years (1916–1971) with but a brief interruption for military service. The publications fall generally into three groups—horticulture, chromosomal studies, and demography—with considerable overlap of the first two areas as much of the cytogenetic and cytotaxonomic work was done on ornamental species in the Arnold Arboretum. The horticultural aspects of Sax's professional career began with his appointment to the Maine Experiment Station, where he was much occupied with improvement of productivity in apples. This interest, which initially involved propagation, crossing, and sterility, was continued at the Arboretum, but the focus of the work was now directed toward an understanding of the origin of the Pomoideae, the production of desirable ornamental hybrids, and the means for dwarfing well-known and useful varieties of nursery stocks. The dwarfing of fruit trees had been practiced empirically for hundreds of years before being introduced into the Americas but the basis of dwarfing was not understood in a scientific sense. By experimenting with a wide variety of intervarietal, interspecific, and even intergeneric combinations of rootstocks and scions; by the use of different interstocks between root and scion; and by single and double bark inversions to block the flow of nutrients through the phloem, Sax contributed significantly to an understanding of the phenomenon, reduced the variability of graft compatibility and growth, and simplified the techniques to the point where the average nurseryman could readily produce his own dwarfs.

In the area of plant breeding, Sax and his students—in particular George Skirm—were successful in creating a number of excellent hybrids that quickly found their way into the ornamental trade. He was especially proud of the graceful cherry "Hally Jolivette," a hybrid between *Prunus subhirtella* and *P. apetela*, which he named for his wife and frequent collaborator. (The fact that Jolivette could be translated from the French into "pretty little one" added icing to the cake of tribute.) The magnolia "Dr. Merrill" honored his predecessor as director of the Arboretum, while the crabapple hybrids "Henry DuPont" and "Henrietta Crosby" were named after two of the loyal Friends of the Arnold Arboretum, who were also his personal friends and research sponsors. The "Blanche Ames" honored a distinguished botanical artist who was also the wife of Professor Oakes Ames; the hybrid "Mary Potter" was so named because one of the parent species was *Malus sargenti*, named after her father, Charles Sargent.

Sax also produced a number of *Forsythia* hybrids. Beatrix Farrand, a well-known landscape architect, Friend of the Arboretum, and designer of the gardens at Dumbarton Oaks in Washington, D.C., was recognized by having a triploid hybrid named after her. This turned out to be a lesser improvement than the tetraploid "Arnold Giant," winner of an award of merit by the Royal Horticultural Society of England. The "Arnold Dwarf" proved to be an interesting ground cover but a meager producer of flowers. Still another of his *Forsythia* hybrids, the "Karl Sax," was subsequently named by a nurseryman who was testing it in his trial plots.

The chromosomal studies fell into two subcategories: cytotaxonomy and the effects of radiation and chemicals on chromosome structure. As indicated earlier, his wheat studies provided him with a doctoral thesis as well as helping to establish what was then the developing field of cytotaxonomy in this country. He shared with the Japanese cytologists Kihara and Sakamura the credit for discovering the role of polyploidy and interspecific hybridization in the origin of certain wheat species, a seminal work of great significance in understanding the nature of some of our basic food plants. Comparable studies, in which Hally Jolivette Sax often participated, were carried out on a wide variety of groups growing or being tested in the Arboretum: Pomoideae, Pinaceae, Rosaceae, Cycladales, Hamamalidaceae, Vitis, Yucca and Agave, Rhododendron, Paeonia, Ulmus, and Platanus. The karyotypes of Yucca and Agave were shown to be sufficiently unique to cause them to be removed from the Liliaceae, and to be given familial status in the Agavaceae; moreover, the complete fertility and regular meiotic pairing in the London plane tree, a hybrid between *Platanus occidentalis* and *P. orientalis*, demonstrated that separation by the Atlantic Ocean for millions of years did not necessarily involve chromosomal rearrangements and accompanying sterility.

It was Sax's interest in the American species of *Tradescantia*, sparked no doubt by his collaboration with Edgar Anderson of the Missouri Botanic Garden, that led to the emergence of radiation cytology out of what began as a cytotaxonomic survey of the Commelinaceae. Sax understood that chromosomal rearrangement must play some kind of role in evolution and speciation and that the large size and small number of *Tradescantia* chromosomes in the readily available haploid microspores made them ideal for experimental purposes. Recognizing that X rays not only induced mutations but chromosomal rearrangements as well, he initiated his radiation studies in 1935. The atom bomb and the horrors of radiation exposure were nearly a decade in the future.

Tradescantia paludosa was the species of choice, and the following two decades witnessed an extraordinary outpouring of papers by Sax and his students—papers that provided qualitative and quantitative information on the frequency of both induced and spontaneous aberrations. The implication and transference of these data to problems of radiation therapy, evolution, and speciation were inevitable, as was additional information related to the effects of temperature, cell cycle, dose rate, and dose fractionation on the final frequency of induced change. Sax was the father of radiation cytology, and he spawned a whole generation of "chromosome busters." In his later years, and particularly after retirement, Sax turned to the chromosomal aspects of aging in seeds, and to the radiomimetic effects of caffeine, insecticides, and chemical food additives.

While he vigorously pursued his horticultural and chromosomal investigations, Sax still managed to take an interest in and make a significant contribution to the area of demography. His initial entry into this field undoubtedly stemmed from his close association with his graduate mentor and now colleague, Professor E. M. East; but it was probably fostered as well by the interest of Castle and Brues in applied eugenics. In 1923 East had published *Mankind at the Crossroads,* a Malthusian indictment of the present and future consequences of unchecked human fecundity in a world of limited resources and agricultural productivity. He advocated a conscious and deliberate practice of birth control; in his words, "parentage must not be haphazard." Sax was similarly Malthusian. (Believing that what he advocated publicly should be first practiced at home, he urged all of his graduate students to read the so-called "Bussey Bible," a collection of articles on birth control.) The first of a continuing flow of articles appeared in *The Scientific Monthly* in 1944, but the gist of his thinking was set forth in his Lowell Lectures. The talks were prepared for book form under the title *Malthus and the Modern World;* this was subsequently altered to *Standing Room Only: The Challenge of Over-Population,* which appeared in 1955 and was reissued in paperback in 1960.

Mild-mannered and retiring as he was in his personal relations, Sax was actively aggressive in the Planned Parenthood League and in his demographic speeches and articles. His local target was the restrictive birth control law of Massachusetts. These laws were subsequently changed by a referendum sponsored by the Planned Parenthood League—but not before Sax had invoked the wrath of many religious leaders and particularly those of the Roman Catholic Church of Boston and its suburbs. (The Church proclaimed to its flock that "birth control is against God's Law" and urged all parishioners to vote down the referendum.) He viewed the harassment that resulted as a measure of the effectiveness of his stand, and so he continued his fight on a national scale—believing, as has proven to be the case, that financial aid to the underdeveloped countries without accompanying information and aid regarding birth control was not only politically immoral but, in a human sense, ultimately self-defeating and cruel as well. He considered India a lost cause in this respect, but he held high hopes for the Latin American countries if aid to them could be tempered with something more than material benefits and weapons.

Sax was a realist and a pragmatist. He was particularly disturbed by demographic and scientific Pollyannas who, through ignorance or design, duped the public with glowing scenes of future happiness and an abundance for all. Consequently Sax reviewed *Enough and to Spare,* a book by Harvard colleague Kirtley Mather, in a tempered but devastating manner to show that both Mather's demography and his biological postulates were utterly without foundation, that his optimism was based largely on pious hopes. Sax himself had a clear vision of the role of science in the betterment of mankind, but he had an equally clear vision of its limitations as well.

In another political direction, Sax took strong exception to the praise that some leading British and American scientists—among them Julian Huxley, J. B. S. Haldane, J. D. Bernal, and L. C. Dunn—accorded Soviet science, particularly genetics. He was too much of a dirt farmer as well as a cytogeneticist to accept Lysenkoism, and he was among the first to call the scientific world's attention to the oppressive treatment given such men as Vavilov, Dubinin, Navaschin, and Timoféeff-Ressovsky.

Retirement in 1959 brought a change of place and of pace. Sax established and maintained an experimental garden on his son's estate in Media, Pennsylvania, but he also traveled and lectured widely. In the years between 1956 and 1966 he held visiting professorships at the Universities of Florida, Tennessee, Georgia, and California at Davis; at Yale University; and at North Carolina State University. For a brief period in 1962, he was resident collaborator at the Brookhaven National Laboratory. In 1961, at the age of sixty-nine, he was a Guggenheim fellow at Oxford University where C. D. Darlington, the dean of British cytologists, held sway.

Darlington and Sax were sharply contrasting scientists. As Sax once wrote, paraphrasing Francis Bacon, he was the ant, the gatherer of quantitative data from which his ideas emerged; Darlington was the spider, the gifted spinner of theories in which facts were often of secondary importance. Both had published on chromosome structure, the mechanisms of crossing over, and the origin of chiasmata, with the Darlingtonian views the more nearly correct. Both were also interested in demography—Sax again the pragmatist, Darlington the theorist, as he wove genetics, race, IQs, mating patterns, and the improvement of mankind into his mental cobwebs. It is regrettable that their conversations were not recorded, for Sax, in his own way, had great respect for Darlington's facile mind—even though he referred to Darlington's *Recent Advances in Cytology* as "a masterpiece of mythogenesis."

In his later years, Professor and Mrs. Sax spent each winter at the University of Georgia. He published regularly during these years, and his papers continued to reflect the breadth of his interests. Fittingly, one of his last journal papers was in response to a request from the Genetics Society of Japan, of which he was an honorary member. Perhaps even more fittingly, it was coauthored by Mrs. Sax, his companion, colleague, and gentle critic for fifty-eight years.

Comparisons are more likely to be invidious than they are to illuminate, but Professor Sax's secure place in his several fields of interest was earned and not thrust upon him: he was an imaginative and dedicated scientist, a plant breeder of note, and a citizen who had a clear vision of the place of science in human affairs. His greatness as a human being, however, was innate. To those of us who gained our scientific stripes under his tutelage, and who came to know him privately as well, he was a father figure: a quiet, decent man who at times was reserved, gruff, even unapproachable; at other times, warmly human and humorous. He treated us all alike, encouraging everyone, but infinitely patient if we could only plod. He was not an eloquent speaker. He let his published papers speak for themselves, or he deferred to his students and colleagues at national and international meetings. But when his deeply held and cherished principles were challenged or misrepresented, he never hesitated to enter the lists. Supported always by Mrs. Sax, he was never an unprepared or unworthy opponent. He rarely dealt in personalities when the subject was controversial, for he could respect another's position or belief even when he disagreed with it; but he was not a compromiser of principles even though, as in the Arnold Arboretum controversy, it might cause him anguish and cost him position and friends.

Karl Sax was survived by his wife, Hally Jolivette, who passed away on March 20, 1979; three sons—Dr. Karl J., an industrial organic chemist, Dr. W. Peter, a psychiatrist, and Edward D., an industrial engineer; nine grandchildren; eight great-grandchildren; and those who, like ourselves, remember him with deep and sincere affection.

BIBLIOGRAPHY

1916

Fertilization in *Fritillaria pudica*. Bull. Torrey Bot. Club, 43:505–22.

1918

The inheritance of doubleness in *Chelidonium majus, L.* Genetics, 3:300–307.

The behavior of the chromosomes in fertilization. Genetics, 3:309–27.

1921

Sterility in wheat hybrids. I. Sterility relationships and endosperm development. Genetics, 6:399–416.

A simple device for weighing seeds. Bot. Gaz., 71:399.

With J. W. Gowen. Productive and unproductive types of apple trees. J. Hered., 12:291–300.

Studies in orchard management. II. Factors influencing fruit development of the apple. Bull. Maine Agric. Exp. Stn., 298:53–84.

Chromosome relationships in wheat. Science, 54:413–15.

1922

With J. W. Gowen. The relation of tree type to productivity in the apple. Bull. Maine Agric. Exp. Stn., 305:1–20.

Sterility relationships in Maine apple varieties. Bull. Maine Agric. Exp. Stn., 307:61–76.

Sterility in wheat hybrids. II. Chromosome behavior in partially sterile hybrids. Genetics, 7:513–52.

Sterility in wheat hybrids. III. Endosperm development and F_2 sterility. Genetics, 553–58.

1923

With H. C. McPhee. Color factors in bean hybrids. J. Hered., 14:205–8.

NOTE: The authors would like to thank Professor William Provine of Cornell University for checking the bibliography.

With J. W. Gowen. The cause and permanence of size differences in apple trees. Bull. Maine Agric. Exp. Stn., 310:1–8.
With J. W. Gowen. Permanence of tree performance in a clonal variety and a critique of the theory of bud mutation. Genetics, 8:179–211.
The association of size differences with seed-coat pattern and pigmentation in *Phaseolus vulgaris*. Genetics, 8:552–60.
Bud and root selection in the propagation of the apple. Proc. Am. Soc. Hortic. Sci., 20:244–50.
With J. W. Gowen. The place of stocks in the propagation of clonal varieties of apples. Genetics, 8:458–65.
The relation between chromosome number, morphological characters and rust resistance in segregates of partially sterile wheat hybrids. Genetics, 8:301–21.

1924

The nature of size inheritance. Proc. Natl. Acad. Sci. USA, 10:224–27.
With E. F. Gaines. A genetic and cytological study of certain hybrids of wheat species. J. Agric. Res., 28:1017–32.
With Hally Jolivette Sax. Chromosome behavior in a genus cross. Genetics, 9:454–64.
The "probable error" in horticultural experiments. Proc. Am. Soc. Hortic. Sci., 21:252–56.
Nursery stock investigations. Proc. Am. Soc. Hortic. Sci., 21:310–12.

1925

Fertilization of apple orchards in Maine. Bull. Maine Agric. Exp. Stn., 322:1–8.

1926

With Iva M. Burgess. Varieties of ensilage corn for Maine. Bull. Maine Agric. Exp. Stn., 330:49–56.
Sweet-corn breeding experiments. Bull. Maine Agric. Exp. Stn., 332:113–44.
Quantitative inheritance in *Phaseolus*. J. Agric. Res., 33:349–54.
A genetical interpretation of ecological adaptation. Bot. Gaz., 82:223–27.

Statistical methods in horticulture. Proc. Am. Soc. Hortic. Sci., 23:141–49.

1928

Bud and root selection in the apple. Bull. Maine Agric. Exp. Stn., 344:21–32.
Chromosome behavior in *Triticum* hybrids. (Verhandl. V. Internat. Kongresses Vererbungs-wissenschaft, Berlin, 1927.) Z. Indukt. Abstamm. Vererbungsl., suppl. 2:1267–84.

1929

Chromosome counts in *Vitis* and related genera. Proc. Am. Soc. Hortic. Sci., 26:32, 33.
Chromosome behavior in *Sorbopyrus* and *Sorbaronia*. Proc. Natl. Acad. Sci. USA, 15:844, 845.

1930

Chromosome number and behavior in the genus *Syringa*. J. Arnold Arbor., 11:7–14.
With D. A. Kribs. Chromosomes and phylogeny in the Caprifoliaceae. J. Arnold Arbor., 11:147–53.
Chromosome structure and the mechanism of crossing over. J. Arnold Arbor., 11:193–220.
Arnold Arboretum cytological laboratory report, 1929–1930. J. Arnold Arbor., 11:237, 238.
Chromosome stability in the genus *Rhododendron*. Am. J. Bot., 17:247–51.

1931

The origin and relationships of the Pomoideae. J. Arnold Arbor., 12:3–22.
Chromosome numbers in the ligneous Saxifragaceae. J. Arnold Arbor., 12:198–206.
Arnold Arboretum cytology laboratory report, 1930–1931. J. Arnold Arbor., 12:299.
The smear technique in plant cytology. Stain Technol., 6:117–22.
Chromosome ring formation in *Rhoeo discolor*. Cytologia, 3:36–53.
Crossing over and mutation. Proc. Natl. Acad. Sci. USA, 17:601–3.

Plant hybrids. Arnold Arbor. Bull. Popul. Inf., 5:17–20.

1932

With E. C. Abbe. Chromosome numbers and the anatomy of the secondary xylem in the Oleaceae. J. Arnold Arbor., 13:37–48.
The cytological mechanism of crossing over. J. Arnold Arbor., 13:180–212.
Chromosome relationships in the Pomoideae. J. Arnold Arbor., 13:363–67.
Arnold Arboretum cytological laboratory report, 1931–1932. J. Arnold Arbor., 13:450, 451.
Meiosis and chiasma formation in *Paeonia suffruticosa*. J. Arnold Arbor., 13:375–84.
The cytological mechanism for crossing over. In: *Proceedings of the Sixth International Genetics Congress*, vol. 1, pp. 256–73. Brooklyn: Brooklyn Botanic Gardens.
Flowering habits of trees and shrubs. Arnold Arbor. Bull. Popul. Inf., 6:14–16.
Review of *Recent Advances in Cytology*, by C. D. Darlington. Collecting Net, 7:201–3.

1933

With Edgar Anderson. Segmental interchange in chromosomes of *Tradescantia*. Genetics, 18:53–67.
With Hally Jolivette Sax. Chromosome number and morphology in the Conifers. J. Arnold Arbor., 14:356–75.
With H. W. Edmonds. Development of the male gametophyte in *Tradescantia*. Bot. Gaz., 95:156–63.
Species hybrids in *Platanus* and *Campsis*. J. Arnold Arbor., 14:274–78.
Chromosome behavior in *Calycanthus*. J. Arnold Arbor., 14:279–81.
The origin of the Pomoideae. Proc. Am. Soc. Hortic. Sci., 30:147–50.
Chromosome numbers in *Ulmus* and related genera. J. Arnold Arbor., 14:82–84.
With Susan Delano McKelvey. Taxonomic and cytological relationships of *Yucca* and *Agave*. J. Arnold Arbor., 14:76–81.

1934

Interlocking as a "demonstration" of the occurrence of crossing over. Am. Nat., 68:95, 96.
With Edgar Anderson. A cytological analysis of self-sterility in *Tradescantia*. Bot. Gaz., 95:609–21.
With J. M. Beal. Chromosomes of the Cycadales. J. Arnold Arbor., 15:255–58.
With Edgar Anderson. Interlocking of bivalent chromosomes in *Tradescantia*. Genetics, 19:157–66.
With L. M. Humphrey. Structure of meiotic chromosomes in microsporogenesis of *Tradescantia*. Bot. Gaz., 96:353–62.
Cytology for students. (Review of *Introduction to Cytology*, by L. W. Sharp.) Science, 80:407.

1935

With Edgar Anderson. Chromosome numbers in the Hamamelidaceae and their phylogenetic significance. J. Arnold Arbor., 16:210–15.
Chromosome structure in the meiotic chromosomes of *Rhoeo discolor* Hance. J. Arnold. Arbor., 16:216–24.
The cytological analysis of species-hybrids. Bot. Rev., 1:100–17.
Variation in chiasma frequencies in *Secale, Vicia* and *Tradescantia*. Cytologia, 6:289–93.
The effect of temperature on nuclear differentiation in microspore development. J. Arnold Arbor., 16:301–10.
With Hally Jolivette Sax. Chromosome structure and behavior in mitosis and meiosis. J. Arnold Arbor., 16:423–39.

1936

The experimental production of polyploidy. J. Arnold Arbor., 17:153–59.
With Ladley Husted. Polarity and differentiation in microspore development. Am. J. Bot., 23:606–9.
Polyploidy and geographic distribution in *Spiraea*. J. Arnold Arbor., 17:352–56.
Chromosome coiling in relation to meiosis and crossing over. Genetics, 21:324–38.
With Edgar Anderson. A cytological monograph of the American species of *Tradescantia*. Bot. Gaz., 97:433-76.

1937

Effect of variations in temperature on nuclear and cell division in *Tradescantia*. Am. J. Bot., 24:218–25.
Chromosome inversions in *Paeonia suffruticosa*. Cytologia, Fujii Jubilee Volume:108–14.
With Hally Jolivette Sax. Stomata size and distribution in diploid and polyploid plants. J. Arnold Arbor., 18:164–72.
Chromosome behavior and nuclear development in *Tradescantia*. Genetics, 22:523–33.
Review of *Recent Advances in Cytology*, by C. D. Darlington. J. Hered., 28:217–19.

1938

The relation between stomata counts and chromosome number. J. Arnold Arbor., 19:437–41.
Chromosome aberrations induced by X-rays. Genetics, 23:494–516.

1939

The time factor in X-ray production of chromosome aberrations. Proc. Natl. Acad. Sci. USA, 25:225–33.
With K. Mather. An X-ray analysis of progressive chromosome splitting. J. Genet., 37:483–90.
With E. V. Enzmann. The effect of temperature on X-ray induced chromosome aberrations. Proc. Natl. Acad. Sci. USA, 25:397–405.

1940

An analysis of X-ray induced chromosomal aberrations in *Tradescantia*. Genetics, 25:41–68.
The effect of radiation on chromosome structure. Am. Philos. Soc. Yearb., 1940:240, 241.

1941

With J. G. O'Mara. Mechanism of mitosis in pollen tubes. Bot. Gaz., 102:629–36.
With C. P. Swanson. Differential sensitivity of cells to X-rays. Am. J. Bot., 28:52–59.

The behavior of X-ray induced chromosomal aberrations in *Allium* root tip cells. Genetics, 26:418–25.
Types and frequencies of chromosomal aberrations induced by X-rays. Cold Spring Harbor Symp. Quant. Biol., 9:93–101.

1942

The distribution of X-ray induced chromosomal aberrations. Proc. Natl. Acad. Sci. USA, 28:229–33.
The mechanisms of X-ray effects on cells. J. Gen. Physiol., 25:533–37.
Diffusion of gene products. Proc. Natl. Acad. Sci. USA, 28:303–6.

1943

The effect of centrifuging upon the production of X-ray induced chromosomal aberrations. Proc. Natl. Acad. Sci. USA, 29:18–21.
With Robert T. Brumfield. The relation between X-ray dosage and the frequency of chromosomal aberrations. Am. J. Bot., 30:564–70.

1944

Population problems of a new world order. Sci. Mon., 58:66–71.
Soviet biology. Science, 99:298–99.

1945

The demographic dilemma. Science, 101:325–26.
Lilac species hybrids. J. Arnold Arbor., 26:79–84.
Population problems. In: *The Science of Man in the World Crisis*, ed. Ralph Linton, pp. 258–81. New York: Columbia University Press.

1947

How new plants are made. Horticulture, 25(n.s.):127, 128.
Mechanism of heredity. Am. Fruit Grow., 67:16, 28, 29.
Plant breeding at the Arnold Arboretum. Arnoldia, 7:9–12.
Temperature effects on X-ray induced chromosome aberrations. Genetics, 32:75–78.
Soviet science and political philosophy. Sci. Mon., 65:43–47.

The Arnold Arboretum during the fiscal year ended June 30, 1947. J. Arnold Arbor., 28:447–52.
The Arnold Arboretum of Harvard University. Arnold Arbor. Bull., 10(3):9, 10, 24.
The Bussey Institution. Arnoldia, 7:13–16.
With Hally Jolivette Sax. The cytogenetics of generic hybrids of *Sorbus*. J. Arnold Arbor., 28:137–40.

1948

The Arnold Arboretum during the fiscal year ended June 30, 1948. J. Arnold Arbor., 29:422–28.

1949

The Arnold Arboretum during the fiscal year ended June 30, 1949. J. Arnold Arbor., 30:450–55.
John George Jack, 1861–1949. J. Arnold Arbor., 30:345–47.
The use of *Malus* species for apple rootstocks. Proc. Am. Soc. Hortic. Sci., 53:219–20.

1950

Rootstocks for lilacs. Arnoldia, 10:57–60.
The cytological effects of low intensity radiation. Science, 112:332–33.
Dwarf trees. Arnoldia, 10:73–79.
Oakes Ames, 1874–1950. J. Arnold Arbor., 31:335–49.
The effect of X-rays on chromosome structure. J. Cell Comp. Physiol., 35 (suppl. 1):71–81.
The Arnold Arboretum during the fiscal year ended June 30, 1950. J. Arnold Arbor., 31:430–34.
The effect of the rootstock on the growth of seedling trees & shrubs. Proc. Am. Soc. Hortic. Sci., 56:166–68.
Population and agriculture. In: *Twentieth Century Economic Thought*, ed. Glen Hoover, pp. 647–68. New York: Philosophical Library.

1951

Biological resources as a factor in international understanding. Sci. Mon., 72:300–305.
Can the earth feed its millions? UN World, 5:22–25.

Photosynthetic energy via agriculture. Proc. Am. Acad. Arts Sci., 79:205–11.
The Arnold Arboretum during the fiscal year ended June 30, 1951. J. Arnold Arbor., 32:412–16.
Food resources and population growth. Bull. At. Sci., 7:105–7.
Population problems in world development. In: *Social Progress Through Technology: The Human Conditions of Economic Growth*, pp. 4–6. (A week-end conference in four panels.) MIT Foreign Student Summer Project. Cambridge, Mass.: MIT Press.

1952

With Henry Luippold. The effect of fractional X-ray dosage on the frequency of chromosome aberrations. Heredity, 6:127–31.
With E. D. King and H. A. Schneiderman. The effects of CO and O on the frequency of X-ray induced chromosome aberrations in *Tradescantia*. Proc. Natl. Acad. Sci. USA, 38:34–43.
The Arnold Arboretum during the fiscal year ended June 30, 1952. J. Arnold Arbor., 33:403–9.

1953

Interstock effects in dwarfing fruit trees. Proc. Am. Soc. Hortic. Sci., 62:201–4.
Enough for all? (Review of *The Road to Abundance*, by J. Rosin and M. Eastman.) J. Hered., 44:203, 204.
The Arnold Arboretum during the fiscal year ended June 30, 1953. J. Arnold Arbor., 34:412–16.
Review: Symposium on chromosome breakage. Science, 118:658, 659.
With H. Kihara. Genetics in the U.S.S.R. J. Hered., 49(4):132, 158.

1954

The control of tree growth by phloem blocks. J. Arnold Arbor., 35:251–58.
Here's an easy way to dwarf trees. Better Fruit, 49:9, 10.
Population problems of Central America. Ceiba, 4:153–64.
Stock and scion relationship in graft incompatibility. Proc. Am. Soc. Hortic. Sci., 64:156–58.

1955

With E. D. King. An X-ray analysis of chromosome duplication. Proc. Natl. Acad. Sci. USA, 41:150–55.

The effect of ionizing radiation on plant growth. Am. J. Bot., 42:360–64.

With E. D. King and H. Luippold. The effect of fractionated X-ray dosage on the frequency of chromatid and chromosome aberrations. Radiat. Res., 2:171–79.

Evaluation of the recombination theory. J. Cell. Comp. Physiol., 45(suppl. 2):243–47.

Plant breeding at the Arnold Arboretum. Arnoldia, 15:5–12.

With A. G. Johnson. Induction of early flowering of ornamental apple trees. J. Arnold Arbor., 36:110–14.

Dwarf trees with bark inversion. Am. Fruit Grow., 75(3):38, 39.

Standing Room Only: The Challenge of Overpopulation. Boston: Beacon Press.

Pflanzenzuchtung im Arnold Arboretum. Dtsch. Baumsch., 7:177–83.

1956

What's new in plant propagation? Natl. Hortic. Mag., 35:116–18.

With Alan Q. Dickson. Phloem polarity in bark regeneration. J. Arnold Arbor., 37:173–79.

Paste the poison ivy. Arnoldia, 16:5–8.

The story behind dwarf fruits. Horticulture, 34(n.s.):203, 233.

The population explosion, pp. 3–61. Headline Series, Foreign Policy Association no. 120.

Review of *Chromosome Botany*, by C. D. Darlington. Science, 124:688.

1957

The control of vegetative growth and the induction of early fruiting of apple trees. Proc. Am. Soc. Hortic. Sci., 69:68–74.

The effect of ionizing radiation on chromosomes. Q. Rev. Biol., 32:15–26.

Dwarf ornamental and fruit trees. Proc. Plant Propagators Soc., 7:146–55.

1958

The juvenile characters of trees and shrubs. Arnoldia, 18:1–6.
The genetic future of man. In: *The Population Ahead,* ed. Roy G. Francis, pp.87–97. Minneapolis: University of Minnesota Press.
Experimental control of tree growth and reproduction. In: *The Physiology of Forest Trees,* ed. K. Thimann, pp. 601–10. New York: Ronald Press.
Forsythia "Beatrix Ferrand." Natl. Hortic. Mag., 37:112, 113.
Breeding ornamental trees and shrubs. Proc. Plant Propagators Soc., 8:120–26.

1959

The cytogenetics of facultative apomixis in *Malus* species. J. Arnold Arbor., 40:289–97.

1960

Meiosis in interspecific pine hybrids. For. Sci., 6:135–38.
Standing Room Only: The World's Exploding Population, rev. ed. (paper). Boston: Beacon Press.

1961

With Hally Jolivette Sax. The effect of age of seed on the frequency of spontaneous and gamma ray induced chromosome aberrations. Radiat. Bot., 1:80–83.
Radiation sensitivity of *Tradescantia* microspore chromosomes to a second exposure of X-rays. Radiat. Res., 14:667–73.

1962

With Hally Jolivette Sax. The effect of X-rays on the aging of seeds. Nature, 194:459, 460.
Aspects of aging in plants. Annu. Rev. Plant Physiol., 13:489–506.

1963

The stimulation of plant growth by ionizing radiation. Radiat. Bot., 3:179–86.
With Lloyd A. Schairer. The effect of chronic gamma irradiation on apical dominance of trees. Radiat. Bot., 3:283–85.
With Hally Jolivette Sax. The effect of chronological and physiological aging of onion seeds on the frequency of spontaneous

and X-ray induced chromosome aberrations. Radiat. Bot., 4:37–41.

1964

The world's exploding population. Perspect. Biol. Med., 7:321–30.
Population problems. Topic, 8:5–19.

1965

With H. J. Teas and Hally Jolivette Sax. Cycasin: Radiomimetic effects. Science, 149:541, 542.

1966

Biological problems of the age of science. Wash. State Rev., 10:5–9.
The Bussey Institution: Harvard University's Graduate School of Applied Biology. J. Hered., 57:175–78.
With Hally Jolivette Sax. Radiomimetic beverages, drugs and mutagens. Proc. Natl. Acad. Sci. USA, 55:1431–35.
Radiomimetic effects of beverages, drugs and insecticides. Cranbrook Inst. Sci. Newsl., 36:46–49.
The world population explosion. Medicine Today, 1:8–14.

1968

With Hally Jolivette Sax. Possible mutagenic hazards of some food additives, beverages and insecticides. Jpn. J. Genet., 43:89–94.
With Hally Jolivette Sax and Wayne Binns. Radiomimetic effects of veratrum. Toxicon, 6:69–70.

1969

Ethical aspects of the population crisis. BioScience, 19:303.

1970

With Hally Jolivette Sax and W. B. Itturian. Effects of sonic energy on chromosomes. Environ. Mut. Soc. Newsl., 5:24, 25.

GERHARD SCHMIDT
December 26, 1901–April 30, 1981

BY HERMAN M. KALCKAR

IN THE MID-1920s, during the more hopeful years of the Weimar Republic, Gerhard Schmidt seemed destined for a distinguished scholarly career in biochemistry. In 1926 he received the M.D. degree from the University of Frankfurt am Main, an institution that enjoyed considerable esteem, both nationally and internationally. In that same year, he accepted a postgraduate research fellowship in the biochemistry department there, the first step in a career progression that brought him eventually to the position of *Privatdozent* in the school's Department of Pathology. But Schmidt's career—like those of so many other scholars of Jewish extraction—was suddenly interrupted by the rise to power of the Nazis in 1933. He left Germany, and after a few years of "wandering"—years that took him to Italy, Sweden, and Canada—he finally settled permanently in the United States. There, he continued his work: first, briefly, at the Rockefeller Institute for Medical Research and Washington University School of Medicine in St. Louis, and then, for nearly forty years, at Tufts University School of Medicine in Boston.

Gerhard Schmidt was born December 26, 1901, in Stuttgart, the capital of the kingdom of Würtemberg, which was part of imperial Germany. His father, Julius, was a professor of chemistry at the Technische Hochschule in Stuttgart and the author of a textbook on organic chemistry; Gerhard's later zeal for sound analytical chemistry was probably influenced by his father's interests and scientific orientation. His mother, Isabella (née Gombrich), was an excellent pianist; her work undoubtedly stimulated her son's active participation in chamber music, an aspect of his life to which we shall return later.

Gerhard attended the Eberhardt Ludwig Gymnasium in Stuttgart, where he was valedictorian of his class at commencement exercises in the spring of 1919. That autumn he enrolled in the University of Tübingen and elected to study medicine; in 1922, however, he transferred to the medical school of the University of Frankfurt am Main. His early interests included not only chemistry and medicine but also general biology and particularly zoology—one of his favorite books was Brehm's popular zoology text, *Tierleben*.

After he received his medical degree in 1926, Schmidt accepted a research fellowship in the laboratory of Gustav Embden. While preparing for work on the so-called "nuclein deaminase," which was generally thought to liberate ammonia from various purine nucleosides, he selected (among various tissues) skeletal muscle for a special study. Parnas and his group had already described ammonia formation in skeletal muscle after tetanic contractions. Schmidt observed that muscle dispersions or extracts catalyzed the release of ammonia from muscle adenylic acid preparations, a phenomenon recently described by Embden and Zimmerman in early 1928; according to the physical and chemical methods they used for evaluation, the crystals were supposedly identical to the adenylic acid that Levene and his group had isolated from yeast nucleic acid by alkaline hydrolysis. A few months later, however, Schmidt was to revise this view profoundly. He found that the adenine ring in Embden's muscle adenylic acid was rapidly deaminated by the muscle deaminase, whereas Levene's yeast adenylic acid was not at all deaminated by the muscle enzyme.

The young Gerhard Schmidt may well have had sleepless nights after these initial observations. To reinforce his new findings, he designed the following control. Since Levene's yeast adenylic acid was obtained by subjecting yeast nucleic acid to a prolonged alkaline hydrolysis, Schmidt subjected muscle adenylic acid to the same type of hydrolysis. The deaminase preparation remained equally active on the treated as well as the untreated muscle adenylic acid. Schmidt wrote: "Therefore there can be no doubt about the chemical difference of the two substances (muscle and yeast adenylic acid). This will be illustrated also by physical and chemical methods, in a subsequent report by G. Embden and G. Schmidt."[1]

These crucial enzymatic findings were published in 1928 by Schmidt alone—but with the keen interest and enthusiasm of his mentor Gustav Embden; the chemical data were published by Embden and Schmidt in 1929 in the same journal—*Zeitschrift für physiologische Chemie*. (It is interesting to note that the next yeast adenylic samples sent to Schmidt and Embden were not only sent personally by P. A. Levene but were also prepared by him.) Schmidt's article emphasized that another deaminase in muscle catalyzed the liberation of ammonia from adenosine, regardless of whether this nucleoside originated from yeast or muscle adenylic acid. Hence the position of the phosphoric acid in the adenine nucleotide was essential for the specificity of the muscle adenylic acid deaminase. Although a few specific enzymes (such as urease) had been described several years earlier, Schmidt's new finding in the case of muscle adenylic acid deaminase may be the first example

---

[1] G. Embden and G. Schmidt, "Berichtigung," *Zeitschrift für Physiologische Chemie*, 197:191–92. This paper corrects one of their mathematical oversights.

of the importance of conformational differences (beyond the local target groups) for enzyme specificity. This principle was to be used successfully by Gerhard Schmidt and later by other investigators for the characterization of nucleic acids and their fragments.

Because inosinic acid, the deamination product of muscle adenylic acid, had been identified by Levene as a 5' nucleotide, muscle adenylic acid had to be considered a 5' nucleotide. Conversely, yeast adenylic acid, which is now known to be simply an artifact of the alkaline degradation, had to be assigned a different structure—either as a 2' or 3' (or both) nucleotide. Although Schmidt followed further developments with active interest, from the beginning he was careful not to categorize the nucleotides (as 2', 3', or 5') until further chemical and biochemical evidence became available.[2]

Schmidt's and Embden's investigations, however, were soon interrupted, as outside political events began to impinge on scientific research programs and institutions all over Germany. With the rise of Hitler and the Nazis, virulent anti-Semitism began to spread rapidly, and many German scholars and artists of Jewish extraction were forced to leave the country. At many German universities, Nazis began to infiltrate the academic community, and the persecution and harassment of Jewish scholars in the sciences and the humanities began to accelerate. This was certainly the case at the University of Frankfurt where Gustav Embden and Gerhard Schmidt were pursuing their important research. Finally, in 1933, during one of the frequent clashes of Nazi stormtroopers and their opponents in the streets near the university, a

---

[2] Soon after Schmidt's discovery of muscle adenylic acid, Fiske, Subarrow, and Lohmann described ATP and ADP. These pyrophosphate derivatives of muscle adenylic acid were not direct substrates for the deaminase. However, the latter enzyme became a crucial tool for this author in the description in 1942 of adenylate kinase (myokinase), the enzyme responsible for the reversible formation of 5' adenylic acid and ATP from two molecules of ADP.

uniformed stormtrooper was killed. The man arrested for the act, allegedly a "communist," was tried before a tribunal that in its verdicts usually favored the Nazi cause. But the verdict on this occasion was "not guilty" because the coroner's report from the pathology department stated that the victim had been shot in the chest and not in the back, as claimed by the Nazis. (Their story had been that the victim was fleeing and was then shot; instead, the pathology report indicated active aggression.)

The Nazis confronted the chairman of the pathology department, Dr. Fischer-Wasels, and accused the young "Jewish doctor" Gerhard Schmidt of falsifying the findings of the autopsy. Since Gerhard was engaged exclusively in medical research and had no responsibility whatsoever for autopsies, Fischer-Wasels immediately suspected a plot and with deep sorrow urged Schmidt to leave Nazi Germany. At first, Gerhard found the accusations too absurd to be alarmed. But finally, when Fischer-Wasels insisted on accompanying him to the next train for Switzerland, Gerhard became convinced of the imminent danger of the conspiracy. With only a few belongings (perhaps including his beloved cello), he left Germany for neutral Switzerland. (Fischer-Wasels, a conscientious scholar and administrator who abhorred anti-Semitism, is said to have rescued other Jewish medical scholars; apparently, however, Gustav Embden was not one of them. Embden's early death in Frankfurt, after he was forced out of his department by the Nazis at the height of one of his most creative scientific periods, remains a riddle.) Gerhard always felt grateful for Fischer-Wasels's resolute and courageous action, and American scientists as well have the old chief to thank for preserving Schmidt's research and teaching abilities for the scholars—both old and young—of this nation.

Schmidt's flight from Germany marked the beginning of years of displacement, a period that saw him moving among appointments at universities in Italy, Sweden, and Canada. As a refugee, Gerhard Schmidt preserved his enthusiasm for the study of phosphorus compounds and for the enzymology of the bases of nucleic acids. He and his last pupil in Frankfurt, Ernest Bueding, had been studying guanase, a deaminase of the base guanine that they found to be abundant in the spleen and liver. As a guest researcher in the institute of Hans von Euler in Stockholm from 1933 to 1934, Schmidt was encouraged to continue his studies on guanase in rat livers from normal animals and from rats deficient in vitamin A. On von Euler's suggestion, Schmidt and his coworker I. Rydh-Ehrensvärd investigated the effect of carotenes on guanase levels in the spleens of vitamin A-deficient rats; they found that administration of β-carotene brought about a doubling of the guanase levels. During 1934, Schmidt was able to publish some other results from his research, such as the isolation of a dipeptide phosphoric acid and a study of purine bases in nonfertilized sea urchin eggs. These topics seem to be related to the work of another prominent Stockholm biochemist, Einar Hammarsten, but it is not known whether the two researchers met during Schmidt's sojourn in Stockholm.

In 1934 Schmidt moved to join Pontimalli in the Department of General Pathology at the University of Florence. With tumor research his main focus during this stay, Schmidt's interest in phosphoproteins was greatly stimulated. In the studies he conducted, his findings indicated that chickens carrying Rous sarcoma released phosphoproteins to the blood plasma. In addition, the phosphoprotein fractions were subject to partition.

In 1935 Schmidt obtained a Carnegie Foundation research fellowship for displaced German scholars. With it came his first chance to visit the Western Hemisphere, where he was invited to set up his own research program in the

Chemistry Department of Queens University in Ontario, Canada. There, in 1936, Schmidt initiated his first systematic studies of nucleic acids and nucleohistone, topics to which he would return later in his research career. For the biochemical resolution, he chose a partly purified alkaline phosphatase preparation from calf intestine. Free nucleic acid incubated with this enzyme released the main part of the phosphorus of the nucleic acid; in contrast, upon enzymic incubation, nucleohistone released only 20 percent of its phosphorus, presumably from the fraction corresponding to the free nucleic acid. If, however, the nucleohistone was preincubated with pancreas extract and then incubated with phosphatase, all the phosphorus was released as inorganic phosphate. Purified trypsin had no effect on nucleohistone.

Schmidt published his findings in 1936, two years before he joined P. A. Levene's laboratory in New York. An additional study (in 1937) on the growth of chicken embryos, and the dependence of growth on egg white (even in rather high dilutions) and on glucose, testifies to Schmidt's interest in general biology. As one of his conclusions, he states that development is resumed after substitution of the inorganic salt solution with egg white.

Schmidt's 1936 studies of and interest in nucleohistone prompted him to apply to P. A. Levene at the Rockefeller Institute for Medical Research in New York. As mentioned earlier, Levene had provided valuable assistance while Schmidt was still in Embden's laboratory in Germany by sending him pure yeast nucleic acid adenylate as a reference compound to muscle adenylic acid. At the time of Schmidt's application, Levene was studying stepwise depolymerization of pure yeast nucleic acid by means of enzymes. Schmidt's exercise of 1936 in this field had already made him familiar with the literature and also with many of the techniques needed for this work. Thus, in 1937, Schmidt left Queens

University and joined Levene as an assistant in the Research Laboratory of Chemistry of the Rockefeller Institute.

Schmidt and Levene first reinvestigated the action of a thermostable pancreatic enzyme preparation capable of depolymerizing yeast nucleic acid. They fully confirmed previous reports of this phenomenon by W. Jones as well as by R. J. Dubos. The heat-stable pancreas enzyme preparation did in fact catalyze a gradual depolymerization of yeast nucleic acid, yielding fractions that were still unable to pass through a cellophane membrane. They termed the digestion product "tetranucleotides of high molecular weight." During this period, Levene held the firm belief that nucleic acids were polymers of tetranucleotides, containing the four different bases (two purines, two pyrimidines).

Another of their joint papers included E. G. Pickels, one of the leading experts in ultracentrifugation techniques and the interpretation of such data. It is in this context and at this point that Einar Hammarsten and his school in Stockholm became standard references. According to Schmidt and his coworkers, the only nucleic acid preparations (from thymus gland and fish sperm) in connection with proteins (histone and protamine, respectively) that they considered "naive" or "genuine" nucleic acids (more specifically, deoxyribonucleic acids) were the nucleic acid preparations from the Hammarsten group. They quote the Stockholm group's assessment of the molecular weight of the native nucleic acid (the term DNA was not in use at that time) as of the order of 10^6. Schmidt, Pickels, and Levene also assessed the so-called Neuman preparation—termed the "a" form of nucleic acid—and determined that it had a molecular weight of 2×10^5 to 10^6. Finally, they confirmed R. Feulgen's suggestion that the enzymatic conversion of the "a" form to the "b" form is a depolymerization.

The year Schmidt spent in Levene's laboratory was probably profitable in several respects. However, Levene's conclusion that the so-called tetranucleotide was the basis for nucleic acid structure gradually came to have less validity for Schmidt, and in later years he discreetly dismissed it.

In 1938 Schmidt received an invitation to join Carl Cori, professor of pharmacology at Washington University School of Medicine in St. Louis. Carl and Gerty Cori by that time had discovered α-glucose-1-phosphate and the enzyme glycogen phosphorylase, and they felt they were at the beginning of an exciting scientific development. Carl Cori had visited Gustav Embden in his laboratory before 1933 and had admired his work and that of his associates, including Gerhard Schmidt. So Schmidt went to St. Louis, and the year 1939–1940, which he spent in the Cori laboratory, must have reminded him of the exciting years with Embden. During the year Schmidt was fortunate enough to work with Carl as well as Gerty Cori, and also with a gifted young doctoral student, Sidney Colowick.

In St. Louis Schmidt became involved in studies of the enzymatic fission of glycogen by muscle phosphorylase, as well as the enzymatic resynthesis of polysaccharides. The Coris had found that muscle adenylic acid was needed for the enzymatic action of muscle phosphorylase. Schmidt was familiar with several purification techniques, some of which he had used in 1928 for the fractionation of muscle adenylic deaminase; the deaminase was used for the determination of adenylic acid. (The adenylic acid used for the work in the Cori laboratory was a gift from Pawel Ostern, the Polish researcher, shortly before his death during the Nazi attack on Poland in 1939.) The role of muscle adenylic acid (5' AMP) in the phosphorolytic splitting of glycogen remained a puzzling problem, however, because it was not consumed in the enzyme-catalyzed phosphorolysis.

In 1939 Walter Kiessling, one of Meyerhof's former associates who had remained in Heidelberg, briefly reported that glucose-1-phosphate added to a crude yeast enzyme fraction was converted to glycogen. The Coris and Schmidt were puzzled that their muscle enzyme fraction, which was incubated with glucose-1-phosphate (and the other ingredients needed for the phosphorylase), did not catalyze any detectable amounts of glycogen. Among Schmidt's incubates was one that he had absentmindedly left at room temperature overnight. It was included among those being studied for glycogen, and it was found that only this sample gave an iodine color for the presence of polysaccharides—and it was blue-red. To Schmidt and the Coris, this was exciting news indeed, not merely because they had finally succeeded but because of the aberrant way in which the polysaccharide biosynthesis ensued. In addition, Carl Cori strongly suspected that primer formation was at work as a precursor step before the polysaccharide biosynthesis could take place, an idea that was instrumental in the success of their later work. It was an exciting year!

Despite these successes, Gerhard Schmidt was still in search of a permanent scientific home, and in the spring of 1940 he found one at the Tufts University Medical Center. S. J. Thannhauser, head of the Boston Dispensary of the Tufts Medical School, asked Schmidt to set up a section on basic biochemical research. Thannhauser had been a well-known clinician in internal medicine in Freiburg, specializing in the diagnosis and treatment of metabolic disorders. In 1939, a few months before the outbreak of World War II, he escaped from Germany and arrived in Boston. The director of the university hospital medical center, Joseph Pratt, had invited several German-Jewish refugee scholars involved in medical research or in internal medicine to the medical center. Thannhauser was among them; interested in securing a first-rate researcher in biochemistry for his unit, he in turn approached Schmidt, who agreed to come to Tufts.

Considering Thannhauser's policies as laboratory chief, he was indeed fortunate to persuade Gerhard Schmidt to join his staff. Every publication from the laboratory carried Thannhauser's name, although he was listed as primary author only if he was actively engaged in the lab work as well. Schmidt agreed to this dictum, and for eighteen years the Thannhauser name appeared on every Schmidt publication.[3] Schmidt may not have been particularly pleased with the persistence of this policy, but he was too busy with research and teaching to spend any time challenging the rule.

Be that as it may, Thannhauser brought Schmidt to the Tufts Medical Center and helped him get started on his research, probably with several grants-in-aid. It is also likely that Thannhauser introduced Schmidt to the field of lipid biochemistry, or at the least encouraged experimental work by Schmidt in this field.

During his almost forty years of research at the Tufts Medical Center, Gerhard Schmidt chiefly explored two broad biochemical fields, both dealing with phosphorus compounds: nucleic acids and phospholipids. He addressed himself to both disciplines during his early years at Tufts, as well as during his later years. The succeeding paragraphs will deal first with his work on nucleic acids, a field he had already cultivated when he arrived in this hemisphere.

[3] This author may occasionally have guessed who led in programming the diverse pieces of research. I am assuming that a few publications that carried Thannhauser's name first must have been initiated and largely carried out by him; since the bibliographies in these memoirs do not make that clear, however, I will try to indicate this in the text. In any case, Schmidt was in his late fifties and well into his more embracing and distinguished tenure as a full professor before he had the opportunity to publish and present his name in a style that clearly indicated who was in charge of the research program. Although his colleagues knew, the next generation of scholars may need some orientation.

Gerhard Schmidt had an unusual ability to develop sturdy analytical methods for quantitative determinations of some of the main constituents of the cell, especially the phosphorus compounds. By 1945 the need for quantitative methods of investigating the nucleic acids had intensified to a point that called for skilled action. Schmidt's familiarity with pentose color reactions from his work on purine nucleotides was not of help for the new task; as he himself emphasized, pyrimidine nucleotides are too acid resistant—in terms of releasing pentose—and deoxyribose is destroyed during the protracted acid hydrolysis needed for release. Schmidt therefore designed a new method for nucleic acid analysis around the determination of phosphorus. The use of dilute alkali brought about the most useful resolution. If tissue extracts (as tissue powder free of lipids) are dissolved in dilute KOH- (1 N) and incubated at 37°C for 20 to 24 hours, a clear solution is usually obtained. A small aliquot of this solution can be used to determine total phosphorus. On the addition of excess trichloroacetic acid (TCA), fortified with 0.2 volume of 6 N HCl, precipitation of the DNA occurs. DNA that lacks the hydroxyl group in the "2" position possesses alkaline-stable diester bonds and remains in the macromolecular, acid-insoluble state; whereas RNA containing hydroxyl groups in the "2" as well as the "3" position is alkaline labile and hydrolyzes to soluble ribonucleotides.

The characteristics of this alkali lability and the mode of action of various nucleases were later explored by Schmidt and others. Schmidt's strategy for the analyses was as follows. The clear filtrate (by now, acid) contained a mixture of inorganic phosphate from the alkaline-labile phosphoserine ester bonds, and purine and pyrimidine nucleotides. The latter were determined as total P (ashing procedure). The total macromolecular phosphorus in the precipitate that appeared following acidification of the alkaline digest represents DNA.

Schmidt described these important methods once more in Colowick and Kaplan's *Methods in Enzymology* (vol. III), which also contains several of Schmidt's enzymatic methods.

During 1946 and 1947, Schmidt returned to one of his favorite fields: the use of specific enzymes to explore nucleotide and especially polynucleotide structure. As mentioned earlier, the tetranucleotide concept was not based on sturdy analyses, yet nobody had produced convincing evidence against the tetranucleotide model. The use of ribonuclease was very much on Schmidt's mind, especially since the Kunitz crystalline ribonuclease had become available. In masterly symposium articles published in 1947 and 1951, Schmidt summarized his experience with the enzymatic degradation of yeast ribonucleic acid and the characterization of its products and pointed out the few options available to obtain new insight. Earlier investigators had used crystalline ribonuclease together with various phosphatase preparations in excess, but they were unable to characterize the products. Schmidt and his coworkers decided on a somewhat different strategy. Yeast ribonucleic acid was first treated with crystalline ribonuclease, which they prepared themselves; but this procedure did not release any inorganic phosphate. Subsequently, a powerful "acid phosphatase" prepared from human prostates (delivered from the Department of Surgery of Massachusetts General Hospital) was successfully employed. Schmidt, however, warned against using an excess of the crude prostate phosphatase because it contained traces of ribonuclease activity. Addition of dilute prostate phosphatase preparations brought about a release of approximately 25 percent of the organic phosphate of the ribonucleate preparation.

But what type of 2' or 3' nucleotides released by ribonuclease corresponded to the 25 percent fraction that was so readily dephosphorylated through the action of prostate phosphatase? Acid hydrolysis in 1 N sulfuric acid at 100°C revealed that they were not the acid-labile type of purine-2' or -3' nucleotides; the fraction released by ribonuclease showed an acid hydrolysis curve characteristic of pyrimidine nucleotides. Apparently, ribonuclease had released a mixture of pyrimidine mononucleotides, and the remaining polynucleotides contained all the purines. In addition, other investigators—especially H. S. Loring—had arrived at similar conclusions using different techniques. These results spelled the end of the era of the tetranucleotide hypothesis and paved the way for concepts that could be emancipated from the earlier symmetry model.

Also in 1946, Schmidt and coworkers studying phosphate uptake in bakers yeast and the accumulation of phosphoric esters found an acid-hydrolyzable fraction that was precipitable with barium acetate. (This fraction was particularly conspicuous if the yeast cells had been starved for phosphate prior to its addition.) The accumulated phosphoric ester was identified as metaphosphate in a paper Schmidt et al. prepared reporting their work. Independently, Wiame in Belgium observed metachromatic staining in yeast cells that were subjected to the same physiological conditions (see the review of this research by Gerhard Schmidt in 1951). Schmidt and his coworkers soon found that the uptake of phosphate into yeast (previously starved for phosphorus) and its subsequent accumulation as metaphosphate require the presence of potassium ions. In addition, they discovered that potassium and magnesium ions are cotransported in preference to any other cations (see Schmidt, Hecht, and Thannhauser, 1949). The accumulation as well as the turnover of the metaphosphate fraction were also found to be enhanced by the addition of nitrogen sources to the medium, a response reminiscent of that of RNA-P.

In other research, published by Schmidt and coworkers

in 1951, periodate oxidation was used as a tool for stepwise degradation of ribonucleic acids and oligonucleotides released after digestion of RNA with pancreas ribonuclease. J. M. Gulland and W. E. Cohn had shown that certain nucleases can release 5' adenylic acid from RNA digests. The labilization of the 5' phosphoric ester bond of ribonucleotides by periodate oxidation of the 2' and 3' hydroxyl groups (to aldehyde groups) was used. In the process, the amine forms a complex with the oxidized oligonucleotide. Schmidt emphasized that the conditions used are relatively mild; yet prolonged exposure to pH 9 for 90 minutes at 45°C—the step needed to release the base—may gradually bring about alterations in the macromolecule. He therefore recommended that this preliminary method rather be used on oligonucleotides not exceeding 8 to 10 units.

It appears that this early edition of purine-pyrimidine sequencing was not further pursued by Schmidt. The "revolution" in nucleic acid biochemistry had begun, and Schmidt followed these developments with admiration. They became an important part of his teaching, however, rather than his research. When he returned later to the nucleic acid field, he revived his early interest in thymus nucleohistone.

In a 1972 study of the amount of binding of divalent ions —Ca^{++} and Mg^{++}—to the phosphoric ester groups of thymus nucleohistones, Schmidt et al. identified the following features. Thymus nucleohistone (ThyNuHi) binds Mg^{++} in up to 50 percent of its phosphoric (P) groups. This corresponds to the capacity to bind toluidine blue. Accordingly, only half of the DNA phosphoric groups of ThyNuHi can be bound to the cation groups of its histone components. ThyNuHi is hydrolyzed slowly by crystalline pancreas DNAase (deoxyribonuclease I), which is much slower than DNA. The remaining macromolecular residue containing the histone does not bind Mg^{++}, and DNAase is unable to catalyze further splitting. The molecular weight of the resistant residues was determined by Clark and Felsenfeld (1971) and found to be approximately 100,000. Clark and Felsenfeld, as well as Schmidt et al., suggested that the DNA-bound histone might occur as discrete clusters (of similar chain length), alternating with histone-free segments along the DNA chain; only the histone-free segments can bind divalent ions and are susceptible to DNAase, releasing acid-soluble oligonucleotides.

Schmidt, however, found it wise to express some caution concerning interpretations of their findings. He emphasized that the amount of DNA digested was to some extent a function of the amount of DNAase used; large excesses of DNAase after longtime incubation will split nearly 100 percent of the nucleohistone. This reservation, however, was not meant to belittle the potential importance of their findings and those of Clark and Felsenfeld. Because the opus by Schmidt et al. contained fragments that were to be used in a Ph.D. thesis, Schmidt felt that self-criticism was well justified.

The other broad biochemical field of particular interest to Schmidt was phospholipids. Schmidt's interest in lipid research was undoubtedly influenced by Thannhauser; together they produced a number of papers describing observations that in turn stimulated other researchers in the field. Much of their work was done before the introduction of modern chromatographic procedures. To circumvent this limitation, Schmidt tried to devise a scheme by which the partition of lipid phosphorus would provide separate determinations of the sphingomyelin, plasmalogen phosphoglycerides, and diacyl phosphoglycerides in tissue samples of moderate sizes. The total lipid extract was saponified under mild alkaline conditions that deacylated phosphoglycerides. The phosphorus of the aqueous extract represented diacyl glycerophosphatides (containing nitrogenous constituents like choline, ethanolamine, or serine). Schmidt found it noteworthy that the plasmalogens remained in the nonsaponifiable fraction. He, however, was able to obtain water-soluble phosphorus by a brief treatment with mercuric chloride. He soon realized that saponification as well as hydrolysis of this product with $HgCl_2$ were needed to obtain water-soluble plasmalogen phosphorus.

Schmidt therefore proposed that native plasmalogen contained an additional lipid chain that was removed by saponification. This structural problem was solved several years later by Maurice Rapport. Rapport discovered the existence of an ($\alpha\beta$)-unsaturated ether that on acid hydrolysis gave rise to an aldehyde, thus showing that the acetal structure originally proposed by Feulgen is not the native structure. It is probably needless to state that Schmidt followed Rapport's elegant work with delight.

As a result of these investigations, some structural work, mainly led by Thannhauser, had to be revised, such as the report that the sulfate in cerebroside sulfate was attached to the C_6 of the galactose moiety. Later work by T. Yamakawa established that the sulfate was actually attached to the C_3 carbon.

In a 1970 paper, Schmidt, together with E. L. Hogan and K. C. Joseph, described his studies of the composition of cerebral lipids in murine sudanophilic leucodystrophy. The research involved measurement of the cerebrosides and sphingolipids in brains of mice with genetically determined disorders of myelination. In normal myelination during development, sphingolipids and cerebrosides increase by a factor of approximately four; phospholipids increase twofold. "Jimpy mutants," a mouse mutant described by R. Sidman, have defective myelination in the central nervous system. In these mice, cerebrosides are highly defective, and sphingolipids are also lowered; phospholipid composition remains unaltered. In 30-day-old jimpy mice with seizures, the cerebrosides were almost totally lost (only 5 to 10 percent were left); sphingolipids were below 20 percent; and only phospholipids were preserved.

At the time of development when myelination is most active, the leucodystrophic mice mutants showed increased levels of cerebrosides in the brain. The ensuing relative deficit points against a defect in the biosynthesis of cerebrosides. The quaking mouse mutants, a less fulminant form, showed a more moderate loss of cerebrosides.

In addition to his research responsibilities, Schmidt taught at the Tufts Medical School, and this duty he not only fulfilled but greatly treasured. His lectures for first-year medical school biochemistry students covered structural macromolecules, preferably proteins and nucleic acids. At least, this was the case during the middle 1960s, according to Schmidt's son Milton, who attended his father's lectures at that time. According to Milton Schmidt, the lectures were ". . . exquisitely lucid and logical. Details were present . . . as a way of getting across a point. In spite of logic and clarity, he was never dry or dull. As in his cello-playing, he was truly rhapsodic when he lectured, conveying intense enthusiasm to everyone."

Gerhard's devotion to music was a very important feature of his personality and certainly deserves mention here. His approach to art centered on music, a choice that had probably been influenced by his mother, Isabella Schmidt (née Gombrich), who was a talented pianist and teacher. (When only in her late teens, she went to Berlin and was invited as a pianist to the rehearsals of the preeminent Joachim string ensemble; the late Dr. Ernest Bueding, a colleague of Gerhard's and an active viola player himself, praised Frau Isabella's perceptive and brilliant piano playing in chamber music.)

Gerhard played his cello with gusto, especially in chamber music; the great works of Mozart, Beethoven, and Schubert were perhaps closest to his heart. What inspired him in music was not only beauty but strength and originality. I shall never forget when I received a special gift from him, a record of one of Schubert's most demanding and magnificent string quartets (the great G major), which is only very rarely played in concert halls. Gerhard had told me about its special "texture," exemplifying Schubert's genius at its greatest. He was pleased to know how deeply my wife and I appreciated his gift.

Gerhard enjoyed great popularity among young as well as older colleagues. His warm humor shone through, especially in his happy family circle[4] but also among his friends. He could and often did make fun of his own absentmindedness. In his youth he enjoyed the German humorist Wilhelm Busch, and he could still cite long passages from Busch's work in his later years. He of course found and enjoyed many humorists in this country, even those bordering on slapstick; many of us recall Gerhard's laughter over Laurel and Hardy.

In later years, Gerhard Schmidt remained as active in the lab as in his earlier career. He arrived early and stayed late in the evening, regardless of snowstorms and lack of public transportation. As one of his former students, Dr. Peter Cashions, puts it: "I can't recall a day in five years that he missed, excluding vacations and meetings. I recall once when during a blizzard all traffic was stopped—he apparently nonchalantly walked home to his apartment along the Fenway and Mission Hill—some of the toughest districts of the city. . . . His typical workday had the serene, unhurried ca-

---

[4] Gerhard Schmidt was married in 1940 to Edith Straus-Horkheimer. They had two sons: Michael, who is a social worker in a psychiatric hospital in New York City, and Milton, a psychiatrist in the Boston area. Schmidt greatly enjoyed his family life, which in later years included two grandchildren.

dence that might be associated with, or more akin to, the pressure of a glacier rather than the frenetic state of agitation, more often linked to high achievers. A particularly good example of this was when he'd go out and buy a 10-pound lobster, dissect out one of the nerves from which he'd extract sphingomyelin. Then he would melt down a pound of butter, boil the rest of the lobster, and everyone would have a feast at about 8 p.m. in the lab."

In the lab, Schmidt insisted on doing practically everything with his own hands, and when his modest dexterity began slipping during his later years, former students recall many an evening loaded with a highly charged atmosphere. He was not always able to convey to his students in the lab his frustrations with his own manual mistakes. Sometimes after a number of attempts at a particular technique, the frowning professor would be breathing heavily; but he might still be unable to convey to a student when the instrument would be available. Arguments with him about lab procedures were spare and laconic, however, since Schmidt, a veteran of many bold lab experiments, did not think that anybody else's advice was warranted.

Some of this tension during Gerhard Schmidt's last years in the lab may have been related to a particularly intense and important project that he discussed with me. This project, which involved a return to the study of thymus nucleohistones, was very close to his heart. And although the study was never completed to his own satisfaction, Schmidt's energy and enthusiasm persisted to the last.

Gerhard Schmidt was a member of several scientific societies including the American Society of Biological Chemists, Canadian Physiological Society, New York Academy of Sciences, American Chemical Society, and American Association for the Advancement of Science. Among the honorary societies that elected him as a member were Sigma Xi, the American Academy of Arts and Sciences, and the National Academy of Sciences. There have also been posthumous honors as well. Volume 100 of Colowick and Kaplan's *Methods in Enzymology* is dedicated to the memory of Gerhard Schmidt as a scholar and artist; it includes a photograph of him playing his beloved cello and a charming little dedication by Sidney Colowick and Nathan Kaplan. In 1981, the president of Tufts University established an annual Gerhard Schmidt lectureship commemorating Schmidt's long and distinguished service to the Tufts University School of Medicine. Four distinguished lectures thus far have been delivered at Tufts University Medical School in Boston.

IN PREPARING this biographical memoir, my thanks are due to many friends of the late Gerhard Schmidt. At the Tufts University Medical School, Drs. R. L. Kisliuk and H. Mautner rendered much help. Regarding Gerhard's terminal year at the University of Frankfurt, the late Dr. Ernest Bueding of Johns Hopkins University provided important information. In trying to formulate the section on lipid research, my thanks are due to Drs. George Hauser, Harvard Medical School; Norman Radin, University of Michigan; and M. M. Rapport, New York State Psychiatric Institute. Concerning such aspects of his life as teaching and lab work with students, I am grateful to Drs. Milton Schmidt of Boston and Peter Cashions of the biology department of the University of New Brunswick. The late Dr. Sidney P. Colowick of Vanderbilt University gave me particularly valuable encouragement, criticism, and stimulation in general in my efforts to formulate the memoir. And finally, special thanks are due Mrs. Edith Schmidt for her help and advice, and for her generous encouragement as well.

ACADEMIC HISTORY

1919–1922　Student of Medicine, University of Tübingen, Germany
1922–1924　Student of Medicine, University of Frankfurt, Frankfurt am Main, Germany (State Board)
1924–1925　Intern in Medicine, Municipal Hospital, Stuttgart, Germany
1925　Intern in Medicine, University Hospital, Frankfurt
1925–1926　Graduate Student in Medicine, University of Frankfurt
1926　M.D. Degree Awarded (Thesis in Biochemistry; Supervisor: Professor G. Embden)
1926–1929　Postgraduate Research Fellow, Department of Biochemistry, University of Frankfurt
1929–1931　Assistant and Director of Biochemical Research Laboratory, Department of Pathology, University of Frankfurt
1931–1933　Instructor (*Privatdozent*) in Pathological Chemistry, Department of Pathology, Faculty of Medicine, University of Frankfurt
1933　Dismissed on April 1 by the Hitler government because of "Jewish race"
1933　Research Biochemist, Marine Biological Laboratories, Naples, Italy; Department of Biochemistry, University of Naples (April through September)
1933–1934　Research Fellow, Department of Biochemistry, University of Stockholm, Sweden
1934–1935　Research Fellow, Department of General Pathology, University of Florence, Italy
1935–1937　Carnegie Foundation Research Fellowship for Displaced German Scholars, Department of Chemistry, Queens University, Kingston, Ontario, Canada
1937–1938　Assistant, Research Laboratory of Chemistry, Rockefeller Institute for Medical Research
1938–1940　Research Fellow, Department of Pharmacology, Washington University School of Medicine, St. Louis, Missouri

1940–1948 Research Associate, Thannhauser Research Laboratory, Boston Dispensary, Tufts University School of Medicine
1948–1955 Research Professor of Biochemistry, Department of Biochemistry, Tufts University School of Medicine
1955–1972 Professor of Biochemistry, Department of Biochemistry, Tufts University School of Medicine
1972–1981 Professor Emeritus of Biochemistry and Research Biochemist, Department of Biochemistry and Pharmacology, Tufts University School of Medicine

BIBLIOGRAPHY

1928

Über Kolloidchemische Veranderungen bei der Ermuding des Warmblutermuskels. Arbeitsphysiologie, 1(2):136–53.

Über fermentative Desaminierung im Muskel. Z. Physiol. Chem., 179:243–69.

1929

With G. Embden. Über Muskeladenylsäure und Hefeadenylsäure. Z. Physiol. Chem., 181:130–39.

Lactacidogen (Review). In: *The Enzymes,* vol. 3, *Methodology,* ed. Carl Oppenheimer, p. 1189. Berlin: George Thieme.

1930

With G. Embden. Über die Bedeutung der Adenylsäure für die Muskelfunktion; weitere Untersuchungen über die Herkunft des Muskelammoniaks. Z. Physiol. Chem., 186:205–11.

1931

With G. Embden. Berichtigung. Z. Physiol. Chem., 197:191–92.

Über die Abbau des Guaninkerns durch die Fermente der Kaninchenleber. Klin. Wochenschr., 10:165–67.

1932

Mikrobestimmungen von Purinsubstanzen in Gewebe, I. Mitteilung: Die Bestimmung des Guanins von Ernst Engel. Z. Physiol. Chem., 108:225–36.

Enzymic breakdown of guanylic acid by rabbit liver. Z. Physiol. Chem., 208:185.

1933

Mikrobestimmungen von Purinsubstanzen in Gewebe, II. Mitteilung Die Bestimmung des Adenins und der Oxypurine. Z. Physiol. Chem., 219(5/6):191–206.

1934

Preparation and composition of a dipeptide phosphoric acid obtained by enzymatic hydrolysis of casein. Z. Physiol. Chem., 223:86.
On the binding of the purine bases in the non-fertilized sea urchin egg. Z. Physiol. Chem., 223:81.
With H. von Euler. Purine content and the normal and pathological growth of tissues. Z. Physiol. Chem., 223:215.
With H. von Euler. Nucleoproteins of fish testicles. Z. Physiol. Chem., 225:92.
With I. Rydh-Ehrensvaard. Influence of carotenes on guanase content of rat spleen. Z. Physiol. Chem., 227:177.

1935

With F. Pontimalli. Partition of the P-fractions in blood plasma of chickens with Rous sarcoma. Biochem. Z., 282:62–73.

1936

Chemical differences between protein-linked and free nucleic acids. Science, 83:15.
Action of enzymes on proteins with prosthetic groups: Action of nucleophosphatase on thymus nucleohistone. Enzymologia, 1:135–41.

1937

Growth-stimulating effect of egg white and its importance for embryonic development. Enzymologia, 4:40–48.

1938

With P. A. Levene. Effect of nucleophosphatase on "native" and "depolymerized" thymonucleic acid. Science, 88:172–73.
With P. A. Levene. Ribonucleodepolymerase (the Jones-Dubos enzyme). J. Biol. Chem., 126:423–34.

1939

With E. G. Pickels and P. A. Levene. Enzymic depolymerization of deoxyribonucleic acids of different degrees of polymerization. J. Biol. Chem., 127:251–59.

With C. F. Cori and G. T. Cori. Synthesis of a polysaccharide from glucose-1-phosphate in muscle extract. Science, 89:464.
With G. T. Cori and C. F. Cori. Role of glucose-1-phosphate in the formation of blood sugar and synthesis of glycogen in the liver. J. Biol. Chem., 129:629–39.

1943

With S. J. Thannhauser. Intestinal phosphatase. J. Biol. Chem., 149:369.

1945

With B. Hershman and S. J. Thannhauser. Isolation of (alpha)-glycerylphosphorylcholine from incubated beef pancreas and its significance for the intermediary metabolism of lecithin. J. Biol. Chem., 161:523.
With S. Proger, D. Decaneas, and B. Wadler. Effect of anoxia and injected cyctochrome C. on the easily hydrolyzable phosphorus in rat organs. J. Biol. Chem., 160:233.
With S. J. Thannhauser. A method for the determination of desoxyribonucleic acid, ribonucleic acid and phosphoprotein phosphorus in tissues. J. Biol. Chem., 161:83.

1946

With J. Benotti, B. H. Swartz, and S. J. Thannhauser. Partition of phospholipide mixtures into monoaminophosphatides and sphingomyelin. J. Biol. Chem., 165:505–11.
With L. I. Hecht and S. J. Thannhauser. Enzymic formation and accumulation of metaphosphate in baker's yeast under certain nutritional conditions. J. Biol. Chem., 166:775–76.
With S. J. Thannhauser. Lipids and lipidoses (Review). Physiol. Rev., 26:275.

1947

With R. Cubiles and S. J. Thannhauser. Action of prostate phosphatase on yeast ribonucleic acid. Cold Spring Harbor Symp. Quant. Biol., 12:161.
With R. Cubiles, B. H. Swartz, and S. J. Thannhauser. Action of ribonucleinase on yeast ribonucleic acid. J. Biol. Chem., 170:759–60.

1948

With L. I. Hecht and S. J. Thannhauser. Behavior of the nucleic acids during the early development of the sea urchin egg (Arbacia). J. Gen. Physiol., 31:203.
With S. J. Thannhauser. The chemistry of the lipids (Review). Annu. Rev. Biochem., 12:233.
With J. Fischmann, H. A. Chamberlain, and R. Cubiles. Determination of acid phosphatase in various normal and pathological specimens of prostate gland. J. Urol., 59:194.

1949

With L. I. Hecht and S. J. Thannhauser. Effect of potassium ions on the absorption of orthophosphate and the formation of metaphosphate by baker's yeast. J. Biol. Chem., 178:733–42.
With B. Ottenstein and S. J. Thannhauser. Pathogenesis of Gaucher's disease. Blood, 3:1250.

1950

Nucleic acids, purines and pyrimidines (Review). Annu. Rev. Biochem., 19:149.

1951

Biochemistry of inorganic pyrophosphates and metaphosphates. In: *Proceedings of a Symposium on Phosphorus Metabolism,* vol. 1, ed. W. McElroy and B. Glass, pp. 443–75. Baltimore: Johns Hopkins University.
With R. Cubiles and S. J. Thannhauser. Nature of the products formed by the action of crystalline ribonuclease on yeast ribonucleic acid. J. Cell Comp. Physiol., 38(suppl. 1):61.
With R. Buciles, N. Zoellner, L. I. Hecht, N. Strickler, K. Seraydarian, M. Seraydarian, and S. J. Thannhauser. Action of ribonuclease. J. Biol. Chem., 192:715–26.
With S. J. Thannhauser and N. F. Boncoddo. Procedure for the isolation of crystallized acetal phospholipides from brain. J. Biol. Chem., 188:417.
With S. J. Thannhauser and N. F. Boncoddo. The (α)-structure of the acetal phospholipides of brain. J. Biol. Chem., 188:423.

1952

With L. I. Hecht, P. Fallot, L. M. Greenbaum, and S. J. Thannhauser. Amounts of glycerylphosphorylcholine in mammalian tissues. J. Biol. Chem., 197:601–9.

1953

With M. Bessman and S. J. Thannhauser. Hydrolysis of L-(α)-glycerylphosphorylethanolamine. J. Biol. Chem., 203:849.

1955

With L. M. Greenbaum, P. Fallot, A. C. Walker, and S. J. Thannhauser. Amounts of glycerylphosphorylesters in tissues. J. Biol. Chem., 212:869.
With M. Liss and S. J. Thannhauser. Guanine, the principal nitrogenous constituent of the excrements of certain spiders. Biochim. Biophys. Acta, 16:533.
With R. Cubiles. Occurrence of the carnosine-anserine fraction in skeletal muscle and its absence in heart. Arch. Biochem. Biophys., 58:227.
With S. J. Thannhauser and J. Fellig. Structure of the cerebroside sulfuric acid ester of beef brain. J. Biol. Chem., 215:211.
Acid prostatic phosphomonoesterase (Review). In: *Methods in Enzymology*, vol. 2, ed. S. P. Colowick and N. O. Kaplan, pp. 523–30. New York: Academic Press.
Nucleases and enzymes attacking nucleic acid components (Review). In: *The Nucleic Acids*, vol. 1, ed. E. Chargaff and J. N. Davidson, p. 555. New York: Academic Press.

1956

With M. J. Bessman, M. D. Hickey, and S. J. Thannhauser. Concentrations of some constituents of egg yolk in its soluble phase. J. Biol. Chem., 223:1027.
With H. M. Davidson. *In vitro* incorporation of labeled phosphate into phosphoproteins by lactating mammary gland. Biochim. Biophys. Acta, 19:116.
With K. Seraydarian, L. M. Greenbaum, M. D. Hickey, and S. J. Thannhauser. Effect of certain nutritional conditions on the formation of purines and ribonucleic acid in baker's yeast. Biochim. Biophys. Acta, 20:135.

1957

In: *Methods in Enzymology*, vol. 3, ed. S. P. Colowick and N. O. Kaplan: Preparation of phosphopyruvic acid, pp. 223–28; Preparation of O-(L-(alpha)-glyceryl) phosphorylcholine, phosphorylcholine, O-(L-(alpha)-glyceryl) phosphorylethanolamine and phosphorylethanolamine, pp. 346–58; Determination of nucleic acids by phosphorus analysis, pp. 671–79; Preparation of ribonucleic acid from yeast and animal tissues, pp. 687–91; Chemical and enzymatic methods for the identification and structural elucidation of nucleic acids and nucleotides, pp. 747–75; and Colorimetric and enzymatic methods for the determination of some purines and pyrimidines, pp. 775–81. New York: Academic Press.

With B. Ottenstein, W. A. Spencer, C. Hackethal, and S. J. Thannhauser. Quantitative partition of acetal phospholipides and free lipide aldehydes. Symposium on Chemistry and Metabolism of Phospholipides. Fed. Proc., 16:816.

With M. J. Bessman and S. J. Thannhauser. Enzymatic hydrolysis of cephalin in rat intestinal mucosa. Biochim. Biophys. Acta, 23:127.

1959

Nucleoproteins and cancer (Review). In: *Physiopathology of Cancer*, 2d ed., ed. F. Homburger, p. 707. New York: P. B. Hoeber.

With B. Ottenstein, W. A. Spencer, K. Keck, R. Blietz, J. Papas, D. Porter, M. L. Levin, and S. J. Thannhauser. The partition of tissue phospholipides by phosphorus analysis. AMA Am. J. Dis. Child., 97:691.

1961

With L. Fingerman and S. J. Thannhauser. Incorporation of labeled orthophosphate into the phosphatidyl compounds, plasmalogens, and sphingomyelins of brain, skeletal muscle and heart of the intact rat. (Proceedings of the Deuel Conference on Lipidoses and Hyperlipemic Conditions, San Diego, California, 1960.) Am. J. Clin. Nutr., 9:124.

With H. Weicker, J. A. Dain, and S. J. Thannhauser. Chromatographic fractionation of gangliosides. Conference on Sphingolipidoses, New York.

1962

With H. Weicker, J. A. Dain, and S. J. Thannhauser. Chemical composition and physical properties of gangliosidic components isolated by adsorption chromatography on silica gel columns. In: *Cerebral Sphingolipidoses*, pp. 289–99. New York: Academic Press.

1963

With G. Barisch, M.-C. Laumont, T. Herman, and M. Liss. Acid phosphatase of bakers' yeast: An enzyme of the external cell surface. Biochemistry, 2:126–31.

1965

With G. Barisch, T. Kitagawa, K. Fujisawa, J. Knolle, J. Joseph, P. DeMarco, M. Liss, and R. Haschemeyer. Isolation of a phosphoprotein of high phosphorus content from the eggs of brown brook trout. Biochem. Biophys. Res. Commun., 18:60.

1966

With E. I. Hogan, A. Kjeta-Fyda, T. Tanaka, J. Joseph, N. I. Feldman, R. A. Collins, and R. W. Keenan. Determination of the lipid bases in the lipids of spinal cord, optic nerve, and sciatic nerve of some species. In: *Inborn Errors of Sphingolipid Metabolism*, ed. S. M. Aronson, pp. 325–59. Elmsford, N.Y.: Pergamon Press.

1968

With K. Okabe and R. W. Keenan. Phytosphingosine groups as quantitatively significant components of the mucosa of the small intestines. Biochem. Biophys. Res. Commun., 31:137.

R. W. Keenan and K. Okabe (from the Thannhauser Research Laboratory, Tufts University School of Medicine, Director: G. Schmidt). Metabolic degradation of tritiated dihydrosphingosine in the liver of the intact rat. Biochemistry, 7:2696.

1970

With E. L. Hogan and K. C. Joseph. Composition of cerebral lipids in murine sudanophilic leucodystrophy. J. Neurochem., 17:75–83.

1972

With P. J. Cashions, S. Suzuki, J. P. Joseph, P. DeMarco, and M. E. Cohen. The action of pancreas deoxyribonuclease I (deoxyribonucleate oligonucleotidohydrolase, EC-number 3.1.4.5.) on calf thymus nucleohistone. Arch. Biochem. Biophys., 149:513–27.

1975

With M. E. Cohen and P. DeMarco. The action of staphylococcal nuclease (EC-number 3.1.4.7.) on thynucleohistone and on some nucleoprotamines. Mol. Cell. Biochem., 6:185–94.

LESLIE SPIER

December 13, 1893–December 3, 1961

BY ROBERT F. SPENCER

A QUARTER CENTURY has gone by since Leslie Spier's death. Yet he remains a major figure in American anthropology: references to his scholarship are widely made, and his influence is still strongly felt.

However hesitantly, I cannot help but begin this memoir with a personal note. In preparing to write this summary, I went of course to the various sources of information on Spier—not only the professional obituary appearing shortly after his passing[1] but also to the lecture notes I had taken as a student in his courses at the University of New Mexico in 1939–40. A second-year graduate student in anthropology, I had enrolled in his course, "Culture Provinces of Western North America." I recall the rather anxious discussions, reflecting then as now graduate student paranoia, attempts to grasp precisely what it was that Spier was expounding. House types, cradle boards, clothing and footgear, containers, transport, and so through a host of highly factual listings of the elements—material, social, and religious—that make up the cultural systems of western native American peoples. What were we, as students, expected to do with such detail? Was it

[1] Harry W. Basehart and W. W. Hill, "Obituary: Leslie Spier, 1893–1961," *American Anthropologist*, 67(165):1258–77.

a question of memorizing, of somehow regurgitating this plethora of facts in an examination? But then Spier called for an evaluation of the material: in a paper to be written in lieu of an examination, we were asked to provide an analysis, to put forth the perspectives we had derived from the course.

Well, by the end of the term something had jelled. Suddenly it all fell into place. Spier's view of ethnology, his scientific concerns, his delineation of problems and his explanatory solutions somehow became clear. I look back on the paper I wrote, at the prized comments in the instructor's own hand, and I note with no little sense of pride that he gave me an A+. However remote in time or space, the Indian tribes of aboriginal California, of the Great Basin, the Southwest, or the intermontane Plateau, assumed new significance. It was at this point, as a result of taking Spier's course, that I can say I became an anthropologist. Spier offered the student a virtual conversion experience. Students might be interested in ethnology, in the varied customs, habits, and practices of aboriginal peoples, but until they experienced the *Aufklärung*—the enlightenment—that Spier could impart, they had not quite made the grade. Few students have had such gifted teaching.

But clearly there is much more to Spier than his superiority as a teacher. True, those students like myself retain the most vivid recollections of his classroom presence, but few teachers succeeded so well in wedding teaching with empirical research. Indeed, this was Spier's forte. He is best remembered for his extensive field work, his descriptive analyses of the precontact cultures, those aboriginal forms of American Indian life in western North America. Not that his interests related solely to American ethnology: he possessed a profound knowledge of human achievements and organizations across the world. Africa, for example, remained one of his strong interests. But it was his firsthand acquisition of knowledge of the content of the social and cultural systems of native American life that established his ethnographic place.

As may be surmised, implicit in Spier's empirical studies of various tribal groups is an underlying body of theory. Yet one cannot call Spier a theorist, at least in terms of his developing a special school or following. His contribution represents a perfecting of a technique of history, one usually identified—not wholly accurately—with the "school" of American anthropology ascribed to Franz Boas (d. 1942) and his students at Columbia University. The problem to which Spier addressed himself most pointedly concerned a history without documentation, a historicist perspective not so much in terms of a search for origins as in a sense of discovering processes of culture building among comparable peoples. Basically, Spier's interest lay in demonstrating relationships between cultural systems in definable areas and positing interrelations and growths. And he carried it off to perfection.

Spier's theoretical orientations are perhaps best seen against the period in which he was most active and the climate in anthropological research that was then operative. One can thus see how he arrived at his specific place in the forefront of American ethnographers.

Leslie Spier was born in New York City on December 13, 1893, one of the four children of Simon F. Spier and Bertha Adler Spier. He went to school in the city itself, a circumstance that drew him into urban life and an interest in the burgeoning technology of the day. It is not surprising that he was a student in applied mathematics and engineering, fields in which he took his B.S. degree at the City College of New York. Yet by happy accident in 1913, when he was employed as an engineering assistant for the New York Public Service Commission, he was assigned to the New Jersey Archaeological and Geological Survey. His interest in anthropology stemmed from this experience, and his early career was marked by a series of publications in archaeology, most notably an evaluation of the prehistoric Trenton Argillite culture of the eastern United States. But archaeology and prehistory were not to be Spier's métier. It was rather that for him this initial field experience opened up undreamed of horizons—the continent inhabited by native Americans, as it was before the arrival of the Europeans.

Drawn to the powerful personality of Franz Boas, Spier came to Columbia University in 1916 as a graduate student in anthropology. He shared with his mentor an interest in archaeology, to be sure, but he was also attracted by physical anthropology (human biology), linguistics, and ultimately cultural anthropology through the avenue of ethnology. In later years Spier was to demonstrate his command of all branches of the holistic discipline of anthropology, studying native American languages as well as conducting a study of physical changes among the descendants of Japanese immigrants. But ethnology remained his first commitment. As an assistant anthropologist at the American Museum of Natural History, he had ample opportunity to become familiar with the artifacts of cultures spread across the world. And with his bent for technology, Spier never lost interest in the material side of human achievements in their respective cultures.

In 1920 Spier was awarded a doctorate from Columbia. The Ph.D. dissertation that Spier submitted to Boas was essentially a library problem combined with some field research. Although he had visited the Pueblo of Zuni in New Mexico in 1916 and had, in 1918 and 1919, begun his significant work with the Havasupai group in Arizona, he spent some time in the latter year with the Kiowa, Wichita, and Caddo, all peoples of the American Plains. His thesis related to the Plains area: it was a comparative study of the dramatic Sun Dance, the most important ritual of the American bison hunters. The focus of the study was historical, raising the question of the sources of a ceremonial complex deeply entrenched in Plains Indian life. Often quoted, Spier's Sun Dance monograph provided a model not only for historical inquiries of other scholars but also for his own future work.

In 1920 Spier accepted his first teaching post at the University of Washington, remaining there until 1929. In New York in 1920 he had married a fellow anthropologist, Dr. Erna Gunther, like himself a student of Boas and a major figure in northwest American anthropology until her death in 1982. The Spiers had two children, Robert and Christopher. The latter is still resident in the Seattle area; the former received his Ph.D. from Harvard in 1954 and—following in his parents' footsteps—is professor of anthropology at the University of Missouri. Spier remarried in 1931; his second wife was Dr. Anna H. Gayton, an equally gifted anthropologist trained by A. L. Kroeber and Robert H. Lowie at the University of California. Dr. Gayton-Spier died in 1977.

Spier's productivity in teaching and research continued over the next three decades. His academic appointments were many: they were often on a visiting basis, but he also held chairs at Yale (1933–39) and at the University of New Mexico (between 1939 and 1955). These appointments often left him free to engage in his extensive field investigations. Other institutions at which he served included the University of Oklahoma (on leave from Washington in 1927 and 1929); the University of Chicago (1928 and 1930); and Harvard University (1939 and 1949). In addition he was occupied with summer teaching over many years with appointments at Columbia and the University of California at both Berkeley and Los Angeles. Spier also held research associateships at California and Yale, and he directed field studies at Chaco Canyon, New Mexico, and field training programs in both the Southwest and Northwest.

Although Spier's wide range of teaching experience influenced many who then moved into professional anthropology, it was in the ethnographic field that he made his name as a scientist. His abiding interest in the native peoples of America stemmed, as may be seen, from his initial endeavors in the Plains and in the Southwest. One finds him moving extensively through the diverse western American Indian cultures—from the Southwest to the Great Basin and California and into the intermontane Plateau. In all these regions are to be found a congeries of native peoples, each group or tribe in its own way distinct, and each, at the time Spier contacted them, retaining elements of an aboriginal way of life. Spier saw his task as eliciting—essentially descriptively—the components of these various native cultures. Implicit in his reasoning as he approached the material and social content of the groups he studied was a sense of historicism, his query being basically directed to the origins and comparisons of cultural systems.

It is at this point that one becomes aware of Spier as a scientific ethnographic field worker. It is by no means an easy task to settle into a remote area (especially given the problems of transport and travel in the preflight era), establish rapport with the members of a tribal group, and ask the kinds of questions that field ethnography requires. Spier's extensive experience, however, made him a master of ethnographic techniques. He acquired a speaking knowledge of various native languages, interested himself in all facets of the cultural and social system in question, and above all brought a keen and sensitive awareness to bear. Those of us who have sometimes followed Spier, asking different questions of the same people, retain our amazement that thirty and forty years later the oldsters in a community recall him with affection and respect: "That man could talk our language." "He could make a basket just like we used to in the old days." "He figured out all the people in my family." The lessons that were imparted are not lost today; in Spier's work there is a superb model for gathering information on the human experience in culture. Moreover, none of his collected data has required revision.

Like other fields, the discipline of anthropology has, over the years, had its ups and downs, problem orientations that may change with each decade, new horizons and perspectives. But, however much the research goals and purposes of cultural and social anthropology become subject to modification, the field remains at base a comparative one, dependent on an awareness of the human potential for cultural difference. In other words, ethnology still underlies the conclusions of whatever theoretical avenue contemporary anthropologists elect to follow.

Spier's studies rested on an awareness of cultural difference rooted in time, the uniqueness of each system. But such uniqueness is to be seen in the context of historical relationships. With other American anthropologists generally active at the time of Boas, Spier rejected any notion of a unilineal evolutionary development of culture—and thus, ultimately, any Marxist position. He held no brief for the so-called "functionalist" schools, that of Malinowski, for example, or Radcliffe-Brown. He tended instead to follow Boas's functional approach, which posits relationships between the components of a culture. Similarly he was generally indifferent to the sense of an all-pervading ethos or configuration, a notion that characterized the famous work of Ruth Benedict. In Spier's work there is a clear idea of what constitutes culture among humans. Because every cultural system depends on time for its growth and development, those features that offer insights into the rise of various cultures are the ones to be analyzed.

Like his mentor Franz Boas, Spier retained throughout his career a strongly defined sense of caution. He was often impatient with conclusions drawn by his contemporaries, arguing that they went too far without sufficient evidence. It was, in fact, this reserve that heightened Spier's brilliance as a field worker. Beginning with his analysis of the Plains Indian Sun Dance, he displayed a meticulousness that carried into all his later work and became his hallmark. In his view a cultural system was made up of parts, discernible elements that, taken together, form a total complex. The components of a culture permitted an evaluation—not only of the way in which they interrelated within the system but in terms of the comparative and implicitly historical relations between cultures.

An example or two of Spier's empirical approach may serve to highlight his contribution to anthropology–ethnology and the kinds of concerns with which he was preoccupied. As stated earlier, he saw himself as a culture-historian; basically he questioned how a particular cultural system developed as it did. The most striking example of Spier's ethnographic method unquestionably appears in the Sun Dance monograph. But because this ceremonial complex moves so deeply into an area of some esoterica, the theoretical stance perhaps may be more readily illuminated in more encompassing studies, such as that of the Havasupai or the Klamath Indians of southern Oregon. Spier worked with the Klamath tribe, a group numbering about 1,500 people, during both 1925 and 1926. His task, as he saw it, was to place the Klamath in "western"—that is, native American—culture. To resolve this issue—seeing the Klamath in relation to native California, the rest of the Plateau-Basin, and the Northwest—Spier set about obtaining an inventory of the components of the culture. As listed in his monograph, these ranged from all material items—houses, clothing, weaponry, transport, containers, and so to economic life generally—on through the array of nonmaterial features—settlements, chieftainship, warfare, social classes, kinship and family structure, and ceremonials.

The result is an account of Klamath life, one that involves a description of how the native system was put together. In this study, as indeed in nearly all his works, the ethnography is complete, the intent clear. Spier tells us what is there in native Klamath life. Contemporary critics might argue that this is a "shopping list," an account in which all component elements are given essentially equal weight. A "modern" anthropologist, fifty years later, might want to stress the ways in which the component elements are put together and so seek to move more deeply into the dynamic aspects of Klamath life. This does Spier an injustice. He was well aware of the problems inherent in native American systems. To him, for example, a ceremony, a bit of ritual, involved a vast number of elements coming together: the locus of the ritual, the participants, their clothing, and their artifacts—and so to the ultimate meaning of the pattern. Several points obtrude in this regard. On the one hand, Spier felt it important to record the content of those native American cultures he investigated before the cultures themselves disappeared. Moreover, he had a rather different concept in mind.

The fundamental issue in the Klamath and other studies was the problem of cultural relations. As in his later works—those on the Yuman tribes or the Havasupai, among others—he drew tightly knit comparisons. Consequently, having described Klamath dwellings (both an earth lodge for winter use and a mat lodge for warmer seasons), he notes the form and general function of these structures. Then, employing comparative ethnographic materials, he traces the distribution of these house types—and finds them spread from the middle Columbia to central California. The same procedure is followed with regard to other elements and complexes; Spier notes the points that are characteristic of the Klamath but that are apparent as well among other tribes in both adjacent and remoter areas. What, then, is the permissible conclusion? It is that the Klamath share with other peoples over a wide geographic area elements of common culture. In other words, a shared history is inferred.

But clearly this is not all. The common elements—whether house types or chieftainship, for example—are given different weighting in different local settings, differences that are slight, perhaps, but none the less perceptible. In short, when the distributions of elements in space are analyzed, they reveal a slightly different integration from group to group. Comparison of the overt discernible features suggests the presence of a major theme, the spread of an idea or thing over a wide area. But, however much demonstrably related groups may possess a common history, each one makes of the elements it possesses something peculiarly its own. To employ a musical analogue, each culture offers its own variations on a theme. One cannot, of course, discover the point of origin of such shared or borrowed traits. But when a vast area of aboriginal America is shown to possess features in common, there is the implication of a broad historical base. Spier's inductive methodology sheds light on the rise of areas of culture in the native New World and indeed elsewhere.

To Spier the concept of culture was primary. His detailed penetration of material and societal institutions affirms the proposition that although human cultural entities are distinct from each other, yet they may share a common cultural base. The ultimate conclusion makes for an essentially relativistic perspective on the nature of culture. Spier's disciplined empirical studies are built on a sense of the properties and processes implicit in a concept of culture. But Spier never sought to develop any elaborate cultural hypothesis, however much his contemporaries—not to mention anthropologists today—agonized over definitions and formulations. Rather than compressing the idea of culture in mankind into some definable and limited frame, Spier was content to let the empirical data speak for themselves. Obviously there are propositions and assumptions, self-evident truths, that color all of Spier's writings. Culture to him was made up of people; his writings show a concern with the role of the individual in culture.

Is the human being free to make choices, or are modes of behavior that are characteristic of cultural systems determined, directed, and limited by the system itself? According to Spier, humans act in their social and natural environments within a framework conditioned by time, i.e., history. Men are free within the limits of historically derived cultural systems. Equally, Spier was much preoccupied with the question of cultural growth as dependent on accident. A culture, he notes, is not accidental or random. Provision can be made for individual choices and their effects, but at the same time the cultures of mankind are always influenced by what has gone before. The patterns of understanding that are characteristic of members of a given culture derive from the factors that have built it.

There are also discernible processes that are operative in the building of culture. Individually made inventions do occur, to be sure, but these—given the frequent absence of verifiable circumstances—come generally from history. Spier devoted considerable time to an analysis of the Prophet Dance of the American Northwest, a messianic revivalistic movement that marked the tribes of the area. Here Spier could demonstrate the innovative in a social movement that drew on both the aboriginal context and on the imposition of ideological elements drawn from Christian missionization. Two processes were shown to be at work. On the one hand, there is the employment of native symbols that gave rise to the Prophet Dance idea; on the other, there is the problem of the spread, the diffusion of the invented rituals from one group to another.

It is the latter point—the diffusion and integration of cultural elements—that becomes problematic for Spier. To Spier, traits and features come out of time; they are invented—but always within the limiting context of a given cultural system—or they are diffused with the same limitation applying. For such reasons, western North America assumed a special place for Spier. The area provided a living laboratory in which major related complexes could be shown to exist, where a common history was evident, and where each culture gave its particular twist, its idiosyncratic interpretation, to the things, material and social, derived from history. Spier remained impatient with the idea of cultural holism, an idea that in the 1920s and 1930s became a watchword and that still reflects a major preoccupation of many anthropologists. The integration of the elements that make up a system is understandable in terms of history and not in terms of a preconceived structure or a psychological bent. By letting the data speak for themselves, Spier's formulations convey a vitality, an objective sense of the real world of ethnographic analysis. In short, the collected data fall into their own niche, offer their own explanation, and never, as Spier employed them, stray from a scientific historicism.

There is one remaining side of Spier's many-faceted career. He saw it as most important to spread the message of a scientific anthropology. Teaching and research were expanded by his work as an editor. And he insisted that every opportunity be given to colleagues and students to publish solid and informative work. As editor of the *American Anthropologist* (the official organ of the American Anthropological Association) from 1934 to 1938, he took a broad and eclectic view: he often published papers—if they were well argued—whose perspective clearly might not dovetail with his own. Open to nuance but insistent on the highest scholarly standards, Spier exerted considerable influence on anthropological publishing for a long time. Eager to further publications, in 1935 he founded a short-lived *General Series in Anthropology,* which was designed to issue monographs on various ethnographic topics. Continuing financial support for this venture proved difficult to obtain; he was able somewhat later, however, in 1945, to found the *Southwestern Journal of Anthropology,* a major journal that Spier continued to edit until his death. (Although still in existence as the *Journal of Anthropological Research,* after Spier's death the *Southwestern Journal* was never able to recapture the vitality he injected.) As an editor, both in his selection of manuscripts and in his treatment of them, he was without peer. Every sentence, reference, and diagram were carefully combed. Indeed, it was this same meticulous quality that appeared in his teaching. Having begun his career in engineering, Spier made full use of his drafting skills and artistic gifts, sometimes going so far as to redraw diagrams and similar items for his contributors. One can recall, as an example, his skills at the blackboard. To illustrate an artifact, he would draw it; and if it were a pot, a basket, or some other symmetrical object, he would take a piece of chalk in each hand and draw a perfect shape.

Lamentably, Spier and the majority of his contemporaries are gone. Quite apart from the sense of loss that must be felt, there is the question of what has happened to the discipline of anthropology, and particularly of ethnology/ethnography since those historicist days. There are some today who are still appalled at the diffuseness of the discipline as it is now practiced and the consequent decline in scholarly excellence. Spier perhaps saw it coming but remained faithful to the field as he knew it. He was and remains one of the "greats."

HONORS AND DISTINCTIONS

DEGREES

1915 B.S. (engineering), College of the City of New York
1920 Ph.D. (anthropology), Columbia University

PROFESSIONAL RECORD

1912–1914 Assistant Anthropologist, New Jersey Archaeological and Geological Survey
1916–1920 Assistant Anthropologist, American Museum of Natural History
1919 Cutting Fellowship, Columbia University
1923 National Research Council Fellowship
1920–1929 Professor, University of Washington
1930, 1934 Director, Anthropology Field Training Program, Pacific Northwest, Okanagon and Modoc
1932–1933 Research Associate, Yale University
1933–1939 Professor, Yale University
1936, 1937, 1939, 1941 Research Director, University of New Mexico Chaco Canyon Field Sessions
1939–1955 Professor, University of New Mexico
1960–1961 Research Associate, University of California, Berkeley

Visiting Professor:

1927–1929 University of Oklahoma
1928, 1930 University of Chicago
1939, 1949 Harvard University
1921, 1923, 1925, 1932 Columbia University (summer)
1924, 1925, 1927, 1932, 1933, 1948 University of California, Berkeley (summer)
1947 University of California, Los Angeles (summer)

HONORARY SOCIETIES

1946 National Academy of Sciences
1946 American Philosophical Society

1953 Fellow, Academy of Arts and Sciences
1955 Fellow, California Academy of Science
1960 Honorary Fellow, Royal Anthropological Institute of Great Britain and Ireland

HONORS

1946 Townsend Harris Medal
1960 Viking Fund Medal and Award

PROFESSIONAL SOCIETIES

American Anthropological Association, President (1943); Editor (1934–1938)
American Association for the Advancement of Science, Vice-President, Section H (1943, 1946)
Andean Institute
Society for American Folklore
National Research Council
Sigma Xi

BIBLIOGRAPHY

1913

Results of an archaeological survey of the state of New Jersey. Am. Anthropol., 15:675–79.

1915

Review of "The double-curve motive in Northwestern Algonkian art," by Frank G. Speck. Am. Anthropol., 17:344–46.
Review of "On the shell heaps of Maine," by F. B. Loomis and D. B. Young. Am. Anthropol., 17:346–47.
Location of archaeological remains on Manhattan Island. In: *The Indians of Manhattan Island and Vicinity*, by Alanson Skinner. American Museum of Natural History, Guide Leaflet Series, no. 41. New York.
Review of *The Indians of Greater New York*, by Alanson Skinner. Am. Anthropol., 17:581–82.
Blackfoot relationship terms. Am. Anthropol., 17:603–7.
Indian remains near Plainfield, Union County, and along the Lower Delaware Valley. Geological Survey of New Jersey, Bulletin 13. Union Hill, N.J.

1916

New data on the Trenton Argillite culture. Am. Anthropol., 18:181–89.
Review of "Composition of California Shellmounds," by Edward Winslow Gifford. Am. Anthropol., 18:282–84.
Review of "A Pre-Lenape Site in New Jersey," by E. W. Hawkes and Ralph Linton. Am. Anthropol., 18:564–66.

1917

Zuni chronology. Proc. Natl. Acad. Sci. U.S.A., 3.
An outline of a chronology of Zuni ruins. Anthropol. Pap. Am. Mus. Nat. Hist., 18(part 3).

1918

The growth of boys: Dentition and stature. Am. Anthropol., 20:37–48.

Notes on some Little Colorado ruins. Anthropol. Pap. Am. Mus. Nat. Hist., 18(part 4).
Physiological age: The relation of dentition to body growth. The Dental Cosmos, 60:899–905.
The Havasupai of Cataract Cañon. Am. Mus. J., 18:637–45.
The Trenton Argillite culture. Anthropol. Pap. Am. Mus. Nat. Hist., 22(part 4).

1919

Ruins in the White Mountains of Arizona. Anthropol. Pap. Am. Mus. Nat. Hist., 18(part 5).
The growth of Porto Rican boys, with special reference to the relation between their stature and dentition. J. Dent. Res., 1:145–57.

1920

Review of *Primitive Society,* by Robert H. Lowie. Pac. Rev., 1:425–26.
Note on letters of a Javanese princess by Raden Adjeng Kartini. Pac. Rev., 1:427.

1921

Review of *Peoples of the Philippines,* by A. L. Kroeber. Pac. Rev., 2:348–49.
Notes on the Kiowa Sun Dance. Anthropol. Pap. Am. Mus. Nat. Hist., 16(part 6).
The Sun Dance of the Plains Indians: Its development and diffusion. Anthropol. Pap. Am. Mus. Nat. Hist., 16(part 7).
Review of *The Ila-Speaking Peoples of Northern Rhodesia,* by Edwin W. Smith and Andrew Murray Dale. Am. Anthropol., 23:372–74.

1922

Havasupai days. In: *American Indian Life,* ed. Elsie Clews Parsons. New York.
Review of *The American Indian,* by Clark Wissler. Wash. Hist. Q., 13:300–301.
A suggested origin for gentile organization. Am. Anthropol., 24:487–89.

Review of *Early Civilization*, by A. A. Goldenweiser. The Book Review, New York Herald-Tribune, October, p. 22.

1923

Southern Diegueno customs. Univ. Calif. Berkeley Publ. Am. Archaeol. Ethnol., 20(Phoebe Apperson Hearst Memorial Volume): 297–358.

Note appended to "A Blackfoot Version of the Magic Flight," by Robert H. Knox. J. Am. Folklore, 36:401.

1924

Zuñi weaving technique. Am. Anthropol., 26:64–85.

Havasupai (Yuman) texts. Int. J. Am. Linguistics, 3:109–16.

Wichita and Caddo relationship terms. Am. Anthropol., 26:258–63.

Review of *Studies in Evolution and Eugenics*, by S. J. Holmes. Am. Anthropol., 26:264–67.

Review of *A History of Magic and Experimental Science During the First Thirteen Centuries of Our Era*, by Lynn Thorndike. Am. Anthropol., 26:277–78.

1925

Reviews of *The Bagesu and Other Tribes of the Uganda Protectorate*, by John Roscoe; *Ashanti*, by R. S. Rattray; *Race Problems in the New Africa*, by W. C. Willoughby. Am. Anthropol., 27:330–31.

Anthropology. In: *New International Year Book for 1924*, ed. Frank Moore Colby and Herbert Treadwell Wade, pp. 38–45. New York: Dodd, Mead and Company.

Review of *Growth of Chinese*, by S. M. Shirokogoroff and V. B. Appleton. Am. Anthropol., 27:469–70.

The distribution of kinship systems in North America. Univ. Wash. Publ. Anthropol., 1(2):69–88.

An analysis of Plains Indian parfleche decoration. Univ. Wash. Publ. Anthropol., 1(3):89–112.

1926

Anthropology. In: *New International Year Book for 1925*, ed. Herbert Treadwell Wade, pp. 37–43. New York: Dodd, Mead and Company.

Review of "Archaeological Investigations in the Aleutian Islands," by Waldemar Jochelson. Wash. Hist. Q., 17:145.
Are savages people? Reviews of *My Crowded Solitude*, by Jack McLaren, and *In Unknown New Guinea*, by W. J. V. Saville. In: New York Herald-Tribune Books, August 22, p. 11.
Are savages people? Review of *Crime and Custom in Savage Society*, by B. Malinowski. New York Herald-Tribune Books, September 19, p. 16.

1927

Review of *Les Origines de l'Humanité*, by René Verneau. Am. Anthropol., 29:116.
Review of *Religion and Folklore in Northern India*, by William Crooke. Am. Anthropol., 29:119.
Review of *Process of Physical Growth Among the Chinese*, vol. 1, by S. M. Shirokogoroff. Am. Anthropol., 29:119–20.
Anthropology. In: *New International Year Book for 1926*, ed. Herbert Treadwell Wade, pp. 40–47. New York: Dodd, Mead and Company.
The association test as a method of defining religious concepts. Am. Anthropol., 29:267–70.
With Dorothy A. Smith. The dot and circle design in Northwestern America. J. Soc. Américanistes Paris, 19:47–55.
Review of *Mythology of Puget Sound*, by Hermann Haeberlin. Wash. Hist. Q., 18:149.
The Ghost Dance of 1870 among the Klamath of Oregon. Univ. Wash. Publ. Anthropol., 2(2):39–56.
Tribal distribution in southwestern Oregon. Oreg. Hist. Q., 28:1–8.
Review of *Culture: The Diffusion Controversy*, by G. Elliot Smith, Bronislaw Malinowski, Herbert J. Spinden, and Alexander Goldenweiser. J. Am. Folklore, 40:415–16.

1928

Concerning man's antiquity at Frederick, Oklahoma. Science, 67:160–61.
Review of *The Story of the American Indian*, by Paul Radin. The Daily Oklahoman (Oklahoma City), March 11, p. 9.

Havasupai ethnography. Anthropol. Pap. Am. Mus. Nat. Hist., 29 (part 3).
Anthropology. In: *New International Year Book for 1927*, ed. Herbert Treadwell Wade, pp. 43–51. New York: Dodd, Mead and Company.
Review of *Primitive Man As Philosopher*, by Paul Radin. The City College Alumnus (New York), 24:73–74.
Review of various Publicaciones de la Secretariá de Educación Pública, Mexico. In: *Books Abroad*, vol. 2, no. 3, pp. 40–41. Norman: University of Oklahoma Press.
Review of *Totenmasken*, by Richard Langer. In: *Books Abroad*, vol. 2, no. 3, pp. 71–72. Norman: University of Oklahoma Press.
A note on reputed artifacts from Frederick, Oklahoma. Science, 68:184.
Measurements of quadruplet girls. Am. J. Phys. Anthropol., 12:269–72.

1929

Review of *The Building of Cultures*, by Roland B. Dixon. Am. Anthropol., 31:140–45.
Review of *The Ancient Inhabitants of the Canary Islands*, by Earnest A. Hooten. Am. Anthropol., 31:169–75.
Problems arising from the cultural position of the Havasupai. Am. Anthropol., 31:213–22.
Review of *Auf der Suche nach dem Pithekanthropus: Dem "Affenmenschen vor Java,"* by Emil Carthaus. In: *Books Abroad*, vol. 3, no. 3, p. 287. Norman: University of Oklahoma Press.
Growth of Japanese children born in America and in Japan. Univ. Wash. Publ. Anthropol., 3(1):1–30.
Anthropology. In: *New International Year Book for 1928*, ed. Herbert Treadwell Wade, pp. 39–46. New York: Dodd, Mead and Company.
Review of *Religion and Art in Ashanti*, by R. S. Rattray. Am. Anthropol., 31:521–25.

1930

Anthropology. In: *New International Year Book for 1929*, ed. Herbert Treadwell Wade, pp. 33–44. New York: Dodd, Mead and Company.

Contributions to *New International Encyclopedia Supplement:* Anthropology, vol. 1, pp. 87–89; Ethnography, vol. 1, pp. 513–18; Ethnology, vol. 1, pp. 518–22; Eugenics, vol. 1, pp. 523–24; Indians, vol. 1, pp. 783–85; Prehistoric races of man, vol. 2, pp. 976–78; Race problems, vol. 2, pp. 1306–10. New York: Dodd, Mead and Company.

Ethnology. In: *Nelson's Perpetual Loose-Leaf Encyclopedia,* vol. 4, pp. 490–94.

Review of *Materials for the Study of Inheritance in Man,* by Franz Boas. Am. Anthropol., 32:321.

With Edward Sapir. Wishram ethnography. Univ. Wash. Publ. Anthropol., 3(3):151–300.

Review of *The Prehistory of Aviation,* by Berthold Laufer. Am. Anthropol., 32:556–57.

Review of *Anthropology and Modern Life,* by Franz Boas. Am. J. Sociol., 35:1117–18.

Slave raid. Southwest Rev., 15:515–23.

Klamath ethnography. Univ. Calif. Berkeley Publ. Am. Archaeol. Ethnol., 30:1–338.

1931

Perfectly natural. Atl. Mon., 147:133–36.

N. C. Nelson's stratigraphic technique in the reconstruction of prehistoric sequences in Southwestern America. In: *Methods in Social Science,* ed. Stuart A. Rice. Chicago: University of Chicago Press.

Historical interrelation of culture traits: Franz Boas' study of Tsimshian mythology. In: *Methods in Social Science,* ed. Stuart A. Rice. Chicago: University of Chicago Press.

Anthropology. In: *New International Year Book for 1930,* ed. Herbert Treadwell Wade, pp. 37–43. New York: Dodd, Mead and Company.

Plains Indian parfleche designs. Univ. Wash. Publ. Anthropol., 4(3):293–322.

1932

Anthropology. In: *New International Year Book for 1931,* ed. Herbert Treadwell Wade, pp. 39–43. New York: Dodd, Mead and Company.

Notes and queries on *Anthropology*, 5th ed. (Edited for the British Association for the Advancement of Science by a committee of Section H.) Am. Anthropol., 34:516.

1933

Review of *Social Anthropology*, by Paul Radin. Am. J. Sociol., 38:775–76.
Anthropology. In: *New International Year Book for 1932*, ed. Frank H. Vizetelly, pp. 35–40. New York: Funk and Wagnalls Company.
Yuman Tribes of the Gila River. Univ. Chicago Publ. Anthropol., Ethnol. Ser. Chicago: University of Chicago Press.

1934

Review of *The Peninsula of Yucatan: Medical, Biological, Meteorological and Sociological Studies*, by George Cheever Shattuck and collaborators. Am. J. Sci., 27:237.
Anthropology. In: *New International Year Book for 1933*, ed. Frank H. Vizetelly, pp. 34–39. New York: Funk and Wagnalls Company.
Review of *The Long Road from Savagery to Civilization*, by Fay-Cooper Cole. Am. Anthropol., 36:302–3.

1935

Anthropology. In: *New International Year Book for 1934*, ed. Frank H. Vizetelly, pp. 33–37. New York: Funk and Wagnalls Company.
The prophet dance of the Northwest and its derivatives. General Series in Anthropology, no. 1, pp. 1–74.

1936

Cultural Relations of the Gila River and Lower Colorado Tribes. Yale Univ. Publ. Anthropol., no. 3, pp. 1–22.
Tribal Distribution in Washington. General Series in Anthropology, no. 3, pp. 1–43.
Anthropology. In: *New International Year Book for 1935*, ed. Frank H. Vizetelly, pp. 31–35. New York: Funk and Wagnalls Company.

1937

Review of *The Comparative Ethnology of Northern Mexico Before 1750,* by Ralph L. Beals, and *The Distribution of Aboriginal Tribes and Languages in Northwestern Mexico,* by Carl Sauer. Am. Anthropol., 39:146–48.

1938

Preface. In: *The Sinkaietk or Southern Okanagon of Washington,* by Walter B. Cline and others. General Series in Anthropology, no. 6, pp. 3–5.

1939

Edward Sapir obituary. Science, 89:237–38.
Illustration in Anthropological Publications. Full-Tone Collotype for Scientific Reproduction, Supplement no. 12. Meriden, Conn.: The Meriden Gravure Company.
Edward Sapir: 1884–4 February 1939 obituary. Man (London), 39:92–93.
Ed. *Songs for a Comox Dancing Mask,* by Edward Sapir. Ethnos, 4:49–55.

1940

Review of *An Ethnic Map of Australia* and *A Preliminary Register of Australian Tribes and Hordes,* by D. Sutherland Davidson. Am. Anthropol., 42:159–60.
Review of *The Kiliwa Indians of Lower California,* by Peveril Meigs, III. J. Am. Folklore, 53:198–200.
The Pueblos since Coronado. El Palacio (Santa Fe, N.M.), 47:201–4.

1941

With A. Irving Hallowell and Stanley S. Newman, eds. Foreword. In: *Language, Culture, and Personality: Essays in Memory of Edward Sapir,* p. x. Menasha, Wisc.: Sapir Memorial Publication Fund.
Completion of an extended ethnography of the Modoc Indians of Oregon. In: *American Philosophical Society, Year Book for 1940,* pp. 253–54. Philadelphia.

1942

Review of *Ceremonial Costumes of the Pueblo Indians: Their Evolution, Fabrication, and Significance in the Prayer Drama*, by Virginia More Roediger. Pac. Hist. Rev., 11:220–21.
Elsie Clews Parsons, 1875–1941. (Obituary.) Am. Counc. Learned Soc. Bull., 35:46–49(716–18).

1943

Review of *Pima and Papago Indian Agriculture*, by Edward F. Castetter and Willis H. Bell. N.M. Q. Rev., 13:99–100.
Addenda to bibliography of Elsie Clews Parsons. J. Am. Folklore, 56:136.
Review of *The Eyak Indians of the Copper River Delta*, by Kaj Birket-Smith and Frederica de Laguna. Am. J. Archaeol., 47:152–53.
With A. L. Kroeber. Elsie Clews Parsons. (Obituary.) Am. Anthropol., 45:244–51.
Franz Boas and some of his views. (Obituary.) Acta Americana: Rev. Inter-Am. Soc. Anthropol. Geogr. (Mexico City), 1:108–27.
With Edward Sapir. Notes on the culture of the Yana. Anthropol. Rec., 3:239–98.

1945

Review of *Racial Prehistory in the Southwest and the Hawikuh of Zuni*, by Carl C. Seltzer. N.M. Hist. Rev., 20:101–3.

1946

Comparative vocabularies and parallel texts in two Yuman languages of Arizona. Univ. N.M. Publ. Anthropol., no. 2, pp. 1–150.

1947

Review of *Papago Indian Religion*, by Ruth M. Underhill. Sci. Mon., 65:170–72.

1949

A study of cultural selectivity. In: *American Philosophical Society, Year Book for 1948*, pp. 207–8. Philadelphia.

1950

Contributions to *Collier's Encyclopedia:* Amuck, vol. 1, p. 515; Anthropology, vol. 2, pp. 37–38; Cannibalism, vol. 4, pp. 467–68; Civilization, vol. 5, pp. 295–96; Couvade, vol. 6, p. 75; Ethnology, vol. 7, pp. 451–52; Infanticide, vol. 10, p. 406; Potlatch, vol. 16, p. 252; Primitive culture (with a section on primitive industry by Harry Tschopik, Jr.), vol. 16, 317–29; primitive religion, vol. 16, pp. 329–34; Primitive society, vol. 16, pp. 334–43. New York: P. F. Collier and Sons Corporation.

1953

With Harold E. Driver, John M. Cooper, Paul Kirchoff, Dorothy Ranier Libby, and William C. Massey. Indian Tribes of North America. Ind. Univ. Publ. Anthropol. Linguist., Memoir 9, Int. J. Am. Linguist. Suppl., Int. J. Am. Linguist., 19(3):1–30.

Some observations on Mohave clans. Southwest. J. Anthropol., 9:324–42.

1954

Ancestor worship. In: *The Encyclopedia Americana,* vol. 1, pp. 651–52. New York: The Americana Corporation.

Some aspects of the nature of culture. First Annual Research Lecture, University of New Mexico, April 23, 1954. N.M. Quarterly, 24(3):301–21. (Also printed separately, pp. 1–21.)

1955

Mohave Culture Items. Mus. N. Ariz. Bull., no. 28, pp. 1–35. Flagstaff: Northern Arizona Society of Science and Art, Inc.

1956

Invention and human society. In: *Man, Culture, and Society,* ed. Harry L. Shapiro, pp. 224–46. New York: Oxford University Press.

1957

The Horse Comes to the Great Plains. Radio Script no. 12, The World of the Mind Series. (Arranged in collaboration with the American Association for the Advancement of Science and the American Council of Learned Societies.) New York: Broadcast Music, Inc.

1958

Invention. In: *Collier's Encyclopedia,* vol. 11, pp. 93A–93F. New York: P. F. Collier and Sons Corporation.
Cannibalism. In: *The Encyclopedia Americana,* vol. 5, pp. 502–3. New York: The Americana Corporation.
Contributions to *Collier's Encyclopedia:* Fire, vol. 8, pp. 56–57; Primitive industry, vol. 16, pp. 593–95; Sign language, vol. 17, pp. 320–27; Wheel, vol. 19, p. 458A. New York: P. F. Collier and Son.

1959

With Wayne Suttles and Melville J. Herskovits. Comment on Aberle's thesis of deprivation. Southwest. J. Anthropol., 15:84–88.
Some central elements in the legacy. In: *The Anthropology of Franz Boas,* ed. Walter Goldschmidt. Am. Anthropol. Assoc. Mem., 89:148–55.

1960

Note on Maricopa origin of the term Nixoras. In: *What Were Nixoras?* by Henry F. Dobyns and others. Southwest. J. Anthropol., 16:233–34.
Contributions to *Collier's Encyclopedia:* Anthropology, vol. 1, pp. 657–58; Anthropogeography, vol. 1, p. 658; Ethnology, vol. 7, pp. 185–86; Primitive and professional hunting, vol. 9, pp. 640–44. New York: P. F. Collier and Son.

1961

Geophagy. In: *Collier's Encyclopedia,* vol. 8, p. 358. New York: P. F. Collier and Son.
Sun dance. In: *The Encyclopaedia Britannica,* vol. 21, p. 565. London and New York: The Encyclopaedia Britannica Company, Ltd.

1962

Contributions to *Collier's Encyclopedia:* Bachofen, Johann Jakob, vol. 3, p. 439; Bastian, Adolf, vol. 3, p. 697; Lowie, Robert Heinrich, vol. 15, p. 60; Sapir, Edward, vol. 20, pp. 425–26. New York: P. F. Collier and Son.

1963

Contributions to *The Encyclopaedia Britannica:* Cocopa, vol. 6, p. 7; Dwellings, primitive, vol. 7, pp. 809–12; Mohave, vol. 15, p. 655. London and New York: The Encyclopaedia Britannica Company, Ltd.

Contributions to the *Harper Encyclopedia of Science:* Fire, vol. 2, p. 7; Primitive technology, vol. 3, pp. 956–57; Wheel, vol. 4, p. 1257. New York: Harper and Row.

1964

Contributions to *The Encyclopaedia Britannica:* Weapons, vol. 28, pp. 531–32; Wheel, vol. 28, pp. 700–702. London and New York: The Encyclopaedia Britannica Company, Ltd.

HANS-LUKAS TEUBER

August 7, 1916–January 4, 1977

BY LEO M. HURVICH,
DOROTHEA JAMESON,
AND WALTER A. ROSENBLITH

O N WEDNESDAY, January 19, 1977, Hans-Lukas Teuber was scheduled to deliver a James R. Killian Faculty Award Lecture entitled "Mood, Motives, Memory and Values."[1] Instead there assembled in the Kresge Auditorium of MIT a memorial gathering of family, colleagues, students, and friends to remember and share recollections of this extraordinary person. They were there to express their affection, admiration, and love for him, and to assuage the grief prompted by his untimely and unexpected death at the age of sixty. Professor Teuber—or Luke, as he was known to his many friends—lost his life on January 4 while swimming off Virgin Gorda in the British Virgin Islands where he was vacationing with his wife Marianne. He had been at MIT since 1961 and in 1964 had founded the Department of Psychology and was appointed its first head. Within a few years the department had grown into a center of psychology and the brain sciences that came to be known and admired the world over.

Only a man of his brilliance, scholarly acumen, and warm personal qualities could have accomplished such a feat in one

[1] The first lecture, which was to have been delivered January 12, 1977, was entitled "From Perception to Action."

decade. A magnetic human being—summarized once in the phrase of a ten-year-old child of a colleague: "He twinkles"[2]—Luke was a gifted experimenter, teacher, and administrator. Above all, throughout his busy professional life, he expressed a warmth for people: gentleness, consideration, and concern for others. His colleague Professor Nauta said of him: "Luke was that rare person, described by Camus, as the true poet who would have no choice at all but to make poetry—even in the desert."[3] Whence came this magical, "highly improbable and very lovable man," as he was described by a brilliant young colleague, Ann Graybiel.[4]

Hans-Lukas Teuber was born August 7, 1916, in Berlin, the son of Dr. Eugen Teuber and Rose Knopf Teuber. His parents were exceedingly musical—both were excellent pianists—and his younger brother became an organist and music historian. His father, who was his greatest single influence during Luke's early years, had studied under Wilhelm Wundt and Carl Stumpf; under the sponsorship of the Prussian Academy of Sciences, he set up a primate station on Tenerife (Canary Islands) for the study of anthropoid apes. (While there, Eugen Teuber also collected folk melodies for Stumpf's "Tonarchiv.") In early 1914 he returned to Germany to serve as a communications officer during World War I. After a brief period during which they overlapped at Tenerife, Wolfgang Köhler took over the direction of the station from Luke's father and went on to conduct the famous chimpanzee experiments that he described in *The Mentality of Apes*. After the war, Luke's father became interested in calculating devices and joined a business machine firm called Adrema, first as director of research and later as director of exports.

---

[2] Transcript of a gathering to remember Hans-Lukas Teuber, Kresge Auditorium, Massachusetts Institute of Technology, Cambridge, January 19, 1977, p. 16.
[3] Ibid., p. 4.
[4] Ibid., p. 13.

In 1938 Lukas's parents and brother moved to Denmark; he continued his studies at the University of Basle in Switzerland, where he was a student from 1935 to 1939.

Lukas spent his youth with the family partly on the Baltic and partly in Berlin. His first schooling was in a private preparatory school in Berlin, and he subsequently attended the Collège Français (a Huguenot school) in Berlin for eight years, graduating in 1934 with a *baccalauréat*. His classical education emphasized the humanities—Latin, Greek, and ancient history—and all subjects, including the natural sciences, were taught in French. Lukas shared his father's disparate interests in Greek and Roman literature, the comparative study of animal behavior, and the application of mathematics to problems of communication. They took long hikes together, first into the Harz Mountains and later in the Alps. Lukas's older son Andreas documented the influence of his father's classical education when he told us at the memorial convocation: "I remember . . . when I was four years old, he thought it would be splendid if I heard *Antigone* by Sophocles—hard enough for a four-year-old—except that my father thought I would not truly appreciate it unless he read it to me in Greek. And so there I was, four years old—I had this teddy bear—and I sat there and listened to Sophocles in Greek."[5] (The going was not always that rough for Andreas and his younger brother Christopher. Although the English translations of the Greek myths and the recounting of the entire *Odyssey* were part of their bedtime fare, so were Dr. Doolittle and Winnie the Pooh.)

Lukas wrote poetry and plays in his youth and had contemplated a career as a poet. In later years, he continued to write occasional verse (he often quoted relevant poetry in his lectures), but while he was at the University of Basle, philos-

---

[5] Transcript of a gathering to remember Hans-Lukas Teuber, p. 10.

ophy became his primary interest—particularly, philosophy of science. His early interest in the comparative study of behavior continued, and he took courses and received laboratory training in biology and zoology, comparative anatomy, and embryology. His teacher in physical chemistry was Professor Bernoulli, and he worked with Professor Portman in the Zoological Institute. Hans Spemann, who came from nearby Freiburg to lecture on embryology, was still another influence. And it was here that Lukas's interest in problems of central nervous system physiology was first engaged.

An important aspect of Lukas's Basle years was the small interdisciplinary workshop in which he participated with several young instructors and fellow students. One of the latter was Marianne Liepe. Discussions at the workshop focused on the methodologies of the diverse sciences and ways to bridge the gap between the biological and social sciences. But the intellectual interests of the group ranged wide. At one time the group read Dante's *Divina Commedia* and works such as Bachofen's *Mutterrecht und Urreligion*—the sort of book that later led Robert Graves to extol matriarchal societies.

On receiving the Holtzer Fellowship at Harvard in 1939, Lukas prepared to come to the United States, but the outbreak of World War II delayed his arrival here until 1941. Marianne Liepe had come to the United States two years earlier to study at Vassar College, and she and Lukas were married in 1941. Marianne's background was similar to Lukas's in many ways. Her parents were Wolfgang and Gertrud (Neustadt) Liepe. Her father had been chairman of the Department of German Literature at the University of Kiel in Germany and later became a professor at the University of Chicago. The Teubers's two sons, Andreas Wolfgang and Christopher Lawrence, were born in 1942 and 1946. Andreas is now an associate professor of philosophy at Brandeis University and Christopher is a structural designer in Venice,

California. The Teubers became naturalized American citizens in 1944. In recent years Marianne has devoted more of her intellectual energies to her contributions to art history, particularly the Bauhaus period; but throughout Lukas's career, she was an integral part of the international intellectual life that moved freely and hospitably from his laboratory or seminar room to their home.

Teuber received his Ph.D. in psychology from Harvard University in 1947. His graduate training at Harvard and research at the Cabot Foundation in Cambridge were interrupted by two years of service in the U. S. Naval Reserve from 1944 to 1946. According to a perhaps apocryphal story, Lukas at first failed the mandatory German language examination at Harvard because, as a recent arrival to the United States, he did not know enough English into which to translate the German text. His Navy stint, however, and a part-time position as assistant boys secretary at the Cambridge YMCA while he was a Harvard graduate student accelerated his Americanization. He eventually acquired a superb command of the English language, and throughout his academic career his rapt audiences enjoyed his eloquence and gentle humor.

During his stay at Harvard, Lukas's interests were divided between the physiology of sensation and the application of experimental methods to the study of small social groups. His appointment to the research staff of the Cabot Foundation turned him temporarily in the direction of experimental sociology and led to his doctoral dissertation—"Dyadic Groups—A Study in Counseling Relationships"—under Gordon Allport's sponsorship. This study was part of a ten-year experiment in the "prevention of delinquency" by providing guidance, counseling, and psychotherapy to 325 underprivileged boys. Treatment consisted of intensive, face-to-face interactions between the boys and some thirty counsellors; these counsellors saw the boys at weekly to monthly intervals for periods ranging from two-and-a-half to eight years. A control group of 325 similarly underprivileged boys—matched in pairs with the members of the treatment group but left entirely untreated—was also set up at the beginning of the experiment.

The importance of control groups to evaluate such social intervention programs was borne out by the outcome. Ten years after the start of the experiment and after all treatment had been terminated, the research staff compared the incidence of delinquency between the treated and control groups. Even though all but one of the counsellors thought their treatment efforts highly successful, the frequency of offenses turned out to be slightly higher in the treatment group. The use of large matched control groups was to be a dominant feature of Teuber's later research on brain-damaged patients.

After his death, an autobiographical sketch that Lukas had prepared in either 1952 or 1953 was found among his papers. In summarizing his career to that point, he wrote:

> My original biological interests had been fostered at Harvard through contacts with Lashley, and through avid reading of the work of J. W. Gibbs, L. J. Henderson, and W. B. Cannon. The possibility that the logic of Gibbsian systems (set up for physical chemistry) might be equally applicable to biological and social systems, was considered more and more seriously.
> A more direct influence was that of Kurt Goldstein, who at that time (1941) was Visiting Professor and William James lecturer at Harvard. Frequent personal contacts made me aware of the strategic role of experimental neurology within the framework of general biological science, and suggested a reconsideration of the earlier German work (Bethe, Uexkull, Weiss) in comparative physiology of nervous systems and problems of sensorimotor integration.
> The final and decisive push in the direction of my chosen field was provided almost fortuitously by a two-year period in the U.S. Navy. In 1944, I arrived at the San Diego Naval Hospital where Dr. M. B. Bender

was in charge of the neurology wards. He was interested in studying peripheral nerve injuries, causalgia, and sensory disturbances after cerebral injury. Hearing of my acquaintance with Goldstein's work, he suggested that I stay with him at the Naval Hospital. An improvised laboratory was set up early in 1945, and men with acute battle injuries of the nervous system were studied by us for nearly two years. The unique opportunity of observing effects of acute brain injuries resulted in a number of joint papers . . . In these papers, we tried to continue the tradition of Goldstein and Gelb, of Poppelreuter, of Head and Holmes, considering the injuries as experiments of nature and studying the disturbances of brain function as a clue to normal modes of central nervous functioning.

This type of research was to remain a consuming interest of Luke's until the end. Dr. Weiskrantz, an Oxford colleague and friend, has written: "He contributed a unique and distinctive personal approach to a tradition that had its roots in 19th century neurology."[6]

Following his discharge from the Navy and completion of his graduate work at Harvard, Lukas went to the New York University College of Medicine. Under the sponsorship of Bender and S. B. Wortis, he built up a small laboratory to continue studying the effects of penetrating brain injuries. Successively he was appointed research associate in the College of Medicine and in the Department of Psychology in the Graduate School of Arts and Science, associate professor, and professor. Throughout this period he headed the Psychophysiological Laboratory at the NYU Bellevue Medical Center and with his colleagues and students established that laboratory as a vital and creative research center that attracted international attention. Teuber's research collaborators during these years included Josephine Semmes, Lila Ghent, Rita Rudel, Sidney Weinstein, William Battersby, Joseph Altman, Mortimer Mishkin, Stephan Chorover, Florry Proctor, and others.

[6] L. Weiskrantz, "Hans Lukas Teuber," *Nature,* 2(1977):485–86.

Although his teaching at NYU was primarily in specialized courses such as neuroanatomy and physiological psychology, Teuber's interdisciplinary interests persisted. He also taught a course on the social psychology of small groups and became a member of the Macy Foundation multidisciplinary group. This group held a series of conferences in an area that became known—after the title of Norbert Wiener's book—as cybernetics; the discussions dealt with feedback theory and communication theory and their possible relevance to the study of central nervous function.

In 1961 Teuber left New York University for MIT—but with certain misgivings: he had had a long association with his group of brain-injured patients, and he was strongly attached to his attractive home in Dobbs Ferry just outside New York City. The early transition to MIT was, in his own words, "somewhat turbulent." But even after the move to the Boston area, Luke was able to maintain his contacts with the New York patient group, and in fact the association lasted some thirty years. He had a clear and uncompromising conception of the type of psychology department he wanted to develop at MIT, and he saw to it that his plan became reality.

In 1961, psychology at MIT was a section in the Department of Economics and Social Science. But Luke moved rapidly to reorganize psychology staffing, to plan a research building, and to develop a doctoral program. In contrast to a proposed interdepartmental arrangement that would have overseen all scientists and engineers at MIT involved or interested in psychology, Teuber and his colleagues stressed the need for psychology as a core concept. Their aim was a strong and cohesive program with both educational and research components. Luke's view was supported by the visiting committee of the "parent" department and the MIT administration; by the end of the 1964 academic year, the MIT corporation conferred departmental status on psychology.

From its very beginning the department focused its efforts on what is now commonly called brain sciences. Three related parallel lines of interest were vigorously pursued: (1) brain and behavior (neuropsychology, neuroanatomy, and neurophysiology); (2) experimental psychology (perception and learning); and (3) social and developmental psychology, with an emphasis on comparative aspects (sensorimotor development, cognition and language acquisition, and psycholinguistics).

Weiskrantz has succinctly summarized the department's further development under Teuber's leadership:

> To it he attracted scientists of great distinction from a variety of disciplines, as well as younger persons whose promise later was fulfilled; the contributions of his colleagues were as important in neurophysiology as in experimental psychology. He worked unceasingly to attract funds for their endeavors and to promote a genuinely interdisciplinary atmosphere, warm and paternalistic, in which he and his colleagues could flourish. The MIT department became an almost compulsory stopping-off point in the U.S.A. for scientists from throughout the world with interests in brain function and psychology; they were invariably greeted with great hospitality and kindness, their seminars almost always continuing at the Teubers' home late into the evening, surrounded by a formidable but enthusiastic circle of graduate students.[7]

To this day the full-time faculty of the department includes Walle J. H. Nauta (Institute Professor), who came from the Walter Reed Institute of Research; Emilio Bizzi, whom Lukas brought from the National Institutes of Health; Richard Held and Alan Hein from Brandeis University; Stephan L. Chorover, who came with Teuber from NYU; and Ann M. Graybiel, Whitman Richards, Peter H. Schiller, and Gerald E. Schneider, all of whom received their doctoral degrees at MIT.

Teuber's scientific interests are succinctly summarized in

[7] L. Weiskrantz, "Hans-Lukas Teuber," p. 486.

the title of one of his many invited addresses, "The Brain and Human Behavior": "What we want to know," he said, "is nothing less than what goes on within ourselves (and by that we mean within our central nervous system) when we perceive, when we move, when we feel (or express emotions), and when we learn or remember."[8] In pursuit of this ambitious goal, his research, which was usually a collaborative effort, can be divided into roughly three periods.[9]

The first phase—with Bender in San Diego—has already been mentioned. It dealt mainly with visual and perceptual changes related to occipital injuries in a small number of brain-damaged individuals. This work was characterized by three qualities: (1) an emphasis on how different examination procedures provide different answers regarding the nature of the deficits; (2) a de-emphasis on the localization aspect of the effects; and (3) the necessity of complementing clinical studies with precise, detailed laboratory investigations. The French neuropsychologist Hecaen has underscored the impact Teuber's approach has had on contemporary neurological procedures.

The work carried out in New York University's Psychophysiological Laboratory constitutes the second phase. When Teuber went to New York in the spring of 1947, he persuaded the Veterans Administration to allow him to draw up lists of World War II veterans who had relatively stable and chronic lesions after receiving penetrating head wounds. After preliminary interviews at VA hospitals, selected patients were invited to participate in the research project at the New York University Medical School. The traumatized

---

[8] H.-L. Teuber, "The Brain and Human Behavior," in *Handbook of Sensory Physiology*, ed. R. Held, H. W. Leibowitz, and H.-L. Teuber, vol. 8, *Perception* (Heidelberg: Springer-Verlag, 1978), p. 880.

[9] H. Hécaen, "H.-L. Teuber et la Fondation de la Neuropsychologie Experimentale," *Neuropsychologia*, vol. 17, no. 2(1979):119–24.

veterans were not chosen on the basis of clinical needs or complaints but simply because they had suffered a head injury. Prior to the head injury they had been healthy young men with no signs of brain pathology.

Working with a large brain-injured population, Teuber and his colleagues developed a battery of precise tests encompassing the tactile, auditory, and visual domains. The resulting data led them to an increased recognition of the importance of problems of functional localization and functional hemispheric lateralization. It became possible to specify the unilateral or bilateral nature of the difficulties; and, as Hécaen points out, by demonstrating the significant associations among the symptoms, it became possible to reveal the functional deficit responsible for the various behavioral manifestations.

A unique feature of this research, and one strongly influenced by Teuber's early work, was the introduction of a large, matched control group. This group was made up of veterans with peripheral nerve wounds; their performance on the battery of tests was used to establish norms. Matched control groups today are de rigueur in scientific studies, and Lashley had used control groups in his animal studies on the effects of brain lesions, but their use was not standard procedure in human neurological testing and diagnosis. Another instance of Teuber's awareness of the importance of control groups came later when he served as a member of the Biosciences Subcommittee of the National Aeronautics and Space Administration. He insisted that matched controls be identified on earth in experiments that involved sending single monkeys—who belong to a naturally gregarious group—off into space. The single, isolated space-borne monkey did die (as Teuber had predicted), but so did several similarly isolated monkeys in the control group on earth.

Another important Teuber contribution—the principle

of the "double dissociation of symptoms"—was designed to offset the uncertainty of verifying a lesion site. In order for a particular deficit to be considered attributable to a particular lesion, the lesion has to "determine" the deficit to the exclusion of another type of deficit, caused by a lesion at a different site that does not involve the first deficit. This principle quickly became a fundamental tenet in animal and human neuropsychological methodology by serving as a check on the validity of experimental results.

As his work progressed, Teuber came to see the principles of cerebral localization in a broader perspective. As evidence accumulated, he drew the conclusion that bilateral hemispheric lesions could produce consequences that were not the equivalent of simply adding two unilateral lesions. On the other hand, disorders of hemispheric interaction could result from unilateral lesions. Ultimately, the brain-injured population that Teuber worked with totaled 520 cases; the original World War II group of veterans had been augmented by cases from both the Korean and the Vietnam wars.

The third phase of Teuber's research contributions began with his recognition of the importance of the concept of corollary discharge. This hypothesis derived from formulations by von Holst and Mittelstaedt[10] and, independently, by Sperry,[11] and it led Teuber to begin rethinking the relationships between perceptual and motor behavior and their cerebral correlates. He advanced the hypothesis that mechanisms of internal stimulation, as distinct from external sensory stimulation, could provide the necessary stability for human perceptions and the spatial and temporal framework

[10] E. von Holst and H. Mittelstaedt, "Das Reafferenzprinzip (Wechselswirkungen zwischen Zentralnervensystem und Peripherie)," *Naturwissenschaften*, 37(1950):464–76.

[11] R. W. Sperry, "Neural Basis of the Spontaneous Optokinetic Response Produced by Visual Inversion," *Journal of Comparative and Physiological Psychology*, 43 (1950):482–89.

for action, a notion that helped to throw light on a variety of frontal lobe disorders.

Teuber described corollary discharge as follows:

> Specifically, we postulate that when we make deliberate voluntary movements (e.g., shift our eyes across the room), *two* streams of signals are initiated within our nervous system, and not only one. One of these two is of course the classical motor outflow to the effector organs. The other set of signals is sent, directly and centrally, to the sensory systems, so that the consequences of the intended action can be taken into account.
>
> We call these discharges "corollary" when they are essentially derivations of momentary motor commands, and "anticipatory" when more remote consequences of the impending action are being computed. In either case, these signals . . . involve an information flow that is the reverse of the classical Sherrington one: not from sensory to motor, from back to front, so to speak, but in the opposite direction, from motor and premotor to sensory and therefore from front to back.[12]

The concept was used to interpret results related to visual searching behavior, curious abnormalities in the reversal of certain types of reversible figures, and breakdowns in sorting and categorizing behavior. As was his wont, Teuber sought to give the notion a solid base in neurophysiology by relating the concept to single cell studies of his own colleagues and related research in other laboratories.

Teuber's move to MIT coincided with rapid advances in electrophysiology and neuroanatomy in laboratories throughout the world. He and his colleagues, however, who were at the forefront of this specialized research, went beyond relating new data from anatomy, physiology, and studies of single neurons to perceptual-motor behavior. They attempted to relate these findings to simple and complex perceptual events (e.g., facial recognition), to problems of language (e.g., acquisition and impairments of production or reception of speech), and to problems of mood and memory (e.g., am-

---

[12] H.-L. Teuber, "The Brain and Human Behavior," p. 900.

nesias). The relative innateness and limits of modifiability of the postulated neurophysiological mechanisms were major concerns of Teuber's in each of the problem areas he touched on.

Teuber recognized that "the key questions about perception and movement, memory and mood remain unanswered"; but he was confident that the "converging evolution of experimental psychology, physiology and microanatomy together with comparative and developmental studies are bound to take us ever closer to our common goal: that of gaining a rational understanding of ourselves."[13] In moving toward this goal he was untiring in his efforts as researcher, administrator, teacher, and promoter of neuropsychology—both at home and abroad.

More than anyone else he helped bring together scientists—both young and old—with diverse backgrounds but mutual interests, hosting their discussions at his departmental colloquia, seminars, scientific meetings, and symposia. He lectured fluently with wit, humor, and brilliance in three languages: German, French, and English. As an "insightful, popular, and expansive reviewer at international meetings—even as a helpful translator for foreigners, the duration of his commentaries was apt to exceed, by a considerable amount, that occupied by the original speaker."[14] As Ann Graybiel reminds us, Lukas was often teased about this trait, but as she says, "He was by nature impish"; "he was a tease, and he loved to be teased."[15] His summations were usually brilliant, his introductions always entertaining and informative, and his classroom lectures—he was among MIT's most popular lecturers—drew standing-room-only audiences. In presentations as well as in conversation, he made no effort to

---

[13] H.-L. Teuber, "The Brain and Human Behavior," p. 912.
[14] L. Weiskrantz, "Hans-Lukas Teuber," p. 486.
[15] Transcript of a gathering to remember Hans-Lukas Teuber, p. 13.

suppress his contagious delight, but his listeners always needed to keep a close watch on his expressive eyebrows, which often punctuated—or punctured—a point.

His gentleness, his warmth and consideration for others, are epitomized by his advocating and helping to institute at MIT the first committee to protect human subjects from untoward effects of psychological and other forms of experimentation. The MIT Review Committee on Human Subjects antedates by several years the university review committees set up under the supervision of the National Institutes of Health.

His concern for the unethical use of scientific knowledge led him to resign as chairman of the Advisory Committee to the Surgeon General of the U.S. Army when his committee was asked to develop a policy for the use of LSD and other mind-altering drugs. Moral decisions must always be primary, he claimed. And when it comes to the application of science, scientists must be citizens first and, together with others, protect all human beings from the abuses of science and from ignorance.

Professor Hécaen paid Teuber the highest tribute when he wrote that Teuber's works made him "the founder and guiding spirit of contemporary neuropsychology."[16] Teuber's posthumously published address, "The Brain and Human Behavior," which was delivered on July 20, 1976, at the 21st International Psychology Congress in Paris, concludes:

> For millennia, we have tried to comprehend the universe around us; the time has come, during this last century, and is now here, to attempt to comprehend ourselves. To this end, all the sciences have to be put to the service of man's understanding of man. Psychology finds its identity, I propose, by its subject matter, not by its methods.
>
> It is clear that our particular science is as central as physics, and ulti-

---

[16] H. Hécaen, "H.-L. Teuber et la Fondation de la Neuropsychologie Experimentale," p. 122.

mately more so. But it is also capable of as much abuse as physics. As Lord Adrian once said, "He who can first explain and control paranoia will have found the means of producing it." Yet just for that reason, all of us here who are concerned with furthering man's understanding of man will have to abide by a new kind of hippocratic oath, never to do harm, always to heal rather than hinder, to make human life richer, and to make it free.[17]

It seems appropriate to conclude this memoir with two brief excerpts from the citation prepared by his MIT colleagues for the James M. Killian Faculty Achievement Award (1976–77):

> Hans-Lukas Teuber, Professor of Psychology, founder and head of the Department of Psychology at the Massachusetts Institute of Technology, is a man who joins the instincts of a penetrating experimenter and the experience of a brain scientist with the consummate style of a gifted teacher. In that many-sided image, he has created the Department where he never ceases to support, by precept and example, his three-fold ends: informed observation, keen experiment, and the generosity and wit to make the fruits of science available to all. . . . Even that is not all. Many of us do not forget his long hours of talking and sharing with troubled and angry students during the terrible years of the war in Southeast Asia. He displays two high gifts, that of a scientist's perpetual wonder at the mysteries of brain and behavior, and that of an artist's compassion for the springs of thought and action in his fellow human beings.

THE AUTHORS would like to thank Marianne Teuber for her generous assistance in the preparation of this memoir.

---

[17] H.-L. Teuber, "The Brain and Human Behavior," p. 913.

HONORS AND DISTINCTIONS

HONORARY DEGREES

Université Claude Bernard, Lyon, France, Doctor of Medicine, 1975
Université de Genève, Switzerland, Doctor of Psychology, 1975

VISITING LECTURESHIPS AND PROFESSORSHIPS

Eastman Professor, University of Oxford, England, 1971–1972
Christmas Lecturer, Illinois Science Lecture Series, Chicago, 1974
Philips Lecturer, Haverford College, Pennsylvania, 1975

AWARDS

Karl Spencer Lashley Award for Research in Neurobiology, American Philosophical Society, 1966
Apollo Achievement Award, NASA, 1969
Kenneth Craik Award in Experimental Psychology, St. Johns College, Cambridge, England, 1971
James R. Killian Faculty Achievement Award, Massachusetts Institute of Technology, 1976–1977

HONORARY AND ELECTED MEMBERSHIPS

National Academy of Sciences, 1972
American Academy of Arts and Sciences, 1962
Society of Experimental Psychologists, 1960
National Institute of Neurology Faculty, Mexico, 1967
French Neurological Society, 1968
Institute of Medicine, 1975–1977
Sigma Xi

SCIENTIFIC AND PROFESSIONAL SOCIETIES

American Academy of Neurology
American Association for the Advancement of Science
American Neurological Association
American Psychological Association
Association for Research in Nervous and Mental Diseases
Eastern Psychological Association
European Brain and Behavior Society
French Psychological Society (associé étranger)

International Brain Research Organization
Psychonomic Society
Society for Neuroscience

EDITORIAL POSITIONS

Coeditor, *Experimental Brain Research,* 1965–1977
Berlin Editorial Board, Springer-Verlag, *Handbook of Sensory Physiology,* 1967
Consulting editor, *Journal of Comparative and Physiological Psychology,* 1956–1968
Consulting editor, *Journal of Nervous and Mental Disease,* 1961–1964
Editorial Board, *Journal of Psychiatric Research,* 1961–1964
Neuropsychologia, 1962–1977

PROFESSIONAL AND ADVISORY AFFILIATIONS

Professional Advisory Committee, Boston University Aphasia Center, 1975
Board of Directors, Foundations Fund for Research in Psychiatry, 1966–1969
International Brain Research Organization: Central Council Representative, 1968–1970; Chairman, 1970–1973; Chairman, Committee on Symposia, 1968–1974
Scientific Advisory Board, Massachusetts General Hospital, 1971–1974
Task Force in Behavioral Biology, National Academy of Sciences, 1965–1968
Biosciences Subcommittee, National Aeronautics and Space Administration, 1963–1970
National Institutes of Health:
Mental Health Study Section, National Institute of Mental Health, 1955–1958 and 1960–1961; Experimental Psychology Study Section, National Institute of Mental Health, 1961–1964; Neurology A Study Section, NINDB, 1964–1968
Behavioral Sciences Training Committee, National Institute of General Medical Sciences, 1969–1973
Head Injury Section, National Institute of Neurological Diseases and Blindness, 1967–1969
Scientific Advisory Committee, New England Regional Primate Center, 1971–1977

Biological and Behavioral Sciences Panels, Office of Scientific Research, U.S. Air Force, 1962–1965
Advisory Committee on Psychophysiology, Office of the Surgeon General: Member, 1958–1960; Chairman, 1960–1963
Research Advisory Committee, United Cerebral Palsy Association, 1959–1969
Area Consultant in Psychology, U.S. Veterans Administration, 1947–1960
Research Group on Head Injuries, World Federation of Neurology and the World Federation of Neurological Sciences, 1967–1969

BIBLIOGRAPHY

1946

Nystagmoid movements and visual perception (their interrelation in monocular diplopia). Arch. Neurol. Psychiatry (Chicago), 55:511–29.

With M. B. Bender. Phenomena of fluctuation, extinction and completion in visual perception. Arch. Neurol. Psychiatry (Chicago), 55:627–58.

With M. B. Bender. Ring scotoma and tubular fields: Their significance in cases of head injury. Arch. Neurol. Psychiatry (Chicago), 56:300–326.

With M. B. Bender. Disturbances in the visual perception of space after brain injury. Trans. Am. Neurol. Assoc., 71:159–61.

1947

The dyadic group: A study in counselling relationships. Ph.D. thesis, Harvard University.

With M. B. Bender. Spatial organization of visual perception following injury to the brain. Arch. Neurol. Psychiatry (Chicago), 58:721–39.

1948

With M. B. Bender. Spatial organization of visual perception following injury to the brain. Arch. Neurol. Psychiatry (Chicago), 59:39–63. (Continued from Arch. Neurol. Psychiatry [Chicago], 58[1947]:721–39.)

1949

With M. B. Bender. Alterations in pattern vision following trauma of occipital lobes in man. J. Gen. Psychol., 40:37–57.

With M. B. Bender and L. T. Furlow. Alterations in behavior after massive cerebral trauma (intraventricular foreign body). Confin. Neurol., 9:140–57.

With W. S. Battersby and M. B. Bender. Changes in visual searching performance following cerebral lesions. Am. J. Physiol., 159:592–93.

With M. B. Bender. Disturbances in visual perception following cerebral lesions. J. Psychol., 28:223–33.

With M. B. Bender. Psychopathology of vision. In: *Progress in Neurology and Psychiatry*, ed. E. A. Spiegel, pp. 163–92. New York: Grune & Stratton.
With M. B. Bender and M. F. Shapiro. Allesthesia and disturbance of the body scheme. Arch. Neurol. Psychiatry (Chicago), 62:222–31.

1950

Neuropsychology. A summary of recent advances in diagnostic methods. In: *Recent Advances in Diagnostic Psychological Testing: A Critical Summary*, pp. 30–52. Springfield, Ill.: C. C. Thomas.

1951

Review of *Recovery from Aphasia* by J. M. Wepman. J. Abnorm. Soc. Psychol., 46:610.
With M. B. Bender. Neuro-ophthalmology: The oculomotor system. In: *Progress in Neurology and Psychiatry*, vol. 6, ed. E. A. Spiegel, pp. 148–78. New York: Grune & Stratton.
With W. S. Battersby and M. B. Bender. Performance of complex visual tasks after cerebral lesions. J. Nerv. Ment. Dis., 114:413–29.
With W. S. Battersby and M. B. Bender. Effects of total light flux on critical flicker frequency after frontal lobe lesion. J. Exp. Psychol., 42:135–42.
With M. B. Bender and W. S. Battersby. Visual field defects after gunshot wounds of higher visual pathways. Trans. Am. Neurol. Assoc., 76:192–94.

1952

Some observations on the organization of higher functions after penetrating brain injury in man. In: *The Biology of Mental Health and Disease*, pp. 259–62. (Proceedings of the twenty-seventh Annual Conference of the Milbank Memorial Fund.) New York: Hoeber.
With M. Mead and H. Von Foerster. Introduction. In: *Cybernetics*, ed. L. W. Neustedt. New York: Macy.

1953

With E. Powers. Evaluating therapy in a delinquency prevention program. In: *Psychiatric Treatment*, pp. 138–47. Baltimore: Williams & Wilkins.

With W. S. Battersby and M. B. Bender. Problem-solving behavior in men with frontal or occipital brain injuries. J. Psychol., 35:329–51.

1954

With M. Mishkin. Judgement of visual and postural vertical after brain injury. J. Psychol., 38:161–75.

With M. Mishkin. Performances on a formboard-task after penetrating brain injury. J. Psychol., 38:177–90.

With E. B. Krueger and P. A. Price. Tactile extinction in a parietal lobe neoplasm. J. Psychol., 38:191–202.

With J. Semmes, S. Weinstein, and L. Ghent. Performance on complex tactual tasks after brain injury in man: Analyses by locus of lesion. Am. J. Psychol., 67:220–40.

1955

Physiological psychology. Annu. Rev. Psychol., 6:267–96.

With L. Ghent, S. Weinstein, and J. Semmes. Effect of unilateral brain injury in man on learning of a tactual discrimination. J. Comp. Physiol. Psychol., 48:478–81.

With J. Semmes, S. Weinstein, and L. Ghent. Spatial orientation in man after cerebral injury. I. Analyses by locus of lesion. J. Psychol., 39:227–44.

1956

With S. Weinstein. Ability to discover hidden figures after cerebral lesions. Arch. Neurol. Psychiatry (Chicago), 76:369–79.

With S. Weinstein, J. Semmes, and L. Ghent. Spatial orientation in man after cerebral injury. II. Analysis according to concomitant defects. J. Psychol., 42:249–63.

1957

With S. Weinstein. Effects of penetrating brain injury on intelligence test scores. Science, 125:1036–37.

With S. Weinstein. The role of preinjury education and intelligence level in intellectual loss after brain injury. J. Comp. Physiol. Psychol., 50:535–39.

1958

Appréciation de la récupération de fonction après lésions cérébrales. Revue Psychol. Appl., 8:129–41.
With R. S. Liebert. Specific and general effects of brain injury in man. Arch. Neurol. Psychiatry (Chicago), 80:403–7.

1959

Some alterations in behavior after cerebral lesions in man. In: *Evolution of Nervous Control from Primitive Organisms to Man*, ed. A. D. Bass, pp. 157–94. Washington, D.C.: American Association for the Advancement of Science.
Report and discussion. In: *Conference on the Central Nervous System: Transactions of the First Conference*, ed. M. A. B. Brazier, pp. 393–99. New York: Macy.

1960

Perception. In: *Handbook of Physiology*, sec. 1, vol. 3, ed. J. Field, H. W. Magoun, and V. E. Hall, pp. 1595–668. Washington, D.C.: American Physiological Society.
The premorbid personality and reaction to brain damage. Am. J. Orthopsychiatry, 30:322–29.
Review of *Einführung in die Pharmakopsychologie* by H. Lippert. Contemp. Psychol., 5:357–58.
Alterations in perception after brain injury in man. In: *Perception and Psychopathology, Proceedings of the third Annual University of Kansas Institute on Research in Clinical Psychology*, ed. M. E. Wright, pp. 89–121. Lawrence: University of Kansas Press.
With W. S. Battersby and M. B. Bender. *Visual Field Defects After Penetrating Missile Wounds of the Brain*. Cambridge, Mass.: Harvard University Press.
With R. G. Rudel, R. S. Liebert, and S. Halpern. Localization of auditory midline and reactions to body tilt in brain-damaged children. J. Nerv. Ment. Dis., 131:302–9.
With J. Semmes, S. Weinstein, and L. Ghent. *Somatosensory Changes After Penetrating Brain Wounds in Man*. Cambridge, Mass.: Harvard University Press.

1961

Sensory deprivation, sensory suppression and agnosia: Notes for a neurologic theory. J. Nerv. Ment. Dis., 132:32–40.

Summation. In: *Brain and Behavior, Proceedings of the First AIBS Conference,* ed. M. A. B. Brazier, pp. 393–420. Washington, D.C.: American Institute of Biological Science.

Some observations on the superior colliculi of the cat (report on the work of J. Altman). In: *Neurophysiologie und Psychophysik des visuellen Systems,* ed. R. Jung and H. Kornhuber, pp. 217–20. Heidelberg: Springer.

Neuere Beobachtungen über Sehstrahlung und Sehrinde. In: *Neurophysiologie und Psychophysik des visuellen Systems,* ed. R. Jung and H. Kornhuber, pp. 256–74. Heidelberg: Springer.

1962

Memory. N.Y. Med., 18:248–50.

Perspectives in the problems of biological memory—a psychologist's view. In: *Macromolecular Specificity and Biological Memory,* ed. F. O. Schmitt, pp. 99–107. Cambridge, Mass.: MIT Press.

Effects of brain wounds implicating right or left hemisphere in man: Hemisphere differences and hemisphere interaction in vision, audition and somesthesis. Discussion. In: *Interhemispheric Relations and Cerebral Dominance,* ed. V. B. Mountcastle, pp. 203–8. Baltimore: Johns Hopkins Press.

With R. G. Rudel. Behavior after cerebral lesions in children and adults. Dev. Med. Child Neurol., 4:3–20.

With R. G. Rudel. Effects of brain injury in children and adults. In: *Clinical Psychology: Proceedings of the Fourteenth Congress of Applied Psychology,* vol. 4, pp. 113–39. Copenhagen: Munksgaard.

With L. Ghent and M. Mishkin. Short-term memory after frontal-lobe injury in man. J. Comp. Physiol. Psychol., 55:705–9.

1963

Space perception and its disturbances after brain injury in man. (For W. Köhler, *Festschrift,* 1962.) Neuropsychologia, 1:47–57.

Discussion. In: *Brain and Behavior: Proceedings of the Second AIBS Conference,* ed. M. A. B. Brazier, pp. 146–51, 247. Washington, D.C.: American Institute of Biological Science.

Personality and reaction to brain damage. In: *Contributions to Modern Psychology,* 2d ed., ed. D. E. Dulaney, R. L. DeValois, D. C. Beardslee, and M. R. Winterbottom, pp. 406–14. New York: Oxford University Press.

Discussion of "Polyopia and palinopia in homonymous fields of vision" by M. B. Bender and A. J. Sobin. Trans. Am. Neurol. Assoc., 88:58.

Discussion of "Perceptual defects in both visual fields in attention hemianopia" by S. Horenstein and T. R. Carey. Trans. Am. Neurol. Assoc., 88:63–64.

With R. G. Rudel. Decrement of visual and haptic Muller-Lyer illusion on repeated trials: A study of crossmodal transfer. Q. J. Exp. Psychol., 15:125–31.

With R. G. Rudel. Discrimination of direction of line in children. J. Comp. Physiol. Psychol., 56:892–98.

With V. Myer and C. G. Gross. Effect of knowledge of site of stimulation on the threshold for pressure sensitivity. Percept. Mot. Skills, 16:637–40.

With F. Proctor, M. Riklan, and I. S. Cooper. Somatosensory status of parkinsonian patients before and after chemothalamectomy. Neurology, 13:906–12.

With J. Semmes, S. Weinstein, and L. Ghent. Correlates of impaired orientation in personal and extrapersonal space. Brain, 86:747–72.

1964

The riddle of frontal lobe function in man. In: *The Frontal Granular Cortex and Behavior,* ed. J. M. Warren and K. Akert, pp. 410–44. New York: McGraw-Hill.

Speech as a motor skill. In: *The Acquisition of Language,* ed. U. Bellugi and R. W. Brown, pp. 131–38. Monographs of the Society for Research in Child Development.

Discussions. In: *Disorders of Language,* ed. A. V. S. De Reuck and M. O'Conner. Transactions of the Ciba Foundation Symposium. London: Churchill.

Discussion. In: *Learning, Remembering and Forgetting: The Anatomy of Learning,* vol. 1, ed. D. P. Kimble. Washington, D.C.: American Institute of Biological Science.

Discussion of "Effects of different cortical excisions on sensory

thresholds in man" by S. Corkin, B. Milner, and T. Rasmussen. Trans. Am. Neurol. Assoc., 89.
Discussion of "Impaired delayed response from thalamic lesions in monkeys" by S. Schulman. Trans. Am. Neurol. Assoc., 89.
With F. Proctor. Some effects of basal ganglia lesions in subhuman primates and man. Neuropsychologia, 2:85–93.
With R. G. Rudel. Crossmodal transfer of shape discrimination by children. Neuropsychologia, 2:1–8.
With F. Proctor, M. Riklan, and I. S. Cooper. Judgement of visual and postural vertical by parkinsonian patients. Neurology, 14:287–93.

1965

Alterations of perception after brain injury. In: *Semaine d'Etude sur Cerveau et Expérience Consciente*, pp. 269–310. Pontificae Academiae Scientiarum Scripta Varia. Rome: The Vatican.
Disorders of higher tactile and visual functions. Neuropsychologia, 3:287–94.
Postscript: Some needed revisions of the classical views of agnosia. Neuropsychologia, 3:371–78.
Effects of occipital lobe lesion on pattern vision. In: *Proceedings of the Eighth International Neurological Congress, Supplement*, Vienna, September, pp. 79–102.

1966

Alterations in perception after brain injury. In: *Brain and Conscious Experience*, ed. J. C. Eccles, pp. 182–216. New York: Springer.
The frontal lobes and their function: Further observations on rodents, carnivores, subhuman primates, and man. Int. J. Neurol., 5:282–300.
Kurt Goldstein's role in the development of neuropsychology. Neuropsychologia, 4:299–310.
Some behavioral consequences of frontal-lobe lesions in rodents, carnivores and primates. In: *Proceedings of the Eighteenth International Congress on Psychology*, Moscow, vol. 10, pp. 90–96.
The lesson of focal brain injury. In: *Proceedings of the Eighteenth International Congress on Psychology*, Moscow, vol. 26, pp. 12–18.
Preface. In: A. R. Luria, *Highest Cortical Functions in Man*. New York: Basic Books.

Preface. In: A. R. Luria, *Human Brain and Psychological Processes.* New York: Harper.
Summation: Convergences, divergences, lacunae. In: *Brain and Conscious Experience,* ed. J. C. Eccles, pp. 575–83. New York: Springer.
With R. G. Rudel and T. E. Twitchell. A note on hyperesthesia in children with early brain damage. Neuropsychologia, 4:351–66.
With T. E. Twitchell, A. R. Lecours, and R. G. Rudel. Minimal cerebral dysfunction in children: Motor deficits. Trans. Am. Neurol. Assoc., 91:353–55.

1967

Lacunae and research approaches to them. In: *Brain Mechanisms Underlying Speech and Language,* ed. F. L. Darley, pp. 204–16. New York: Grune & Stratton.
Wolfgang Köhler zum Gedenken. Psychol. Forsch., 31:1–14.

1968

Disorders of memory following penetrating missile wounds of the brain. Neurology, 18:287–88.
With B. Milner and H. Vaughan. Persistent anterograde amnesia after stab wound of the basal brain. Neuropsychologia, 6:267–82.
With B. Milner. Alteration of perception and memory in man: Reflections on methods. In: *Analysis of Behavioral Change,* ed. L. Weiskrantz, pp. 268–375. New York: Harper & Row.
With B. Milner and S. Corkin. Further analysis of the hippocampal amnesic syndrome: 14-year follow-up study of H. M. Neuropsychologia, 6:215–34.

1969

Wahrnehmung, Willkürbewegung und Gedächtnis. Stud. Gen., 22:1135–78.
Neglected aspects of the post-traumatic syndrome. In: *The Late Effects of Head Injury,* ed. A. E. Walker, W. F. Caveness, and M. Critchley, pp. 13–34. Springfield, Ill.: C. C. Thomas.
Recommendations (post-traumatic syndrome). In: *The Late Effects*

of *Head Injury*, ed. A. E. Walker, W. F. Caveness, and M. Critchley. Springfield, Ill.: C. C. Thomas.

1970

Discussions. In: *Psychotomimetic Drugs*, ed. D. H. Efron, pp. 215–16, 220–28, 312–15, 338–43. New York: Raven Press.
Sensation and perception. In: *Biology and the Future of Man*, ed. P. H. Handler, pp. 416–28. New York: Oxford University Press.

1971

Mental retardation after early trauma to the brain: Some issues in search of facts. In: *Physical Trauma as an Etiological Agent in Mental Retardation*, ed. C. R. Angle and E. A. Bering, Jr., pp. 7–28. Bethesda, Md.: National Institutes of Health.
L'hypothèse des décharges corollaires. In: *La Fonction du Regard*, ed. A. Dubois Poulson, G. C. Lairy, and A. Remond. Paris: INSERM.
Subcortical vision: A prologue. In: *Brain, Behavior and Evolution*, ed. W. Riss, pp. 7–15. Basel: S. Karger.
Perception et mouvement. In: *Neuropsychologie de la Perception Visuelle*, ed. H. Hecaen, pp. 187–221. Paris: Masson & Cie.
With R. G. Rudel. Spatial orientation in normal children and in children with early brain injury. Neuropsychologia, 9:401–7.
With R. G. Rudel. Pattern recognition within and across sensory modalities in normal and brain injured children. Neuropsychologia, 9:389–99.

1972

Effects of focal brain lesions. III. Neurophysiology. Neurosci. Res. Program Bull., 10:381–84.
Unity and diversity of frontal lobe functions. Acta Neurol. Exp., 32:615–56.

1973

With F. Koerner. Visual field defects after missile injuries to the geniculo-striate pathway in man. Exp. Brain Res., 18:88–113.
With J. Lackner. Alterations in auditory fusion thresholds after cerebral injury in man. Neuropsychologia, 11:408–15.
With B. T. Woods. Early onset of complementary specialization of

cerebral hemispheres in man. Trans. Am. Neurol. Assoc., 98:113–17.

1974

Why two brains? In: *The Neurosciences: Third Study Program*, ed. F. O. Schmitt and F. G. Worden, pp. 71–74. Cambridge, Mass.: MIT.

Psychological effects of trauma. In: *Study of Injured Patients*, pp. 79–81. Trauma Research Programs. Bethesda, Md.: National Institute of General Medical Sciences.

Recovery of function after lesions of the central nervous system: History and prospects. In: *Functional Recovery After Lesions of the Nervous System*, ed. E. Eidelberg and D. G. Stein. Neurosci. Res. Program Bull., 12:197–209.

Concluding session: Motor programs. (Presented at the Colloque du Centre National de la Recherche Scientifique, no. 226: Comportement moteur et activités nerveuses programmés.) Brain Res., 71:535–68.

Contribution. In: *Transactions of the Common Session and Round Table: Eighth International Congress of Electroencephalography and Clinical Neurophysiology.* Electroencephalogr. Clin. Neurophysiol., 36:561–76.

With R. G. Rudel and T. E. Twitchell. Levels of impairment of sensorimotor functions in children with early brain damage. Neuropsychologia, 12:95–108.

1975

Recovery of function after brain injury in man. In: *Outcome of Severe CNS Damage*, Ciba Foundation Symposium, pp. 159–90. Amsterdam: Elsevier.

Effects of focal brain injury on human behavior. In: *The Nervous System, The Clinical Neurosciences*, vol. 2, ed. D. B. Tower, pp. 457–80. New York: Raven Press.

With G. Ettlinger and B. Milner. The Seventeenth International Symposium of Neuropsychology. Neuropsychologia, 13:125–33.

With W. Marslen-Wilson. Memory for remote events in anterograde amnesia: Recognition of public figures from newsphotographs. Neuropsychologia, 13:353–64.

1976

Complex functions of the basal ganglia. In: *The Basal Ganglia*, ed. M. D. Yahr, pp. 151–68. New York: Raven Press.

De la perception à la mémoire: Problèmes persistantes de la neuropsychologie. Lyon Med., 236:661–71.

Plasticité nerveuse et début du développement. Bull. Psychol., Paris, 30(Piaget *Festschrift*):376–86.

With S. Corkin and T. E. Twitchell. *A Study of Cingulotomy in Man.* (A report to the National Commission for the Protection of Human Subjects of Biomedical and Behavioral Research.) Bethesda, Md.: National Institutes of Health.

1977

Shades of blindness. Neurosci. Res. Program Bull., 15:346–48.

With S. Corkin and T. E. Twitchell. A study of cingulotomy in man: A summary. In: *Neurosurgical Treatment in Psychiatry, Pain and Epilepsy*, ed. W. H. Sweet, pp. 355–62. Baltimore: University Park Press.

With B. T. Woods. Changing patterns of childhood aphasia. Trans. Am. Neurol. Assoc., 102:36–38.

1978

The brain and human behavior. In: *Proceedings of the Twenty-First International Congress on Psychology*, Paris, pp. 119–63.

The brain and human behavior. In: *Handbook of Sensory Physiology*. vol. 8, *Perception*, ed. R. Held, H. Leibowitz, and H.-L. Teuber, pp. 879–920. Heidelberg: Springer-Verlag.

With B. T. Woods. Changing patterns of childhood aphasia. Ann. Neurol., 3:273–80.

With B. T. Woods. Mirror movements after childhood hemiparesis. Neurology, 28:1154–58.

WARREN WEAVER

July 17, 1894–November 24, 1978

BY MINA REES

INTRODUCTION

WARREN WEAVER died on November 24, 1978, at his home in New Milford, Connecticut. The New Milford house in the Connecticut countryside was a haven of beauty and peace. It had been conceived and planned and built with full concern for all the little details that were important to him and to Mary, his wife of many years, as they looked forward to the happy years together after Warren's retirement. They had been fellow students at the University of Wisconsin—she was Mary Hemenway then—and their marriage a few years after their graduation brought them an affectionate family life, shared by their son, Warren Jr. (and his family), and their daughter, Helen.

Warren Weaver started his career as a teacher of mathematics. But before his thirty-eighth birthday he became a foundation executive when he accepted the post of director of the Division of Natural Sciences of the Rockefeller Foundation. In that role he exercised a profound influence on the development of biology worldwide, and it was probably for this that he was best known during his lifetime. During his years as an officer of the Rockefeller Foundation, however, and during his service as an officer of the Sloan Foundation after his retirement from the Rockefeller post, his influence on many other aspects of science expanded and its impact was broadly felt.

Weaver assumed the vice-presidency of the Sloan Foundation immediately after his statutory retirement from the Rockefeller Foundation in 1959. But he reduced the amount of time he spent at his office so that he would have more time for his family and the extensive property at his New Milford home. He liked intellectual work, but he also loved to do physical work—chopping wood, moving rocks, gardening, puttering in his shop. He worked all the time: in a doctor's office (whether the wait was five minutes or half an hour) or on a commuter train—and he commuted regularly. He found these bits of time important. And he found the work that he was able to do in these moments very rewarding.

These personal qualities, combined with his great pleasure in working with and absorbing new ideas in physics and new results across a broad spectrum of scientific research, made possible his extraordinarily productive life. His performance as a philanthropoid (his term) was exemplary; in addition to the Rockefeller and Sloan Foundation positions, he also held responsible posts in the civilian scientific effort that supported the military services during World War II. After the war his achievements as an expositor of science gave him a distinctive role in the growing movement to promote the understanding of science on the part of the nonscientific public.

These are the main themes to which I shall devote this memoir.

CAREER CHOICE, ARMY SERVICE, AND MARRIAGE

Weaver was born on July 17, 1894, in the little town of Reedsburg, Wisconsin (population circa 2,000). As a child he was shy, introspective, unskilled in sports, and often lonesome. His fondness for his elder brother Paul, which became a warm and important part of both their lives, developed only after their graduation from college. Paul took a job in banking—as a result of parental pressure—but soon rebelled and pursued his own vocation, becoming an accomplished pianist-organist and ending his career as head of the School of Music at Cornell. Warren's career had a more intriguing genesis.

When Warren was a youngster, his father, who was a pharmacist, made an annual buying trip to purchase the drugstore's supply of Christmas toys for the coming holiday season. It was traditional for him to return with a gift for each of the boys. After one of these trips, Warren received a small electric motor that was powered by a dry cell. It was labeled "Ajax" and cost a dollar. As Warren wrote some sixty years later in a paper on careers in science:

> Within a few weeks I had built, with spools and similar household objects, all the little devices that could be run with the tiny torque of this motor. I took off the field winding, re-wound it—and it would still run! Getting more adventuresome, I took off the armature winding and discovered how it had to be put back on so as to recapture the miracle of movement.
>
> I promptly decided that this was for me. I didn't know any name to apply to this sort of activity—I didn't know (or care, I suspect) whether anyone could earn his living doing this kind of thing. But it was perfectly clear to me that taking things apart and finding out how they are constructed and how they work was exciting, stimulating, and tremendous fun.
>
> It may well be the case that in the small rural village where I lived ... there was not a single person who had any real concept of what the word "science" meant. I was accordingly told that this was "engineering"; and from that time until I was a junior in college, I assumed without question that I wanted to be an engineer.[1]

---

[1] Warren Weaver, "Careers in Science," in *Listen to Leaders in Science*, ed. Albert Love and James Saxon Childers (Atlanta: Tupper & Love/David McKay, 1965), p. 276.

It was at the University of Wisconsin that Warren—studying "Advanced Mathematics for Engineers"—realized that his enthusiasm was for science rather than for engineering. He decided to pursue a graduate degree in mathematics and theoretical physics as soon as this proved feasible. Immediately after receiving a degree in civil engineering in 1917 (he had earned a B.S. in mathematics in 1916), he accepted an invitation from Robert A. Millikan to become an assistant professor of mathematics at Throop College (soon to be renamed the California Institute of Technology). Millikan was just shifting his interests from Chicago to Pasadena and was planning to spend one academic quarter there each year. Max Mason, a brilliant mathematical physicist who had been Weaver's teacher and close friend at Wisconsin, suggested Weaver to Millikan. Mason and Charles Sumner Slichter, professor of applied mathematics at Wisconsin, were the two professors who most influenced Weaver's choice of a career. Mason would continue to be an important influence in his life in the years immediately ahead.

Weaver had been at Throop for less than a year when he was drafted into the Army at the request of Charles E. Mendenhall, chairman of the Physics Department at Wisconsin. Mendenhall was then serving as a major in the Army's unit associated with the newly formed National Research Council. Weaver was assigned to participate in one of the technical efforts, carried on chiefly at the National Bureau of Standards, to develop effective equipment to assist U.S. aviators in the air battles of World War I. He was discharged as a second lieutenant in about a year. After a brief interlude teaching at Wisconsin, he returned to Pasadena—but not before marrying Mary Hemenway and taking her back with him.

THE LIFE OF A PROFESSOR OF MATHEMATICS

The next year at Pasadena was delightful and stimulating. But in the spring of 1920, as the end of the academic year approached, a letter from Madison invited Weaver to join the faculty at Wisconsin. There was also a most important letter from Max Mason, who urged Warren to accept Wisconsin's offer and suggested that they work together on a book on electromagnetic field theory. For Warren this was irresistible—the opportunity to collaborate with Mason, whose insights, brilliance, and imagination he so greatly admired. And his own power as an expositor would be given full rein because Mason had no fondness for committing ideas to paper.

By the fall of 1920, the newlyweds were established in Madison, where they were to remain for the next twelve years. In 1921 Warren earned his Ph.D. His collaboration with Mason began promptly and was vigorously pursued. In 1925, however, Mason left to become president of the University of Chicago, while Weaver carried on alone in Madison, sending drafts to Mason in Chicago. In 1928 Weaver succeeded Edward Burr Van Vleck as chairman of the Department of Mathematics.

The Mason–Weaver book, *The Electromagnetic Field*, was published in 1929. For some years thereafter, it was the book from which many graduate students in physics learned Maxwell's field equations and the associated theory. For occasional physicists whom he met in later years, Warren Weaver became "Weaver, of Mason and Weaver."

Although his most important writing in the years at Madison was the collaboration with Mason, Weaver also published occasional papers in mathematics, chiefly in probability theory and statistics, subjects for which he continued to have great enthusiasm throughout his life. And in 1924 he published—jointly with Max Mason—what he called "a really good mathematical paper" that turned out to contain the fundamental analytical theory of the supercentrifuge.

The publication in 1963 of *Lady Luck,* his little book on probability, is an indication of his continuing interest in the subject and of his conviction that it should be accessible to laymen, particularly young students. *Lady Luck* is an instance of Weaver's rare gift of exposition. But his own estimate of most of the mathematical papers he published during his stay at Wisconsin was that they were routine solutions of specific problems, not real additions to mathematical knowledge. He complained that he never seemed to get a first-class original idea for advancing mathematics itself.

THE LURE OF THE ROCKEFELLER FOUNDATION

In 1931 a disturbing and unexpected invitation arrived from Max Mason, an invitation that raised the possibility of Weaver's leaving what he and his wife considered a nearly idyllic life in Madison. Mason had left the presidency of the University of Chicago in 1928 to take on responsibility for the work in the natural sciences that was supported by the Rockefeller Foundation; in 1930, he assumed the presidency of the foundation. In the fall of 1931, Mason invited Weaver to come to New York to discuss the possibility of his joining the staff of the Rockefeller Foundation as head of its program in the natural sciences. Weaver was reluctant to accept the invitation for many reasons. But the fact that it came from Mason and included a free trip to New York (which he had never seen) settled the matter. Weaver was off to New York.

The city itself proved at least as alluring as he had imagined—and the visit to the Rockefeller Foundation as tempting. Here we must stop to consider, on the one hand, the organizational situation in the Rockefeller Foundation at that time and, on the other hand, the ideas about the state of science that had been brewing on many of the country's campuses in the late 1920s and early 1930s.

On the campuses there was talk that the century of biology was upon us. At Wisconsin, for example, there was a lively program in biology at the School of Agriculture as well as in the College of Arts and Sciences. Mason and Weaver had often discussed a new thrust in biology and the opportunities that would open up if some of the most imaginative physical scientists turned their attention—and some of the sophisticated instruments they had developed—to the examination of biological problems. Weaver complained about the lack of really good ideas in the biological literature and its failure to produce the intellectual ferment characteristic of much of the work in the physical sciences. At the time of his first visit to New York, he hoped to interest the trustees of the Rockefeller Foundation in a substantial shift in direction: he wanted to bring to reality a change in the major thrust of biological research worldwide—no mean ambition. Happily, his timing was fortuitous.

The Rockefeller Foundation had recently been reorganized, absorbing several other Rockefeller agencies that had been founded for special purposes that no longer required separate settings. The foundation's aim, "to promote the well-being of mankind throughout the world," was interpreted by the trustees as being best served, in the immediate future, by the support of the scientific research of individuals. (This contrasted with their practice in the immediate past, when large sums were spent on plant and endowment, chiefly at a few major institutions, or on the funding of new research establishments such as the Woods Hole Oceanographic Institution.)

The newly created Division of Natural Sciences thus would be faced with deciding how "the well-being of mankind throughout the world" could best be served through the support of science. The amount then available—roughly $2 million a year—was substantial; in 1932, it constituted a large percentage of the funds available for the support of research in the United States. But although the funds available were substantial, they were nonetheless limited, particularly since the foundation defined its program in the natural sciences as concerned broadly with anything that was science but not medicine. Some principles of selection would need to be established.

In the discussions with the trustees on his visit to New York, Weaver was asked for his ideas on the Rockefeller program for the support of scientific research. He expressed his satisfaction with his own experience in the physical sciences, a field that had been a principal beneficiary of Rockefeller support. But he also stated his conviction that the most striking progress in science would soon occur in the biological field. There, he thought, the Rockefeller Foundation would have a great opportunity. He urged that it undertake a long-range program of support of quantitative biology—a program that would seek to apply to outstanding problems of biology some of the methods and machines that had been so successful in the physical sciences.

Although he urged his point of view with his customary persuasiveness, Weaver also insisted that he was not the man to preside over the proposed program; he was, after all, not trained as a biologist. He did, however, have the background in the physical sciences that he himself had argued should be brought into the picture; and he returned to Madison with an invitation to become the director of a newly defined Division of Natural Sciences of the Rockefeller Foundation. Thus he and his wife were faced with the difficult decision that made so complete a change in their lives. In his autobiography, Weaver says of one of the elements in their decision:

I think ... that I was both realistic and accurate about my abilities and my limitations. I loved to teach, and knew that I had been successful at it. I had a good capacity for assimilating information, something of a knack for organizing, an ability to work with people, a zest for exposition, an enthusiasm that helped to advance my ideas. But I lacked that strange and wonderful creative spark that makes a good researcher.

Thus I realized that there was a definite ceiling on my possibilities as a mathematics professor. Indeed, I think I realized that I was already about as far up in that profession as I was likely to go.[2]

THE PROGRAM IN EXPERIMENTAL BIOLOGY

After much soul-searching, the Weavers decided that the opportunities opening up in New York could not be refused. In January 1932, Weaver was elected director for the natural sciences of the Rockefeller Foundation.

Shortly thereafter, Weaver translated the discussions that had led to his appointment into a formal proposal to the trustees. In it he suggested that the foundation's science program be shifted from its previous preoccupation with the physical sciences to an "interest in stimulating and aiding the application, to basic biological problems, of the techniques, experimental procedures, and methods of analysis so effectively developed in the physical sciences." The trustees adopted this recommendation.

Commenting on this action, Dean Rusk—president of the foundation from 1952 to 1960—wrote in his introduction to the 1958 president's report (the last before Weaver's retirement):

In 1932–33 the Rockefeller Foundation elected to center its major scientific effort in the sciences concerned with living things. . . . [This] major emphasis . . . which continues to characterize the Foundation's science program, rested upon four considerations. First, [the life sciences] could

[2] Warren Weaver, *Scene of Change, a Lifetime in American Science* (New York: Charles Scribner & Sons, Inc.), p. 62.

be expected to add significantly to a better understanding of man himself, whose well-being is a basic charter concern of the Foundation. Second, the life sciences were intimately linked with medicine and public health, the central interests of the Foundation in its opening decades. Third, in the early 1930's the several sciences concerned with living things seemed to be poised for a historical surge forward, with exciting possibilities opening up in all directions. Finally, it seemed at the time that the life sciences were not receiving the public interest and financial support which were warranted by their intellectual promise and by their potential capacity to contribute brilliantly to man's practical needs. The decisions gave The Rockefeller Foundation a modest share in a great adventure which is continuing to unfold.[3]

The trustees' decision involved a major change in the modus operandi of the foundation. In 1933 the program statement formulated for the Natural Sciences Division articulated this change and set forth these general principles to provide the desired direction as well as the necessary flexibility to the program of the division:

A highly selective procedure is necessary if the available funds are not to lose significance through scattering. In the past, this selection has consisted chiefly of a choice of scientific leaders, among both men and institutions, although there has always been some selection on the basis of fields of interest. It is proposed, for the future program, that interest in the fields play the dominant role in the selection process. Within the fields of interest, selection will continue to be made of leading men and institutions.

In general, this narrowing of purpose in the specialized program should result in greater emphasis on the biological and related fields, and especially in greater emphasis on the study of man himself.

A small provision should be made in the budget of the program to care for unpredictable but unquestionable opportunities.

The program should always be kept flexible.

The immediate and underlying values in science justify a continuation of general support to the development of science.[4]

---

[3] The Rockefeller Foundation, *President's Review and Annual Report, 1958* (New York: The Foundation), p. 5.

[4] The Rockefeller Foundation, *President's Review and Annual Report, 1958*, p. 26.

Progress with the program was so prompt and promising that the foundation's 1938 annual report began its natural science section with a sixteen-page discussion headed "Molecular Biology." It began: "Among the studies to which the Foundation is giving support is a series in a relatively new field, which may be called molecular biology, in which delicate modern techniques are being used to investigate ever more minute details of certain life processes." This was probably the first use of the term *molecular biology*.

Some years later (1949), Weaver expressed his confidence in the importance of the research going on in molecular biology:

> The century of biology upon which we are now well embarked is no matter of trivialities. It is a movement of really heroic dimensions, one of the great episodes in man's intellectual history. The scientists who are carrying the movement forward talk in terms of nucleoproteins, of ultracentrifuges, of biochemical genetics, of electrophoresis, of the electron microscope, of molecular morphology, of radioactive isotopes. But do not be misled by these horrendous terms, and above all do not be fooled into thinking this is mere gadgetry. This is the dependable way to seek a solution of the cancer and polio problems, the problems of rheumatism and of the heart. This is the knowledge on which we must base our solution of the population and food problems. This is the understanding of life.[5]

With the passage of time, Warren Weaver's career involved him in major responsibilities far from molecular biology, both during World War II and afterward, but he continued his enthusiasm for research in this field. In 1970 he wrote in his autobiography:

> I believe that the support which the Rockefeller Foundation poured into experimental biology over the quarter century after 1932 was vital in encouraging and accelerating and even in initiating the development of

---

[5] Letter from Warren Weaver to Mrs. J. M. H. Carson, June 7, 1949. Published in Raymond B. Fosdick, *The Story of the Rockefeller Foundation* (New York: Harper & Brothers, 1952), p. 166.

molecular biology. Indeed, I think that the most important thing I have ever been able to do was to reorient the Rockefeller Foundation science program in 1932 and direct the strategy of deployment of the large sums which that courageous and imaginative institution made available. It was indeed a large sum, for between 1932 and my retirement from the Rockefeller Foundation in 1959 the total of the grants made in the experimental biology program which I directed was roughly ninety million dollars.[6]

Weaver, however, also sought some objective basis to support his view that the Rockefeller Foundation program for the support of molecular biology played an important role in the emergence of this field as one of the most exciting in present-day science. He reported that George Beadle, in the late 1960s, identified eighteen Nobel laureates between 1954 and 1965 who had been involved in one or another aspect of molecular biology; fifteen had received assistance from the Rockefeller Foundation. Weaver remarks, sagely, that what was significant was not that they received this assistance, but that they received it, on the average, more than nineteen years before the Nobel prize was awarded.

Weaver's assessment of the excellence and importance of the Rockefeller Foundation program was shared by the trustees and by the scientists whose work gave the program its shape and significance. These scientists have commented on the importance of the support they received and on the skill and understanding with which it was given. Such comments are, of course, hard to assess. One of the most persuasive was made by Max Delbruck, a physicist turned biologist, in a letter to Weaver in 1967: "I can only testify as far as I am concerned, and here very strongly and unambiguously: without the encouragement of the Rockefeller Foundation received in 1937 and their continuing support through the mid-forties I believe I would hardly have been able to make my contributions to biology."[7]

[6] Weaver, *Scene of Change*, p. 72.
[7] Weaver, *Scene of Change*, p. 74.

It seems clear that the procedures Weaver developed for identifying the most promising young men in Europe and America and providing them with support before their quality was generally recognized were strikingly effective. Weaver's establishment and management of the Rockefeller Foundation's program in molecular biology accelerated the movement of physicists and chemists into biology and was of major significance for the development of biology.

Robert E. Kohler, a historian of contemporary science, had this to say in an article in *Minerva* about the decision that was reached by the trustees of the Rockefeller Foundation in the early 1930s concerning their program in the natural sciences:

> In the United States the large private foundations, most notably the Rockefeller Foundation, pioneered in establishing the general institutional traditions and the specific administrative techniques for the patronage of individual research on a large scale. Warren Weaver's programme in the natural sciences division of the Rockefeller Foundation in the 1930s is an exemplary case of this new relationship between a promoter of science and academic scientists. Weaver played an active role in selecting areas of research to be developed, yet he did not intrude on the actual process of research. He developed research grants for individuals and projects and mastered the art of conducting a large programme of relatively modest grants—skills which Foundation leaders doubted could be perfected. The organization and style of the programmes of the Rockefeller Foundation played a significant role in forming the mode of operation of federal science agencies after the Second World War.[8]

THE PUBLIC UNDERSTANDING OF SCIENCE

While he was still at Wisconsin, Weaver had begun a program of self-education in biology because he was convinced that the most exciting developments in science in the years

---

[8] Robert E. Kohler, "A Policy for the Advancement of Science," *Minerva: A Review of Science, Learning, and Policy*, vol. 16, no. 4(Winter 1978):480–81.

ahead would lie in that field. The limitations imposed by his inability to conduct the experimental program that was so essential to an adequate education in biology were somewhat mediated by his transfer to the Rockefeller Foundation. There his close identification with the often inspired experimental work of his many associates in Rockefeller-supported research in molecular biology provided him with a rare education in the character and status of work in that field. This background and his experience in administering the Rockefeller Foundation program were called upon by the National Academy of Sciences in 1955.

The country's newspapers during that time had been persistently asking, "What effects will the atomic age have on the human race?" The public was hopelessly confused by the conflicts of opinion being expressed by people it viewed as qualified specialists. At a meeting of the Board of Trustees of the Rockefeller Foundation in 1954, several members asked whether there was any way in which the foundation could help to clear up the confusion. Consequently, the Board asked one of its members, Detlev W. Bronk, who was at that time president of the National Academy of Sciences, whether the Academy would be willing to address itself to some of the scientific aspects of this question. Would the Academy be willing to carry out a survey of the biological effects of atomic radiation and prepare a report that would set forth the best information then available in a form accessible to seriously concerned citizens?

After consulting his colleagues at the Academy, Bronk agreed to undertake the study. He appointed six committees: genetics, pathology, meteorology, oceanography and fisheries, agriculture and food supplies, and disposal and dispersal of radioactive wastes. The first committee was chaired by Weaver, who successfully mediated the opposing positions of the two groups of geneticists who were members of the committee and prepared a report that had their unanimous support. After the first summary report was published in 1956, there was virtual editorial unanimity in the nation's newspapers that "the report should be read in its entirety to be appreciated" and that it deserved the close attention of all concerned citizens.

In 1957, the National Academy of Sciences announced the award of its Public Welfare Medal to Warren Weaver "for eminence in the application of science to the public welfare." The statement that was issued said, in part:

> Dr. Weaver ... has recently performed ... a task of immense significance to the general public. Making use of his unusually broad scientific experience in mathematics and biology, Dr. Weaver served as chairman of a committee of distinguished geneticists asked by the Academy to appraise the genetic effects of atomic radiation.
> That the committee's report, published in 1956, was able to fashion the various points of view expressed by geneticists into agreement on most of the fundamental issues has been attributed, in large measure, to the leadership, breadth of vision, and insight contributed by Dr. Weaver. The summary report of the Academy committee has been generally accepted in the United States as an authoritative assessment of the genetic hazards involved in atomic radiation.

Weaver's leadership in preparing this report was one of his most widely acclaimed contributions to the public understanding of science, but he made other such contributions with possibly more far-reaching results. One of his major efforts in his continuing commitment to the promotion of the public understanding of science was undertaken toward the end of World War II. At that time the U.S. Rubber Company was sponsoring the Sunday afternoon radio broadcasts of the New York Philharmonic Symphony Orchestra. They asked Weaver to serve as chairman of a committee of scientists who would undertake to provide an intermission program. U.S. Rubber was committed to the idea that these discussions should treat material of substantial concern to a public whose anticipation of the end of the war was darkened by anxiety about the future. As Weaver said: "What the future would be, no one could forecast. But one thing was sure: science would be a mighty and pervasive force in helping to shape that future.... The time had clearly come when everyone ought to have a broader and a more authentic understanding of what science is and how it operates."

The committee assembled by Weaver provided seventy-nine intermission talks, each given by a research scientist who cited his own work. These talks treated a wide range of sciences as well as the relations of science to such things as health, war, and the values of our society. In 1947 these talks were assembled in a book, *The Scientists Speak,* which was edited by Weaver.

Nearly a decade later, Weaver arranged a comparable series for television for the Bell Telephone Science Series. Once again he recruited a committee of scientists who planned a series of eight television programs. Each program dealt with a single field such as genetics or astronomy. The committee's work continued from the fall of 1954 until the fall of 1963. Each program was broadcast twice on a national network, and copies of the filmed programs were distributed free of charge to schools, colleges, clubs, churches, and other groups. The total viewing audience for each program was estimated at more than 60 million people.

These are but two instances of the variety of ways in which Weaver participated in formulating public statements about science—the kind of statements that have appeared with increasing frequency in recent years. In fact, Weaver himself played an important role in bringing about this increased public attention to developments in science. During his membership on the Executive Committee (now called the Board of Directors) of the American Association for the Advancement of Science, the decision was made to reexamine the association's policy and program of activities. The object of this reexamination was to attempt to achieve a better fit between these activities and the changing situation of science in the United States. It was Weaver who formulated a statement for the AAAS membership that expressed the Executive Committee's hopes for a conference on this subject to be held at Arden House in September 1951; it was Weaver who drafted the "Arden House Statement of Policy for the AAAS"; and, after he was elected president of AAAS, it was Weaver who implemented the Arden House recommendations.

Although the Arden House conference in no sense changed the objectives of AAAS—objectives that had long been a part of its constitution—it did change the emphasis that was placed on some of these goals. One of the changes was the role assigned to programs to increase public understanding and appreciation of the importance and promise of the methods of science in human progress. In his retiring presidential address at a AAAS meeting on December 28, 1955, Weaver said:

> It is hardly necessary to argue, these days, that science is essential to the public. It is becoming equally true, as the support of science moves more and more to state sources, that the public is essential to science. The lack of general comprehension of science is thus dangerous both to science and to the public, these being interlocked aspects of the common danger that scientists will not be given the freedom, the understanding, and the support that are necessary for vigorous and imaginative development.

The variety of ways in which AAAS has succeeded in implementing this new emphasis in its purposes would not be appropriately summarized here. But it is appropriate to mention that Warren Weaver became the first chairman of the AAAS Committee on the Public Understanding of Science and was influential in organizing the Council for the Advancement of Science Writing. Moreover, the AAAS magazine *Science* has provided a training ground for a group of gifted science writers. In many ways the Weaver influence has been felt in the excellent science reporting now seen in U.S. newspapers, journals, and broadcasts. In particular, in the late 1940s, he was an enthusiastic supporter of Gerard Piel and Dennis Flanagan who undertook to convert the long-established *Scientific American* into a vehicle for reporting on recent important scientific results—using the scientists themselves as the prime reporters.

Piel and Flanagan had been science editors on the staff of the magazine *Life* and viewed the intermission talks on science that Weaver had arranged for the New York Philharmonic Symphony performances as a model worth emulating. They planned to use his method: to get the scientist to tell the story and then to help him retell it, using their skills in communicating with a nonscientific public to "pool two relevant competences," a Weaver description.

Financially, the magazine barely survived the period after they had gotten it "off the pad," but before long it was safely in the black. With Weaver's continuing help, the venture capitalists who had originally backed the enterprise were induced to continue their support until the magazine had established itself. It is now, arguably, the source of firsthand information about new scientific work that is most respected by nonscientists.

Weaver was widely recognized for his activities "at the interface of science and society" (as he described it). In a single year—1965—he received the two most prestigious prizes awarded for contributions to the public understanding of science. The first, the Kalinga Prize, was awarded for literary excellence in scientific writing by an international committee set up by UNESCO. It was established through the generosity of one of India's industrial leaders, B. Patnaik, to honor particularly meritorious contributions to the popularization of science. Weaver was the last winner of that prize and the first winner of the Arches of Science Award, which was intended to stimulate "the interpretation of what science as a high form of intellectual activity means to man and to the society and the world in which he lives and works and dreams and thinks." The citation that accompanied the Arches of Science Award concluded with a quotation from Weaver's own writings:

> As a natural social activity science belongs to all men. It is well for us that this is true. For it tells us that science need not be regarded as the possession of some select inner priesthood, but that its essential nature can be understood by all literate persons. This is the proposition which assures that the citizens of a free democracy, understanding and prizing the work of science, will provide the support and terms of support that will cause science to prosper and bring its benefits, power and beauty to the service of the people.

THE SLOAN FOUNDATION

Weaver's great facility in making scientific issues accessible to nonscientists was related to his enjoyment of words, his skill in using them, and his consistent willingness to be the member of a committee or board who wrote the summarizing statement or the final report. He was a member of the Board of Trustees of the Sloan Kettering Institute for Cancer Research and chairman of its Committee on Scientific Policy; as such, he regularly presided over the committee's detailed study of recommendations submitted for board action and presented the committee's findings on relevant scientific issues to the board. The majority of board members, including Alfred P. Sloan, Jr., were nonscientists. The effectiveness of Weaver's presentations and his success in coupling the institute's research with its clinical work were impressive—and Sloan was one of those who was most impressed. It was through increasingly frequent contacts of this kind that Weaver became one of Sloan's most trusted advisers.

In 1959, at the time of Weaver's retirement from the Rockefeller Foundation after nearly thirty years of service, he began a much shorter career as vice-president of the Sloan Foundation. Although Alfred P. Sloan's ideas and energy continued to dominate the foundation's program, Weaver was able to set up an internal structure under which the work of the foundation proceeded smoothly after Sloan's death in 1966. Weaver had retired as vice-president and a member of the foundation's board in 1964. At that time the board acknowledged its good fortune in having been able to call on his extraordinary experience and judgment in the practice of the arts of philanthropy and on his uncommon imagination and integrity. Board members also expressed their gratitude for his role in giving them a keener sense of the meaning and responsibilities of truly professional philanthropy. And they emphasized the enduring value of his broad view of the importance of science to our national life and his conviction that the beauty and power of science are meant to elevate the human condition in both an aesthetic and a practical sense.

One of Weaver's most gratifying activities during his Sloan years resulted in the construction (with partial support from the Sloan Foundation) of a building at New York University that was christened Warren Weaver Hall. This building houses the now-famous Courant Institute of the Mathematical Sciences, the second such institute created through the imagination and drive of Richard Courant. His energetic leadership at Göttingen, Germany, before World War II, was supported by the Rockefeller Foundation: it resulted in the establishment of the world-renowned Göttingen Mathematics Institute, which suffered severely during the Hitler regime. The Courant Institute at New York University is a worthy companion to the Institute at Göttingen.

TWO PAPERS OF SPECIAL INTEREST

Weaver combined his enjoyment of words with his enthusiasm for statistics and probability theory in two efforts that were of particular interest to him: an article entitled "Recent Contributions to the Mathematical Theory of Communication" and a memorandum on machine translation, both published in 1949. The first made Claude E. Shannon's work in communication theory available to a larger audience than could be reached by Shannon's more technical presentation. The memorandum, "Translation," is credited by William N. Locke and A. Donald Booth (in their book[9] on the subject, which was published in 1955) with providing the original stimulus to the field of machine translation. Weaver himself believed that this second paper embodied one of the two or three ideas he ever had that were both original and important.

There was a good deal of work in the field worldwide in the early 1950s. In the United States, part of this work had Rockefeller Foundation support, and much of it had government support until the mid-1960s. At that time the so-called Pierce Report[10] suggested that the field of machine transla-

---

[9] William N. Locke and A. Donald Booth, eds., *Machine Translation of Languages* (New York: Wiley Technical Press, 1955), p. 15.

[10] Division of Behavioral Sciences, National Academy of Sciences–National Research Council, *Language and Machines: Computers in Translation and Linguistics. A Report by the Automatic Language Processing Advisory Committee*, NAS–NRC Publication no. 1416 (Washington, D.C.: NAS–NRC, 1966). The *Recommendations* of the NAS–NRC Automatic Language Processing Advisory Committee are given on p. 34. The main thrust of the Advisory Committee's position on fully automatic translation is suggested on p. 24 of the report, where significant invited comments by Victor H.

tion would be unproductive in the foreseeable future and that government support should be redirected to the support of linguistics as a science. As a result, the use of computers for natural-language processing became and continues to be a lively subfield of linguistics. Lately, however, research in machine translation has been attracting renewed attention. Current interest at the universities is in the use of artificial intelligence techniques applied to machine translation problems, and there is also work going on in industry.

THE WAR YEARS

From the beginning, Warren Weaver's duties at the Rockefeller Foundation required fairly regular travel to Europe—and later to other parts of the world. During his trips in the early 1930s, he became acquainted with many of Europe's leading scientists whose work lay in the areas of the foundation's interest. His conversations with German scholars in those years convinced him of the imminence of worldwide conflict.

In 1940, at the invitation of President Roosevelt, Vannevar Bush set up an organization, the National Defense Research Committee (NDRC), to aid the military services with their scientific problems. Weaver wrote to Bush, offering his services on a full-time basis. He also took a step motivated by his memory of World War I and the destruction of European libraries that ensued. With the support of the Rockefeller Foundation trustees, he arranged for the American Library Association to administer a grant "for the purchase or reproduction of American scholarly journals for institutions in areas of war damage, chiefly in Europe and Asia." A first-rate librarian was employed, and a large empty loft was

---

Yngve, then of the MIT Research Laboratory of Electronics, are also quoted. Appendix 19 on pp. 121–123 deals with machine translation and linguistics.

rented in Washington. The librarian made a list of university libraries in Europe and the developing countries, including those with Socialist governments—the total was around 5,000—and entered subscriptions to all the professional journals in the United States. As the journals were published, copies were deposited in bins marked "Library of the Sorbonne," "Library of the University of Heidelberg," "Library of the University of Louvain," and so on. At the end of the war, the complete series of journals was boxed and ready for shipment to these libraries as the rubble was being cleared.

In July 1940, Bush invited Weaver to set up the fire-control section of NDRC. Weaver accepted and planned to resign from the Rockefeller Foundation. But he was persuaded to retain his appointment there, carrying on some of his usual duties while giving first priority to NDRC functions.

In fact, Weaver had few opportunities to perform Rockefeller functions, but those that occurred were important. One such opportunity during a wartime mission to England in the spring of 1941 proved of exceptional importance. Weaver received a note from Howard Florey of Oxford, saying that he would like to call on Weaver in London. Florey had begun experiments with molds—experiments that ultimately led to the production and widespread use of penicillin. At that time Florey and his colleagues could only produce very small amounts of a mold from which they were obtaining an important active ingredient. Florey was convinced that this ingredient had antibiotic properties so effective that it might play a major role not only in general medicine after the war but also, perhaps, in the immediate medical emergencies of the war. But it was impossible to produce larger amounts of the mold in England because resources were so completely taken up with pressing war needs. Florey hoped to get to the United States and persuade one or more of the American companies with large resources for handling fermentation problems to cultivate enough of the organism to permit the necessary human tests and eventually the practical application of the drug. Weaver undertook to arrange to finance the trip, Florey got permission from the British authorities to leave, and the rest is history. The Rockefeller Foundation continued its association with Florey after the war.

Meanwhile the NDRC fire-control section headed by Weaver was working on sighting systems to be used for directing the guns of an airplane against enemy aircraft and on bombsights for such uses as low-level attacks on submarines. But the largest and most useful of the projects sponsored by the section was the design and development of a successful electrical antiaircraft director.

For Army Ordnance, the most pressing problem when the war began was to furnish good fire control for a weapon that was capable of shooting down high-altitude planes. The mechanical methods based on gears and cams that had been used previously were neither rapid enough nor accurate enough to cope with the fast, high-flying targets of World War II. It was evident that a new approach was needed.

Bell Telephone Laboratories came forward with a novel concept: they would develop an electrical gun director whose computation process would rely on several electrical devices, none of whose designs had been proven. A compensating feature, however, was the expectation that the electrical instrument could be produced in large numbers by comparatively unskilled labor. This was in contrast to the existing requirements for precision machine tools and machine-tool skills in the manufacture of precision equipment using gears and cams.

After a conference between the fire-control section's executive committee and personnel at Bell Laboratories, Weaver made his recommendation: he advised the technical staff of Army Ordnance, traditionally skeptical about the use under battle conditions of anything electrical, to proceed with the proposed director. Finally, on November 4, 1940, Ordnance requested NDRC to begin work and to take all responsibility for technical supervision and direction. Work on the electrical antiaircraft director continued throughout 1941. In February 1942, the revolutionary instrument was accepted by the Army as the M-9 Director. It was ready in time to join radar and the proximity fuze, which was also developed by Bush's organization, in reversing the tide of the Battle of Britain—saving London from the worst of the destruction threatened by the German "buzz-bombs" that began to rain down on the city on June 12, 1944.

By late 1942, Bush had identified the increasing need for sophisticated mathematical studies, and the greatly expanded need for mathematical assistance in NDRC. He established the Applied Mathematics Panel (AMP) with Weaver as its chief; Harold Hazen of MIT became chief of the fire-control division.

The Applied Mathematics Panel was in need of a large group of mathematicians to provide assistance in military research. To meet this need the panel invited the participation of a broad array of able mathematicians, without regard to their field of specialization.

Several hundred mathematicians, whose peacetime work was often in the purest of "pure" mathematics, worked in groups set up at ten universities across the country to help with AMP problems. In these efforts the groups demonstrated both versatility and effectiveness in meeting military requirements, qualities that were much admired by the military officers with whom they worked. This was true also of the economists and others skilled in statistical techniques who joined in the work of the panel. Many of those associated with the panel left their own universities to join in the effort. The problems ranged from those calling for mathematical expertise even though they involved no new mathematical results (e.g., some problems dealing with optimum employment of equipment) to those requiring the creation of a new theory (e.g., inspection sampling of materials that were destroyed during testing—sequential analysis was born during World War II). Later, a number of these wartime developments in mathematics were enhanced by the postwar growth of federally financed research. Such research encouraged further exploration of some wartime beginnings, such as operations research and computer construction and use, and expanded the ongoing mathematization of a number of fields.

Warren Weaver's skill in the administration of research and his effectiveness in dealing with military officers and with the Washington bureaucracy greatly facilitated the work of the Applied Mathematics Panel. During the war, the panel received many letters of appreciation from military commands; at war's end, several of the war-born research projects were continued with support from interested military agencies. Weaver continued to serve on boards and commissions in Washington, including the Naval Research Advisory Committee (he was its first chairman), the War Department Research Advisory Panel, and the Research and Development Board of the U.S. Department of Defense. For his war work, he received the British King's Medal for Service in the Cause of Freedom and the Medal for Merit of the United States. In 1950 he was made an Officer of the Legion of Honor of France. The citation that accompanied the award of the U.S. Medal for Merit read, in part: "He revolutionized antiaircraft fire control. He made brilliant contributions to the effectiveness of bomber aircraft. The work of his Panel showed the full possibilities of the application of mathematics to the problems of war."

In 1952, in a reorganization of the Rockefeller Foundation, Weaver's responsibilities were enlarged when he was appointed vice-president for the natural and medical sciences. It was at about this time that he became active on several committees dealing with medical research. In 1952 he was also chairman of the board and nonresident fellow of the Salk Institute for Biological Studies; and in 1954 he was president of AAAS. He was a member of the American Philosophical Society (elected in 1944), a fellow of the American Academy of Arts and Sciences (1958), and a member of the National Academy of Sciences (1969). From 1956 to 1960 he served on the National Science Board.

During the war years the Rockefeller Foundation embarked on its major program to address the problems of hunger around the world. This work was the beginning of the effort that expanded from Mexico to a broader base in Latin America, Asia, and Africa and has been referred to as the "Green Revolution." For several years the Rockefeller Foundation called this program the "Conquest of Hunger," and it is still committed to a major undertaking to help improve agriculture-led development in Third World countries.

The agriculture program was initiated in 1941 after Raymond B. Fosdick, then president of the Rockefeller Foundation, returned from a visit to Washington. During the visit he had lunched with Henry A. Wallace, vice-president of the United States and an agricultural expert. Wallace had been appalled by the inferior quality of the cornfields he had just seen in Mexico, particularly because corn holds so central a position in the Mexican diet. He remarked that if anyone could increase the yield per acre of corn and beans in Mexico, it would contribute more effectively to the welfare of the country and the happiness of its people than any other plan that could be devised. Fosdick consulted Weaver about the possibility that the foundation could do something useful.

An extensive preliminary study was carried out by a group

of three specialists—E. C. Stakman (plant pathology), Richard Bradfield (soils), and Paul Mangelsdorf (corn genetics and plant breeding)—who visited all the regions of Mexico at the request of the Rockefeller Foundation. They determined that a great deal could be done and outlined basic principles for the conduct of the work. After careful preparation the project was set up in Mexico in 1942 with the participation of the Mexican government; it was headed by J. George Harrar.

The work in Mexico prospered, and in 1950 a similar program was established in Colombia. Then Chile and other Central and South American countries entered the program. Improved varieties of wheat were bred in Mexico and successfully introduced into a number of African and Asian countries. With the cooperation of the Ford Foundation, an International Rice Research Institute was created in the Philippines on land furnished by the Philippine government. Sturdy, high-yielding rice was successfully bred there and distributed widely in Asia.

Commenting on the dwarf wheat strain developed in Mexico and the improved rice strain developed in the Philippines, an editorial in *Nature* (August 10, 1968) said, "They have provided countries which were perennially faced with starvation with the means not only to become self-sufficient, but equally important, to regain their self-respect and national pride."

Although Warren Weaver had continuing contact with this program during the war, his associates in the Rockefeller Foundation assumed the principal day-by-day responsibility. At the end of the war, after he had recovered from radical surgery necessitated by repeated and painful attacks of Ménière's disease, he devoted much of his time and energy to this expanding agricultural program. In 1970, looking back on his nearly thirty years of service to the Rockefeller Foundation, he expressed satisfaction at having been associated with two programs, "in both of which I had the privilege of major administrative responsibility: the program in experimental biology which played a significant role in initiating and developing the present-day field of molecular biology; and the agricultural program."[11]

OTHER ENTHUSIASMS

This account has focused on Warren Weaver's professional career over a period of nearly fifty years. Although his professional life was demanding, he had many hobbies, one of which was collecting. For a time, his chief interest in collecting was in acquiring a library that would represent the historical landmarks in the development of the physical sciences. But when he realized that his interest in *Alice in Wonderland*—and in her friend the Reverend Charles Dodgson (a.k.a. Lewis Carroll)—was competing with his plans for this library, he faced the inevitable: he had to choose to which of these delights he would dedicate his limited resources. *Alice* won, with the result that at the end of his life, Warren Weaver's Lewis Carroll collection, now at the University of Texas in Austin, was among the important private collections in the world.

Weaver derived great pleasure and satisfaction from his Carroll collection, and some of his enthusiasm found its way into print. Probably the most interesting of these publications is a book called *Alice in Many Tongues*. The book in part reports on the problems and fun of acquiring so many different translations of *Alice*. But it also discusses the problems that must be faced in trying to come to grips—in many different tongues—with the difficulties introduced by a text that relies on parodied verse, puns, nonsense words, jokes involving

[11] Weaver, *Scene of Change*, p. 103.

logic, and twists of meaning for much of its delight. When *Alice in Many Tongues* was written, translations had been made into forty-seven languages; there were over 300 translated editions. The total number of languages represented in the Weaver collection was forty-two (although he had 160 different translations).

The pursuit of *Alice in Wonderland* and other aspects of Dodgson's activities was what Weaver called one of his minor enthusiasms. Religion was a major enthusiasm after his family, which came first, and his work, which came second. From earliest childhood, church was a family ritual, and in adulthood, it had become a cherished part of Sunday's special quality. For years there seemed to be no need to question the interrelationship between science and religion; each played an important role in Weaver's life, but he felt no conflict between them. When he decided in the 1950s that he should examine the conflict many other people did feel, his conclusion was that he could find none between a properly humble science and a properly intelligent religion. He became the scientist par excellence who was often invited to speak at churches and at religious gatherings. Whenever he published an article on this subject, it was widely reprinted. One article, "A Scientist Ponders Faith," was published in the *Saturday Review* of January 3, 1959, and was reprinted by nine other publications during the next two years. Weaver was convinced that there was a permanent core of truth in religion as there is in science and that religious ideas, like scientific ones, evolve with the acquisition of new knowledge. He was perfectly comfortable with his conclusions, realizing full well that they did not conform with the bulk of religious opinion.

CONCLUSION

How to sum up the account of this extraordinary man? Witty, forthright, a superb raconteur, skilled in the use of words as few of us can hope to be, Warren Weaver was a man whose company was a constant source of stimulation to those who were closely associated with him. He was a prodigious worker and a man for whom the conquest of a new and difficult idea, particularly in science, was an event of importance. He viewed science as the most successful of man's intellectual adventures, and in some senses his whole life was devoted to science.

He bore the discomforts of declining health with fortitude, and lived the last of his years with a grace that made them as admirable as the many years before them—years rich in enjoyment and achievement.

IT IS DIFFICULT TO EXPRESS adequately my appreciation of the kindness and hospitality of Warren Weaver's immediate family in helping me to arrive at an adequate understanding of his multifaceted life, some parts of which were quite outside my personal experience of him. Mrs. Weaver put at my disposal his personal records filed at their Connecticut home, including a copy of the oral history interview recorded for the Columbia University Oral History Project in the spring of 1961. In addition, she responded to my questions by calling upon her experience and her own recollections.

The Rockefeller Foundation has been generous with its help and has provided me with access to the Weaver files at the Rockefeller Archive Center at Pocantico Hills, New York. Assistance with this memoir also was generously given by a number of people associated with diverse phases of Warren Weaver's life. These include, in addition to the Weaver family, Dennis Flanagan, H. H. Goldstine, Alexander Hollaender, Robert S. Morison, Gerard Piel, E. R. Piore, Nan S. Robinson, and Dael Wolfle. For all of this help, I express my great appreciation.

BIBLIOGRAPHY

1920

Forecast. Am. Math. Mon., 27(May):205–9.
The average reading vocabulary; an application of Bayes's Theorem. Am. Math. Mon., 27(October):347–54.
The pressure of sound. Phys. Rev., 15(5):399–404.
The kinetic theory of magnetism. Phys. Rev., 16(5):438–48.

1924

With Max Mason. The settling of small particles in a fluid. Phys. Rev., 23(3):412–26.

1925

Elementary Mathematical Analysis, a Textbook for First-year College Students, by Charles S. Slichter, 3d rev. ed., ed. Warren Weaver. New York: McGraw-Hill.

1926

The duration of the transient state in the settling of small particles. Phys. Rev., 27(4):499–503.

1927

Die Diffusion kleiner Teilchen in einer Flüssigkeit. Z. Phys., 43:296–98.

1928

Die Sedimentationszeit kleiner Teilchen in einer Flüssigkeit. Z. Phys., 49:311–14.
With H. W. March. Diffusion problem for a solid in contact with a stirred liquid. Phys. Rev., 31(6):1072–82.

1929

With Max Mason. *The Electromagnetic Field*. New York: Dover Publications (University of Chicago Press).
Review of *A Debate on the Theory of Relativity* by R. D. Carmichael et al. Am. Math. Mon., 27(January):38–42.
Science and imagination. Sci. Mon., 29(November):425–34.

1930

Geophysical prospecting. Bull. Assoc. State Eng. Soc., 5(3):76–90.
Mathematics and the problem of ore location. Am. Math. Mon., 27(April):165–81.
The reign of probability. Sci. Mon., 31(November):457–66.

1932

Conformal representation, with applications to problems of applied mathematics. Am. Math. Mon., 39(October):448–73.
Uplift pressure on dams. J. Math. Phys. (MIT), 11(2):114–45.

1938

Lewis Carroll and a geometrical paradox. Am. Math. Mon., 45(April):234–36.

1947

Chapter 1 and the introductions to all 15 chapters. In: *The Scientists Speak*. New York: Boni & Gaer.

1948

Probability, rarity, interest, and surprise. Sci. Mon., 67(December):390–92.
Science and complexity. Am. Sci., 36(4):536–44.
Statistical freedom of the will. Rev. Mod. Phys., 20(1):31–34.

1949

The mathematics of communication. Sci. Am., 181(July):11–15.
Recent contributions to the mathematical theory of communication. In: *The Mathematical Theory of Communication*, by Claude Shannon and Warren Weaver, pp. 93–117. Urbana: University of Illinois Press.

1950

Probability. Sci. Am., 183(October):44–47.
Reply to Professor McConnell's letter regarding extrasensory perception (correspondence on probabilities). Sci. Mon., 70(February):138–40.

1951

Alice's Adventures in Wonderland, its origin, its author. Princeton Univ. Libr. Chron., 13(1):1–17.

Protein structure studies. Sci. Mon., 73(December):387–90.

1952

Statistics. Sci. Am., 186(January):60–63.

1953

Fundamental questions in science. Sci. Am., 189(September):32, 47–51.

Probability and statistics, the mathematical way of estimating risk. (Delivered at the 200th Anniversary of the Mutual Insurance Companies of America, New York, 1952.) In: *Facing the Future's Risks*, ed. Lyman Bryson, pp. 34–58. New York: Harper & Brothers.

1954

The mathematical manuscripts of Lewis Carroll. Proc. Am. Philos. Soc., 98(5):377–81.

People, energy, food. Sci. Mon., 78(June):359–64.

Who speaks for whom or for what? (Editorial.) Science, 119 (February 26):3A.

1955

Can a scientist believe in God? In: *A Guide to the Religions of America*, ed. Leo Rosten, pp. 158–65. New York: Simon & Schuster, Inc.

Foreword and chapter 1 (entitled "Translation" and based on a memorandum drawn up for the Rockefeller Foundation in July 1949). In: *Machine Translation of Languages*, ed. William N. Locke and A. Donald Booth, pp. v–vii, 15–23. New York: Wiley Technical Press.

The Patent Office problem. (Delivered before a joint meeting of the American Patent Law Association and the New York Patent Law Association, New York, April.) Am. Doc., 6(3):129–33.

Science and faith. (Delivered on Layman's Sunday in the Congregational Church of New Milford, Connecticut, May 1954.) Christian Century, 72(January 5):10–13.

Science and people. Science, 122(December 30):1255–59.

1956

Lewis Carroll: Mathematician. Sci. Am., 194(June):36, 116–20.
The Parrish collection of Carrolliana. Princeton Univ. Libr. Chron., 17(2):85–91.
Report of the Committee on Genetic Effects of Atomic Radiation. In: *The Biological Effects of Atomic Radiation—Summary Reports*, pp. 3–31. Washington, D.C.: National Academy of Sciences, National Research Council.

1957

Radiations and the genetic threat. J. Franklin Inst., 263(4):283–93.
Science and the citizen. Science, 126(December 13):1225–29.

1958

Communicative accuracy. (Editorial.) Science, 127(March 7):499.
The encouragement of science. Sci. Am., 199(September):50, 170–76.
How big is too big? (Editorial.) Science, 128(July 18):113.
A quarter century in the natural sciences. In: *The Rockefeller Foundation Annual Report*, pp. 3–122. New York: The Rockefeller Foundation.

1959

Dither. (Editorial.) Science, 130(August 7):301.
Purposes and innovations in science teaching. Daedalus (Boston), 88(1):182–85.
Report of the Special Committee. Science, 130(November 20):1390–91.
A scientist ponders faith. Saturday Review, 42(January 3):8–10.

1960

The attractiveness of dessert. (Editorial.) Science, 132(November 25):1521.
The disparagement of statistical evidence. (Editorial.) Science, 132(December 23):1859.
A great age for science. In: *Goals for Americans* (Report of the President's Commission on National Goals, administered by the American Assembly, Columbia University), pp. 103–24. New York: Prentice-Hall.

The imperfections of science. Proc. Am. Philos. Soc., 104(5):419–28.
Issues of man and his environment. (Excerpts from remarks made at the Great Issues Convention, Dartmouth College, September.) Dartmouth Alumni Magazine, 53(1):22; 53(2):4, 22.
Medicine: The new science and the old art. J. Med. Educ., 35(4):313–18.
Moment of truth. (Editorial.) Science, 131(January 29):267.
Science and the World of Scholarship. Welch Found. Res. Bull., no. 6 (January). 19 pp.
Words. (Speech delivered at the midwinter dinner of the Citizens Advisory Committee of the New York Public Library, January 19.) New York: The New York Public Library. 11 pp.

1961

Chester Irving Barnard. Biographical memoir. Yearb. Am. Philos. Soc.: 106–10.
Facing up to the odds. Sci. Digest, 50(July):18–24.
Introductory remarks (to an address by Sir C. P. Snow on the moral unneutrality of science, given at AAAS annual meeting, 1960). Science, 133(January 27):255–56.
Science for citizens. (Speech delivered at Conference on Communication between Science and the General Public, Gainesville, Florida, February.) Pride (Am. Coll. Publ. Relat. Assoc.), 5(5):11–12.
Why is science important? Chem. Eng. News, 39(7):144–48.

1962

Cancer research: Where are we? Fourfront (Memorial Hospital Newsletter), 5(6):3–4.
The emerging unity of science. Ann. Jpn. Assoc. Philos. Soc., 2(2):98–113.
New Institute for Biological Sciences at San Diego. (Editorial.) Science, 136(June 1):747.
Science for everybody. Saturday Review, 45(July 7):45–46.
Stability and change. (Editorial.) Science, 137(September 28):1025.
Thoughts on philanthropy and philanthropoids. Foundation News (Bull. Found. Libr. Center), 3(3):1–6.
What a layman needs to know about science. (Report and com-

mentary by John Lear of a speech given by Weaver at a symposium at Oakland State College, Michigan State University, May.) New Sci., 14(291):579.
What a moon ticket will buy. Saturday Review, 45(August 4):38–39.

1963

Dreams and responsibilities. Bull. At. Sci., 19(May):10–11.
Lady Luck: The Theory of Probability. Garden City, N.Y.: Anchor Books.
Max Mason. In: Biographical Memoirs of the National Academy of Sciences, vol. 37, pp. 205–36. Washington, D.C.: National Academy of Sciences.
The New Biology and health, sickness, aging. Think (IBM), 29(2):2–5.
Science for everybody. In: Science in the College Curriculum, pp. 11–33. (Report of a conference sponsored by Oakland University with the support of the National Science Foundation.) Rochester, Mich.: Oakland University Press.

1964

Alice in Many Tongues. Madison: University of Wisconsin Press.
Mathematics and Philanthropy. New York: Alfred P. Sloan Foundation. (n.d.). 30 pp.
Scientific explanation. Science, 143(March 20):1297–300.

1965

Careers in science. In: Listen to Leaders in Science, ed. Albert Love and James Saxon Childers, pp. 267–78. Atlanta: Tupper & Love/David McKay.
The "India" Alice. The Private Library, 6(1):1–7.

1966

Four pieces of advice to young people. Tennessee Teacher, 33(6):9.
Good teaching. (Editorial.) Science, 151(March 18):1335.
The inner nature of science. (Excerpted from the Kalinga Prize Speech, October 1965.) UNESCO Cour., 19(January):34.
Some moral problems posed by modern science. Zygon, 1(3):286–300.

Why is it so important that science be understood? (modified version of the Kalinga Prize Speech, October 1965). Impact Sci. Soc. (UNESCO), 16(1):41–50.

1967

The art of giving money to science (appearing as an untitled article in the "Matter of Opinion" column). Sci. Res. (McGraw-Hill), 2(7):32–36.
Philanthropic foundations and grants to universities. (Letter.) Science, 158(December 1):133–34.
Science and Imagination. New York: Basic Books, Inc.
U.S. Philanthropic Foundations: Their History, Structure, Management, and Record. New York: Harper & Row.

1968

Confessions of a scientist-humanist. In: *What I Have Learned; A Collection of Twenty Autobiographical Essays . . . from the "Saturday Review,"* pp. 298–309. New York: Simon & Schuster.

1970

Scene of Change: A Lifetime in American Science. New York: Charles Scribner's & Sons, Inc.

1971

The first edition of *Alice's Adventures in Wonderland;* a census. Pap. Bibliog. Soc. Am., 65(1):1–40.

1975

Alfred P. Sloan, Jr., Philanthropist. New York: Alfred P. Sloan Foundation.

Cumulative Index

VOLUMES 1 THROUGH 57

A

Abbe, Cleveland   8:469-508
Abbot, Henry Larcom   13:1-101
Abel, John Jacob   24:231-57
Adams, Comfort Avery   38:1-16
Adams, Leason Heberling
  52:3-33
Adams, Roger   53:3-47
Adams, Walter Sydney   31:1-31
Adkins, Homer Burton
  27:293-317
Agassiz, Alexander   7:289-305
Agassiz, Louis   2:39-73
Aitken, Robert Grant   32:1-30
Albert, Abraham Adrian
  51:2-22
Albright, Fuller   48:3-22
Alexander, John H.   1:213-26
Alexander, Stephen   2:249-59
Allee, Warder Clyde   30:3-40
Allen, Charles Elmer   29:3-15
Allen, Eugene Thomas   40:1-17
Allen, Joel Asaph   21*(1):1 20
Ames, Joseph Sweetman
  23:181-201
Anderson, Edgar   49:3-23
Anderson, John August   36:1-18
Anderson, Rudolph John
  36:19-50
Angell, James Rowland
  26:191-208

Armsby, Henry Prentiss
  19:271-84
Astwood, Edwin Bennett
  55:3-42
Atkinson, George Francis
  29:17-44
Avery, Oswald Theodore
  32:31-49

B

Babcock, Ernest Brown   32:50-66
Babcock, Harold   45:1-19
Bache, Alexander Dallas
  1:181-212d
Bachmann, Werner Emmanuel
  34:1-30
Badger, Richard McLean
  56:3-20
Baekeland, Leo Hendrik
  24:281-302
Bailey, Irving Widmer   45:21-56
Bailey, Solon Irving   15:193-203
Bain, Edgar Collins   49:25-47
Baird, Spencer Fullerton
  3:141-60
Balls, Arnold Kent   41:1-22
Barbour, Thomas   27:13-45
Barnard, Edward Emerson
  21*(14):1-23
Barnard, Frederick Augustus
  Porter   20:259-72

531

INDEX

Barnard, John Gross 5:219-29
Barrell, Joseph 12:3-40
Bartelmez, George William 43:1-26
Bartlett, William H. C. 7:171-93
Barus, Carl 22:171-213
Bateman, Harry 25:241-56
Beams, Jesse Wakefield 54:3-49
Becker, George Ferdinand 21*(2):1-19
Beecher, Charles Emerson 6:57-88
Bell, Alexander Graham 23:1-29
Benedict, Francis Gano 23:67-99
Benedict, Stanley Rossiter 27:155-77
Benioff, Victor Hugo 43:27-40
Berkey, Charles Peter 30:41-56
Berry, Edward Wilber 45:57-95
Bigelow, Henry Bryant 48:51-80
Billings, John Shaw 8:375-416
Bishop, George Holman 55:45-66
Blackwelder, Eliot 48:83-103
Blake, Francis Gilman 28:1-29
Blakeslee, Albert Francis 33:1-38
Blalock, Alfred 53:49-81
Blichfeldt, Hans Frederik 26:181-89
Bliss, Gilbert Ames 31:32-53
Boas, Franz 24:303-22
Bogert, Marston Taylor 45:97-126
Bolton, Elmer Keiser 54:51-72
Boltwood, Bertram Borden 14:69-96
Bonner, Tom Wilkerson 38:17-32
Boring, Edwin Garrigues 43:41-76
Borthwick, Harry Alfred 48:105-22
Boss, Lewis 9:239-60
Bowditch, Henry Pickering 17*:183-96
Bowen, Ira Sprague 53:83-119
Bowen, Norman Levi 52:35-79
Bowie, William 26:61-98
Bowman, Isaiah 33:39-64
Bradley, Wilmot Hyde 54:75-88
Bramlette, Milton Nunn 52:81-92
Branner, John Casper 21*(3):1-20
Bray, William Crowell 26:13-24
Breasted, James Henry 18:95-121
Brewer, William Henry 12:289-323
Bridges, Calvin Blackman 22:31-48
Bridgman, Percy Williams 41:23-67
Brillouin, Léon Nicolas 55:69-92
Britton, Nathaniel Lord 19:147-202
Bronk, Detlev Wulf 50:3-87
Brooks, William Keith 7:23-70
Brouwer, Dirk 41:69-87
Brown, Ernest William 21:243-73
Brown-Séquard, Charles Edouard 4:93-97
Brush, George Jarvis 17*:107-12
Bucher, Walter Hermann 40:19-34
Buckley, Oliver Ellsworth 37:1-32
Buddington, Arthur Francis 57:3-24
Bueche, Arthur M. 56:23-40
Bumstead, Henry Andrews 13:105-24
Burgess, George Kimball 30:57-72
Burkholder, Paul Rufus 47:3-25
Bush, Vannevar 50:89-117
Byerly, Perry 55:95-105

C

Campbell, Angus 56:43-58
Campbell, Douglas Houghton 29:45-63

INDEX

Campbell, William Wallace 25:35-74
Cannan, Robert Keith 55:107-33
Carlson, Anton Julius 35:1-32
Carmichael, Leonard 51:25-47
Carothers, Wallace Hume 20:293-309
Carty, John Joseph 18:69-91
Casey, Thomas Lincoln 4:125-34
Castle, William Ernest 38:33-80
Caswell, Alexis 6:363-72
Cattell, James McKeen 25:1-16
Chamberlin, Rollin Thomas 41:89-110
Chamberlin, Thomas Chrowder 15:307-407
Chandler, Charles Frederick 14:127-81
Chaney, Ralph Works 55:135-61
Chapman, Frank Michler 25:111-45
Chauvenet, William 1:227-44
Child, Charles Manning 30:73-103
Chittenden, Russell Henry 24:59-104
Clark, Henry James 1:317-28
Clark, William Bullock 9:1-18
Clark, William Mansfield 39:1-36
Clarke, Frank Wigglesworth 15:139-65
Clarke, Hans Thacher 46:3-20
Clarke, John Mason 12:183-244
Clausen, Roy Elwood 39:37-54
Cleland, Ralph Erskine 53:121-39
Cleveland, Lemuel Roscoe 51:49-60
Clinton, George Perkins 20:183-96
Cloos, Ernst 52:95-119
Coblentz, William Weber 39:55-102
Cochran, William Gemmell 56:61-89
Cochrane, Edward Lull 35:33-46
Coffin, James Henry 1:257-64

Coffin, John Huntington Crane 8:1-7
Coghill, George Ellett 22:251-73
Cohn, Edwin Joseph 35:47-84
Cole, Rufus 50:119-39
Compton, Arthur Holly 38:81-110
Comstock, Cyrus Ballou 7:195-201
Comstock, George Cary 20:161-82
Conant, James Bryant 54:91-124
Condon, Edward Uhler 48:125-51
Conklin, Edwin Grant 31:54-91
Cook, George Hammell 4:135-44
Cooke, Josiah Parsons 4:175-83
Coolidge, William David 53:141-57
Cope, Edward Drinker 13:127-317
Cottrell, Frederick Gardner 27:1-11
Coues, Elliott 6:395-446
Coulter, John Merle 14:99-123
Councilman, William Thomas 18:157-74
Crafts, James Mason 9:159-77
Craig, Lyman Creighton 49:49-77
Crew, Henry 37:33-54
Cross, Charles Whitman 32:100-112
Curme, George Oliver, Jr. 52:121-37
Curtis, Heber Doust 22:275-94
Cushing, Harvey 22:49-70

D

Dall, William Healey 31:92-113
Dalton, John Call 3:177-85
Daly, Reginald Aldworth 34:31-64
Dana, Edward Salisbury 18:349-65
Dana, James Dwight 9:41-92

Danforth, Charles Haskell 44:1-56
Davenport, Charles Benedict 25:75-110
Davidson, George 18:189-217
Davis, Bergen 34:65-82
Davis, Charles Henry 4:23-55
Davis, William Morris 23:263-303
Davisson, Clinton Joseph 36:51-84
Day, Arthur Louis 47:27-47
Debye, Peter Joseph Wilhelm 46:23-68
DeGolyer, Everette Lee 33:65-86
Demerec, Milislav 42:1-27
Dempster, Arthur Jeffrey 27:319-33
Dennison, David Mathias 52:139-59
Detwiler, Samuel Randall 35:85-111
Dewey, John 30:105-24
Dobzhansky, Theodosius 55:163-213
Dochez, Alphonse Raymond 42:29-46
Dodge, Bernard Ogilvie 36:85-124
Dodge, Raymond 29:65-129
Donaldson, Henry Herbert 20:229-43
Dragstredt, Lester Reynold 51:63-95
Draper, Henry 3:81-139
Draper, John William 2:349-88
Dryden, Hugh Latimer 40:35-68
Duane, William 18:23-41
DuBois, Eugene Floyd 36:125-45
Duggar, Benjamin Minge 32:113-31
DuMond, Jesse W. 52:161-201
Dunn, Gano Sillick 28:31-44
Dunn, Leslie Clarence 49:79-104
Durand, William Frederick 48:153-93

Dutton, Clarence Edward 32:132-45

E

Eads, James Buchanan 3:59-79
East, Edward Murray 23:217-42
Echart, Carl Henry 48:195-219
Edison, Thomas Alva 15:287-304
Eigenmann, Carl H. 18:305-36
Einstein, Albert 51:97-117
Eisenhart, Luther Pfahler 40:69-90
Elkin, William Lewis 18:175-88
Emerson, Alfred Edward 53:159-75
Emerson, Ralph 55:231-45
Emerson, Robert 35:112-31
Emerson, Rollins Adams 25:313-23
Emmet, William Le Roy 22:233-50
Emmons, Samuel Franklin 7:307-34
Engelmann, George 4:1-21
Erlanger, Joseph 41:111-39
Evans, Griffith Conrad 54:127-55
Evans, Herbert McLean 45:153-92
Ewing, James 26:45-60
Ewing, William Maurice 51:119-93

F

Farlow, William Gilson 21*(4):1-22
Fenn, Wallace Osgood 50:141-73
Fermi, Enrico 30:125-55
Fernald, Merritt Lyndon 28:45-98
Ferrel, William 3:265-309
Fewkes, Jesse Walter 15:261-83
Fischer, Hermann Otto Laurenz 40:91-112

INDEX

Fisk, James Brown 56:91-116
Fleming, John Adam 39:103-40
Folin, Otto (Knut Olaf) 27:47-82
Foote, Paul Darwin 50:175-94
Forbes, Alexander 40:113-41
Forbes, Stephen Alfred 15:3-54
Francis, Thomas, Jr. 44:57-110
Frazer, John Fries 1:245-56
Fred, Edwin Broun 55:247-90
Freeman, John Ripley 17:171-87
Frost, Edwin Brant 19:25-51

G

Gabb, William More 6:345-61
Gamble, James Lawder 36:146-60
Gay, Frederick Parker 28:99-116
Genth, Frederick Augustus 4:201-31
Gerald, Ralph Waldo 53:179-210
Gesell, Arnold Lucius 37:55-96
Gherardi, Bancroft 30:157-77
Gibbon, John Hersham, Jr. 53:213-47
Gibbs, Josiah Willard 6:373-93
Gibbs, William Francis 42:47-64
Gibbs, Wolcott 7:1-22
Gilbert, Grove Karl 21*(5):1-303
Gill, Theodore Nicholas 8:313-43
Gilliland, Edwin Richard 49:107-27
Gilliss, James Melville 1:135-79
Gilluly, James 56:119-32
Gödel, Kurt 56:135-78
Goldmark, Peter Carl 55:293-303
Goldschmidt, Richard Benedict 39:141-92
Gomberg, Moses 41:141-73
Gooch, Frank Austin 15:105-35
Goodale, George Lincoln 21*(6):1-19
Goode, George Brown 4:145-74
Goodpasture, Ernest William 38:111-44

Gorini, Luigi 52:203-21
Gortner, Ross Aitken 23:149-80
Gould, Augustus Addison 5:91-113
Gould, Benjamin Apthorp 17*:155-80
Graham, Clarence Henry 46:71-89
Graham, Evarts Ambrose 48:221-50
Gray, Asa 3:151-75
Gregory, William 46:91-133
Guyot, Arnold 2:309-47

H

Hadley, James 5:247-54
Hague, Arnold 9:21-38
Haldeman, Samuel Stedman 2:139-72
Hale, George Ellery 21:181-241
Hall, Asaph 6:241-309
Hall, Edwin Herbert 21:73-94
Hall, Granville Stanley 12:135-80
Hallowell, Alfred 51:195-213
Halsted, William Stewart 17:151-70
Handler, Philip 55:305-53
Hanson, William Webster 27:121-37
Harkins, William Draper 47:49-81
Harned, Herbert Spencer 51:215-44
Harper, Robert Almer 25:229-40
Harrar, J. George 57:27-56
Harrison, Ross Granville 35:132-62
Hart, Edwin Bret 28:117-61
Harvey, Edmund Newton 39:193-266
Hassid, William Zev 50:197-230
Hastings, Charles Sheldon 20:273-91

Haworth, Leland John
55:355-82
Hayden, Ferdinand Vandiveer
3:395-413
Hayford, John Fillmore
167:157-292
Hektoen, Ludvig   28:163-97
Henderson, Lawrence Joseph
23:31-58
Hendricks, Sterling Brown
56:181-212
Henry, Joseph   5:1-45
Herget, Paul   57:59-86
Herrick, Charles Hudson
43:77-108
Herskovits, Melville Jean
42:65-93
Herty, Charles Holmes, Jr.
31:114-26
Hess, Harry Hammond
43:109-28
Hewett, Donnel Foster
44:111-26
Hibbert, Harold   32:146-80
Hilgard, Eugene Woldemar
9:95-155
Hilgard, Julius Erasmus
3:327-38
Hill, George William   8:275-309
Hill, Henry Barker   5:255-66
Hillebrand, William Francis
12:43-70
Hitchcock, Edward   1:113-34
Hoagland, Dennis Robert
29:123-43
Holbrook, John Edwards
5:47-77
Holdren, Edward Singleton
8:347-72
Holmes, William Henry
17:223-52
Hoover, Herbert Clark
39:267-91
Horsfall, Frank Lappin, Jr.
50:233-67
Houston, William Vermillion
44:127-37

Hovgaard, William   36:161-91
Howard, Leland Ossian
33:87-124
Howe, Henry Marion
21*(7):1-11
Howe, Marshall Avery   19:243-69
Howell, William Henry
26:153-80
Hrdlička, Aleš   23:305-38
Hubbard, Joseph Stillman
1:1-34
Hubble, Edwin Powell
41:175-214
Hubbs, Carl Leavitt   56:215-49
Hudson, Claude Silbert
32:181-220
Hulett, George Augustus
34:83-105
Hull, Albert Wallace   41:215-33
Hull, Clark Leonard   33:125-41
Humphreys, Andrew Atkinson
2:201-15
Hunt, Edward B.   3:29-41
Hunt, Reid   26:25-41
Hunt, Thomas Sterry   15:207-38
Hunter, Walter Samuel
31:127-55
Huntington, George Summer
18:245-84
Hyatt, Alpheus   6:311-25

I

Ipatieff, Vladimir Nikolsevich
47:83-140
Isaacs, John Dove III   57:89-122
Ives, Herbert Eugene   29:145-89

J

Jackson, Charles Loring
37:97-128
Jackson, Dunham   33:142-79
Jacobs, Walter Abraham
51:247-78
Jennings, Herbert Spencer
47:143-223

Jewett, Frank Baldwin 27:239-64
Johnson, Douglas Wilson
  24:197-230
Johnson, Samuel William
  7:203-22
Johnson, Treat Baldwin
  27:83-119
Jones, Donald Forsha 46:135-56
Jones, Lewis Ralph 31:156-79
Jones, Walter (Jennings)
  20:79-139
Jordan, Edwin Oakes
  20:197-228
Joy, Alfred Harrison 47:225-47
Julian, Percy Lavon 52:223-66

K

Kasner, Edward 31:180-209
Keeler, James Edward 5:231-46
Keith, Arthur 29:191-200
Kelley, Walter Pearson
  40:143-75
Kellogg, Remington 46:159-89
Kellogg, Vernon Lyman
  20:245-57
Kelly, Mervin Joe 46:191-219
Kelser, Raymond Alexander
  28:199-221
Kemp, James Furman 16:1-18
Kendall, Edward C. 47:249-90
Kennelly, Arthur Edwin
  22:83-119
Kent, Robert Harrington
  42:95-117
Kettering, Charles Franklin
  34:106-22
Kharasch, Morris Selig
  34:123-52
Kidder, Alfred Vincent
  39:293-322
Kimball, George Elbert
  43:129-46
King, Clarence 6:25-55
Kirtland, Jared Potter 2:127-38
Kluckhohn, Clyde Kay Maben
  37:129-59

Knopf, Adolf 41:235-49
Kofoid, Charles Atwood
  26:121-51
Kohler, Elmer Peter 27:265-91
Kok, Bessel 57:125-48
Kompfner, Rudolf 54:157-80
Kraus, Charles August
  42:119-59
Krayer, Otto 57:151-225
Kroeber, Alfred Louis
  36:192-253
Kunkel, Louis Otto 38:145-60

L

Lamb, Arthur Becket 29:201-34
Lambert, Walter Davis
  43:147-62
La Mer, Victor Kuhn 45:193-214
Lancefield, Rebecca Craighill
  57:227-46
Landsteiner, Karl 40:177-210
Lane, Jonathan Homer 3:253-64
Langley, Samuel Pierpont
  7:245-68
Langmuir, Irving 45:215-47
LaPorte, Otto 50:269-85
Larsen, Esper Signius, Jr.
  37:161-84
Lashley, Karl Spencer
  35:163-204
Lasswell, Harold Dwight
  57:249-74
Latimer, Wendell Mitchell
  32:221-37
Laufer, Berthold 18:43-68
Lauritsen, Charles Christian
  46:221-39
Lauritsen, Thomas 55:385-96
Lawrence, Ernest Orlando
  41:251-94
Lawson, Andrew Cowper
  37:185-204
Lazarsfeld, Paul F. 56:251-82
Lea, Matthew Carey 5:155-208
Le Conte, John 3:369-93

538 INDEX

Le Conte, John Lawrence 2:261-93
Le Conte, Joseph 6:147-218
Leidy, Joseph 7:335-96
Leith, Charles Kenneth 33:180-204
Lesley, J. Peter 8:155-240
Lesquereux, Leo 3:187-212
Levene, Phoebus Aaron Theodor 23:75-126
Leverett, Frank 23:203-15
Lewis, George William 25:297-312
Lewis, Gilbert Newton 31:210-35
Lewis, Howard Bishop 44:139-73
Lewis, Warren Harmon 39:323-58
Lillie, Frank Rattray 30:179-236
Lim, Robert Kho-Seng 51:281-306
Linton, Ralph 31:236-53
Little, Clarence Cook 46:241-63
Loeb, Jacques 13:318-401
Loeb, Leo 35:205-51
Loeb, Robert Frederick 49:149-83
Long, Cyril Norman Hugh 46:265-309
Long, Esmond R. 56:285-310
Longcope, Warfield Theobald 33:205-25
Longstreth, Miers Fisher 8:137-40
Longwell, Chester Ray 53:249-62
Loomis, Alfred Lee 51:309-41
Loomis, Elias 3:213-52
Lothrop, Samuel Kirkland 48:253-72
Lovering, Joseph 6:327-44
Lucas, Howard Johnson 43:165-76
Lueschner, Armin Otto 49:129-47

Lush, Jay Laurence 57:277-305
Lusk, Graham 21:95-142
Lyman, Theodore 5:141-53
Lyman, Theodore 30:237-56

M

MacCallum, William George 23:339-64
Macelwane, James B., S. J. 31:254-81
MacInnes, Duncan Arthur 41:295-317
Mackin, Joseph Hoover 45:249-62
MacLeod, Colin Munro 54:183-219
MacNider, William deBerneire 32:238-72
Mahan, Dennis Hart 2:29-37
Mall, Franklin Paine 16:65-122
Mann, Frank Charles 38:161-204
Marsh, George Perkins 6:71-80
Marsh, Othniel Charles 20:1-78
Marshall, Eli Kennerly, Jr. 56:313-52
Mason, Max 37:205-36
Maxcy, Kenneth Fuller 42:161-73
Mayer, Alfred Marshall 8:243-72
Mayer, Maria Gappert 50:311-28
Mayor, Alfred Goldsborough 21*(8):1-14
Mayo-Smith, Richmond 17*:73-77
McCollum, Elmer Verner 45:263-335
McElvain, Samuel Marion 54:221-48
McLean, William B. 55:399-409
McMaster, Philip Dursee 50:287-308
McMath, Robert Raynolds 49:185-202
Mead, Warren Judson 35:252-71

Meek, Fielding Bradford
  4:75-91
Meek, Walter Joseph   54:251-68
Mees, Charles Edward Kenneth
  42:175-99
Meggers, William Frederick
  41:319-40
Meigs, Montgomery
  Cunningham   3:311-26
Meltzer, Samuel James
  21*(9):1-23
Mendel, Lafayette Benedict
  18:123-55
Mendenhall, Charles Elwood
  18:1-22
Mendenhall, Thomas Corwin
  16:331-51
Mendenhall, Walter Curran
  46:311-28
Merica, Paul Dyer   33:226-40
Merriam, Clinton Hart   24:1-57
Merriam, John Campbell
  26:209-32
Merrill, Elmer Drew   32:273-333
Merrill, George Perkins
  17:33-53
Merrill, Paul Willard   37:237-66
Meyer, Karl Friedrich
  52:269-332
Meyerhof, Otto   34:153-82
Michael, Arthur   46:331-66
Michaelis, Leonor   31:282-321
Michelson, Albert Abraham
  19:121-46
Midgley, Thomas, Jr.   24:361-80
Miles, Walter Richard   55:411-32
Miller, Alden Holmes
  43:177-214
Miller, Dayton Clarence
  23:61-74
Miller, George Abram
  30:257-312
Millikan, Clark Blanchard
  40:211-25
Millikan, Robert Andrews
  33:241-82

Minkowski, Rudolf Leo
  Bernhard   54:271-98
Minot, Charles Sedgwick
  9:263-85
Minot, George Richards
  45:337-83
Mitchell, Henry   20:141-50
Mitchell, Samuel Alfred
  36:254-76
Mitchell, Silas Weir   32:334-53
Modjeski, Ralph   23:243-61
Moore, Carl Richard   45:385-412
Moore, Eliakim Hastings
  17:83-102
Moore, Joseph Haines   29:235-51
Moore, Stanford   56:355-85
Morgan, Lewis Henry   6:219-39
Morgan, Thomas Hunt
  33:283-325
Morley, Edward Williams
  21*(10):1-8
Morse, Edward Sylvester   17:3-29
Morse, Harmon Northrop
  21*(11):1-14
Morton, Henry   8:143-51
Moulton, Forest Ray   41:341-55
Mueller, John Howard
  57:307-21
Murphree, Eger Vaughan
  40:227-38
Murphy, James Bumgardner
  34:183-203

N

Nef, John Ulric   34:204-27
Newberry, John Strong   6:1-24
Newcomb, Simon   17*:1-69
Newton, Hubert Anson   4:99-124
Newton, John   4:233-40
Nicholas, John Spangler
  40:239-89
Nichols, Edward Leamington
  21:343-66
Nichols, Ernest Fox   12:99-131

Nicholson, Seth Barnes 42:201-27
Niemann, Carl 40:291-319
Nissen, Henry Wieghorst 38:205-22
Norris, James Flack 45:413-26
Norton, William A. 2:189-99
Novy, Frederick George 33:326-50
Noyes, Arthur Amos 31:322-46
Noyes, William Albert 27:179-208

O

Oliver, James Edward 4:57-74
Opie, Eugene Lindsay 47:293-320
Osborn, Henry Fairfield 19:53-119
Osborne, Thomas Burr 14:261-304
Osterhout, Winthrop John Vanleven 44:213-49

P

Packard, Alpheus Spring 9:181-236
Palache, Charles 30:313-28
Parker, George Howard 39:359-90
Patterson, Bryan 55:435-50
Patterson, John Thomas 38:223-62
Paul, John Rodman 47:323-68
Pearl, Raymond 22:295-347
Pecora, William Thomas 47:371-90
Peirce, Benjamin Osgood 8:437-66
Penfield, Samuel Lewis 6:119-46
Peters, John Punnett 31:347-75
Pickering, Edward Charles 15:169-89
Pierce, George Washington 33:351-80

Pillsbury, Walter Bowers 37:267-91
Pincus, Gregory Goodwin 42:229-70
Pirsson, Louis Valentine 34:228-48
Pitts, Robert Franklin 57:323-44
Pourtalés, Louis François de 5:79-89
Powell, John Wesley 8:11-83
Prudden, Theophil Mitchell 12:73-98
Pumpelly, Raphael 16:23-62
Pupin, Michael Idvorsky 19:307-23
Putnam, Frederic Ward 16:125-52

R

Ransome, Frederick Leslie 22:155-70
Ranson, Stephen Walter 23:365-97
Raper, John Robert 57:347-70
Reeside, John Bernard, Jr. 35:272-91
Reid, Harry Fielding 26:1-12
Remsem, Ira 14:207-57
Rich, Arnold Rice 50:331-50
Richards, Alfred Newton 42:271-318
Richards, Theodore William 44:251-86
Richtmyer, Floyd Karker 22:71-81
Riddle, Oscar 45:427-65
Ridgway, Robert 15:57-101
Ritt, Joseph Fels 29:253-64
Rivers, Thomas Milton 38:263-94
Robertson, Howard Percy 51:343-64
Robertson, Oswald Hope 42:319-38
Robinson, Benjamin Lincoln 17:305-30

INDEX

541

Rodebush, Worth Huff
  36:277-88
Rodgers, John   6:81-92
Rogers, Fairman   6:93-107
Rogers, Robert Empie   5:291-309
Rogers, William Augustus
  Part I,   4:185-99
  Part II,   6:109-17
Rogers, William Barton   3:1-13
Romer, Alfred Sherwood
  53:265-94
Rood, Ogden Nicholas   6:447-72
Rosa, Edward Bennett
  16:355-68
Ross, Frank Elmore   39:391-402
Rossby, Carl-Gustaf Arvid
  34:249-70
Rous, Francis Peyton   48:275-306
Rowland, Henry Augustus
  5:115-40
Royce, Josiah   33:381-96
Rubey, William Walden
  49:205-23
Ruedemann, Rudolf   44:287-302
Russell, Henry Norris   32:354-78
Russell, Richard Joel   46:369-94
Rutherford, Lewis Morris
  3:415-41
Ryan, Harris Joseph   19:285-306

S

Sabin, Florence Rena
  34:271-319
Sabine, Wallace Clement Ware
  21*(13):1-19
St. John, Charles Edward
  18:285-304
Sargent, Charles Sprague
  12:247-70
Saunders, Frederick Albert
  29:403-16
Sauveur, Albert   22:121-33
Savage, John Lucian   49:225-38
Sax, Karl   57:373-97
Saxton, Joseph   1:287-316
Scatchard, George   52:335-77

Schiff, Leonard Isaac   54:301-23
Schlesinger, Frank   24:105-44
Schmidt, Gerhard   57:399-429
Scholander, Per Fredrik
  Thorkelsson   56:387-412
Schott, Charles Anthony
  8:87-133
Schuchert, Charles   27:363-89
Schultz, Adolf Hans   54:325-49
Schultz, Jack   47:393-422
Scott, William Berryman
  25:175-203
Scudder, Samuel Hubbard
  17*:81-104
Seares, Frederick Hanley
  39:417-44
Seashore, Carl Emil   29:265-316
Setchell, William Albert
  23:127-47
Shaffer, Philip Anderson
  40:321-36
Shapley, Harlow   49:241-91
Shedlovsky, Theodore
  52:379-408
Sherman, Henry Clapp
  46:397-433
Shope, Richard Edwin
  50:353-75
Silliman, Benjamin, Sr.   1:99-112
Silliman, Benjamin, Jr.   7:115-41
Sinnott, Edmund Ware
  54:351-72
Slater, John Clarke   53:297-321
Slipher, Vesto Melvin   52:411-49
Small, Lyndon Frederick
  33:397-413
Smith, Alexander   21*(12):1-7
Smith, Edgar Fahs   17:103-49
Smith, Erwin Frink   21:1-71
Smith, Gilbert Morgan
  36:289-313
Smith, Homer William
  39:445-70
Smith, James Perrin   38:295-308
Smith, John Lawrence   2:217-48
Smith, Sidney Irving   14:5-16
Smith, Theobald   17:261-303

Sperry, Elmer Ambrose
  28:223-60
Spier, Leslie   57:431-58
Squier, George Owen   20:151-59
Stadler, Lewis John   30:329-47
Stebbins, Joel   49:293-316
Steenrod, Norman Earl
  55:453-70
Stein, William H.   56:415-40
Steinhaus, Edward Arthur
  44:303-27
Stejneger, Leonhard Hess
  24:145-95
Stern, Curt   56:443-73
Stern, Otto   43:215-36
Stevens, Stanley Smith
  47:425-59
Stewart, George W.   32:379-98
Stieglitz, Julius   21:275-314
Stillwell, Lewis Buckley
  34:320-28
Stimpson, William   8:419-33
Stock, Chester   27:335-62
Stone, Wilson Stuart   52:451-68
Stratton, George Malcolm
  35:292-306
Stratton, Samuel Wesley
  17:253-60
Streeter, George Linius
  28:261-87
Strong, Theodore   2:1-28
Sullivant, William Starling
  1:277-85
Sumner, Francis Bertody
  25:147-73
Sumner, James Batcheller
  31:376-96
Sutherland, Earl W.   49:319-50
Swain, George Fillmore
  17:331-50
Swanton, John Reed   34:329-49
Swasey, Ambrose   22:1-29
Szilard, Leo   40:337-47

T

Taliaferro, William Hay
  54:375-407

Tate, John Torrence   47:461-84
Taylor, Charles Vincent
  25:205-25
Taylor, David Watson   22:135-53
Tennent, David Hilt   26:99-119
Terman, Lewis Madison
  33:414-61
Thaxter, Roland   17:55-68
Thom, Charles   38:309-44
Thompson, Thomas Gordon
  43:237-60
Thomson, Elihu   21:143-79
Thorndike, Edward Lee
  27:209-37
Thurstone, Louis Leon
  30:349-82
Timoshenko, Stephen   53:323-49
Tolman, Edward Chace
  37:293-324
Tolman, Richard Chace
  27:139-53
Torrey, John   1:265-76
Totten, Joseph Gilbert   1:35-97
Tozzer, Alfred Marston
  30:383-97
Trelease, William   35:307-32
Trowbridge, Augustus
  18:219-44
Trowbridge, John   14:185-204
Trowbridge, William P.   3:363-67
Trumbull, James Hammond
  7:143-69
Tuckerman, Edward   3:15-28
Tueber, Hans-Lukas   57:461-90
Turner, Richard Baldwin
  53:351-65
Tyzzer, Ernest Edward
  49:353-73

U

Ulrich, Edward Oscar   24:259-80
Utter, Merton Franklin
  56:475-99

V

Van Hise, Charles Richard
  17*:145-51

INDEX 543

Van Slyke, Donald Dexter
  48:309-60
Van Vleck, Edward Burr
  30:399-409
Van Vleck, John Hasbrouck
  56:501-40
Vaughan, Thomas Wayland
  32:399-437
Veblen, Oswald 37:325-41
Verrill, Addison Emery 14:19-66
Vestine, Ernest Harry 51:367-85
Vickery, Hubert Bradford
  55:473-504
Vigneaud, Vincent du 56:543-95
von Bekesy, Georg 48:25-49
von Kármán, Theodore
  38:345-84
von Neumann, John 32:438-57

W

Walcott, Charles Doolittle
  39:471-540
Walker, Francis Amasa 5:209-18
Warren, Gouverneur Kemble
  2:173-88
Washburn, Edward Wight
  17:69-81
Washburn, Margaret Floy
  25:275-95
Watson, James Craig 3:43-57
Watson, Sereno 5:267-90
Weaver, Warren 57:493-530
Webster, Arthur Gordon
  18:337-47
Webster, David Locke II
  53:367-400
Welch, William Henry 22:215-31
Wells, Harry Gideon 26:233-63
Wells, Horace Lemuel 12:273-85
Werkman, Chester Hamlin
  44:329-70
Wetmore, Alexander 56:597-626
Wheeler, William Morton
  19:203-41
White, Abraham 55:507-36
White, Charles Abiathar
  7:223-43

White, David 17:189-221
White, Henry Seely 25:17-33
Whitehead, John Boswell
  37:343-61
Whitman, Charles Otis 7:269-88
Whitmore, Frank Clifford
  28:289-311
Whitney, Willis Rodney
  34:350-67
Wiggers, Carl John 48:363-97
Wilczynski, Ernest Julius
  16:295-327
Williams, John Harry 42:339-55
Willier, Benjamin Harrison
  55:539-628
Willis, Bailey 35:333-50
Williston, Samuel Wendell
  17*:115-41
Wilson, David Wright 43:261-84
Wilson, Edmund Beecher
  21:315-42
Wilson, Edwin Bidwell
  43:285-320
Wilson, Henry Van Peters
  35:351-83
Wilson, Ralph Elmer 36:314-29
Wilson, Robert Erastus
  54:409-34
Winlock, Joseph 1:329-43
Winstein, Saul 43:321-53
Wolfrom, Melville Lawrence
  47:487-549
Wood, Horatio C. 33:462-84
Wood, William Barry, Jr.
  51:387-418
Woodruff, Lorande Loss
  52:471-85
Woodward, Joseph Janvier
  2:295-307
Woodward, Robert Simpson
  19:1-24
Woodworth, Robert Sessions
  39:541-72
Worthen, Amos Henry 3:339-62
Wright, Arthur Williams
  15:241-57
Wright, Frederick Eugene
  29:317-59

Wright Orville 25:257-74
Wright, William Hammond 50:377-96
Wyman, Jeffries 2:75-126

Y

Yerkes, Robert Mearns 38:385-425

Young, Charles Augustus 7:89-114

Z

Zinsser, Hans 24:323-60

NOTE: An asterisk (*) indicates volumes 17 and 21 of the scientific *Memoir* series, which correspond to volumes 10 and 11, respectively, of the *Biographical Memoirs*.

RAYMOND H. FOGLER LIBRARY
DATE DUE

**BOOKS ARE SUBJECT TO
RECALL AFTER TWO WEEKS**